THE COLD WAR ERA

Problems in American History

Series editor: Jack P. Greene

Each volume focuses on a central theme in American history and provides greater analytical depth and historiographic coverage than standard textbook discussions normally allow. The intent of the series is to present in highly interpretive texts the unresolved questions of American history that are central to current debates and concerns. The texts will be concise enough to be supplemented with primary readings or core textbooks and are intended to provide brief syntheses of large subjects.

THE COLD WAR ERA

Fraser J. Harbutt

Emory University

First published 2002

2 4 6 8 10 9 7 5 3 1

Blackwell Publishers Inc.
350 Main Street
Malden, Massachusetts 02148
USA

Blackwell Publishers Ltd
108 Cowley Road
Oxford OX4 1JF
UK

Library of Congress Cataloging-in-Publication Data

Harbutt, Fraser J.
    The Cold War era / Fraser Harbutt
        p.   cm. — (Problems in American history ; 6)
    Includes bibliographical references and index.
    ISBN 1–57718–051–8 (alk. paper) — ISBN 1–57718–052–6 (pbk. : alk. paper)
    1. United States—Foreign relations—1945–1989.   2. Cold War.   3. United States—Politics and government—1945–1989.   4. United States—Social conditions—1945–.   5. Cold War—Social aspects—United States.   I. Title. II. Series.

    E744 .H36 2001
    973.92—dc21

                                                                            2001035368

British Library Cataloguing in Publication Data

A CIP catalogue record for this book is available from the British Library.

Typeset in 11 on 13 pt Sabon
by Ace Filmsetting Ltd, Frome, Somerset
Printed in Great Britain by T.J. International, Padstow, Cornwall

This book is printed on acid-free paper.

For my Mother

Contents

Preface

This book presents a brief historical synthesis of the Cold War era, defined roughly as the period between the Yalta Conference of 1945 and the dissolution of the Soviet Union in 1991. It is one of a series of books about major problems in American history. The series editor has set out three authorial tasks. The first is to give the reader a sense of the ways in which historians, academic and otherwise, have defined and explained the compelling issues raised by the topic. Secondly, the scholarly arguments are to be lodged within a sufficiently coherent narrative treatment to give the venture a sense of direction. Finally, I am invited to offer my own views of the period.

The Cold War itself functions substantively as the primary event of this era and, conceptually, as its logical framework. It dominated American thought and action for almost half a century. Its origins and character have been exhaustively analysed and passionately debated. This is partly because, in its early stages, the Cold War seemed to offer Americans a choice: to engage with the potential European antagonist (for the third time in 30 years) or to stand aside. But after 1949, when the Soviet Union first acquired nuclear weaponry, the engagement had the sanction of necessity. In the event, to the surprise of many, the bomb kept the peace, but at the cost of permanent tension. And the United States–Soviet confrontation remained inescapably the touchstone of world politics, even as the Cold War itself went on to take a variety of new forms.

The impact of the Cold War upon American life is hardly measurable in a short study. It seems, on balance, to have been stimulative economically, despite the vast diversions to military and related costs. It was certainly a primary agent of social cohesion, at least until the shattering experience of the Vietnam War. It was at all times a powerful cultural and intellectual presence. At the political level it greatly inflated the power of the presidency. Most of the nation's successful leaders focused sharply on what they saw as an epic struggle. Those who downplayed it in favor of a domestic emphasis, like Lyndon Johnson, or tried to escape its political compulsions, like Jimmy Carter, paid a heavy price.

None of this is to suggest that the Cold War explains everything. At certain times, the McCarthy years and the Vietnam upheavals between 1968 and 1973 for instance, its impact on the national life was palpable and profound. But many important modern developments – the traditional tug of war between liberals and conservatives, the significant, if incomplete, ameliorations in racial relations, the loosening of cultural constraints in the 1960s – derive from long-rooted impulses in American history and are still working themselves out today. Here the Cold War functioned mainly as a temporary context, often a very influential one, but not by any stretch of the imagination as a comprehensive explanation.

I have therefore tried, in what is inevitably a politically oriented account (the Cold War was after all essentially a struggle for world power), to do some admittedly scant justice to ancillary socio-economic and cultural issues. Given the limited scope of this book I have not sought to advance any striking thematic innovation. But I have, here and there, attempted to present some new perspectives. I view American diplomacy, for example, as in the main the expression, not of a warrior or imperial culture, but of a compulsively managerial ethos. I am intrigued by the uneasy co-existence of a conservative political structure and a private realm of techno-business volatility and radical popular culture. In general I would like to invoke the expansible but neglected concept of generational change to supplement (one cannot expect to displace) the hallowed trinity – class, race, and gender – of modern historiography. It seems particularly applicable to a fluid, effusive society that is largely governed by cultural rather than political dynamics, and is marked less by hierarchies and rigid ideologies on the European model than by free-floating thought and emotion that only very occasionally crystallize into policy or law.

But the reader will find that these notions are insinuated rather than fully explored here. My primary purpose is simply to review this deceptively familiar period (about which we all have our own ideas) in friendly but sometimes questioning association with the many historians, journalists, novelists, and others who have taught me much and eased my path. I am deeply indebted to them all. I also have some personal acknowledgments to make. I thank Professor Jack P. Greene for the invitation to write this volume. I am particularly grateful to Professor Richard Polenberg of Cornell University who gave the manuscript a very helpful critical reading. I am, of course, fully responsible for the shortcomings that remain. My thanks to the staff at Blackwell, especially to Susan Rabinowitz, Ken Provencher, Tessa Hanford, and to Emory University for a helpful sabbatical leave. Above all I must thank my long-suffering family. The work is dedicated to my mother, who first gave me a love of books and of history.

1

Harry S. Truman and the Creation of a Postwar Order

Beginnings

On April 12, 1945, 139 million Americans received the shocking news that President Franklin D. Roosevelt had died. In 12 years of highly personalized leadership he had wrestled in turn with the challenges of depression and world war. He had only recently been re-elected to a fourth term to manage the transition to peace. The epic and controversial character of his unique presidency is implicit in the widely varying judgments of historians: that, for instance, he saved democracy and capitalism; that his vast new federal government undermined American values and vitality; that he made the United States into a dominant world power.

It is undeniable that Roosevelt found America in an advanced state of socio-economic crisis and left it victorious and prosperous, the economic depression apparently cured by the demands of war. Inevitably all this profoundly influenced the Cold War era that followed. But Roosevelt's America, even in 1945, was very different from our own. The population was about half its present size. The country must therefore have seemed larger and, in this pre-television age, infinitely more mysterious. We would recognize the familiar social diversity and the effusively democratic political culture, its persistent tensions only partly tempered by wartime unity. But we might be startled by a range of socially conservative hierarchies and widely observed codes of behavior that have all but vanished today. Despite wartime upheavals there was, to name but one notable difference, a more rooted sense of place. The mobile, self-indulgent, high consumption, urban–suburban lifestyle still lay ahead. In many ways, the imprint of the nineteenth century, with its characteristic small town ethos, was still strong.

Yet more than any other twentieth-century statesman FDR had transformed the character and substance of American life. One of his accomplishments was that, as historian William Leuchtenburg puts it, "He created the expectation that the chief executive would be a primary shaper of his time – an expectation with which each of his successors has had to deal."[1] The new president, Harry S. Truman of Independence, Missouri seemed initially an unpromising heir to that legacy. Physically unimposing and somewhat distinctive in his taste for history and music (though like all but a few Americans of his generation without a college education) he had some early struggles in the semi-frontier society of western Missouri. But he rose steadily, working the family farm, serving with distinction as an artillery captain in France during World War I and then, after a business failure, refusing to declare bankruptcy and going on to pay his debts in full. Promoted by the notorious Pendergast political machine of Kansas City, he remained personally incorruptible and became an outstanding county judge and eventually a respected United States senator. Contrary to legend he was quite widely regarded as a viable vice-presidential candidate in 1944. And though he had no personal constituency and was virtually ignored by Roosevelt before and after the election, he went on to have a remarkable, transformative presidency of his own.

Inevitably, given this saga of success against the odds, there is a modern tendency to sentimentalize Harry Truman. David McCullough's successful 1992 biography, *Truman* extols his simplicity, patriotism, and common sense. As Alonzo Hamby aptly puts it in his later, more scholarly study, *Man of the People*, "to celebrate him is to celebrate ourselves" – always a congenial task. The question is whether these favoring judgments are a fair measure of his achievements, or simply an exercise in nostalgia inspired by the post-Watergate malaise and a revulsion against the media politics and celebrity culture of recent years.[2]

For as any student of the postwar era quickly realizes Truman was not, except for brief periods, a popular president. His feisty provincialism, so humanly appealing in distant retrospect, grated on millions at the time. Many found the contrast with Roosevelt painful. Nor has Truman received an easy passage from scholars. Even mainstream liberal historians, who have generally warmed to his strong policies toward the Soviet Union and his promotion of New Deal reformism, have found many faults in the detailed record. The most powerful criticisms, however, have come from the left-liberal quarter where it is widely felt that he missed unique opportunities to secure a reasonable peace with the Soviet Union and, at home, to reshape American society along more progressive lines. Meanwhile, right-wing critics have produced a persistent stream of disapproval, citing among other complaints his failure to deal with communist penetration of sensitive government agencies, his supposed responsibility for the success of communism in China, and his dismissal of General Douglas MacArthur during the Korean War.

Many of these academic controversies are still raging today. The Truman generation after all, even as it struggled with the complicated problems of economic conversion and postwar international relations, was also wrestling with profound, far-reaching issues. Could future depressions be avoided? Could growth be created and sustained without the stimulus of war? What would be the role of the federal government? Would business or labor dominate the factory floor, or even management decisions? And, reflecting the new primacy of foreign relations, how should the Soviet and communist problem be met? Its answers to these questions would create a powerful framework for the next half-century, narrowing options where it did not foreclose alternative scenarios. It is not surprising then that the historical explorations of this period have been unusually searching, or that the academic postmortems have sometimes been bitter. There was so much at stake.[3]

Any fair judgment of Truman's record, however, must take account of his difficult inheritance. Consider first the domestic arena. In a general way, to be sure, Truman could rely on the now well-rooted tradition and progressive outlook of the New Deal, which he had long supported. And indeed many accounts, including Steve Fraser and Gary Gerstle's *The Rise and Fall of the New Deal Order, 1930–1980* and William Leuchtenburg's *In the Shadow of FDR* tend to view the postwar era variously as the unfolding fulfillment or modification of Roosevelt's vision.[4]

But when we turn from the general to the particular that sense of lineal descent and continuity fades. Take for instance the crucial issue of business–labor relations. Moving as he said from "Dr. New Deal" to "Dr. Win the War" Roosevelt had focused during the hostilities almost exclusively on a united effort for victory and tried, so far as he was able, to remain aloof from political squabbles. Significantly, he avoided, at least until late 1944, any serious postwar planning. The result of all this was that two very purposeful antagonists marched into the political vacuum. Business thrived during the war on the government's generous cost-plus contracts and labor's reluctant and sometimes violated "no-strike" pledge. In return it performed miracles of production (gross national product rising from about $91 billion in 1939 to about $212 billion in 1945) and looked with rising confidence to a postwar free of government controls and labor harassment. Labor saw it very differently. It too prospered during the war with full employment, high wages, and a union membership that grew from 9 million in 1940 to 15 million in 1945. Angered by what they saw as excessive business profit-taking, and confident in their new powers to redress the situation, the trade unions frequently led work stoppages in actions that many saw as a foretaste of postwar industrial violence.[5]

These looming business–labor struggles, and the associated Democrat–Republican battles in Congress, fit compatibly into a conventional liberal versus conservative conceptualization of a wartime political arena that was full of both extravagant hopes and deep anxieties. There were ambivalent feelings about the powerful, federal state that FDR had created. Many liberals were conscious of their waning influence and some feared the resurgent conservatism might lead to some form of fascism, though others were more temperamentally inclined to see the war simply as an interruption in the onward march of reform. Conservatives welcomed the opportunity the war offered business to redeem itself after the disasters of the previous decade, but here too there were deep concerns among many who saw Roosevelt's war-enhanced state as a harbinger of socialism. Each side produced a widely read manifesto. Vice-President Henry A. Wallace's book *The Century of the Common Man* (1943) expressed a liberal sense of American mission in the world that answered the more power-oriented approach developed in Republican press magnate Henry Luce's 1941 editorial in *Life* magazine advancing the influential conception of an "American Century." At a more rarified level liberal economists spread the strong state doctrine of British economist John Maynard Keynes, while conservatives played up F. A. Hayek's warning in his 1944 best-seller *The Road to Serfdom*, that state intrusion in the economy led inexorably toward totalitarianism.[6]

Truman's problems cannot be explained simply in terms of industrial tensions and discordant ideas. The war also exacerbated social tensions. Historians Richard Polenberg and John Blum, among others, have shown that beneath the government-fostered image of solidarity there was an abundance of division and suspicion in the wartime United States. In the same spirit James Patterson's apt characterization of a "segmented society" captures the intensified social differentiation of the period. Even consolidating power groups like business and labor were in many ways uneasy coalitions: of manufacturers and financiers, of large and small corporations, of traditional and radical industrial unions. In rural America agri-business struggled with the small farmer. The political parties were often little more than acrimonious partnerships: the Republicans a tense marriage of East Coast internationalists and mid-western and western agrarians; the Democrats still an illogical, mutually antagonistic amalgam of northern left-liberals, urban ethnics, labor, and southern conservatives. Behind these institutional instabilities the movement of millions of women and blacks into the labor market inevitably meant a high degree of social dislocation, made worse by inflamed racial tensions in some cities and by anxious speculations about the capacity of the postwar economy to maintain those jobs, let alone find places for 12 million returning veterans.[7]

But the heart of Truman's difficulties lay not only in the general character of conditions in wartime America than in the very ambiguous legacy he received from Roosevelt himself. For, so far as the postwar prospect was concerned the great champion of American liberalism sounded an unclear note to his following through most of the war. Until the 1944 election forced a clarification he did not appear to be greatly concerned by the conservative revival or the growing divergences we have just noted. In large part this was doubtless due to his determination to focus on wartime unity and production. But it was also a matter of personality. If FDR was indeed the social architect of modern America it was more by fortuitous circumstance than philosophical design. True, he created a massive federal machine involving an unprecedented degree of regimentation in American life. But he himself was unsystematic in his habits and policy-making, and artistic rather than bureaucratic in his political temperament. He disliked planning and blueprints and, partly no doubt in deference to wartime political realities, he did not trouble to defend the liberal-oriented National Resources Planning Board which an increasingly pro-business Congress destroyed in 1943. He also allowed congressional conservatives to gut the Farm Security Administration (a New Deal agency established to help small farmers) without significant protest and failed to support efforts to broaden the reach of Social Security. By mid-1944 many liberals would have agreed with one liberal publication's reproachful comment, "Franklin Roosevelt is no New Dealer."[8]

Roosevelt's exact intentions are still somewhat mysterious. He may have been undergoing a significant transition himself.

Alonzo Hamby is no doubt right to claim that the president continued to believe in reform in a general sense. But historian James Gilbert, citing his approval of the business-oriented Plan for Demobilization and Industry Reconversion in early 1944 saw his goal as being "a speedy reconversion to private ownership and production and a dismantling of controls." Most significant, perhaps, is Alan Brinkley's intriguing recent argument that FDR had been converted to a new economic philosophy by the alarming experience of the 1937 depression. He henceforth tended toward a proto-Keynesian belief in the importance of government-promoted demand as a crucial condition of the economic growth that must sustain future reforms. The demand-led wartime prosperity reinforced the case and, it is argued, steadily led the New Dealers away from traditional class and redistributive politics toward high levels of consumption and, inevitably, an acceptance of business as the indispensable creator of wealth.[9] All this sounds plausible, though the case is vitiated somewhat by the fact that Roosevelt never clearly acknowledged any such sea-change in his thought, and indeed went on to fight the 1944 election on more or less traditional New Deal lines. And it was from that campaign, rather than any elusive intellectual transformation, that Truman would take his line in the approaching transition.

A strong case can be made, I think, that whether or not he underwent any substantial intellectual conversion, it was mainly Roosevelt's habitual and very visible style of political leadership that caused most of Truman's difficulties in 1945. Truman himself noted later "President Roosevelt often said he was no administrator. He was a man of vision and ideas."[10] His general approach was inspirational and opportunistic. While his substantive bent as president was toward reform and social justice, these causes were advanced in spasmodic rather than steady incremental fashion. His *modus operandi*, especially during the war years, was essentially improvisational. Rather than conform to plans he liked to work off events. Thus, with characteristically consummate timing he kept potentially controversial plans for the postwar United Nations from public view until the moment Allied troops had landed safely in France in June 1944, and then launched them on a tide of celebration and optimism that gave the proposals irresistible momentum. He took a similar approach to his fundamental domestic and foreign problems, using the November 1944 presidential election to lay out a reform-minded domestic scenario for the postwar, and the Yalta conference in February 1945 to define the constituent elements of a postwar order that Truman would feel obliged to try to institutionalize. But in these crucial instances he was much less successful. The clarifications came too late to give any chance of a harmonious transition and in each case, domestic and foreign, were significantly at variance with political realities.

Let us look at each of these in turn, for they effectively set the stage for a problematic aftermath to the war. Consider first Roosevelt's 1944 re-election campaign. He took a much more radical reform line than he had exhibited during the war. There were, to be sure, a number of generally accepted postwar measures, such as the famous G.I. Bill giving extensive benefits to returning veterans, that suggested a strong state role. And Republicans and most conservatives also conceded the inevitability of a brief extension of wartime economic controls, including the much-disliked Office of Price Administration, for a period of six months after hostilities ended. But even allowing for this the Democratic campaign had a distinctly left-wing cast. Roosevelt allowed labor, including some of its most radical elements, to take a prominent role. Left-progressive intellectuals also played an active part. This emphasis, together with the stress on an Economic Bill of Rights, on government's responsibility to ensure a full employment economy, on a continuing Fair Employment Practices Commission and on enlarged Social Security coverage, and a variety of other welfare reforms all implied both a liberal revival and a strong role for the state in postwar America. Business and Republican leaders condemned these "socialistic" nostrums as a dangerous return to the redistributionist excesses of the mid-1930s. A standard account sees Roosevelt "committing himself squarely to a full resumption of progressive policies in the postwar era." Another historian, William Chafe, comments "FDR revived progressive hopes and seemed to promise that the end of the war would bring a return to the social and economic agenda of the liberal New Deal." Roosevelt was triumphantly re-elected. But the effect of all this revived radicalism was to cut across the successful government–business wartime collaboration and leave Truman to navigate a difficult transition to the peacetime economy with an aroused, increasingly hostile business community on one side and a highly expectant leftist coalition on the other.[11]

The Rooseveltian legacy in foreign relations was similarly contradictory and even more problematic. In domestic affairs, after all, Truman had some experience and could look to some breathing space before the final victory. He could also draw on post World War I precedents to address issues that were out in the open and eased by some degree of public understanding. The diplomatic difficulties, however, which were completely new to him, demanded immediate attention and presented themselves in a form completely at odds with the harmonious image Roosevelt had created after his supposed success with the Soviets at the February 1945 Yalta conference. FDR had led Americans to think that the planning for peace was going well. In fact it was on the verge of collapse.

How did this come about? Many historians have tried to capture the essence of Roosevelt's wartime diplomacy but, despite an enormous documentary record, there is little basic agreement. The titles of some leading books dealing with Roosevelt's 12 years of international statesmanship – James McGregor Burns' *The Lion and the Fox*; Warren Kimball's *The Juggler* – bear ample witness to the difficulty scholars have had in trying to find a defining principle.[12] There is, however, one observable recurring tendency that will help us understand this protean statesman. As in domestic politics, so in diplomacy, Roosevelt preferred during the war to detach himself from political complications. Thus he kept himself, so far as he could, aloof from the politics of wartime anti-Nazi Europe. It is true that he formed a uniquely intimate strategic and military partnership with British Prime Minister Winston

Churchill; that he made spasmodic efforts to create a personal relationship with Soviet leader Josef Stalin; and that he gave birth to a steady stream of visionary declarations and embryonic international institutions that seemed to promise a peaceful postwar. These initiatives gave Americans at the time (and many historians since) the impression of a robust American activism. In fact they obscured a vacuum at the heart of American diplomacy. For FDR systematically avoided any real engagement with the political problems of Europe that emerged as the war wound down. Apart from the limited initiatives inspired by the exigencies of war, by flickers of irritation at provoking figures like the French leader, Charles de Gaulle, or by the demands of American domestic politics (solicitude for Italy, for example), Roosevelt carefully kept his distance.

In all this FDR was doubtless exhibiting the old American reluctance to get entangled with Europe's politics. And, as with importunate liberal domestic reformers during the war, he sometimes justified himself to critics by saying that he wanted no distraction from the war effort. But here too the explanation is partly personal. He did not believe that this detachment would impair his ability to act decisively at the end of the war. His self-confidence, his tendency to procrastinate, and his acute distaste for European politics (recently illuminated by historian John Lamberton Harper), all pushed him in the same direction.[13]

But detachment had consequences in diplomacy too. Just as his comparative disengagement on the home front allowed both business and labor to strengthen their political influence, so his aloofness from the wartime politics of anti-Nazi Europe encouraged Europeans to look (as most would probably have done anyway) to some kind of Anglo–Soviet understanding for their postwar security. The character of that neglected relationship was largely misread by Americans at the time, and many historians since, as one of political and ideological confrontation. This may be due partly to the influence of Winston Churchill's exculpatory memoirs, written in the heat of the early Cold War, which portrayed their author as Stalin's persistently skeptical and only reluctant colleague-by-necessity. Eventually, after the Yalta conference of February 1945 had effectively brought the United States more fully into the arena and Stalin's conduct had become politically insupportable, the two European allies did fall out. But Britain and Russia had worked together against Napoleon and the Kaiser, responding to an enduring geopolitical logic rather than ideological differences, and in World War II, their respective interests – a Soviet fixation upon Eastern Europe and a British obsession with the Mediterranean – were still compatible. From June 1941 up to Yalta in early 1945, therefore, they fell again into their collaborative habit, fitfully and with occasional setbacks certainly, but with an increasing degree of mutual understanding and, on the British side at least, a suspension of the moral posturing that had stood in the way of a prewar cooperative stand against Hitler. This culminated in their October 1944 "sphere of influence" deal which effectively divided Europe. Roosevelt saw the reality of the arrangement and initially accepted its logic, though his election-conscious adviser, Harry Hopkins, later led him to disassociate himself formally. One cannot but wonder how matters would have turned out if this Anglo–Soviet "road not taken" had become the basis of a postwar European order, with the United States in its traditional posture of detached onlooker. This was, in Europe at least, a widely expected outcome up to early 1945. In the event the apparent ruthlessness with which the British and Soviets imposed themselves on their respective spheres in late 1944 aroused public alarm and protest in the United States, and jeopardized Roosevelt's plans for a postwar American internationalism, embedded as it was in a United Nations proclaimed but as yet unborn. The president felt obliged to respond.[14]

This is the background to the sudden burst of American diplomatic activity that began in December 1944 with official and public complaints from Washington about British actions in Greece and Italy. A painful Anglo–American crisis ensued. Then, in February 1945, with Hopkins in a preliminary tour of Western Europe conceding that "we have come in too late," FDR made the long trip to Yalta in the Crimea to try and persuade Stalin to pursue more acceptable policies in an Eastern Europe that seemed destined to fall into Soviet hands. This famous summit conference, the symbol for millions of international intrigue and betrayal, still mystifies. It is indicative of this confusion that the era of postwar liberal historiography produced John Snell's *The Meaning of Yalta*, a collection of articles mostly blaming Stalin; that the revisionist 1960s brought Diane S. Clemens' *Yalta*, holding the United States responsible for subverting a reasonable transaction after Roosevelt's death; and that the Reagan era of the 1980s yielded Russell Buhite's portrait of Soviet duplicity and Rooseveltian naiveté. It is perhaps this kind of historiographical variety that led the Czech intellectual Milan Kundera to declare a few years ago, "We still don't know what happened at Yalta."[15]

Yalta is clearly a difficult subject, badly in need of re-examination. There is, however, one important exchange between Roosevelt and Stalin at their earlier meeting at Teheran in Iran during November 1943 which gives us a tantalizing clue to the confusions of the Yalta meeting and its disastrous aftermath. Roosevelt asked Stalin, in effect, to impose a light hand on the Baltic States and, by implication, on Eastern Europe. Stalin, in turn, asked the president to "educate" American public opinion. These simple exchanges lay bare the essential problem in United States–Soviet relations, giving us a sudden illumination of precisely what each leader thought the other must do to ensure postwar cooperation.[16] Had each leader acted as the other requested the Cold War may well have been averted. In fact neither leader went on to perform as asked. Stalin's Red Army and its baggage train of political commissars and economic scavengers had already begun, by the end of 1944, to impose a very heavy hand upon Eastern Europe; and Roosevelt, far from trying to present a realistic picture for Americans to ponder had instead created a distracting vision of postwar harmony and goodwill. Now they were at Yalta, with the political situation in Eastern Europe already crystallized in Stalin's favor and American opinion firmly focused by optimistic Rooseveltian rhetoric on the prospect that the region would henceforth be blessed with free,

independent democracies. The two powers were on a colli-
sion course and Roosevelt was caught between two incompatible realities. He spent the first days of the conference trying
unsuccessfully to persuade Stalin to conform to American
standards. He accepted a Soviet-dominated Polish provisional
government and did not directly challenge the October spheres
"deal'. He then moved to public diplomacy, producing the
State Department's Declaration on Liberated Europe which
pledged the Big Three to create "free and unfettered" governments and "democracy" in the liberated countries. Rather surprisingly, but perhaps because he was already schooled in
FDR's persistent calls for help in sugar-coating various diplomatic pills for home consumption, Stalin ignored his Foreign
Minister Molotov's warnings and signed it.[17]

These ill-judged attempts to cover up for the public the incompatibility of the European and American conceptions of
the new era led to the post-Yalta crisis and to Truman's first
serious problem. For Roosevelt used the spurious Declaration
in public as a full explanation of Yalta, thus giving a falsely
optimistic image of the conference and the future prospect.
He looked to Yalta, he told Congress, to "spell the end of the
system of unilateral action, the exclusive alliances, the spheres
of influence, the balance of power, and all the other expedi-
ents that have been tried for centuries – and have always
failed." Churchill, privately acknowledging "a false prospec-
tus," began to encourage a tougher line with Stalin, thus putting
the Anglo–Soviet understanding at risk. Stalin, infuriated, began immediately to crack down more oppressively in Eastern
Europe, forcing a proto-communist regime on Rumania, im-
prisoning Polish partisan leaders, and refusing to collaborate
with his allies, as he had promised to do, on a modification of
his Polish puppet regime. He also refused to send Molotov to
the San Francisco Conference and soon afterwards began what
came to be known as a "war of nerves" against Britain. An
alarmed Roosevelt now had to face the prospect of explaining
to the American people why he had popularized the Yalta
arrangements. Both Western leaders, anxious to avoid such a
public denouement, tried without success to persuade Stalin

to cooperate, especially on the Polish issue. They were unsuccessful and, when FDR died in April, the ensuing tension was acute and threatening to become public knowledge.[18]

Thus, Truman, who would have found the transition to peace very difficult under the best of circumstances, was left by Roosevelt's late-blooming activism with two distorted perspectives. Thanks to FDR's radical electioneering in the 1944 election he was now the focal point of a highly expectant left-labor revival that was bound to increase political tension and lead to industrial strife that would complicate the whole reconversion process. And by popularizing a falsely optimistic vision of Yalta, for which there was no solid political basis, Roosevelt had saddled his successor with high public expectations in the international arena that were almost certain to be dashed. It would now be Harry Truman's task to try and find some kind of as yet unglimpsed solution to these problems. He could not at the outset see the nature of this flawed legacy as clearly as we can. Later he did. His succinct response to an inquiry some years later about the situation he suddenly confronted in April 1945 – "Heroes know when to die" – suggests a carefully veiled but deeply felt resentment.[19]

Shaping the Postwar World Order

The Cold War, in its turbulent course over nearly half a century, broke down many traditional distinctions between American domestic and foreign affairs. But these remained, of course, separate spheres of action and as a practical matter the historian must decide which to explore first. Most Americans were undoubtedly preoccupied between 1945 and 1947 with personal and local matters, especially with employment prospects. Truman himself, a thoroughly domestic politician, focused mainly on the problems of reconversion, the dramatic labor unrest, and all the issues of national politics. He left foreign affairs mostly to a tiny group of high officials. Nevertheless the international arena has a first claim on our attention. Domestic turbulence, after all, was a familiar, more or less predictable fact of life. The Cold War was new. It created, at some point during the two years following the end of hostilities, the precise moment being a matter of passionate controversy because of its association with the crucial issue of historical accountability, the governing framework for American life over the next four and a half decades. As Truman put it in a January 1953 farewell address, "I have hardly had a day in office that has not been dominated by this all-embracing struggle."[20]

The long debate among historians over the origins of the Cold War reflects generational as well as philosophical divisions. The tensions have abated in recent years but academic arguments persist, enlivened recently by a trickle of new evidence issuing in haphazard, uncoordinated fashion from former Soviet archives. It seems sensible, therefore, before examining the main events of this crucial period, to identify briefly some of the leading points of view. In the early years, say from 1949 to the mid-1960s, the so-called liberal/orthodox school dominated the field. Its work reflected the widespread belief in the United States that the Soviet Union had deliberately set itself against the wholesome postwar vision conjured up by Roosevelt. Years later historians would disinter remarks by such early observers as Alexis de Toqueville and Simon Bolivar predicting that America and Russia would one day confront each other across a prostrate Europe. But while many Americans expected Britain and the Soviet Union to fall out after World War II very few anticipated anything resembling the multi-faceted American involvement, so foreign to rooted tradition, that actually developed. The liberal historians held the Soviets accountable. They admired the Truman administration both for standing up to the Russians (characterized by Arthur M. Schlesinger Jr. as "the brave and essential response of free men to Communist aggression") and for breaking down the considerable reluctance of many Americans to take a leading part in that resistance.[21]

There were other views in these early years. A thin stream of Marxist or populist criticism on the left saw American imperialism exploiting Soviet vulnerability. There was a more substantial and much noisier conservative line blaming

Roosevelt for betraying Eastern Europe and China and berating the early Truman tendency to accommodate or respond only tardily to Soviet expansion. And a sophisticated "realist" interpretation, later associated with the diplomat George F. Kennan and political scientist Hans J. Morgenthau, agreed that the Soviets were basically responsible for the tension but found the American reaction excessively emotional and moralistic where it should have been guided by a sober, more calculated sense of the national interest.[22]

The most substantial challenge to liberal orthodoxy came in the 1960s from a generation of younger scholars who argued that a powerful United States was fully or partially responsible for the Cold War. They were influenced by the general spirit of change and critical self-examination that permeated American historical scholarship in this period, and by the increasingly unpopular Vietnam War, which they tended to view as a logical outcome of earlier American Cold War diplomacy. Revisionism took a number of forms but many scholars were inspired by William Appleman Williams' 1959 book *The Tragedy of American Diplomacy* which, by contrast with the more politically oriented liberal school, emphasized the less visible but arguably more determinative economic compulsions – the world-wide search for raw materials, markets, and investment outlets – that had supposedly driven an expansionist United States foreign policy since the 1890s. Williams' "Open Door" concept of a relentlessly aggressive American capitalism influenced the development of "New Left" thinking about foreign policy. Historians began to emphasize an American insistence upon shaping the new order to its own liking, regardless of, and insensitive to, legitimate Soviet claims to security and recompense.[23]

During the most intense phase of the Vietnam War, between 1965 and 1975, orthodox and revisionist historians of the Cold War's origins often clashed bitterly, their arguments steadily spreading to other areas of the American past as well. Contemporary political passion drove scholarship. After 1975, however, with the Vietnam trauma over and *détente* with China and the Soviet Union blooming, the gladiatorial aspects faded. Basic divisions of opinion certainly have persisted – over American diplomacy, over economic unfairness, over race, civil rights and other social issues, over the character of American life generally – but the emphasis, even in Cold War studies, has steadily moved from accountability to calmer explorations of causation.

In recent years the appearance of British and Soviet documents has internationalized Cold War historiography, tempering the durable Americocentrism of the field. The opening of some Soviet archives after 1990 aroused high expectations. Some gaps have been filled, some large issues (the origins of the Korean War for instance) have been substantially clarified, and we have a better sense of the context in which Soviet policy was made. But unfortunately much of value has been destroyed or withheld, especially documentation of high-level decision making during and immediately after World War II. What we do have tends to validate the orthodox view. Significantly, most modern Russian historians tend to fix Stalin with the primary responsibility.[24] The British records began to emerge, with much less academic fanfare, long before this (in 1972) and some historians – notably Robert Hathaway, Randall Bennett Woods, and Terry Anderson – began to uncover a significant British role in the early stages of the Cold War. My own research led me to suggest in 1986 that there was an initial Anglo–Soviet "Cold War" during 1945–46 which set the British to the familiar task of drawing an initially reluctant United States into a European struggle for a third time in just over 30 years. In the same year the Norwegian historian Geir Lundestad, also sensitive to the European lure, advanced an influential conceptualization – the notion that the United States gained during the early Cold War an "empire by invitation" in Western Europe. This new international outlook, implicit in much recent work and evident in the approach of scholars like Odd Arne Westad and Marc Trachtenberg, is steadily broadening the field.[25]

Here then are a number of sharply differentiated perspectives. It will be immediately clear to the reader that if we tackle this great puzzle head-on – by posing the fundamental question: Why the Cold War? – we face a daunting historiographical problem that, given the variety of impassioned scholarship, can hardly be resolved satisfactorily in a necessarily compressed study. I propose, therefore, to approach the issue obliquely, by asking a less dramatic but crucial and more manageable question: When did the Cold War begin? This strategy will allow us both to get a sense of the main events as they unfolded, and at the same time will show how the various historical interpretations have developed.

Truman's foreign policy difficulties began with the arrival of Molotov at the White House in late April 1945. His appearance was a kind of reconciliatory gesture from Stalin after Roosevelt's death. Truman, briefed by increasingly anti-Soviet officials, berated him for not upholding the Yalta accords. When Molotov took offence Truman apparently told him bluntly to carry out his agreements. He was adopting the public, Rooseveltian view of Yalta, seen as a commitment to democracy and free elections in Eastern and Central Europe, by which standard the Soviets were of course in violation. To strengthen the impression of American displeasure, meanwhile, Truman stopped lend-lease shipments to the Soviets as soon as the fighting ended in Europe, and appointed a known hardliner to the reparations committee about to meet in Moscow. He also communicated increasingly frequently with Churchill and together they strengthened the impression of a growing Anglo–American diplomatic front by sending further concurrent complaints to Stalin about Soviet policy in Poland.

These initiatives and exchanges, so abruptly confrontational after the emollient Roosevelt approach, are a striking illustration of the influence of personality in high-level diplomacy. They reflect Truman's penchant for direct, decisive action. Some historians in the 1960s and later have seen in them the beginnings of the Cold War.[26] A case can certainly be made that the post-Yalta crisis marks the end of the "Grand Alliance," to use Churchill's inspirational but misleading phrase, and the beginning of a difficult transitional period, but not, I think, the start of the United States–Soviet Cold War – a rather more profound event.

The treatment of the post-Yalta crisis reflects some of the difficulties historians have had in finding agreement about the start of the Cold War. The general tendency among diplomatic historians, especially those orthodox liberal scholars who dominated the field until the late 1960s, has been to see the Truman Doctrine of March 1947 as the true beginning of the Cold War and the various earlier points of tension as, in political scientist John Spanier's words, "signposts" along the way. But the unveiling of a fuller documentary record in the late 1950s and beyond, together with the emergence of a new generation of American historians, less celebratory and more critical of United States' foreign policy, has brought closer attention to these earlier, perhaps decisive episodes.

In this case, however, we appear to be looking at a diplomatic skirmish, not the start of the Cold War. Significantly, within a few weeks of Roosevelt's death we find Truman backing away and sending an accommodationist Harry Hopkins to Stalin to patch things up. This he did, with the pleasing result that the founding United Nations Conference in San Francisco was brought to a successful conclusion and a communist-dominated but more representative government took power with American acceptance in Poland.

This paved the way for the Potsdam conference starting in late July. The fate of Germany was now the principal issue. Here too we find historians jumping the gun. The failure to settle the German problem, it is argued, made the Cold War inevitable. It is certainly true, as historian Bruce Kuklick and others have stressed, that the compromise reached at Potsdam made partition much more likely.[27] But everyone concerned at the time recognized the difficulty of this issue and Truman and Stalin, in an atmosphere of mutual cordiality, came to a temporary arrangement with a reparations agreement that seemed to meet everyone's immediate needs and an ambivalent political deal that seemed at the time to leave the door open for a controlled reunification. In fact, as events turned out, this did later evolve into partition. But that outcome was far from certain in mid-1945.

The German issue was a central feature of the early Cold

War as Carolyn Eisenberg and others have emphasized. And in many respects it remained a most dangerous flashpoint. But it was not, I think, a direct cause of the struggle. This is because, while Western relationships with the Soviet Union deteriorated in other arenas the three powers seem, despite much irritation on all sides, to have acknowledged the right of each to be there, to have understood something of each other's difficulties, and to have treated the German issue with some degree of sensitivity and practicality. This ended in the latter part of 1947. But by then the Cold War had already developed from other immediate causes. One significant factor here may be that, as Norman Naimark has argued, Stalin was unsure and undecided what to do about his eastern zone of Germany and that "Soviet officers bolshevized the zone not because there was a plan to do so, but because that was the only way they knew to organize society."

One thing was settled at Potsdam: the fate of Japan, clearly facing defeat but still fighting grimly in the Pacific. For it was here that Truman received word that the atomic bomb, targeted for Hiroshima and, if no surrender followed, for Nagasaki, was ready for a use that had long been intended and which he never seriously questioned. The employment of these weapons had been secretly discussed earlier by certain key officials and a presidentially appointed committee, which endorsed the strikes. Only a few scientists from the Manhattan Project (the name given to the organization that built the weapon) registered a dissent and called for delay or some demonstration for the Japanese.

It was known that the Japanese were putting out peace feelers in Moscow, but no response had been received to Allied calls for unconditional surrender. Meanwhile, the Japanese armed forces continued to fight fiercely and American lives were being lost. Truman and his advisers appear to have believed that unless the weapon was used a costly invasion of the home islands would be necessary at the end of 1945. It was expected that this would meet suicidal resistance. Hiroshima was destroyed on August 6 with perhaps 75,000 immediate and tens of thousands of later deaths. There being no immediate surrender the second bomb was dropped on Nagasaki on August 9 without any intervening policy review. Here there were about 40,000 immediate deaths. At this point the Emperor interceded and overruling his military advisers ordered the surrender that came four days later.[28]

It is perhaps a testament to the privations of war and the almost universal relief when it was finally over that American public opinion overwhelmingly approved Truman's decision (75 percent majority according to the Gallup poll). So did most of the early historians, Herbert Feis urging that the bomb's use was justified because it saved "probably tens of thousands" of American lives. Only in the 1960s when a generation of younger historians began to review this period did a full intellectual critique appear. The most radical skeptic was Gar Alperovitz who argued that the Japanese were known to be about to surrender before Hiroshima and further that the unwarranted attack on Nagasaki came much too quickly thereafter. Moreover, the surrender would certainly have come, he insisted, upon the shortly anticipated Soviet declaration of war. Alperovitz outraged traditionalists by suggesting that the real motive was a desire, suddenly realizable with the successful New Mexico tests that preceded Hiroshima, to end the war before the Soviets could come in and challenge the United States' plans by demanding a large postwar role in East Asia. Stalin would also, it was hoped, become more cooperative in Eastern Europe after this demonstration of American power. This line of thought has not found widespread favor in academic circles. Even historians, like Martin Sherwin and Barton Bernstein, who have been critical of Truman's decision, have acknowledged that his primary motive was to end the war. And he has been vigorously defended by others who point out that the Japanese gave no evidence, other than the weak diplomatic initiative in Moscow, of an intention to surrender until the very end, and also that the real power lay with military fanatics rather than the civilian officials. It is conceded that some American officials, including Secretary of State James F. Byrnes, speculated that the event would make the Soviets more amenable, but this has generally been interpreted as the lesser part of a mixed motive whose principal concern was simply to end the war.[29]

But disturbing questions have stubbornly persisted during the last 56 years. Was the "unconditional surrender" policy reasonable given the widespread belief that the Japanese would surrender if the emperor's status was preserved, something quickly accepted anyway after the war? Was the expectation of up to a million American casualties upon the final invasion, much relied on later by Truman and his associates as a justification for the bomb's use, really genuine? It is known now that military planners never projected such figures and the anticipated Soviet entry into the war raises a further doubt. Why was there so little consultation in the weeks before Hiroshima, given the doubts expressed at the time or later by such key figures as chief of staff Admiral William D. Leahy, General Dwight D. Eisenhower, former President Herbert Hoover, publisher Henry Luce, and columnist Walter Lippmann among others? Was it necessary to bomb an almost exclusively civilian population (96 percent of the casualties for the two cities combined)? How does one explain the destruction of Nagasaki only three days after Hiroshima?

The fateful decisions have been vigorously defended and answers of varying plausibility have been given to all these questions. In a recent historiographical review J. Samuel Walker suggests that the 1970s' consensus – "that the bomb was used primarily for military reasons and secondarily for diplomatic purposes" – continues to prevail. But fresh official and private evidence has stimulated a good deal of recent debate. Robert Messer has found curious ambiguities in Truman's records; James Hershberg has uncovered a coordinated quasi-official attempt to disarm anticipated public criticism; and Michael Sherry has probed the significance of a "technological fanaticism" he finds at the heart of air force bombing policy. Meanwhile the three pace-setting scholars in this field have variously maintained or modified their positions: Alperovitz reasserting his case strongly in a number of ways; Sherwin, who in his earlier acknowledgment of a mixed motive had nevertheless argued that by Potsdam, "the decision to use the bomb to end the war could no longer be distinguished from the desire to use it to stabilize the peace," going on now to suggest that Truman refused to modify the "unconditional surrender" formula because of the "diplomatic dividend" he expected; and Bernstein, conversely, emphasizing in recent work that none of the possible alternative actions could have ended the war as quickly as dropping the bomb.[30]

The debates continue. They erupted publicly as recently as 1995 when a planned Smithsonian Institution commemorative exhibit brought veterans groups and scholars into angry confrontation over the desire of a wide spectrum of diplomatic historians to have the various viewpoints aired as a part of the display. The enduring passions doubtless reflect the fact that, as the Japanese emperor told his people, the atomic bomb was "a cruel weapon." But the Japanese had been exceptionally cruel themselves earlier, and indeed the whole war in 1945 had reached such a crescendo of violence that Dresden in Germany had been destroyed by the British and American air forces with comparable loss of life in February, and one of the many conventional air attacks on Tokyo had already killed more people than died at Hiroshima. These facts help explain the absence of significant moral concern in the immediate aftermath of the atomic explosions.[31]

Many feel, nevertheless, that there is a unique moral imperative at the heart of these events and that no fully satisfactory answer can be found simply by making comparisons and sifting political motives. Doubtless revisionist critics could be more sensitive to the general context of the war in 1945. But few historians approach this subject without qualms. Historian Paul Boyer, who has explored Hiroshima's remarkable significance in American life, especially its cultural effects, urges a full continuing confrontation with the issue. "It is very difficult, to say the least," he argues "to fit Hiroshima into a moral schema rooted in a national mythology of innocence and exceptionalism." The deliberate selection of an overwhelmingly civilian target, populated mainly by the elderly, women, and children; the grotesque flippancy of the title "Little Boy" scribbled on the Hiroshima bomb; the dogged assertion of

President Truman that he never lost a night's sleep over the decision; the exultation of a United States air force general that he was able to get in one more devastating air attack on the ruins of Tokyo just ahead of the anticipated surrender – all this seems to expose a depressing sense of human alienation.

Hiroshima is a pivotal event in modern history. It can be seen as both a horrific climax to half a century of unprecedented international violence and as an overture to another half-century of fragile peace secured very largely by vivid memories of the event. It brought an immediate revolution in consciousness. The Soviets were suddenly brought to see the limits of their hard-won victory, the Americans to recognize the prospective loss of their historic immunity from attack. And as political scientist David Holloway's exploration of the Soviet nuclear weapon program during the war has shown, the two emergent superpowers were already, though few Americans were as yet aware of it, competing in a nuclear arms race.[32] Is Hiroshima, then, the appropriate moment to announce the onset of the Cold War?

I think not. It is better seen as an enormously significant moment in an otherwise confusing stream of events. The bomb's potential as a possible threat to future peace was, of course, immediately recognized and led to the formulation of the Truman administration's so-called Baruch Plan, envisioning a short-term American monopoly followed by a regime of international control. But United States–Soviet negotiations in 1946 broke down, a victim of rising mutual suspicion. The atomic weapon's full ramifications, like those of the post-Yalta tension and the Potsdam decisions over Germany, only became obvious later when the Cold War reached a crystallized stage. Cumulatively events like the post-Yalta differences, the Potsdam conference, and the atomic attack on Japan doubtless diminished hopes for an easy transition to peace and aroused increasing suspicion on both sides of what was not yet known as "the Iron Curtain." But it is surely questionable whether a phenomenon as profound and long-lasting as the Cold War can be said to have started with a period of more or less conventional and predictable diplomatic skirmishing or with a single issue or a unilateral act, whether it be a dramatic one like the advent of the atomic bomb, or a relatively obscure one such as the call by French Communist Party leader, Jacques Duclos, in an April 1946 newspaper article, for the American Communist party to oppose United States foreign policies – identified by some historians as the start of the great conflict.[33]

We should surely be looking for something more structural in character, perhaps for a process or chain of circumstances where we can see fundamental policy on both sides actually changing in response to events and taking on the shape of a mutually recognized confrontation between the two great cohering systems of power. We certainly do not see anything like that in the period immediately after the war, say from August 1945 to March 1946. Truman, and indeed most Americans, were preoccupied as we will shortly see with the difficulties of reconversion and with the erupting industrial strife at home that developed by early 1946 into the largest strike movement in American history. Diplomacy was left mainly in the hands of James Byrnes who, after a negotiating setback at an inconclusive foreign ministers conference in London in September went to Moscow in December 1945 and, very much in the spirit of Rooseveltian accommodation, reached several compromise agreements with Stalin. These included an intimation that the United States would recognize the Soviet satellite regimes in Rumania and Bulgaria conditional on the promise of future elections there.

But now we do begin to see signs of fundamental change. For by this point, nearly half a year after Hiroshima, Truman was receiving criticism from more hawkish Republicans and conservative newspapers were complaining about the lack of coherent principle in American diplomacy. Truman himself was losing patience with the Soviets whose general behavior in Eastern Europe and Iran (where they persisted in occupying the northern part of the country) and in international affairs generally seemed increasingly self-interested and unfriendly. The president was inclined to blame Byrnes, an

adroit deal-maker only lightly burdened by principle, for ap-
peasing Stalin. Truman told the Secretary that he was "Tired
of babying the Soviets." The new militance led to an unhappy
homecoming for Byrnes, explained in fascinating detail by historian Robert Messer, but not to any immediate discernible
change in policy.[34]

Nevertheless we are now, I believe, at the beginning of the
chain of interrelated events that brought on the Cold War. In
December 1945 the Soviets had disappointingly given official
notice that they would not join the World Bank or the International Monetary Fund – two key institutional features of
Roosevelt's postwar vision. Then at the start of 1946 Truman's
re-awakened suspicions about Soviet intentions were sharpened further by a series of shocks. In January we see a show of
belligerence by the Soviet delegation to the first meeting of the
United Nations Security Council in London. When the Iranian government complained, with apparent justification, that
the Soviet Union was illegally prolonging the military occupation of its country Moscow responded with fierce attacks upon
British policies in Greece, Indonesia, and elsewhere. This was
quickly followed by public revelations that the Soviets had
been spying on the wartime Manhattan Project, and by official statements that seemed to acknowledge that Stalin had
extracted territorial concessions at the expense of China and
Japan from Roosevelt at Yalta in return for their brief, self-
serving war effort in that theater. Stalin then made a speech
on February 9 forecasting, very much in the spirit of prewar
ideological hostility, that the imperialists, clearly meaning Britain and the United States, would soon fall out and wage a war
with each other that might endanger Soviet security.[35]

By themselves these developments might have been received
with understanding. But their rapid sequential appearance in
such a compressed period of time suggested an uncooperative
spirit and inevitably gave them a provocative aspect. And they
were especially disturbing because they occurred against a
background of growing Soviet geopolitical expansion in Southern Europe and the Near East. Since the Churchill–Stalin deal
at Moscow in October 1944, it had been more or less ac-

cepted in London and Washington that the Soviets would impose their rule, hopefully in a humane way, in Eastern Europe which, it was widely acknowledged, had been at least since Napoleon's time an easy, congenial staging ground for the invasion of Russia. But since the middle of 1945 Stalin had been steadily moving into areas where the "security" argument was much less compelling. And now he was clearly applying various forms of pressure, including military threats, against three British-protected states to the south: Greece, Turkey, and Iran. It was this move, well beyond the tacitly accepted Soviet sphere, that was now ringing alarm bells in London, and increasingly in Washington also.

This Soviet southern thrust had its origins in the breakdown of the Anglo–Soviet partnership after the Yalta Conference when Churchill, responding to what he clearly saw as a better postwar prospect, aligned himself with a United States that seemed at last to be willing to accept a significant degree of political engagement in postwar Europe. He therefore gave public support to Roosevelt's proclaimed post-Yalta commitment to democracy in Poland and Eastern Europe generally. Stalin retaliated sharply. The threats he now presented to the three states Britain regarded as her indispensable "northern tier" – protecting her interests in the Mediterranean and the oil regions to the East – took different forms: a communist insurgency in Greece that he appears to have had trouble controlling effectively; a more conventional threat to Turkey's independence including massing troops in neighboring Bulgaria; and a prolonged and increasingly menacing occupation of northern Iran seemingly with a view to incorporating that area, and perhaps more of the country, into the Soviet sphere. In addition the Soviets, while carefully avoiding any geopolitical challenge to the United States, developed a campaign to undermine a British leadership in Western Europe that Moscow had encouraged during their wartime association as a natural and even desirable complement to Soviet influence in the East. They also began a world-wide propaganda barrage against British "imperialism." This variegated political onslaught the British had by early 1946 come to regard as a

Soviet "war of nerves." It was a rehearsal in many respects for the United States–Soviet confrontation that followed.[36]

It is important to be aware of these Anglo–Soviet tensions in the European political theater in the nine months or so after Germany's defeat because a vital part of the process of political crystallization early in 1946 was the first substantive American attachment to the British side in this struggle, a development that, by threatening the marriage of American power and Britain's European and world-wide connections, was bound to disturb the leadership in Moscow. Twice already in the twentieth century the United States had moved to confront the dominant, expansionary continental power through the British corridor. Now this path was clearly opening up again, and already perceptive dissenters who saw America once more succumbing to British manipulation were sounding a warning note.

If these Soviet actions and gestures, and the resentment they caused in Washington constituted a first step toward full cold war in early 1946, the second stage was the well-timed appearance of two authoritative definitions of the threat from Moscow and of the steps needed to meet it. The first came from George F. Kennan, United States Charge d'Affaires in Moscow and an acknowledged expert on Soviet policy. Asked by the State Department to explain Moscow's recent aggressive diplomacy he responded on February 22 with what came to be known as the "long telegram" portraying a relentlessly expansionary Soviet state, driven by a messianic ideology. Only an American-led democratic coalition, pursuing a policy of what he would later call "containment," could halt it, save Europe, and ensure security for the United States. His compelling argument greatly impressed Byrnes and was widely circulated in official Washington by Secretary of the Navy James Forrestal. It played a significant part in mobilizing official support for a firmer policy.[37]

Much the same call to action, this time in public and addressed to an American and world audience, came a few days later from Winston Churchill. His party had been defeated in the July 1945 British election and at the beginning of 1946 he was vacationing in Florida. He had spoken out in discreetly measured terms about what he clearly saw as a Soviet menace on earlier occasions as an opposition leader in London. He now came to Westminister College in Fulton, Missouri, accompanied by President Truman, who had sponsored the invitation and introduced the Englishman's presentation on March 5 of what came to be known as the "Iron Curtain" speech. Churchill spelled out, with characteristic eloquence, his perception of the dangers created by the power and "expansionary tendencies" of the Soviet Union, already in command of Eastern and Central Europe and a threat to the rest of the continent and regions beyond. Like Kennan he urged that the only defense short of war was a policy of collective security built around an Anglo–American "fraternal association." This sensational warning, rightly seen as having Truman's prior approval, was a sharp break with the convention of outward cordiality toward the Soviet Union hitherto observed by Western leaders. Many Americans were initially opposed to the thesis, or at least unconvinced. But as press and public debate grew, and as the concurrent crisis over the Soviet occupation of Iran provided daily reinforcement, there was a marked drift in general sentiment toward Churchill's view.[38]

Churchill's initiative was not a unilateral British act, nor was it simply a speech. It was, rather, the visible part of, and in a sense a cover for, a strategy of tentative policy re-alignment on the part of the Truman administration that was executed mainly by Byrnes. As early as 1972 the historian John Lewis Gaddis identified a "re-orientation" of American policy in early 1946. My subsequent explorations tied this in certain ways to Churchill's speech. Both Truman and Byrnes consulted with Churchill before the event and knew the general line he would take well in advance. They found it politic in the immediate aftermath to dissociate themselves somewhat, but neither the Soviets nor most of the American press were deceived. More substantively, Byrnes sent three separate geopolitical messages to Moscow on March 5, the day of the Fulton speech: one demanding copies of all economic agreements the Soviet government had made with the East European states; a second protesting Soviet economic demands on China; and the third complaining of Soviet conduct over the Iranian issue. The *New York Times*, missing the note on Eastern Europe, editorialized on the others: "One would have to go back far to find two U.S. protest notes to one power on two different issues on the same day." The *Washington Star* found the initiatives "obviously part of a general policy." The era of ambiguity in American diplomacy was coming to a close.[39]

Meanwhile, even as Churchill's speech was being digested and discussed, a third crucial element in the evolving consolidation, a vivid demonstration by the Soviet Union of the essential accuracy of the Kennan–Churchill diagnosis, was unfolding in full public view. With the now illegal and ominous-looking Soviet occupation of northern Iran beginning to agitate Western opinion, the Iranian government, with secret British encouragement and active American help behind the scenes, brought the issue before the closely watched United Nations Security Council meeting held in New York in late March. Byrnes, seizing the opportunity to consolidate the new "firm" line that he had already begun to implement without any public acknowledgment, appeared at the head of the American delegation and, in effect, prosecuted the case. The Soviets, failing to grasp the public significance of this theatrical event – the first American appearance of the United Nations with an estimated 200 journalists in attendance for each delegate – resisted stubbornly. As so often in these years they made a bad, "bullying" impression and when they failed to dislodge the Iranian complaint they walked out of the Council meeting, arousing expectations that they might leave the organization altogether. In itself, this was an alarming event. In the inflamed context of March 1946 it seemed to many to present spectacular confirmation of Churchill's portrait of Soviet power and purposes. The Truman administration, newly confident and generally applauded at home for its defense of a small power under threat, was now set on a steady course toward confrontation and cold war.[40]

As we review this process of American policy realignment –

Soviet provocations, authoritative definitions of the threat, confirmation of it through Soviet clumsiness in Iran and the United Nations – we are inevitably left with a question: Why did Stalin, so careful up to this point to avoid bringing the United States and Britain together in an anti-Soviet front (which Roosevelt had repeatedly reassured him he would not allow), now act in a way that was highly likely to unite them? Historians have often suggested that as a totalitarian dictator Stalin was handicapped by his inability to understand democratic sentiment. But the better explanation is that he now felt, after Churchill's speech and Byrnes' diplomatic reinforcement of it, that the feared Anglo–American alliance was already in place and that, in a test of wills over Iran, an area of primary Soviet interest, he should show resolution. After all, the 1930s' lessons about appeasement had universal application. As the former Marxist historian, Isaac Deutscher wrote, "Stalin, playing from terrible weakness, decided to bluff his way out by a show of calm, self-assurance and power." In April, shortly after the United Nations confrontation with the United States, Stalin complained directly to the American ambassador in Moscow that Churchill was instigating war and that an anti-Soviet alliance existed. Years later his successor, Nikita Khrushchev, recalled that after Churchill's speech Soviet relations with Britain and the United States "were, for all intents and purposes, ruined." The Cold War, he noted, "had already set in."[41]

A deceptively quiet year followed these early 1946 eruptions. We see abundant evidence of the Truman administration's commitment to this new firmer policy, only partly tempered by continuing uncertainty about public opinion. We notice, for example, the ostentatious dispatch of the USS *Missouri*, the world's most powerful warship, on a mission of symbolic support to Turkey, and increasing American financial support for the British effort to sustain both Turkey and Greece. The United States kept the pressure on over Iran too, and the Soviets circumspectly withdrew at last in mid-1946. A hard line was taken, as well, at the long Peace Conference, held in Paris during the summer to iron out peace treaties with

Hitler's former satellites. Byrnes, with Republican associates supportively at hand, vigorously defended Western interests in Europe and the Mediterranean. And there was a tougher line at home also, symbolized by the forced resignation of Commerce Secretary and former Vice-President Henry Wallace when he publicly questioned Byrnes' increasingly anti-Soviet approach.[42]

But we see too the early emergence of a well-obscured and little-acknowledged truth about the Cold War: that while it was pre-eminently a passionately contested politico-ideological struggle, with a violent, military outcome always a lively possibility, it was also, both in this early European phase and later, a system of order and stability which the two sides created together and in which each had a fundamental stake. This system, a foundation of what historian John Lewis Gaddis later conceptualized as "the long peace," sometimes broke down, notably over German issues and more generally when the Cold War merged with the dramatic assertiveness of formerly subjected peoples and became a global affair. In the year after the Fulton–Iran crisis, certainly, the two emergent superpowers still made some effort to play down their increasingly confrontational relationship and in Paris, after much acrimonious negotiation, the United States finally recognized the communist governments of Bulgaria and Rumania, in effect conceding Eastern Europe to Stalin, and the Soviets in turn abandoned their long diplomatic effort to secure a foothold in North Africa and a base in the Eastern Mediterranean.[43]

In geopolitical terms this was a consummation of the Stalin–Churchill "deal" of October 1944, recognizing respective spheres in Eastern Europe and the Mediterranean. The profound event in the intervening two years had been the gradual attachment of the United States to the British side, a development precipitated not by direct third party aggression as in 1917 and 1941, but by the essentially political crisis of early 1946. It was eased in the minds of many hitherto dubious Americans in the year following by the popularity of a new conceptualization – "the West" – which steadily subsumed

Churchill's uncomfortably explicit Anglo–American "fraternal association."

The postwar international arena had therefore emerged with some clarity well before March 1947, when British officials appeared at the State Department to declare that their government could no longer afford to maintain the defense of Greece and Turkey. Here, it was immediately understood in Washington, was a crucial test for the Truman administration. It had been waging a kind of diplomatic war against the Soviets for a year without any real public acknowledgement. Now it would have to go public, an action that would critically test the new line. It was one thing to take on the Soviets in the congenial surroundings of the Security Council or the Paris Conference. It was quite another to plunge headlong into European politics with security guarantees. Truman and his advisers consulted the key Republican, Senator Arthur Vandenberg of Michigan, who recommended that the president "scare hell out of the American people." Truman did so. He appeared before a joint session of Congress and called for a $400 million appropriation for aid to Greece and Turkey, justifying it in a fiery speech that dramatized the Soviet and communist threat along the lines laid out by Kennan and Churchill and defining America's mission as the duty "to defend free people everywhere."[44]

The President's bold gamble paid off. Both Congress and the American people responded positively, registering the change in opinion over the previous year and sealing a government–public bond of solidarity concerning the Soviet and communist danger that would last for two decades. There were significant dissentients at the time and later. The influential columnist, Walter Lippmann, found the president's rhetoric dangerously disproportionate, and Schlesinger, in his 1949 book, *The Vital Center*, criticized him for unnecessarily universalizing a regional conflict. Vietnam-era historians like Richard Freeland, looking back for the roots of that disaster, blamed Truman for laying a misleading and flawed philosophical basis for global interventionism. Athan Theoharis, exploring the connections between domestic and diplomatic history, is one of many historians who have also been critical of Truman's clearly related order, only days after his speech to Congress (soon called "the Truman Doctrine") for a loyalty probe of all federal officials by the Federal Bureau of Investigation, an inquisition that examined six and a half million officials, found no major scandals and led to only 600 resignations, mostly voluntary. But all this reflected a new political sensibility in Washington. George Kennan contributed to the drumbeat a few weeks later by publishing an article in *Foreign Affairs* setting out what soon came to be known as "the containment doctrine" – a geopolitical strategy envisaging political, economic, and where necessary forceful resistance to communist expansionism all round the periphery of the Soviet empire. A persuasive distillation of the basic points made by Kennan and Churchill in early 1946, this concept became the dominating intellectual rationale of American policy throughout the Cold War.[45]

The capstone of this sudden, new burst of American activism was the Marshall Plan. General George C. Marshall, former wartime Army Chief of Staff and now, Byrnes having retired, Truman's new Secretary of State, gave a speech at Harvard University in June where he invited European governments to come up with a plan for their economic recovery which, he intimated, the United States would underwrite. This reflected the administration's concern both about the vulnerability of the still terribly weak European economies after the disastrous winter of 1946/47 and the related political danger this presented of communist take-overs in France, Italy, and elsewhere. The motivation was therefore a composite of the humanitarian, the economic, and the political. Events moved quickly. The British and French immediately organized a conference in Paris, which all the interested Europeans, including the Soviet Union and its satellites attended. It is an interesting token of the as yet unconsolidated character of the Cold War that Marshall felt obliged to include the communist states in his ostensibly humanitarian offer. It was calculated, however, that they would withdraw when presented with the prospect of comprehensive American auditing of the proposed aid funds.

So it proved. Molotov and the East European leaders withdrew, leaving the West Europeans to draw up plans that Marshall, after some modifications, submitted to Congress with the remarkable price tag of $17 billion over five years.[46]

Even this was not the end. Shortly afterwards Truman persuaded Congress to pass the National Security Act creating a single Department of Defense, the Central Intelligence Agency, and the National Security Council. Meanwhile, aid was beginning to flow to the French in their effort to reclaim Indo-China, and behind the scenes American intelligence operatives were making contact with anti-communist activists in French and Italian labor circles. What all this means, put simply, is that with the assurance of public support Truman had now worked himself free of the confusions which Roosevelt had left him in foreign policy. America would be internationalist sure enough. But it would function primarily as the leader of a political–military coalition, not as the architect of a harmonious world order.

Historians have, of course, combed over these events. Memoirs by leading figures like Truman, Under-Secretary of State Dean Acheson and George Kennan, among others, together with first-hand accounts such as Joseph Jones' widely read *The Fifteen Weeks: An Inside Account of the Genesis of the Marshall Plan*, formed the initial evidentiary basis of a kind of liberal celebration of this early 1947 period, symbolized by the title of Acheson's book, *Present at the Creation*. Many liberal scholars have followed Schlesinger's approach in characterizing American actions in this period as "the response of free men" to tyranny, or have agreed with John Lewis Gaddis in stressing the American perception of a West European loss of morale in early 1947 so that "the idea was to produce instant intangible reassurance as well as eventual tangible reinforcement." On one important point the orthodox scholars agree. The main impetus came not from internal American pressures but from, in Gaddis' formulation, "a perceived external danger powerful enough to overcome American isolationism." In the same spirit recent studies like David Fromkin's *In the Time of the Americans* and Walter Isaacson's *Six Wise*

Men have emphasized the common values of a heroic generation of leaders and officials rising to a profound challenge.[47]

Revisionists have often taken a more skeptical view, seeing
these initiatives as aggressive, self-serving, internally generated American actions. On this view it is the demands of
American capitalism that constitute the principal dynamic.
Thus scholars like Lloyd Gardner, Walter LaFeber, and
Michael Hogan have stressed the ways in which this politico-
economic activism of 1947 helped achieve American objectives. Hogan's recent, thorough analysis of the Marshall Plan,
for example, identifies a general desire on the part of American leaders, far from fully realized, to remake Europe in the
American image. Whatever their ideological persuasion most
students of the subject agree that the Marshall Plan served as
an economic restorative and Alan Milward's countering thesis that it only marginally stimulated the European recovery
enjoys little support. Not all revisionists stress economic issues. Melvyn Leffler, for instance, characterizes Soviet actions
from 1947 as "reactive" and emphasizes a variety of political,
geopolitical, and ideological as well as economic impulses in a
forward postwar American diplomacy of "national security"
directed to the acquisition and control of "resources, industrial infrastructure, and overseas bases."[48]

What then is the historical verdict on this turbulent transition from war to Cold War? A brave American response to
yet another totalitarian bid for world power? A Greek tragedy of men on both sides caught in a web of history-fostered
illusions and hazy perspectives? The inevitable, or at least logical, outcome of a century of relentless American political and
economic expansion? The consequence, at least in its final
stages, of the crisis of early 1946? Or should it be seen more
positively in a dualistic way as a system, ultimately congenial
for both superpowers, for the control of postwar Europe and
the containment of the nuclear demon, a system that might
have settled down after its early birth-pangs but for the unanticipated eruption of China and the problems unexpectedly
caused by the faltering grasp of the European imperial powers?

One thing seems beyond dispute. By mid-1947 Truman had created a new politically viable framework for American foreign policy in the postwar era. Franklin Roosevelt, with his over-optimistic vision of a harmonious international order shaped by American values, had not prepared the American people to face the possibility of sterner realities. This transformative task fell to his successor. Once he had committed himself in early 1946 to a full political engagement with the perceived threat of Soviet expansionism Truman, even as he struggled with a succession of devastating reverses in domestic politics, moved with growing confidence through the series of consolidating steps we have traced since early 1946 toward the institutionalization of a national security policy at home and the rudiments of an American-led alliance in Europe. And by mid-1947 it was clear that he was carrying the American people with him.

This was a significant achievement. This unlikely president had shattered the old inhibition against an unabashedly political American engagement with the world in peacetime that had ruined Woodrow Wilson's presidency and the hopes of millions in 1919. And he had done it not on the basis of Roosevelt's ingratiatingly rosy scenario but on grounds of harsh necessity. Truman was never a visionary and it is unlikely, the inflated rhetoric of his March 1947 speech notwithstanding, that he expected the American commitment to grow much beyond the political and economic support of Western Europe and the altruistic provision of modest amounts of economic aid to the developing world that he would promise in 1949. But he had in fact taken giant steps toward the creation of a global superpower.

The Postwar Order at Home

The fundamental domestic issue can be stated quite simply: What would be the character of the postwar American order? Roosevelt's 1944 campaign had revitalized the left and set forth the vision of a more widely shared prosperity under a strong, compassionate government. As soon as the war ended this spirited scenario was vigorously challenged from the similarly renascent right: by business in the industrial arena; by the Republican party in the political. The reconversion period is properly seen, therefore, as a struggle for mastery in a moment of crucial transition.

In the longer view historians have also seen it as a struggle for definition. Could labor force business to share industrial power, a process already taking shape in the emerging European social democracies? What would be the role in post-depression, postwar America of Roosevelt's new federal state, created after all to meet a crisis that had now passed? Given the profundity of the issues at stake it is not surprising that while some historians have viewed the Truman era, in domestic affairs at least, as a kind of evolution or haphazard unfolding of themes established in Roosevelt's New Deal (implicit in the titles of Leuchtenburg's *In the Shadow of FDR* and Fraser and Gerstle's *The Rise and Fall of the New Deal Order, 1930–1980*), many others appear to believe that it has a markedly significant importance of its own and some even subscribe to Michael Lacey's estimate that in historical terms the Truman era "is more important than the New Deal."[49]

However that may be, Truman, as his record would eventually show, was not untouched by New Deal idealism. But he appears to have seen and to hope others would see that reconversion was an unavoidable, apolitical problem. He thought he could solve it sensibly by governing the economic transition to general satisfaction with his extended wartime powers, notably the Office of Price Administration (OPA), which, by controlling both prices and wages for a transitional period, would avoid the surge of inflation, perhaps followed by depression, that would clearly develop if the public's pent-up wartime savings were allowed to chase the inevitably small range of consumer items currently available. But politics intruded. In his brief "honeymoon" period after Roosevelt's death, while the public was still distracted by the war's dramatic end, Truman himself, conscious of his limitations, tried to create a suitable political base. This produced a number of early miscues. His quick replacement of several New Deal grandees with less stellar appointees, some of them Missouri cronies of very modest accomplishments, upset Rooseveltian liberals. And an aggressively reformist speech to Congress on September 9 (reflecting his sense of the 1944 Democratic platform as a binding obligation) alienated white Southern leaders by calling for a permanent Fair Employment Practices Commission (FEPC) – cherished by African-Americans. He also angered Republicans even as their business allies were reeling from an epidemic of hastily cancelled wartime orders from Truman's military departments, which were fearful of being left with vast, useless surpluses.[50]

Still, the administration showed marked consideration for the business community's problems. It started negotiations that eventually brought a bonanza to business in bargain price sales of valuable plants and patents. And though Truman refused to allow the general price rises business wanted to tide it over the crisis, rises it justified by pointing to the vast hoard of public wartime savings, he approved Congress' action in appropriating a modest increase in public spending to encourage demand and, in a step he must have regretted later, he did allow some relaxations in price controls in certain, well-publicized cases.

These favors to business, small though they appear, were a dangerous gamble on the patience of a powerful labor movement. It had accepted "no-strike" wartime constraints very reluctantly and had often violated them, seeing them as a gift to business interests which they suspected were salting away enormous profits in unexamined accounts. It is certainly true that during the emergency wages were more rigorously controlled than prices. Richard Polenberg and other historians have shown that high worker income and abundant overtime, at least as much as wartime solidarity, had calmed industrial tensions. But now, with the patriotic spur gone, and with business, unable to raise prices, cutting costs by discharging millions of workers and withdrawing overtime, some kind of serious business–labor confrontation was all but inevitable. It developed alarmingly in the latter part of 1945 as the growing habit of union approved work stoppages evolved inexorably toward a series of major strikes.[51]

This serious industrial action escalated in December when the United Automobile Workers (UAW) struck General Motors. The dispute dragged on well into 1946. Early in the new year nearly a million steel and electrical workers walked off their jobs. The coal miners soon followed and in May the railroad workers struck, effectively paralyzing the national transportation system. By mid-year several million workers were out, most of them in industries vital to the national economy. It was the most substantial industrial dispute in American history, the closest the country has ever come to a national strike.

Here, clearly, was a situation to unnerve the most steadfast president. Truman watched the situation deteriorate in late 1945 and then began to intervene wholeheartedly as he saw his reconversion plans jeopardized. He injected himself particularly into the rail disputes, which threatened to affect most economic activity. He negotiated personally with the rail union leaders, but they refused any compromise. Deeply angered, Truman took to the radio to criticize the union policy and threatened to ask Congress for legislation allowing the government to draft striking workers into the armed forces. This extraordinary action, which even the conservative Republican leader, Senator Robert Taft of Ohio, thought grossly excessive, was shelved when, in a dramatic denouement, Truman was handed a message during an address to a joint session of Congress saying that the unions had decided to end the strike on the president's terms. He was rather less successful with the 400,000 coal miners whose formidable chief, John L. Lewis, a man Truman cordially detested, apparently settled his grievances with the owners in May 1945 only to declare his desire to renegotiate the settlement in November, a threat made especially ominous by the approach of winter. Truman again intervened strongly, securing a court injunction against the strike – a move that led to the imposition of a $3.5 million fine when the union disobeyed. Lewis had offered to negotiate with the president, but Truman refused to meet with him and in December the chastened union called off the strike.

These events have a claim on our attention for several reasons. They were, taken together, an unprecedentedly vigorous push for power by organized labor, hoping to convert the promise of the wartime expansion and the 1944 Democratic platform into a more effectual economic role. Their failure did much to give a conservative twist to the emerging postwar order. For this was not only the high-water mark of the modern American labor movement; it was also, arguably, the best and last chance for a wide degree of popular sovereignty in the American political and economic arenas. It is this sentiment that has inspired sympathetic labor historians like David Brody and Nelson Lichtenstein to lament the unions' defeat and their failure to become what many New Dealers and left-liberals had hoped for and expected: the spearhead of, not simply what political philosopher, Michael Sandel has called "a vision of industrial democracy," but of a practical social agenda that would go far beyond wages and benefits and look to a wider distribution of wealth and social justice.[52]

Clearly, this did not happen. The great labor disruptions of 1945–46 remain, like Roosevelt's refusal to seize the supposed opportunity to create conditions for socialism in the crisis atmosphere of 1933, one of the great "missed opportunities" in American radical left historiography. Some historians, unimpressed by the difficult context he was working in, blame Truman for betraying Roosevelt's 1944 pledges and for playing into the hands of business and the Republicans by so effectively mobilizing public sentiment against the unions. Others, however, point to the fateful decision of Walter Reuther, the influential leader of the United Automobile Workers, to give up the battle for access to General Motors' accounts in return for tempting wage increases and various benefits. He therefore opened the road, not to enhanced social justice, but to that privatization of welfare which remains, in certain respects, a central feature of American life to this day. Here, and in other like instances, labor in effect gave up its right to participate in management decisions, and with that its last real chance to share power in industry.[53]

These charges gain a certain plausibility from the contemporaneous trend in Western Europe toward close management–worker forms of social democracy. But one wonders if this was a realistic prospect at the time in the United States. In Europe, after all, the political and socio-economic crises of 1944–47 compelled a degree of radical innovation. There was no comparable trauma in the United States. Moreover, as the historian James Gilbert has pointed out, there was very little concrete planning inside the wartime labor movement toward a broad social agenda. In any event the early postwar years quickly exposed certain very substantial ideological and structural limits to labor's general appeal. The union movement was split between a moderate American Federation of Labor (AF of L) and the more radical Council of Industrial Organizations (CIO), each of which contained several clashing factions. There was also a strong, entrenched communist element in the leadership of several CIO unions that its opponents and the mostly conservative media played up relentlessly. Labor leaders like Reuther and Philip Murray worked hard to limit if not destroy communist influence and by 1949 several left-wing unions had been expelled from Murray's CIO. Further, vigorous efforts to promote union membership in the South and West during the immediate postwar years (for example the "Operation Dixie" campaign) failed miserably, a setback that later turned into a disaster for the left-wing unions that supported Henry Wallace's 1948 presidential campaign. By that time, according to cultural historian William Graebner, "Irreconcilable differences between workers and owners over production were displaced into the realm of consumption, where issues of ownership and class were softened and attenuated."[54]

Truman's halting, often distracted attempts to shape the postwar domestic order were scarcely more successful. His dramatic strike-breaking sacrificed labor support for ephemeral gains in public esteem that were soon dissipated by his unpopular insistence on controls to carry reconversion through without inflation. Many appear to have thought he was holding back prosperity unnecessarily. OPA's director, Chester Bowles, faced intense public and business pressure to relax price controls. The general director of reconversion, John Snyder, was susceptible to these pressures and Truman himself was often inconsistent. When Congress grudgingly extended OPA's authority in July 1946, but with much reduced powers, Truman impetuously vetoed the flawed bill, effectively destroying the agency. Prices immediately rocketed up causing public alarm. A sobered Congress again presented its barebones bill, which Truman quickly signed. But the damage had been done. There was little option now but to relax controls rapidly. By the end of 1946 OPA, the administration's effort to control reconversion, and indeed the Democratic hold on Congress, were all on the scrap heap.

On the whole historians have been more generous than his contemporaries in their judgments of Truman's handling of reconversion. It is true that he alienated labor by attacking the unions' industrial action, and by sticking to controls for so long he angered business and upset much of the general public. The situation called for a steadier hand and a sharper sensitivity to the economic and political currents, perhaps for a Roosevelt conducting the whole affair grandly from on high rather than a Truman rushing from crisis to crisis like an increasingly demented fire-fighter. But, as Alonzo Hamby has pointed out, this inexperienced new leader had to face "the revolt of every group in American society against those controls that directly affected its interests."[55] Truman was in an almost impossible position and perhaps deserves credit for the fact that the inevitably difficult transition was carried through without any major shocks, with steadily increasing economic growth and employment (after the initial run-down), and, in the circumstances, a lower inflation rate than might have been expected. If Roosevelt had lived all this would probably have been widely hailed as the unfolding design of a master political architect. As it was contemporary critics viewed it as a costly muddle.

Where then, if not to big labor or to the harassed Truman administration, do we look to find the principal shaping force behind the postwar order? It is surely to business and its conservative political allies. Robert Griffiths has shown that

American business began an increasingly sophisticated political mobilization in the late 1930s, adjourned it to some extent during the war, and then expanded it effectively in 1945–46. This campaign was waged, as Griffiths puts it, "on many fronts and by many combatants." We see it most obviously in the fight against the Truman administration's postwar controls and against labor's direct attack on cherished business–management prerogatives. We see it also in the constant effort, through lobbying and congressional pressures, to dismantle or emasculate the government's regulatory apparatus. And we see it in the persistent media celebration of free markets, as well as in the steady stream of abuse directed against controls, government intrusion in the economy and a supposedly burgeoning variety of dangerous "socialistic" tendencies.[56]

It is true that business itself was far from united – another reflection of the fragmenting impulse in many areas of American life that would steadily emerge as a strong counterpoint to the unifying sentiment engendered by the Cold War. In a recent study, political journalist John Judis draws an important distinction between an influential group of moderate leaders of large corporations whom he credits with a responsible public attitude, and the more conservative businessmen who dominated the National Association of Manufacturers (NAM). Led by men like Paul Hoffman of the Studebaker Corporation and the advertising leader William Benton, who had both served on Roosevelt's wartime Business Advisory Council and then in 1943 had founded the consensus-oriented Council on Economic Development, the former group stood for "a middle way". They prevailed over the NAM in securing acceptance of industry-wide union contracts, which suited large corporations but hurt smaller enterprises. And when the NAM called for the postwar abolition of federal regulatory agencies, the more moderate government-oriented corporate chiefs made it clear that they were content simply to limit federal powers. The outcome of the compromise they engineered with the Truman administration was the important Administrative Procedure Act, 1946, which economic historian Robert Reich has aptly called "a pivot" in the period's industrial legislation. It had the effect of converting the government from a direct monitoring party in a given regulatory hearing to little more than a "referee." Moderate business leaders also brokered a compromise with Truman over the Employment bill, lowering its expressed aim from "full employment" to "the promotion of maximum employment, production, and purchasing power." It emerged from Congress in a much restricted form.[57] These were all, to be sure, tokens of a general trend away from the 1944 Democratic mandate and back toward the enduring conservative coalition of Republicans and southern Democrats. We see this in the 1946 session when conservatives combined to pass the Case bill imposing restrictions on labor freedom and a compulsory "cooling-off" period before striking, as well as in the conservative gutting of the Democratic Employment bill.

But the tendency was toward government–business compromise, not congressional or corporate diktats. For instance, even as conservatives were stripping progressive features from his Employment bill Truman was able to make significant additions that actually enhanced, though admittedly from a somewhat different angle, the power and even more strikingly the efficiency of the federal government. These included the establishment of a Council of Economic Advisers (CEA) to counsel the president, and provision for an annual presidential report to Congress on the economy. Meanwhile, he had formed a commission under ex-President Herbert Hoover to improve general government efficiency. This preoccupation with good political housekeeping was very much in character for the tidy-minded Missourian who had long shared the widespread frustration with New Deal administrative chaos. But it had a deeper significance. It meant that, however limited his opportunities to effect reforms might be, Truman was determined to defend and where possible extend the concept of a strong federal government. The way was opening up for a domestic system of "countervailing power."

By the end of 1946 then, the constituent elements of a viable postwar order were beginning to emerge. Business, acknowledged now as the essential creator of wealth, would take a central part. It was beginning to work its will in innumerable ways. But its victory was not absolute. The long anticipated postwar radicalism had been successfully turned and labor was clearly opting for a comfortable junior partnership, but the union chiefs retained the power to disrupt and frustrate. Government was proving to be more collaborative than the 1944 Democratic platform had implied and seemed to be moving away from direct controls. But it retained the power to control the general economic context through its fiscal and monetary instruments and it continued to insist on its right to regulate business activity. Nor, with the Democrats still in power, had it explicitly disavowed its reformist and redistributionist mission. Here then was a developing system of balances and actual and potential checks, allowing for plenty of maneuver and adjustment. It was also animated, for the moment anyway, by a common understanding of the need to find practical solutions in the search for a general prosperity that was going to be seen as conditioned on a high level of consumer demand.

The rationality of this system, whatever moral view one takes of it, only became fully visible in the 1950s, by which time it had become more solidly institutionalized. It was obscured, meanwhile, by a good deal of vigorous agitation in the political arena of the early postwar. Here, we see Truman steadily becoming the focus of frustration and disenchantment for the heterogeneous New Deal coalition of 1944. Despite his fitful and generally unprofitable attempts to unite his party the coalition fell apart in the 1946 congressional elections. Labor blamed him for its many failures, liberals resented his new appointments and the small-town tone of parts of the administration, white southerners were upset by his tentative gestures toward civil rights reform, and there was a general feeling on the left that he had given in too much to big business.

Truman also suffered, as he approached this first test of his popularity, from the frustrations of two other powerful constituencies: women and black Americans. It is difficult to assess accurately the motivations of the millions of women who, often in response to official propaganda, had entered the workplace in 1942 and later. Historians William Chafe and Leila Rupp suggest, however, that by the end of the war many women workers were reluctant to surrender their often life-changing, even life-enhancing, wartime jobs. This issue is the subject of much debate today. What is clear is that the harsh cost-cutting impact of reconversion pushed millions of American women out of work with little ceremony, and that the return of 12 million veterans meant that when many of them did return to work later it was to less remunerative and less prestigious employment, often the familiar treadmill of waitressing and low-level services.[58]

The same churning postwar labor market upset black Americans. As jobs dried up so did the successful militance associated early in the war with A. Philip Randolph's Brotherhood of Sleeping Car Porters, with protest marches, with FEPC agitations, and the support of influential New Dealers like Eleanor Roosevelt and Harold Ickes. The individual heroics of returning black veterans, rediscovered by modern researchers, counted for little in the South, and even in the northern states many forms of discrimination in the job market (where blacks were typically among the first to be discharged), in housing, in admission procedures to college and in other fields, persisted virtually unchallenged by the Truman administration. Here too, then, as with incalculable numbers of women, the president had little prospect of assistance from an increasingly potent, liberal constituency.[59]

In all these circumstances, together with the historical fact that the opposition party normally made gains in a non-presidential election, the Republicans had ample reason to be optimistic as the 1946 campaign opened. They focused on two easy targets: the labor movement and the seemingly incompetent Truman administration. They benefited from the rampant inflation that had developed as controls were lifted (probably the most significant cause of public frustration in the mid-1940s); from the appearance of the anti-communist issue between the parties, a consequence of union radicalism and the first revelations of Soviet atomic espionage; and from the self-evident despair of many Democratic candidates who ostentatiously ignored Truman and appealed to memories of Roosevelt and the New Deal. In the event the Republicans, gaining as well from the general trend toward conservatism since 1944, won control of both houses of Congress for the first time since 1933. Many of them appear to have believed that liberalism was finished.[60] Certainly the new 80th Congress assembled in that spirit, already looking forward to a final triumph in 1948.

Towards 1948

In fact it all turned out rather differently. In what is arguably the most remarkable upset in American political history, Harry Truman was triumphantly re-elected in 1948. The traditional explanation, from historians who focus more or less exclusively on state and national politics, is that after the 1946 debacle Truman found himself confronting two aggressive but clumsy antagonists – the Republican 80th Congress, which set itself stubbornly against reform and worked to try and dismantle key elements of the New Deal; and the Soviet Union together with its naïve or disloyal American "fellow-travelers" who threatened national security – whose errors he exploited to successfully reconstitute the old New Deal coalition and confound all the pundits.

The problem with this is not that it is wrong – there is much truth in it – but that it is only part of the story. For a narrowly political approach emphasizing personalities, interest groups, and campaign tactics is inevitably superficial and even misleading. It contributes to the illusion that politics is a timeless struggle for power that transcends time, space, and the societal context. Moreover the excessively political approach, with its spurious sense of immediacy, brings us too close to the event. The proper corrective is to introduce a social dimension that plays down the individuals somewhat and gives us the broader perspective developed in recent years by historians like William Chafe and James Patterson. They have stressed the social turbulence and economic dislocations of the postwar period, es-

pecially as it affected millions of women, blacks, and returning veterans.

Patterson reminds us that the lifestyle (significantly the word,
evocative of a pleasurable chosen existence far above material
want, was not then in use) of the postwar era was very spartan
by modern standards. Many currently familiar items scarcely
existed in 1948: supermarkets, malls, residential air condi-
tioning, dishwashers, four-lane highways, automatic transmis-
sion, and so on. There was very little civilian air travel. Most
urban residents were renters. Only 44 percent of Americans
owned their homes (rising to 60 percent in 1960 – one of the
great quiet revolutions in American history), and only 46 percent of households owned a telephone. Cities were more com-
pact, more densely peopled, undeformed as yet by the
automobile. Suburbs existed, certainly, and had done since
the nineteenth century as Kenneth Jackson demonstrated in
his 1985 book *The Crabgrass Frontier*. But in 1948 they were
still a comparatively insignificant adjunct to the dominating
cities. Rural America, not the suburb, was still the natural foil
to the city. In 1945 about 25 million Americans (17.5 percent) still got their living from the soil. The move from farm
to city only became a flood in the late 1940s (by 1970 fewer
than 10 million worked the land). It was only then that, with
the postwar prosperity finally beginning to seem a solid prospect, the ever more thickly peopled race to the suburbs began
to look like a stampede.[61]

These socio-economic realities help explain both the preoccupation with the past and the very qualified optimism we
notice in these early postwar years. People were looking anx-
iously for secure employment, for cheap housing, for a safe
social security system. This broader perspective also makes us
more aware of social change as a determinant of political activity, important here because the late 1940s, inevitably perhaps given its transitional character, has an indistinct social
image. We lack here, for example, anything resembling Robert
Wiebe's "island community" conceptualization of a small-
town America in the late nineteenth/early twentieth century
that was driven by a "search for order" in an industrializing

society, although this has become the basis of a useful, more extended historiographical approach called "the organizational synthesis" which envisions twentieth-century American life as stretched out on a spectrum of advancing bureaucratic modernization. Yet in some respects the United States in 1947 was as close to Wiebe's progressive era portrait as it was to what social scientists in the late 1950s, only a decade ahead, impressed by new developments like rapid suburbanization, high consumption, cultural conformity, and television, would begin to call "the mass society." It might be thought that this formulation shortchanges the degree of modernization in the United States between the two wars and unduly dramatizes the pace of change after 1950. But as James Gilbert has written of the immediate postwar, "Americans still thought very much in terms of the 1930s." The impress of the past seems to have remained strong until 1949–50, when a combination of the new political challenges and rising affluence ushered in a discernibly different outlook.[62]

Putting political and social developments together in this way allows us to approach a fundamental question: What were Americans thinking as they approached their verdict in 1947–48? There are many straws in the wind here. The political discourse is certainly a primary source. Statistics are helpful and even polls (whose limitations as a guide to public sentiment would be famously exposed in this election) can be illuminating. One can also very valuably soak oneself in the journalism of the day for this last pre-television era was a kind of golden age for newspapers. A useful insight comes from media historian James Baughman who found a "transformation" after the Japanese surrender in most American newspapers and radio stations as local news quickly reassumed its prewar dominance and international coverage shrank dramatically.[63] The cliché "isolation died at Pearl Harbor" may be a fair comment on American foreign policy but not necessarily on the national psychology, as the incessant efforts of all later Cold War presidents to nourish and preserve a supposedly fragile internationalist outlook amply confirms.

Still, it would be wrong to make too much of this apparently persisting provincialism. George Kennan, a self-confessed elitist and professional diplomat, on venturing nervously into the deep American hinterland during a postwar "educational" lecture tour for the State Department, found audiences that were "attentive and appreciative." And this impression of sophistication is confirmed by the millions who read the serious literature of the late 1940s, much of it pessimistic and even apocalyptic. The presence on best-seller lists of Arnold Toynbee's multi-volume *Study of History*, George Orwell's starkly visionary *1984*, Arthur Koestler's anti-totalitarian novel *Darkness at Noon*, and war novels like Norman Mailer's *The Naked and the Dead* and James Gould Cozzens' *Guard of Honor*, compares favorably with the jostle of celebrity biographies, horror stories, and cookbooks we find there today.[64]

One book that brings this pre-election and pre-television period vividly to life is John Gunther's 1947 best-seller *Inside U.S.A.* Gunther, who visited every state and talked to nearly all the major figures, wanted "to show this most fabulous and least known of countries, the United States of America, to itself." He was by this time a national institution. His prewar books, *Inside Europe* and similar investigations of political life in Asia and Latin America were not profound in the social and cultural sense but their portraits of deceptively familiar power struggles in exotic settings indubitably illuminated – perhaps "domesticated" would be a better word – some of the mysteries of the outside world for many Americans. President Truman's characterization of Stalin at Potsdam as being "as near like Tom Pendergast as any man I know" is a perfect expression of Guntherism in action.[65]

On his home turf, however, Gunther produced a shrewdly observed book that is an excellent guide to representative postwar attitudes. Two themes stand out particularly strongly. One is the vitality of local traditions, institutions, and practices. Almost everywhere he found a high degree of pride and solidarity toward both state and region. The other is the enduring character of traditional American political culture and especially of what we might call the power structure in these far-flung localities. He celebrates "diversity" but of the regional rather than the social variety, telling us more about the local habits and cherished traditions of Virginians and Californians than about the problems of poverty in the cities or women in the workplace. Almost everywhere the white, Anglo-Saxon Protestant elite dominates, challenged only by the occasional Irish aspirant. Here and there the Catholic Church is an influential factor and ethnic figures like New York mayor Fiorello LaGuardia and Bank of America founder A. P. Giannini sometimes break into the picture. Jews are prominent in New York and Hollywood, but clearly their day has not yet fully dawned. African-Americans are apparently not to be found in the North and are a significant presence only in the South where they remain "a problem." Women, except for an occasional paragon, are scarcely visible, their sudden dispossession from the job market unworthy of notice, their feelings left to the imagination.

There is, too, a significant ambivalence about the book that helps explain the mixed feelings of many Americans as they approached the 1948 election, already anticipated as a verdict both on the continuing relevance of the New Deal approach and on Truman's record. It is at once a remarkable panorama (despite the limitations just noted) of a country undergoing great changes but trying to hang on to traditional ways, and a portrait of a society caught between its hopes and its fears. On the whole Gunther claimed to find a stable social structure and a widespread sense of well-being. Most of the states outside the South seemed prosperous and had surplus revenues that their governments were planning to distribute through tax cuts. Interestingly, given the Republican assumption of restlessness and frustrated ambitions, he found warm memories of Roosevelt and the New Deal, especially in the West and South, confirming the more recent conclusions of historians Jordan Schwarz and Numan Bartlett whose respective surveys of these two regions show a high degree of New Deal developmental assistance during the war. But Gunther was very uneasy about the surface of satisfaction and optimism he was portraying. He frequently expressed qualms about the accuracy of his own judgments in the face of such a vast subject, and also the concern that he and many of his interviewees felt about the durability of the war-induced prosperity. Nonetheless, interwoven with the garlands of metaphoric excess ("This nation is at once bull-shouldered and quick as a ballet dancer on its feet") are enough thorns of sharp-edged social commentary, condemnations of corruption, and warnings of moral complacency to bring many features of the period to life.[66]

The title of Mark L. Kleinmann's *A World of Hope, A World of Fear: Henry A. Wallace, Reinhold Niebuhr, and American Liberalism* is a crystallized expression of this contemporary sense of hope tempered by anxiety. As William Graebner aptly puts it, "From the 1946 film *Best Years of Our Lives* to theologian Reinhold Niebuhr's *The Irony of American History* (1952) many of the characteristic products of this culture of uncertainty were either ironic or concerned with the pervasive irony of the American experience, a sign of the society's general failure to work out the most crucial issues before it." He documents the point by reference to the films and books that manifest the haunting effects of the depression, the war experience, the Holocaust, the Hiroshima bomb – all producing a sense of profound contingency about life, about history as progress, and even about the American experiment.[67]

This evidence of ambivalence, which polls and other evidence substantiate, helps us understand the divergent courses of the two main political parties as they prepared for the 1948 campaign. The Republicans chose the optimistic tack. They thought, as their 1946 victory seemed to suggest, that their successful slogan "Had Enough?" reflected the public's repudiation of the Democrats and at least part of the New Deal, rather than simply frustration over postwar government controls. They therefore took the early initiative and projected an aggressive growth-oriented conservatism in the 80th Congress. Their battle cry was the enlargement of freedom – politico-economic freedom of the kind intellectually described by Hayek and others, sanctioned in foreign policy by the libertarian struggle against totalitarian communism, and nourished now at home, they thought, by a growing sense of business-led prosperity.

In that confidence the new Republican majority defined and tried to put into law a number of conservative measures. In hindsight it is easy to make fun of the ill-fated 80th Congress, one of the most cherished exhibits in the trophy room of American liberalism. It has been abused ad nauseam for its "neanderthal" mentality and its ultra-conservative crankiness. This has been overdone. It comes as a surprise after historian William E. Leuchtenburg's quite representative judgment that "the 80th Congress set out to dismantle the New Deal brick by brick," to find that the only basic New Deal constituency it attacked head-on was the now very unpopular labor movement. Its famous Taft–Hartley bill, passed over Truman's veto (and still in effect today, suggesting a less than revolutionary event) capitalized on public resentment to force labor to accept a compulsory cooling-off period of 80 days before striking. It also outlawed the closed shop and the secondary boycott and made unions liable for breach of contract and subject to various restrictions – all to general approval. Otherwise it left most of the basic New Deal edifice untouched. It cut some small programs such as the provision for school milk, but it had little success in its attempts to lower taxes for the wealthy. On the other hand it provided money for public housing (a particular enthusiasm of Taft's) and, with Vandenberg vigorously in the lead, it collaborated with the Truman administration in the institutional build-up of the containment policy. In many ways its bark was much worse than its bite. Having said all that, however, there is no doubt that in their highly partisan character and in their fiery rhetoric extolling freedom and excoriating what they saw as an exhausted liberalism, the Republicans in Congress considered themselves to be the heralds of a fully triumphant conservatism.[68]

If the Republicans tended to see only the hope and vitality that Gunther found in abundance, the Democrats had little choice but to take the other tack and emphasize the anxieties he had also noted. Many were inclined to blame Truman for the 1946 losses and there were several early efforts to replace him with a more attractive candidate in the presidential election. But for most it was not really a matter of personalities.

The New Deal was still the issue and the Democrats steadily worked toward a campaign built around the slogan, "Don't let them take it away!"

The Democratic blueprint is usually traced to a memorandum submitted to Truman by its supposed author, his bright young St. Louis aide, Clark Clifford. Alonzo Hamby has shown that it was really a synthesis developed by a former Roosevelt assistant, James Rowe, and refined by an informal brains trust to which Clifford belonged. Hamby also suggests that it contained no revelations for Truman who was himself the principal architect of his own campaign.[69] However this may be, the strategy correctly anticipated that Governor Thomas Dewey of New York would again be the Republican candidate and looked to defeat him by reconstituting the New Deal coalition with targeted appeals to liberals, labor, ethnic groups, blacks, and small farmers, and, of course, the solid South. The means to unity would be a progressive platform and a vigorous campaign showing up the contrast with Republican conservatives. The approach would be forward-looking in calling for carefully judged further reforms, and shrewdly backward-looking in its loud reminders of the Republican–business failures before 1933.

This sounds brilliantly prophetic in retrospect. At the time it must have seemed to many to be very optimistic and speculative. There was, for example, a dangerous, indeed near-fatal assumption at the heart of the Democratic scenario. Even as they moved to please labor, liberals, and blacks, they seem to have assumed, as Clifford's memorandum put it, that "the South, as always, can be considered safely Democratic." The flaw revealed itself in early February 1948 when Truman, having followed up a dramatic appearance before the National Association for the Advancement of Colored People (NAACP) convention in 1947 with a modest but significant civil rights reform message to Congress, encountered passionate southern resistance and threats to bolt the party. Truman backed off, and indeed, he hoped to keep the South in the fold by a strategy of inaction. Thus, his aides formulated a bland platform commitment at the Democratic convention. But the issue was forced by Minneapolis mayor, Hubert Humphrey, a rising liberal and now Senate candidate who led a successful fight for a strong civil rights plank. Many southern delegates immediately bolted the convention and later met in Birmingham, Alabama to form the States Rights Party with Governor Strom Thurmond of South Carolina, already well advanced in his amazingly long career, as their presidential candidate.

Truman accepted this reverse reluctantly. It should not have been a surprise. For a southern secession from the Democratic Party had been on the cards for several years. Roosevelt had long desired to create a modern northern-based liberal party on broad New Deal principles. To this end he had campaigned vigorously though unsuccessfully against several southern conservative incumbents in the Democratic primaries before the 1938 congressional elections. During the war he tentatively broached the idea with Wendell Willkie, his ideologically moderate liberal Republican opponent in 1940, hinting at a collaborative initiative. Meanwhile, CIO leaders like Walter Reuther of the UAW and David Dubinsky of the International Ladies Garment Workers Union (ILGWU) proselytized to like effect. And now Truman's strategy seemed to reflect a judgment that labor and black votes in the North were more important than the usual monolithic support in the South.

This would have made sense to anxious Democrats if there had been a generally united northern, liberal constituency to rely on. In fact, even before the southern defection the liberal split had widened dramatically and taken on an institutional character as former Vice-President Henry Wallace, with support from leftish liberals, CIO radicals, and others who were upset by the advent of the Cold War and its domestic accompaniment of right-wing Red-baiting, had helped form the Progressive Citizens of America and was later nominated as their candidate. Truman, who had tried hard to keep Wallace within the administration up to his self-induced dismissal in late 1946, made light of these adverse developments in public and soon began to campaign against "Henry and his communists." This was shrewd politics, for domestic anti-communism was already, thanks to Soviet conduct, Truman's coalition-building rhetoric, the House Un-American Activities Committee's hearings, and a few highly publicized spy scandals, a rapidly increasing source of public concern.[70]

Truman was similarly helped by the still deteriorating relationship with the Soviet Union. 1948 was, arguably, the most turbulent year of the early Cold War. Much of the tension derived from the decision of the United States and British governments to unite their German zones for economic and administrative purposes. So far as the Soviets were concerned, however, this was a highly provocative decision for it raised the specter of renewed German power. It is generally believed by historians to have led Stalin to launch, in February, the communist coup that toppled the hitherto tolerated Czech government of Eduard Benes, a self-described "bridge" between East and West, and thus condemned Czechoslovakia to life behind the Iron Curtain.

This event shocked American opinion, which had in any case been hardening against any dealings with the Soviets during the preceding year, and led immediately to passage of the Marshall Plan by Congress, and to the formation by the British-led Western European powers, with American blessings and strong intimations of future participation, of the so-called Brussels Pact – the precursor of the North Atlantic Treaty Organization (NATO).

Here we see the beginning of the third and in some ways most remarkable of the three great initiatives that the United States took in Europe between 1947 and 1949. The Truman Doctrine was an act of political commitment, implying the possibility but decidedly not the certainty of widespread American military engagement in Europe. The Marshall Plan was a highly politicized commitment to Europe's economic recovery. But it took the communist takeover in Czechoslovakia, with its overtones of revived totalitarian aggression and its inevitable intensification of American and Western concern about the safety and viability of the Western zones of Germany, to create the political climate that finally produced a United States-led NATO. Germany was now at last undeniably the basic Cold War issue. Today, with a more comprehensive evidentiary record, we know that, as John Lewis Gaddis has written, "What each superpower most feared was that its wartime enemy might align itself with its Cold War adversary." The merger of the Western zones had been inspired in part by a desire to revive the Ruhr economy and enhance administrative efficiency. It was also viewed by the West as a defensive response (though some scholars have seen it as an aggressive American initiative) to what seemed an increasingly effective Soviet campaign during late 1947 to create a unified Germany under its aegis or at least indirect control. Now the Czech coup suggested that they might try to realize this ambition with military force. The result was a surge of bipartisan collaboration in Washington. After Truman declared in a March 14 speech that the Marshall Plan was "not enough" and publicly endorsed the Brussels Treaty, Vandenberg worked with the administration to present to the Senate on May 19 what became known as "the Vandenberg Resolution." It envisioned American participation in a transatlantic collective security alliance, justifying it as a regional pact under the United Nations Charter. Then, as negotiations with the West Europeans began, Stalin took the next step in the spiraling tension by blocking the land access routes to West Berlin.[71]

Here the Soviets were taking advantage of the failure of the Western Allies, in wartime zonal negotiations, to secure legal road access to Berlin which, deep in Eastern Germany, reproduced in miniature the four-zone occupation of Germany as a whole. Truman responded to the virtual blockade with the spectacular Berlin Airlift, which involved the United States and British air forces flying thousands of tons of supplies into Berlin every day. This kept American eyes on his bold leadership right through the election period.[72]

It is often said that the effect of all this was to take foreign policy out of the campaign. In fact, it converted foreign policy into a prime Democratic asset. As in 1944, when Dewey had felt it politic not to attack Roosevelt's diplomacy, so now he felt obliged to accept the administration's foreign policy in general, thus losing this part of the battle from the start. Truman also benefited from the formation of the increasingly

influential Americans for Democratic Action (ADA) which was
established by well-known liberals like Eleanor Roosevelt, New
York Mayor Fiorello LaGuardia, theologian Reinhold Niebuhr
and historian Arthur M. Schlesinger, Jr. as a vigorously anti-
communist counter to the Wallace movement. The ADA endorsed the president's hard-line foreign policy, as did millions
of Americans of Polish, Hungarian, and other East European
descent. Truman also gained from his decision to recognize
the new state of Israel (overriding Secretary of State Marshall
and other advisers). Meanwhile, a similar coalition-building
impulse was at work on the domestic front. Labor was joining up, impressed by Truman's opposition to Taft–Hartley.
The President courted black voters with civil rights promises,
a campaign appearance in Harlem, and a historic Executive
Order in July to end discrimination in the military (though
the army was not integrated until after the Korean War). The
so-called "Brannan Plan" promised the small farmers of the
West and South various attractive subsidies and price supports.

The other positive feature for the Democrats was Truman's
vigorous leadership. His spirited whistle-stop campaign caught
the public imagination. He artfully ignored the two moderate
internationalists at the top of the Republican ticket – Dewey
and Governor Earl Warren of California – and focused his
attack on the hapless 80th Congress. He electrified the hitherto dispirited audience at the Democratic convention by declaring his intention to recall the Congress before the election
and challenge it to pass the progressive Democratic program.
Of course it failed to do so. But the effect was to dramatize for
all uncommitted voters the persisting hostility of the Republican Party to the whole New Deal tradition.

The Truman strategy worked. Dewey proved, once again, a
dull campaigner. Thoroughly complacent and over-confident
he refused to try and match the president's cross-country
barnstorming. Truman's attacks on "the do-nothing" Congress were the perfect unifying element. In the event he gained
a plurality of two million votes. Post-election analysis showed
that he had made the right choices. Labor support, galvanized

by Truman's redemptive opposition to the Taft–Hartley restrictions and his refusal to truckle to southern conservatives
who were resisting labor recruiting drives in their region, may
have been decisive (Truman himself said later, "Labor did it").
Black support made the difference in several northern states
and, when the chips were down, all but four southern states
remained Democratic. The Progressive movement was a complete flop and Wallace won no electoral votes. It was clear
that, despite all the auguries to the contrary, the New Deal
had survived the loss of its great architect. It had in fact
achieved a historic and decisive vindication.[73]

How sweet the morning after! Who has not seen the photo-
graph of a radiant Truman holding aloft the *Chicago Tribune*'s premature headline "Dewey defeats Truman." It was a
dramatic finale to a unique campaign in American history,
recently brought back to life by historian Zachary Karabell
who celebrates the substantial issues, the heated debates, and
the wide spectrum of ideological opinion on display. The president had confounded all the polls and pundits. It was clear
that the over-confident Republicans had drawn the wrong
conclusions from their 1946 victory.

In retrospect three significant consequences of the 1948 verdict stand out. In the first place Truman had, at least for the
moment, re-established the Democratic Party (and the New
Deal coalition) as the principal political power, though in its
slackening hold on the South the coalition was, as Alonzo
Hamby writes "badly frayed about the edges." Secondly,
Truman had created (though perhaps he did not fully realize
it at the time) a clear and enduring formula that would guide
the Democratic Party and "the liberal reform tradition," as
journalist Godfrey Hodgson has aptly described it, over the
next two decades.[74] The formula had two crucial compatible
parts. At home it envisioned governmental encouragement of
economic growth (with Keynesian methods implicit but not
yet openly acknowledged) allowing the introduction of further social reforms without undue sacrifice or social dislocation; and, in foreign affairs, robust opposition together with
congenial allies to Soviet aggression and communist penetra-

tion. This formula – growth and reform at home; containment of communism abroad – underpinned the policies of the second Truman administration, persisted in its modified form under Eisenhower, re-emerged strongly with John F. Kennedy and Lyndon B. Johnson through the 1960s, and perhaps had its last full-throated expression in the 1976 presidential primary campaign of Senator Henry Jackson of Washington. It received an early airing in Schlesinger's influential 1949 book *The Vital Center*, which is often mentioned as a powerful intellectual vindication of Cold War liberalism. Schlesinger echoed and retrospectively defined Truman's campaign by stressing the twin objects of desirable social reform at home and stout resistance to communist totalitarianism abroad. He gave the credit to Roosevelt and, somewhat immodestly, to ADA type liberals.[75]

If Truman has received less credit than he deserves from liberal historians for establishing the enduring framework of postwar Democratic political principles, it is perhaps partly because of the unanticipated disappointments of his second term. This brings us to the third striking consequence of the 1948 election: the anger of the defeated Republicans, many of whom henceforth devoted themselves to what one scholar has with only slight exaggeration called "the politics of vengeance." Here too Schlesinger showed insight in his 1949 book, predicting that the new liberal synthesis "will continue to be under attack from the far right and the far left." And indeed liberal rejoicings were short-lived. Truman's social agenda, freshened for the election, would make little headway against the enduring congressional conservative coalition, the appearance of new Soviet and other communist challenges would shortly draw the United States into an unanticipated war in Asia, and by 1950 the growing interrelation of conservative bitterness and communist successes had brought on the destructive phenomenon known as "McCarthyism." It is to these fundamental assaults and challenges to the postwar framework so laboriously established since 1946, that our inquiry now turns.

2

The Cold War Breaks Loose, 1949–54

Political historians tend to divide modern American history into presidential segments: the Truman era, the age of Eisenhower and so on, a tribute, no doubt, to the comfortable consistency of the constitutional system. More substantively it is a reflection of the dominance of the executive power during the past half-century which has produced what one scholar, writing in the late 1960s, stigmatized as "the Imperial Presidency."[1] Social and economic historians have long since presented alternative perspectives, emphasizing deep, persisting themes. And occasionally more politically oriented scholars, scenting the illusion of another quadrennial "fresh start", have asserted the unity of distinctive periods and patterns that simply refuse to be encased in constitutionally mandated categories. One of these supervening period occurs, I think, in the years 1949–54, bridging the Truman and Eisenhower administrations.

My rationale, simply put, is that important assumptions and contexts changed in and after 1949, introducing a new era. There is a conceptual unity to the period we have just examined, starting with the economic and political uncertainties of the immediate postwar, and culminating in the 1948 electoral sanction of the solutions found by the Truman administration. These included business-led growth at home, with attendant benefits for labor and the potential for further social reform, and containment abroad of the threat to Europe presented by Soviet communism. There was certainly no complacency in the national mood at the end of 1948. But there was, if only in foreign policy, a fresh sense of purpose and solidarity. The Truman administration was apparently determined to resist the new totalitarian menace. In many respects the problem seemed both familiar and manageable. Once again the antagonist, after some initial haziness, was coming into a clear focus that promoted unity. The danger was seemingly confined to Europe and its environs, which the United States had twice recently defended. As before, the engagement had developed through the well-trodden British corridor and was eased by the presence of other eager allies. And the United States was working from its usual industrial superiority, augmented now by a monopoly of the atomic weapon. Amidst the new, much was recognizable and much was reassuring.

The 1949–54 period, to which we now turn, exposed the illusory nature of such thinking. It produced a more frightening reality, presenting a fundamental challenge to Truman's hard-won postwar equilibrium. It was dominated by two profound and unexpected developments. First, the Cold War arena suddenly expanded, in two distinct stages, far beyond the European theater. In 1949 China turned communist and shortly thereafter the United States found itself embroiled in the defense of South Korea against a powerful communist attack from the north. The Cold War suddenly had a grimly contested Northeast Asian theater. Then, with the advent of the Eisenhower administration in 1953 we see a further enlargement of the arena with significant expressions of American interest in Iran, Latin America and Indochina. This, together with a number of regional commitments in the 1951–54 period, converted the hitherto comparatively localized Europe-centered struggle with the communist states into a truly global contest. Secondly, as the Cold War expanded, it insinuated itself with alarming intensity into the center of American political life. For, as the scope of the struggle unexpectedly widened, the Cold War "came home" to Americans both literally in the form of a rapidly intensifying domestic

politics of anti-communism, and psychologically in a growing realization that the United States was now engaged in a
new, demanding and pervasive kind of warfare that was recognized, after the first successful Soviet atomic test in 1949,
as carrying the threat not just of attack but of total, instanta-
neous defeat if matters were badly handled.

The effect of all these post-1948 developments was both to
raise the stakes of a Cold War struggle that many suddenly
felt was spinning out of control, and to break down the traditional line that, except briefly during the two world wars, had
kept domestic and foreign affairs apart. Until1949 the modern United States had, in its character as a world power, led a
charmed life – comfortably inviolable at home, exerting power
abroad more or less at will through political suasion, economic
pressure, and the occasional projection of expeditionary forces.
In 1949 the barrier between the two spheres began to break
down and with it, at least temporarily, Truman's orderly du-
alism of reform at home and containment in Europe. It led to
a period of unpleasant surprises and reactionary politics, characterized most dramatically by the full political mobilization
of the American people for a new kind of Cold War.

The principal events of this later period will be familiar in
broad outline: in 1949 the fall of China to communism and
the successful Soviet explosion of an atomic bomb; in 1950
the emergence of Senator Joseph McCarthy as the leading and
most influential anticommunist figure, followed by the start
of the Korean war; in 1951 the Truman–MacArthur crisis and
the fading of postwar liberalism, and its replacement in 1953
by a Republican administration ostentatiously pledged to com-
munist-purging and cost-cutting at home and "liberation"
policies overseas.

Each of these developments has its own controversial history. The striking thing is the way they fed into each other to
create a very distinctive, emotionally charged political culture.
A period of bitter politics and public hysteria ensued as the
so-called "Red Scare" gathered force. Not until 1954 did the
firestorm abate and the United States begin, with the discrediting of McCarthy and the deferred ascendancy of Eisenhower

"moderation," to move into the more tranquil years we associate with our image of the 1950s.

The Shocks of 1949

The new dispensation did not reveal itself fully until the middle of 1949. President Truman was able to bask momentarily in his great triumph. His foreign policy initiatives, despite their cost and their radical departure from American tradition, had been overwhelmingly approved. They continued, now under an energetic new Secretary of State, Dean Acheson, to evolve logically. In April Stalin called off the Berlin blockade, another moment of vindication for the administration, and in July the Senate, yielding to Acheson's skilful advocacy, ratified the NATO treaty binding the United States, Canada, and its West European allies together by an 82 to 13 vote. The United States, it was now clear to all, would defend Western Europe. For the rest of the world Truman unveiled in his 1949 inaugural address the Point IV concept promising scientific aid and industrial expertise to the emerging countries. This benevolent idea, more visionary than politically effective, was widely seen as a worthwhile pendant to the security arrangements for Europe and one that furthered the general American aim of a multilateral economic world order.[2]

The refreshed administration showed similar self-confidence and optimism in domestic policy. Truman announced a remarkably comprehensive program of liberal reform before Congress on January 5 – the so-called "Fair Deal." It encompassed both an extension of existing New Deal welfare reforms and the new causes he had added since 1945, notably aid for education, a national health program, the Brannan farm plan, civil rights legislation, and the repeal of the Taft–Hartley law.[3]

In retrospect it was an unduly ambitious scenario. The election result, which brought new Democratic majorities of 54 to 42 in the Senate and 263 to 171 in the House, had not, it was soon clear, displaced the old conservative congressional coalition of anti-labor Republicans and southern segregationist Democrats. This dominant bloc, together with the intense opposition to change mounted by well-financed special interests like the American Medical Association, large farmers, and munificent corporations, presented an insuperable obstacle in most cases. Some felt that Truman, though temperamentally as combative as ever, was being forced to become a political compromiser whose role, as journalist Samuel Lubell put it, was "to raise all issues but to settle none." The 1948 verdict was, it soon appeared, really for a consolidation rather than an expansion into new areas of reform.[4] Just as the Republicans had taken an over-optimistic view of their mandate in 1946, so now Truman seems initially to have misread the meaning of his victory, which was soon undermined from a different direction by the appearance of new foreign difficulties.

These setbacks, which will appear more fully as we proceed, have created a widespread impression among historians that the Fair Deal was a failure. William Chafe, in his influential overview, ignores it altogether. But this is unduly dismissive. In fact, Truman won important legislative battles for increased public housing appropriations (still an urgent problem in 1949), for increases in the minimum wage, and for other extensions of existing programs. His greatest achievement was to secure legislation extending the very limited reach of Roosevelt's social security system to millions more Americans. In these ways Truman enlarged the scope and promise of the liberal reform impulse. James Patterson credits him only with "a modest holding action" in preventing the unraveling of FDR's New Deal design. But given his constrained mandate, the unanticipated difficulties he had to contend with in his second term, and the new harsher interest group pluralism he had to work with, we might be more inclined to accept Hamby's conclusion that Truman left "a record of considerable achievement."[5]

However, the political climate soon turned against the liberal Democrats. Historians often emphasize two external events in 1949 that clearly stand in some kind of causative relationship to the developing "Red Scare." One was the communist victory in China. By the spring it was obvious to officials, who had long foreseen the defeat of Chiang Kai-shek's Nationalist regime, that the final crisis was impending. Chiang's army was breaking up, crippled by massive defections. The communists occupied the capital in April, crossed the Yangtze River soon afterwards, spread into the populous south and by mid-year had virtual control of the mainland. Truman, aware that American war materials mostly fell into enemy hands, had meanwhile terminated aid to the Nationalists. This hastened their fall and exposed the administration to the full fury of the China lobby – a powerful group of media barons, conservative politicians, people with missionary ties, and various long-time supporters of the Nationalist government which, as its fortunes declined, moved to the comparative offshore safety of Taiwan. Hitherto a fringe group, reflecting the primacy of Europe in American thinking to this point, the China Lobby now caught the ear of an increasingly aroused and anxious public with a sharpened indictment of Democratic diplomacy that had actually been initiated years earlier with the Roosevelt administration's alleged "betrayal" of China (and Eastern Europe) at Yalta.[6]

Public concern is easy to understand. The historic American peacetime commitment to the security of Western Europe had finally been accepted – the 1948 election confirmed that. Now, suddenly, the Cold War arena had grown alarmingly to take in the whole Eurasian landmass and, even worse, the odds seem to have tilted heavily in favor of the communists. Inevitably, given the earlier lack of official guidance, given indeed many unwise past expressions of optimism, the question arose: "Who lost China?" In August 1949 Acheson tried to ward off criticism by publishing a White Paper setting out developments in great detail and arguing persuasively that the result came essentially from internal Chinese realities and that the United States could not have avoided the outcome. But this came too late to head off the developing political firestorm.[7]

Historians, looking back on these events, have focused sharply on two questions. First, regarding China, they have tended, while finding much to criticize in the incoherence and confusion of U.S. policy, to endorse Acheson's exculpatory statement, locating the source of the setback in China, rather than Washington, except in the remote sense, suggested by Akira Iriye and Odd Arne Westad, that the civil war result was indeed associated with the breakdown of the Roosevelt–Stalin "Yalta system" for Asia.[8] Secondly, they have asked whether Truman and Acheson should have accepted reality and headed off an unwelcome Sino–Soviet combination by responding more positively to overtures from the Chinese communist leaders suggesting diplomatic recognition and some form of political acceptance. Recognition would have been difficult, especially as Chinese sincerity was never clear. In the fast-moving revolutionary situation various attacks on American property and personnel, as well as strident anti-American propaganda, suggested, if not implacable hostility, an inability to collaborate effectively. But historian Walter LaFeber, characterizing the Chinese revolution as a "turning point in history" has criticized the Truman administration for failing to turn with it. Similarly, William W. Stueck, Jr. has been critical of Washington's decision not to engage in talks with the Chinese leadership. Nancy Bernkopf Tucker, on the other hand, credits Acheson with a genuine effort to create the possibility of negotiations toward recognition.[9]

It is clear, though, that any such initiative would have been difficult in the face of conservative and congressional opposition, and especially after Truman was obliged to acknowledge on September 22 the successful Soviet test of an atomic device. This effectively precluded any surviving chance, from the viewpoint of domestic politics, of an accommodation with the communist Chinese. Acheson announced, on October 12, that the United States would not recognize the communist government of China, a policy quickly sealed by Mao's ensuing month-long trip to Moscow, which seemed to most Americans proof positive of the creation of a communist monolith, now apparently armed with the potential ability to launch a direct attack on their country.

It would be impossible to exaggerate the significance of the

Soviet atomic test. Once again the Truman administration seems to have been caught badly off guard. It had realized that the Soviets would eventually acquire nuclear weapons. But scenarios ranged up to 20 years, and David Rosenberg's studies of U.S. strategy in the short 1945–49 period of American monopoly show how little effort was made to develop stockpiles or encourage research advances. Strategy was dominated by the Air Force, which still thought very largely in World War II terms. In fact, as political scientist David Holloway has recently shown from Soviet records, Stalin had been pressing for research on an atomic weapon since 1943, and had then launched a kind of crash program after Truman's skeletal acknowledgment of the weapon at Potsdam just before the Hiroshima explosion. Now, very suddenly, the American people found themselves contemplating both the "loss" of China and, with this Soviet breakthrough, the imminent loss of their historic immunity from direct attack.[10]

Inevitably, these events caused public concern, though it is difficult to measure this precisely. The historian Lisle A. Rose, has recently argued that there was less public disquiet than earlier scholars, caught up in the later Red Scare excesses, have allowed. But there was certainly enough general alarmism to inspire quick ad hoc responses by the administration that stoked up the Cold War atmosphere and narrowed American options for the future. Thus, the failure to reach some sort of *modus vivendi* with the Chinese communists probably tightened bonds between Moscow and Mao's regime (which might have happened anyway); and the Soviet bomb clearly pressed the Truman administration and its scientific advisers toward an immediate decision to accelerate research for a hydrogen bomb, the easy solution best calculated to allay public fears.[11]

The move from atomic (fission) to hydrogen (fusion) weapons, formalized by Truman's January 31 decision, is another pivotal development. When one considers that a 10 megaton test explosion of the new "super" bomb in 1952 generated hundreds of times more power than the Hiroshima bomb, only the most fanatic Cold Warrior can fail to regret the decision to escalate and the frantic arms race that followed. But here, as with the 1945 atomic bomb decision, Truman saw the problem in simple terms. Once advised by scientific, military, and political advisers that the Soviets may have the capacity to build the "super," and conscious, no doubt, of polls showing a strong public majority for the escalation, he gave the go-ahead. Most Americans appear to have subscribed to the identification in a *Life* editorial of "the elemental fact of 1950: the enemy of the free world is implacably determined to destroy the free world. There can be no compromise and no agreement with Soviet Communism."[12]

Out of all this unforeseen turbulence there came a felt need for some sort of coherent policy declaration that would embrace the new situation. Truman called for an overall policy review. This was carried out early in 1950, mainly by the State Department, whose Policy Planning Staff (PPS) was now led by Paul Nitze. Its previous chief, George Kennan, increasingly restive as U.S. policy hardened, had resigned to take an academic post at Princeton University. Under Acheson's careful monitoring the PPS produced what came to be known as *National Security Council Memorandum 68* (NSC 68) – a paper setting out a series of hard-line policies resting on the notion of a bipolar, international arena, half-free, half-enslaved, with the U.S. called to resist the Soviet bid for "world conquest."

The United States, this significant document declared, "must lead in building a successfully functioning political and economic system in the free world" using both American military and moral resources. In practice, this meant no diplomatic negotiations with the Soviets or other communists, development of hydrogen weapons to counter further Soviet research advances, an enlarged American conventional force to create effective alternatives to nuclear war, a much larger military budget, a powerful alliance system, the mobilization of American public support, and unspecified efforts to undermine the Soviets in their own sphere. Sent to Truman in April 1950 this set of policy prescriptions, essentially containment with teeth, was almost immediately sanctified by the coming of the Korean War and became, as historian Walter LaFeber has said, "the American blueprint for waging the Cold War during the next twenty years."[13]

McCarthyism

At the beginning of the 1950s one becomes ever more acutely aware of the growing interrelationship between domestic politics and foreign affairs. The expansion of the Cold War marks both the occasion and the primary cause of the virulent anticommunism that permeated the national arena from the late 1940s to the mid-1950s, a period characterized by historian Stanley Kutler as "the darkest days of the Cold War." It was an increasingly visible factor up to the 1948 election campaign, though held in check to some degree by the Truman administration's increasingly popular activism in foreign policy which led to a brief period of bipartisanship, if not consensus. But sharp political divisions emerged again in January 1950 when the conviction for perjury of former high State Department official Alger Hiss (discrediting his earlier denials that he had given documents to a communist in the 1930s) exposed liberals to attack. The conviction tied in with the conservative critique of the "betrayals" of Yalta, which meeting Hiss had attended with Roosevelt, inspiring the title of Alastair Cooke's best-selling account *A Generation on Trial*.[14]

The Hiss scandal also acted as a curtain-raiser for the appearance of Republican Senator Joseph McCarthy of Wisconsin who burst upon the national scene with a speech in February at Wheeling, West Virginia announcing that he had the names of 205 communist officials in the State Department. "The reason why we find ourselves in a position of impotency," McCarthy declared, " is not because our only potential enemy has sent men to invade our shores, but rather because of the traitorous actions of those who have been treated so well by this nation."[15] Thus McCarthy addressed rising public anxiety, amplifying the Cold War-driven fear of domestic subversion and adding a provocative touch of class resentment. He then embarked on a remarkable four-year anticommunist crusade of fiery finger-pointing and harsh investigations that pilloried the Truman administration and also blighted innumerable careers in government, the media, the entertainment world, education, and elsewhere.

"McCarthyism," as it soon came to be called, did not emerge out of a clear sky. American anticommunism can be traced back to the nineteenth century when, long before the Bolshevik revolution, we find warnings and indictments in respectable journals. The "Red Scare" phenomenon that followed World War I, with its enigmatic mixture of labor-bashing and antiradicalism, appeared again in similar conditions at the end of World War II. Even before that, in the turbulent 1930s, numerous scare-mongering books contributed to a rising public concern about the fascist and/or communist penetration of American institutions. This helped inspire the formation in 1938 of the House Un-American Activities Committee (HUAC), passage of the Hatch Act in 1939 prohibiting political activity by federal employees, and of the Smith Act of 1940 mandating government registration of all aliens and criminalizing any conspiracy to advocate the overthrow of the U.S. government by force.

With victory in sight, difficulties with the Soviets intensifying and the business–labor struggle for postwar mastery heating up, the anticommunist tempo again became an insistent political factor. Thomas Dewey protested during the 1944 campaign that communists were seizing control of the New Deal. In 1945 the discovery that a left-wing journal, *Amerasia*, had large numbers of unclassified documents in its office, and testimony by a federal clerk called Elizabeth Bentley identifying supposed communists in sensitive offices, energized HUAC which, by 1947, was conducting a highly publicized inquisition into the always vulnerable film industry. Meanwhile, such respectable institutions as the Roman Catholic Church, the U.S. Chamber of Commerce, and Truman's own Justice Department, as well as a number of former communist intellectuals, all contributed to the rising anxiety with a flood of alarming anticommunist literature. As we have seen a number of historians feel that Truman fanned the flames with his loyalty tests and anticommunist rhetoric leading one of them, Garry Wills, to write "it is unfortunate that McCarthyism was named teleogically, from its most perfect product, rather than genetically - which would give us Trumanism."[16]

This seems rather unfair. After all Soviet/communist expansionism was hardly a figment of Truman's imagination. He clearly felt he had to arouse a reluctant public opinion. He won his point, achieving the consensus he needed for action. Moreover, the anti-radical public mood abated somewhat in 1948, as we noted. But it was then stimulated again by the foreign shocks of 1949 and the Hiss verdict of early 1950, which was immediately followed by alarming revelations from British officials that Klaus Fuchs, a wartime scientist of German origin who had been a member of the British team working on the atomic bomb at Los Alamos, was a Soviet spy. This clear intimation that the Soviets had long had a sophisticated atomic weapons program further reinforced Truman's January 31 decision to build the hydrogen bomb. It also led to the exposure of an American spy ring whose most famous members, Julius and Ethel Rosenberg, were now charged with arranging the passage of sensitive scientific secrets to Soviet officials.[17]

This background sets McCarthyism in a wider explanatory framework. The anticommunist issue was on the table long before his Wheeling speech. McCarthy simply picked it up after considering such other possible issues for his then unpromising 1952 re-election campaign as the controversial St. Lawrence Seaway. Moreover, McCarthy's anti-Red campaign did not really begin to catch fire in the country at large until Truman unwisely rescued the sputtering demagogue by attacking him personally, thus inspiring Republican leaders like Taft to defend and politically legitimize him. Even then, as historian Lisle Rose has recently shown, it took the sudden advent of the Korean War in June to bring McCarthyism fully to life. Given also that the senator's crusade ended with his personal humiliation in 1954, one is inclined to look receptively at historian Ellen Schrecker's recent argument that to understand this intensely anticommunist phase properly, we should take account not only of McCarthy's comet-like prominence but also of the extensive, much more coherent and enduring anticommunist network centered on the immovable figure of FBI director, J. Edgar Hoover.[18]

McCarthy was, nonetheless, a deeply significant actor in modern American history. For he took anticommunism out of the committee rooms, the law courts, and the more or less respectable printed page and brought it out into the public domain and then down to a level that was intensely human, accessible, and highly theatrical. He, more than anyone else, emotionalized the issue, tapping with instinctive skill into all sorts of deeply rooted American anxieties. For as he exploited a pre-existing fear of communism and treason he also exacerbated a range of social resentments (especially against the eastern liberal establishment) and phobias. He was successful in large part because he was persistently on the attack. So long as he had an ample number of targets he was successful and remarkably popular. His basic technique, making skilful use of senatorial immunity and an increasingly sensation-hungry press that was just beginning to feel the competitive pressure of television, was the sharp public accusation which, in effect, forced individuals from their private lives into the spotlight of a hostile congressional committee hearing that was itself, in this volatile time, an intriguing kind of political art form. The victim's exculpatory performance was invariably and usually immediately overshadowed by new or vaguer charges, or by a shift in the direction of fresh, even more prominent subjects.

Schlesinger, noting that McCarthy's ambitions were directed at headlines rather than real political power, recently posed the enduring question: "How did this reckless adventurer bring to boil the latent anti-communist panic of so many Americans?"[19] McCarthy's success was largely due to the support he received from conservative newspaper proprietors (at a time when the press enjoyed enormous power over the public mind) and from a Republican leadership, including Taft and other senior senators, that was still smarting from the loss of 1948. Beyond that historians have identified a remarkably wide range of support from groups including politically emergent Catholics, German and Irish Americans and other ethnic groups, newly wealthy Western entrepreneurs, and various status-hungry elements who admired his aggressive style. But one should not exaggerate these particularities. Right up to his disgrace in 1954 he enjoyed, if polls are to be believed, the approval of most Americans.[20]

His impact was profound. His efforts helped create the atmosphere in which the Supreme Court upheld, with only two dissents, several convictions of Communist Party leaders for violations of the Smith Act provision outlawing the "conspiracy to advocate" revolution by violence, the first convictions for sedition in over a century; and in which Congress passed, over Truman's veto, the 1950 McCarran Act, requiring communist or communist-front organizations to register with the Attorney-General, barring communists from entering the United States, and authorizing the construction of secret prison camps for domestic subversives in time of war. Though Truman fought back against McCarthy's assaults upon the patriotism and competence of his administration with characteristic spirit, most Democrats, even staunch liberals like Senator Paul Douglas of Illinois, were intimidated. McCarthy was able to attack not only safe targets like Acheson and "the striped pants brigade" in the State Department, but also such national icons as General George C. Marshall. The fierce new anticommunist spirit was felt far beyond Washington. Hollywood, already worked over by HUAC, now busied itself weeding out numerous left-oriented actors and writers and producing highly patriotic, anti-left movies in large numbers. The "blacklist" approach, pioneered in earlier witch-hunts against Hollywood, was now at work in television (where corporate sponsors frequently responded to active right-wing pressure groups by withdrawing financial support from shows and stations of questionable ideological sanctity) and in most of the public arts. Teachers, especially university professors, were also hounded. Many were obliged to take loyalty oaths. There were numerous dismissals. What is remarkable, perhaps, is the weak, ineffectual support most of these victims received.[21]

Liberals, looking for a silver lining in adversity, hoped that the Republican victory in the 1952 presidential election would damp down McCarthy's influence. In the event, having played an active part in the campaign, he was rewarded with the chairmanship of a new Senate investigative committee. President Eisenhower detested him personally but refused to confront him. In the end McCarthy played a large part in his own decline and discredited the whole anticommunist campaign by recklessly taking on ever more resistant and improbable targets: the Voice of America, the Protestant clergy, and, finally and fatally, the U.S. Army. The televised Army–McCarthy hearings from April to June 1954, ostensibly concerned with Army resistance to McCarthy's investigation of some of its practices, showed up the senator's harsh, unattractive personality. His irresponsibly brutal approach to obviously harmless individuals was exposed for all to see by a clever Army lawyer. Shortly afterwards the Senate, sensing McCarthy's lost power, condemned him for unbecoming conduct. His self-confidence and his health declined rapidly, and he drank heavily. He died in 1957, his forty-ninth year.

Many historians have tried to explain McCarthyism: its origins, its character, and its significance. The earliest biographers tended to focus on his personality. He had forced his way into Wisconsin politics from an impoverished background and then, after brief non-combat war service, he ran successfully, if somewhat fraudulently, for the U.S. Senate in 1946 as "Tail-gunner Joe." From this setting early writers, mostly liberal in their political sympathies, typically moved on to McCarthy's lackluster Washington career, which was generally seen as thoroughly opportunist. Yet there was always some reluctant respect for his shrewdness. Thus Richard Rovere wrote in 1959, "No bolder seditionist ever moved among us – nor any politician with a surer, swifter access to the dark places of the American mind." Many later historians have agreed. Robert Divine, for example characterized him as "a supremely accomplished demagogue" who became "the most dangerous man in public life since Aaron Burr."[22]

But of course one cannot explain McCarthyism by reference to its author alone. The first scholars to study the phenomenon analytically were liberal historians like Richard Hofstadter and the sociologists Daniel Bell and Seymour Martin Lipset. They were intrigued (and appalled) by McCarthy's evident appeal to poorer elements in American society traditionally loyal to the Democratic Party – elements some of them were inclined to see as the heralds of a "mass society" fixated increasingly by status anxieties. These scholars were acutely mindful of recent European totalitarianism. In their methodology they were influenced by European social thought, much of it introduced by the Frankfurt School of German émigré intellectuals re-established in New York during the Nazi era. But there were also, as historian Richard Pells reminds us, complementary intellectual precedents to draw on at home, notably studies in the 1930s by scholars such as Lewis Mumford, Harold Lasswell, and Thurman Arnold, whose often multidisciplinary diagnoses of mass society and behavior helped turn Hofstadter and others toward perspectives in psychology, anthropology, and sociology as well as history.[23]

More recent scholarship has expressed reservations about sweeping searches through history and in other disciplines for appropriate analogies and conceptualizations that tended to detach McCarthyism from its specific context. Norman Pollack and Lawrence Goodwyn, among others, have defended the Populists of the 1890s (characterized by Hofstadter as nativist, backward-looking, and addled by status anxieties), as authentic representatives of the American liberal tradition rather than the unwitting precursors of McCarthy. Schlesinger suggests that status anxiety is a historical constant in American life. And a number of historians, from different viewpoints, have insisted on the primacy of a more or less traditional political explanation of the early 1950s' eruptions. Thus Athan Theoharis, from the left, was joined by Richard Freeland and others in identifying Truman's persistently anti-communist rhetoric and occasional violations of civil liberties as creating a receptive climate for the Wisconsin senator. Michael Paul Rogin (whose detailed research tends to refute the notion of an underlying irrationality behind McCarthyism) and Robert Griffiths are more sympathetic to the embattled president, and place the responsibility more squarely on the frustrated Republican leaders who, from Taft down, were eager to pursue what Alonzo Hamby has characterized as "a politics of revenge."[24]

Despite their substantive and methodological differences virtually all the aforementioned historians have viewed McCarthyism as a national misfortune if not a tragedy. Stephen J. Whitfield, in a wide-ranging 1991 study, made the important point that far from being a purely political phenomenon "the national fetish with anti-communism pervaded American Society." He stressed its powerful impact upon the popular culture of the era. "Literature, movies, art, and the media – particularly the then-new force, television" he wrote, "consistently hammered the theme of an enemy within, working to subvert the American Way of Life." Recently, however, there has been a significant change in perception. The lonely efforts of conservatives like William F. Buckley Jr. to defend McCarthy in the 1950s have been steadily reinforced over the years. One thinks here of Allen Weinstein's persuasive demonstration in the late 1970s of Alger Hiss's guilt (after years of defense by many liberals) and more recently a similar exposure of the Rosenbergs by Ronald Radosh. The end of the Cold War brought access to Soviet documents which Harvey Klehr and others have used to demonstrate the almost total control by Moscow of the leadership of the Communist Party of the United States. These developments have been most recently summarized and reviewed in Arthur Herman's 1999 book, *Joseph McCarthy*, which is sympathetic in tone.[25]

The result has been a degree of liberal rethinking. In a 1998 study Ellen Schrecker, one of McCarthy's scholarly critics, conceded that most of McCarthy's "victims" had been in or close to the Communist Party and that, as Hoover, Nixon, and other conservatives claimed at the time, there was legitimate cause for alarm. But she urges a "pluralistic" view of the Party encompassing both a leadership obedient in the main to Moscow and a distinctly different membership bent sincerely on domestic social reform. Like historian Alan Wolfe she stresses McCarthy's destructive impact both upon individuals and, by virtue of his irresponsible exaggerations and crass behavior, upon the political culture. In October 1998 a continuing liberal skepticism inspired the anxious *New York Times* editorialists to proclaim "Beware the rehabilitation of Joseph McCarthy."[26]

We are not quite at that point yet. Yet clearly there is unfinished business for historians here. We need more closely focused studies in the Rogin–Weinstein mode that examine the impact of McCarthy in specific situations. But this is not to devalue the innovative Hofstadterian approach, which views McCarthyism as a key to deeper truths about American politics and society. Both are needed, for instance, when we try to measure the the long-term effects of this four-year phenomenon. It narrowed the political spectrum. McCarthy's excesses discredited the American Right, so that it took a further quarter century before a conservative president could be elected. More immediately apparent, however, was the damage the senator inflicted on the American Left. Godfrey Hodgson notes that, "Until after 1965, when the Vietnam crisis broke in full force, there was no opposition to orthodox anti-communism from the Left in the Democratic Party, and none worth a President's attention." The result was that "The risks of seeming 'naïve' or 'weak' always far outweighed the danger of seeming too tough."[27]

It is worth noting, however, that the radical left was in retreat long before McCarthy emerged. And one wonders whether anything to the left of Cold War liberalism ever had much of a chance in modern America. A recent analysis by Seymour Martin Lipset and Gary Marks entitled *It Didn't Happen Here: Why Socialism Failed in the United States* cites a host of obstacles. These include constitutional and political barriers, powerful capitalist values, and the failure of union/ socialist collaboration among other reasons, for what can only be seen as a history of recurrent failure.[28] The Cold War was itself a powerfully inhibiting factor.

During much of the post-1945 era there was, in foreign policy at least, a determined, self-conscious impulse in leading American political circles toward a "center" of bipartisanship, consensus, and shared purpose. But sometimes, in moments of great stress, the Cold War failed in its remarkable cohering function, allowing underlying tensions and political extremes to break through. Thus during the right-wing pressures of 1950–54 (and again during the surge of left-wing agitation during the later 1960s) the hitherto steadfast center painstakingly put together by 1948 and laboriously recreated after McCarthy's fall, broke apart to reveal, not indeed a unified people, but rather a cross-hatched society through whose only marginally communicating levels the fumes of credulity, distrust, and unbridled emotionalism could rise rapidly and almost unchallenged to the surface of national life.

Recent scholarship demonstrates a continuing interest in the socio-cultural implications of McCarthyism. William Graebner, for instance, recently characterized McCarthy, together with the innovative economist Joseph Schumpeter, the preacher Billy Graham, and others, as leaders of a 1950s' "revitalization movement" that was "committed to disruptive processes in an effort to break through or transcend barriers to change – in an age in which barriers seemed to be everywhere and change seemed impossible." And Lisle Rose concludes that McCarthyism was not simply, as Truman himself always maintained, a matter of partisan politics, but "was the first and most piercing middle American protest against all the real and apparent soulessness and incompetence of a large, distant, often unresponsive and, above all, liberal government." So the debate over this four-year episode continues, driven by a persisting suspicion that it holds the key to mysteries far beyond the feverish imagination and shrewd manipulations of its principal author.[29]

Korea

We must now factor in another unanticipated crisis during this difficult period. On June 24, 1950 the North Korean Army crossed the 38th parallel and launched an invasion of South Korea. Their rapid advance continued until checked by a desperate infusion of American military aid, which was just enough to hold a small perimeter around the southern port of Pusan. The invasion was yet another unpleasant surprise for the Truman administration. Korea had been a hotbed of unrest since the United States and the Soviet Union had, following prior agreement, occupied the north and south respectively after the Japanese surrender. In 1949 the two great powers withdrew leaving a well-entrenched communist regime under Kim Il Sung in the north confronting an appreciably more democratic but very authoritarian south under Syngman Rhee. There followed a tense period of border skirmishing and threats to invade from both sides.

Despite this the invasion took the Truman administration by surprise. It reacted with remarkable vigor, setting in motion a war that would soon turn into a larger struggle with communist China and go on until mid-1953, costing, according to best estimates, about three million Korean, one million Chinese and 35,000 American combat deaths. With the passage of time it has sometimes been called "the forgotten war." It nevertheless had a dramatic impact on the wider international arena and the United States' role in it.[30] One might get up a good debate whether McCarthyism or the Korean War was the key event in the 1950–54 period. In fact they overlapped and were closely related, with one historian calling the war "the most effective and economical explanation of McCarthyism." The Korean eruption undoubtedly gave McCarthy the vital spur he needed. The backdrop of American fighting men struggling desperately with communist forces on the Asian mainland endowed his campaign with growing credibility. By the same token President Truman's fateful decision to defend South Korea, respectably expressed in the fashionable Cold War determination to avoid a Munich-like appeasement, is fully explanable only in terms of the pervasive domestic climate of anxiety and continuing debate over the "loss" of China, the advent of the Soviet bomb, and the pressure generated by McCarthy's disturbing charges.

The diplomatic origins of the Korean War were a matter of intense debate during the Cold War itself. In the absence of communist sources two general lines of thought dominated American historiography. The principal one, reflecting official thinking and the Moscow-focused outlook common to most American observers, was that this was a deliberate move on the international chessboard by Stalin who, as George Kennan put it in his memoirs, "launched" the Korean struggle. Stalin's precise motivation was, of course, a matter of speculation. Some saw it as an opportunist move that would bring him an easy gain on the assumption that the United States would not intervene. Central to this thesis was a clumsy speech by Acheson on January 12, 1950 defining the American "defense perimeter" as the offshore islands of East Asia, implying that South Korea was expendable. Others have argued that Stalin may have expected the Americans to be inhibited by a fear that this was simply a preliminary feint before a bolder Soviet move in Europe, perhaps against Berlin, perhaps against the errant communist, Tito, in Yugoslavia. This was indeed Truman's view of the situation. Communist success in Korea, according to this reasoning, would be seen in Moscow as a material gain, a geopolitical hedge against the looming transformation of Japan into an American ally, and a propaganda victory after the humiliating back down over Berlin.

Revisionists, from the 1960s on, while not usually denying that the communists had taken the decisive step, were inclined to blame American policy-makers. The basic setting, they argued, was not great power manipulation, but a chronic Korean civil war in which the United States had irresponsibly encouraged the dangerously volatile Rhee. The most vigorous proponent of the "civil war" thesis, Bruce Cumings, stands at the head of a number of writers who have argued that the Truman administration created, or at least unnecessarily intensified the crisis for its own purposes, notably to get support for the invigorated but very expensive defense build-up set out earlier in NSC 68.[31]

Time, reflection, and new evidence from Soviet and other communist sources have in recent years given us a clearer view. It appears that Stalin, for example, was involved with, but was not the initiator of, the North Korean action. The causative sequence apparently began with the communist take-over in China in mid-1949. This, it seems clear, rekindled Stalin's optimism regarding the worldwide prospects of the communist mission. At the same time, until the Acheson speech and the preceding NSC strategy review upon which it was founded (which Stalin may, historian John Lewis Gaddis suggests, have received through British spy Guy Burgess) the Soviet leader had urged caution upon the newly established Chinese communists for fear of American intervention. By early 1950, however, he apparently felt somewhat more confident. More to the point here, the new prospect encouraged Kim Il Sung, impressed by Washington's failure to support Chiang in the final Chinese crisis, to seek support from both Stalin and Mao for the forced reunification by his well-drilled army of the Korean peninsula. Stalin, emotionally sympathetic but characteristically cautious at first, finally promised help and gave a highly conditional green light to Kim in early 1950. He could go ahead, Stalin said, only if Mao agreed, for "if you should get kicked in the teeth, I shall not lift a finger." Kim then gave an exaggerated account of Stalin's enthusiasm to Mao who had also been initially reluctant because, in this consolidating period of his revolution, he feared an American intervention, probably with Nationalist support from Taiwan. Reassured now that his help would not be needed the Chinese leader also went along. A rapid Soviet military build-up, apparently monitored by Stalin himself, brought the communist forces to the point of readiness on June 25. It seems, therefore, that responsibility rests with the communist side with all three leaders having a hand in the crucial decisions.[32]

The war itself quickly raised new problems for all the involved parties. Before examining them it may be well to review quickly the principal developments. The first communist thrust was held finally outside a small perimeter round the southern port of Pusan thanks to Truman's quick decision to send in American troops under the command of World War II hero General Douglas MacArthur who was the American governing authority in Japan. MacArthur regained the initiative a few weeks later with a brilliant amphibious landing at Inchon, a port halfway up the western coast. This produced the liberation of the capital, Seoul, the headlong flight of the outflanked communists, and a new question for American leaders. Should the United Nations forces (for the convenient absence of the Soviet Union from the Security Council during this crisis – to show its objection to the Council's refusal to give the Chinese seat to the communist regime – had allowed the Truman administration to act in the name of the otherwise supportive international body) capitalize on this success by marching north and re-unifying Korea under Western auspices?[33]

The issue came to turn, after much soul-searching, on estimates of a possible Chinese response. Would they come in, as shrill public statements from China suggested they would if the UN forces came close to their border? Truman himself was hesitant. He had said at the outset that the object was simply to restore South Korea. But with this new tempting vista opening up he consulted MacArthur at a hastily arranged conference on Wake Island. The general was eager to advance and reassured Truman that the Chinese would not intervene. If they did they would be defeated easily. It was now Truman's turn, as it had been Stalin's earlier, to defer to the man on the spot.

MacArthur's prophetic gift, it soon turned out, was no better than Kim's. When the UN forces neared the Yalu River and Korea–China border the Chinese forces entered in great numbers and pushed MacArthur's troops, which had been carelessly divided, back below the 38th parallel. A rancorous debate ensued between Washington and MacArthur who now wanted to launch attacks on China proper. He requested 34 atomic bombs and wanted to establish a belt of radioactive cobalt to prevent further Chinese incursions. Truman himself openly raised the possibility that nuclear weapons might be used. This alarmed Britain and other allies and the president was quickly obliged to issue appropriate reassurances. MacArthur became increasingly assertive and insubordinate leading Truman, at great political cost, to dismiss him on April

11, 1951.[34] Meanwhile, the war dragged on, in mercifully conventional fashion but without much advantage to either side, until President Eisenhower was able to bring about an armistice in the spring of 1953. This fixed a provisional border line almost exactly where the communist invasions had begun three years earlier. There, after almost half a century of argument and unresolved issues, delegates from both sides continue to meet.

Before placing all the blame on MacArthur (who is alleged in a recent study to have secretly wanted an all-out military showdown with communist China all along) we must consider recent Chinese and Soviet archival revelations. They show, first, that MacArthur was right in assuming that the prospect of an American advance would cause consternation in the communist camp. Kim, depressed and anxious in the post-Inchon period, called on Stalin for help, only to be told by the Kremlin realist that he should evacuate North Korea. In desperation he then turned to Mao, warning that the future of socialism in North Korea was at stake. Mao also wavered at first but eventually promised to intervene, whereupon Stalin withdrew his evacuation advice. This leads to a second point. The communist records suggest that in this immediate post-revolutionary period Mao expected some sort of American counter-revolutionary intervention, perhaps from Taiwan if not through Korea. He often talked about "the U.S. invasion of Asia" and always declared his intention to resist it forcefully, possibly even at the Korean 38th parallel, almost certainly if it approached the Chinese frontier. The historian John Lewis Gaddis, reviewing the most recent Chinese historical work based on these findings, suggests that quite early in the war Mao decided "that the Korean peninsula would be a good place for Chinese armies to confront the American aggressors."[35]

But none of this was known in Washington and, as UN troops retreated in humiliating fashion down the peninsula the American leadership began to pay the price for its overconfidence. MacArthur, remarkably, came out best with the public, though at the cost both of his career and his historical reputation. He never accepted any responsibility for his faulty predictions or for the carelessness and insubordination associated with his violation of orders to avoid provoking the Chinese as he approached the Yalu River. Playing to the China lobby and other conservative elements at home, he blamed Washington for denying him full strategic freedom and adequate resources. His increasingly public complaints finally gave Truman the opportunity to recall him. He returned to a hero's welcome while Truman's popularity, already much reduced, shrank to around 24 percent and never recovered significantly thereafter.

Truman tried hard to pick up the pieces and, despite continual harassment from McCarthy and the China lobby, he received support from both the Joint Chiefs of Staff (who were thoroughly fed up with MacArthur) and the congressional leadership led by Senator Richard Russell of Georgia, a pay-off for Truman's go-slow on Fair Deal reforms since the war began. But the president, unable now to either enlarge the expeditionary force or use nuclear weapons, could not win a victory in Korea; nor could he orchestrate a satisfactory peace, confronted as he was with conservative resistance at home and the stubborn obduracy of Koreans on both sides. His remaining time in office was unprofitable and unpleasant as Republican charges of corruption and incompetence seemed to herald the final end of the Democratic era.[36]

From the historian's viewpoint the Korean War is an object lesson in the dangers of rushing to judgment. Many myths took hold, only partly purged by the familiar academic/official cycle of orthodox justification, sharp revisionism, and late-arriving fresh evidence. The military historian, Stanley Sandler, has cleared some of this ground effectively, exposing the false notion that the United States fought "with one hand tied behind our backs" by showing the extraordinary level of destruction it achieved against the enemy while enjoying, for the most part, almost complete control of the air space and surrounding sea. It is also clear now that, contrary to widespread impression, the American fighting performance was impressive and that the allegedly vast "tail" of support units behind the combat troops was a myth. The communists, it turns out, had far more backstage personnel. And the notion that the United States engaged in bacteriological warfare, a staple of communist propaganda through the Cold War, has also been largely discredited, though a handful of historians continue to voice suspicion.[37]

In one sense the Korean War could be said to have had a constructive aspect. It provided a small peripheral arena where various assumptions and illusions could be tested, where the superpower antagonists could show each other their basic preoccupations and character and the way in which they might respond to challenges. This seems important in the light of two considerations. First, the United States and the Soviet Union had very little in the way of a historical relationship to guide and inform their diplomacy. Consequently, on both sides, emotion and ideology tended to dominate. The perceptual gulf between the United States and communist China was even greater. Secondly, the potential cost of error was now greatly magnified by new, destructive technology, especially the existence of nuclear weapons. In this sense Korea provided lessons that clarified if they did not reassure. The United States showed a resolution that was bound to encourage more caution from its enemies, and it showed restraint in not using nuclear weapons. The Soviet Union showed restraint in avoiding a direct role and not exploiting the crisis by provocative action in Europe. The Chinese, for their part, showed a clear determination to protect their revolution. This line of thought has been most fully developed by the historian William Stueck Jr. who, in writing an international history of the conflict, presented a chapter entitled "Korea as a Substitute for World War III." He argues that Stalin was probably sobered by the Korea episode into abandoning plans to topple Tito from power in Yugoslavia and also learned from the experience that "to arouse the U.S. from a slumber through blatant military action could prove a costly mistake."[38]

However, if in some deep sense Korea and its quasi-institutionalization of "limited war" gave some promise of human survival in the nuclear age, and was a useful lesson in constraint for all parties, these blessings were hardly apparent to Americans at the time. It was at best a draw, not a victory. The fighting took over 35,000 American lives. It irrevocably enlarged a Cold War that might otherwise, assuming a China bent on internal reconstruction, have remained confined largely to Europe. Thanks in large part to the Korean War the notion of a Soviet–Chinese monolith became a short-term reality and a long-lived article of American faith. The United States now felt obliged to create a new web of alliances to contain it. There was henceforth an increasingly pervasive sense of being engaged in a global struggle. The clear manifestation of this was the enshrinement of NSC 68, approved by Truman shortly after the war began, as official policy. The defense budget was very shortly tripled, the development of the hydrogen bomb was accelerated, American troops were sent on permanent duty to Europe, German rearmament was set in train, the Chinese nationalists in Taiwan were given full American protection, and the French began to receive the much-enhanced help in Indochina that would later lead so logically into a full-scale commitment.

At home too the consequences were profound. Truman had necessarily put the already languishing Fair Deal on the shelf once the war started. The primacy of foreign affairs in American public life was enhanced by the Korean War, a development dramatized by the continuing power of McCarthy whose striking career of anti-communist demagoguery was virtually coterminous with the hostilities. All this spelled the approaching end of the Democratic hold on the presidency.

Eisenhower and the Global Cold War

The logical political outcome of the Truman administration's tribulations since 1949 was, undoubtedly, the Republican victory in 1952, a subject for later examination. But we are justified, I think, in stressing for the first 18 months or so of the new administration, continuity rather than change. In a strictly constitutional or political way Eisenhower's victory introduces a new phase. But in many respects the transition was not sharp and the governing features we have found in American life since 1949 – war abroad and an intense anticommunism at home – persisted. Eisenhower himself noted in his diary in the middle of 1953 that his administration was "immobile" and that the Korean War and Senator McCarthy still dominated the news.[39]

Moreover, we observe well into Eisenhower's first term that steady enlargement of the Cold War which is the primary characteristic of the 1949–54 period. The struggle increasingly permeated domestic politics and steadily expanded its geopolitical scope to a worldwide dimension. It is significant that the Republicans in 1952 stressed their traditional faith in a smaller federal government but otherwise scarcely bothered to make a case against Democratic domestic reformism, hardly a factor since 1949 anyway. Nor was there much debate about the economy, now growing rapidly with the passionate postwar business–labor struggles already a fading memory. The campaign was dominated by the Cold War issues of the Korean War and the supposed communist subversion of the government. It was perhaps most notable for Eisenhower's promises to tighten security at home, to end the shooting war in Korea, and to intensify the political confrontation with the communists by transforming democratic "containment" into a more robust but only vaguely defined "liberation" approach.

Eisenhower skillfully brought the Korean War to a close. He was perhaps fortunate that Stalin's death in March 1953 brought a more amenable communist attitude. Old arguments about the repatriation of Chinese and North Korean prisoners who did not wish to return home delayed a settlement. But in the end, when Rhee unilaterally released thousands of North Korean prisoners, the communists did not break off the negotiations. They may have been influenced by Eisenhower's enigmatic indication through Indian intermediaries that he might employ nuclear weapons to end the war. The president himself appears to have believed that this was a viable option. But historians Roger Dingman and John Lewis Gaddis downplay the impact of American nuclear posturing and believe that the substitution of the new collective leadership for Stalin was the decisive factor for peace on the communist side. In any event, an armistice was signed on July 27, 1953 with a prisoner compromise and a temporary territorial settlement very close to the line the communists had crossed three years earlier.[40]

Ending the Korean imbroglio was one thing. Otherwise the Republican approach was remarkably militant and expansionary. A primary feature of their campaign had been the call for "liberation" with explicit reference to Eastern Europe and implicit undertakings elsewhere. We see this new vitalism in Eisenhower's resistance to the "peace offensive" presented by Georgi Malenkov on behalf of the new Soviet leadership. Many political prisoners were freed and the new regime promised a reorientation from heavy industry to consumer goods. At the same time Malenkov made conciliatory gestures in foreign affairs and declared that there was no issue, even with the United States, that could not be settled to mutual satisfaction. All this was widely seen, especially in Europe (by British Prime Minister Winston Churchill and others) as a possible turning point in relations with the Soviets.

But Eisenhower, despite some vigorous prodding from Churchill, was unmoved. Though he did feel obliged to make some public response to an olive branch he clearly regarded as insincere he confined this to a speech insisting that the Soviets should demonstrate their new goodwill by ending the war in Korea, stopping communist insurgencies in Malaya and elsewhere, and allowing genuinely free elections in Eastern Europe. This all-or-nothing approach, as near as the administration came to pursuing a true "liberation" policy, left little room for diplomacy. It must be said in Eisenhower's defense that he was inevitably influenced by the fact that he had been elected on a harder-line foreign policy platform and was understandably sensitive to pressure from McCarthy and his hawkish supporters. He may also have believed it was necessary to keep up a strong front in the concurrent Korean negotiations. And, as historian Klaus Larres has emphasized, the Soviet "peace offensive" coincided inconveniently with delicate negotiations looking toward a German rearmament that was only acceptable to many West Europeans (especially the French) in the context of a realistic Soviet threat. Secretary of State John Foster Dulles and Federal German Chancellor Konrad Adenauer, close to bringing this policy to fruition in early 1953, were understandably suspicious of the sudden Soviet cordiality. Consequently, the opportunity, if it was indeed that and not a communist "trick," was missed.[41]

There was a similar hard line, and much the same sense of taking the battle to the enemy, in the willingness of the Eisenhower administration to think and act, far more aggressively than the Democrats had done, in global terms. Up to 1953, as we have seen, the American Cold War engagement had moved from the European theater, largely consolidated by 1948, to the wider Europe–North Asia arena of 1949–53. It fell to the Republicans to take, in the early stages of their tenure, the third and final step to a fully global commitment. We see the new expansionary spirit first in Iran where a nationalist leader, Mohammed Mossadeq, had seized power in 1951. In August 1953 the CIA financed and helped organize right-wing army elements to stage a successful coup that restored the pro-American Shah to his throne. And we see it again in Guatemala. Here too a leftist, but not communist reformer, Jacobo Arbenz, had come to power legitimately in 1953. To provide land for the long-oppressed peasantry he had taken some unused property from the American-owned United Fruit Company. The company turned to Washington for help. Arbenz, while hedging over Dulles' demands for compensation for the seizures, took steps to defend his government against American pressure by ordering an arms shipment from Czechoslovakia. This provided a convenient rationale for CIA action which, repeating the Iranian pattern, organized disaffected military elements into the instrument of a successful coup which brought a pro-American dictatorship to power in June 1954.[42]

This new American activism had by then moved on from the Middle East and Central America to Southeast Asia. The sudden surrender of the French forces at Dien Bien Phu in May 1954 brought vigorous international diplomatic action. After a lively debate in the highest reaches of the American political establishment Eisenhower decided not to use nuclear weapons or to enter the struggle with conventional force. At the ensuing Geneva Conference all the interested parties (France, the Soviet Union, China, Britain, and all the Vietnamese factions) agreed that France would give up its struggle to reclaim Indochina and that internationally supervised elections within two years would settle a legitimate Vietnamese government. Only the United States of the major powers stood aside, though promising to support the future election scenario, which was generally expected to produce a communist victory.

In the event, however, the Eisenhower administration took steps to foreclose any such resolution. It quickly replaced the departing French as the anti-communist power in the south. It strongly endorsed a Vietnamese Catholic from the mandarin class, Ngo Dinh Diem, back from self-imposed exile in a New Jersey seminary and placed in power in Saigon by the pro-French emperor, Bao Dai. It sent economic aid and military advisers to help the new leader secure the noncommunist South. When Diem declared in 1955 that he would not allow elections Dulles immediately supported him. With these fateful actions, passing up the opportunity to liquidate a dangerous commitment under the authority of an international cover that not even the China lobby or McCarthy could have seriously discredited, Eisenhower and Dulles set the United States on a course that steadily became less and less tenable.[43]

Revisionist historians in the 1960s and later drew attention to these and other far-flung initiatives as evidence, not simply of the nation's increasingly global reach, but of an "imperial" character in American diplomacy that had been developing since the late nineteenth-century's industrial surge and was coming to a sinister kind of fulfillment under cover of the Cold War. The use of this term, and of the epithet "Amerika" favored by later student radicals, was doubtless intended in many cases to be provocative. Hitherto, except for a few stray Marxists, the pejorative term "empire" had been reserved in American discourse for that British and other European exploitation of the rest of the world that had driven earlier Americans to revolution.

We will return to this issue later but there is something interesting in it that deserves mention here. Whether we call its accelerating engagement with the outside world "the defense of freedom" or "Cold War globalization" or "American imperialism" the enlargement of the United States' commitments had occurred remarkably quickly. Perhaps too rapidly for a society that historically, as the slow turns in domestic affairs toward some kind of welfare state and a more humane approach to civil rights clearly demonstrate, was used to long deliberative preparation before embarking upon fundamental change. As recently as World War II Franklin D. Roosevelt had steadily proclaimed, with only a minimal vagueness as a concession to European sensibilities, that the ultimate objective of American wartime diplomacy was still the creation of a Wilsonian open world free of imperial dominion. But even as the war wound down FDR was cautiously backing away from his prior determination to force the French out of Indochina. By 1950, moreover, the United States was paying most of the costs as France tried desperately to restore herself there. And now we find Eisenhower restoring an apparently reactionary monarchy in Iran, sabotaging a democratically elected, reformist leader in Guatemala, and confounding not just local sentiment but the redemptive homing instincts of the Europeans themselves, in committing the United States to the support of an unabashedly unrepresentative Vietnamese regime led by a seminarian from New Jersey.

Here surely is one of the basic conundrums of American Cold War history. How is it that the United States – historically the scold and hammer of old world imperialism and the champion of freedom everywhere – took upon itself so quickly, one is tempted to say so blithely, and in so many unpromising places, the inevitably conservative if not reactionary role being vacated by the exhausted Europeans. In case after case, from the 1950s on, the United States found itself propping up, at great material and moral cost to itself, old, discredited elites and new oppressive dictators against young, highly motivated, seemingly patriotic rebels whose desire for change was increasingly plausible in the minds of young Americans who had difficulty squaring their own country's traditional ideals with its actions.

Two broad answers have been given. The revisionist explanation, only thinly voiced in the Eisenhower era but becoming a powerful conception by the late 1960s as the Vietnam War intensified, has generally been to say that, as its persistent interventionism demonstrated, the modern United States was never really liberal anyway, and that behind all the smoke-and-mirror moralism of its effusive political culture it has been driven consistently, or at least since its dramatic industrialization in the late nineteenth century, by an imperial outlook inspired throughout by economic self-interest. Thus, to take only the examples cited here, the intervention in Iran was held to have been prompted less by fear of Soviet expansion than by the ambitions of American oil companies; the Guatemala episode was designed not so much to keep communism at bay in this hemisphere, but to allay the anxieties of the United Fruit Company and other watchful investors in Latin America; and the Indochina commitment, ostensibly a defiant challenge to Moscow and Beijing, was really governed by a felt need to meet the economic requirements of Japan and other Asian outposts of the developing American imperium.

Mainstream liberal historians, by contrast, have generally portrayed a well-intentioned and self-sacrificial sense of American mission throughout, maintained with great difficulty in the unprecedented, complex situations created by the Cold War. The Soviet and Chinese communist challenge forced a reluctant United States to play the part, not simply of Europe's liberator but of a traditional great power, meeting force with force on a global scale. The foreign policy leadership (or "establishment" as it came to be known to its critics) found it necessary to practice realism and geopolitics. Yet this was always done with distaste. And it was accompanied throughout by a persistent solicitude for the long-term interests of expectant but threatened peoples round the world that came to be expressed as a commitment to "nation-building." This conception dignified American policies and forged a crucial link to traditional values. It also justified the long-term character of the effort. The typical new nation obviously could not, in the face of a communist challenge masquerading as nationalism, be created in the desired American image overnight. But with time and support it might be. All this was compatible with the deep-rooted American view of history as a steady, progressive evolution, and more immediately with the necessarily patient master-strategy of "containment" to which Eisenhower and Dulles, after their brief, mainly rhetorical flirtation with the hazards of "liberation," quickly returned.

All these initiatives, together with the formulation of a "New Look" military strategy that envisaged a great expansion of the American nuclear arsenal and a highly publicized willingness to use it in the face of any kind of communist attack, gave an aggressive cast to the new administration's diplomacy. In retrospect much of this was a matter of rhetoric and emotion. For in its actual responses to crises we soon find a significant degree of continuity. The illusion of "liberation" for example was dramatically exposed as early as mid-1953 when the administration failed to do anything tangible in support of the violent protests against their communist leaders by workers in East Berlin.

The most striking point of continuity with the previous administration, apart from the generally aggressive diplomacy within a domestic context of rising anti-communism that gives this period its coherence, lies, perhaps, in what we might reasonably call the Eisenhower/Dulles "managerial" diplomacy. Both relied upon collective security with suitable allies enshrined in multinational treaties. Truman and Acheson had already repeated their European method in East Asia by negotiating the United States–Japan peace treaty in 1951. In addition to settling remaining war issues the agreement restored Japanese sovereignty in the home islands but gave the United States bases in Okinawa and the right, expressly denied to third parties, to station troops and planes elsewhere in Japan. When America's wartime allies protested against the prospective revival of Japanese power the United States settled mutual security pacts with the Philippines and with Australia and New Zealand (the ANZUS pact). In all this, as historian Walter

LaFeber has written, "the U.S. was single-handedly preparing Asia for the containment of China."[44]

Dulles, when he took charge of American diplomacy himself, shored up these new commitments and completed the Asian containment perimeter by pressing Britain, France, Australia, New Zealand, Pakistan, Thailand, and the Philippines into the Southeast Asia Treaty Organization (SEATO) signed in Manila on September 8, 1954. The signatories pledged to "consult" rather than unconditionally "resist" (as in the NATO treaty) in the event of an attack, but they did express an additional determination "to prevent and counter subversive activities directed from without." The new treaty, which the Senate approved by a vote of 82 to 1, also contained a protocol promising to protect the nonsignatory states of South Vietnam, Laos, and Cambodia. A remarkable encirclement of the communist powers was now being steadily achieved, on paper at least, from Norway to Japan (the vacant gap between the two major alliances being closed later by a series of bilateral treaties and later by the Central Treaty Organization (CENTO) which was signed in 1959.[45]

All these vigorous initiatives in the late Truman, early Eisenhower period were driven along, if not inspired, by the powerful tide of anti-communist fervor stirred up by McCarthy and his influential political and media supporters. Eisenhower and his leading associates from Dulles down gave every impression of being sincere Cold Warriors. The president, having significantly tightened the criteria for dismissal, proudly boasted early in 1954 that he had removed 2200 security-risk government officials, far more than Truman. He upset liberals by refusing clemency to the Rosenbergs, who were executed in 1953. And he and Dulles allowed McCarthy to force the resignation of several innocent diplomats, and gave him virtual veto power over some key State Department appointments.[46]

But the fall of McCarthy in late 1954 brought the era of acute American anti-communism to a close. After the dramatic humiliation of his televised struggle with the U.S. Army, the senator's star faded rapidly. Eisenhower, responding to this, sent Vice-President Richard Nixon, a former McCarthy promoter and Hiss prosecutor, out to publicly deplore the senator's "reckless talk and questionable methods." Comedian Bob Hope courageously joked early in 1954 that McCarthy had seized a Moscow telephone directory and was about to reveal the names of two million more communists.[47] Everyone sensed a turning point. People were getting tired of the endless charges, few of which seemed to turn up an authentic villain. As the storm died down the Cold War, and its varied forms of communist menace, began to be accepted as a permanent part of American life. Political agitation began to abate. Republicans and Democrats began again to talk, as they had in 1947–8, of bipartisanship in diplomacy. Soon the social critics and historians would be talking of "consensus" as the primary characteristic of American public life. The "Fifties" had arrived at last.

3

The Eisenhower Fifties: Consolidation and Confrontation

Most Americans in the post-McCarthy 1950s, if we judge by the media of the times, seem to have enjoyed a sense of well-being. There were, to be sure, tense moments, such as the frightening nuclear testing by both sides in the Cold War, the economic setbacks in 1954 and 1959, the civil rights confrontations, and the Soviet space successes. But these were widely viewed as episodic expressions of problems that were moving, however slowly, toward resolution. In general, the United States appeared to its citizens to be uniquely successful: secure and respected in the leadership of the pleasingly-defined "free world," free at last of economic depression, and socially at peace with itself under a much-loved leader.

The picture presented by historical scholarship is rather different. Some historians, like Alonzo Hamby, do indeed see "an oasis of placidity between eras of extraordinary turbulence in American politics." But the decade has also been a battlefield between liberals and conservatives. Thus, journalist David Halberstam's best-selling *The Fifties* (1995) recently restated a familiar liberal indictment of weak leadership, social apathy, and festering racial and urban problems left dangerously unaddressed. The 1998 Hollywood film *Pleasantville* presented a similarly dreary, unappealing view of the decade.

On the other hand historian Stephen Ambrose's recent biographical celebration of Eisenhower was well received, and conservatives can find comfort in the social critic Hilton Kramer's assessment of Halberstam's work as "a monstrous compendium of misinformation about one of the most admired epochs in American History."[1]

The historiography is clearly somewhat at odds with the supposed tranquillity of the era. Much of it, one suspects, is rooted in a preoccupation with other times. Many mainstream liberals, for example, though willing enough to concede that Eisenhower was a moderate rather than a Taftian conservative in his political philosophy, have seen the 1950s as a lamentable interruption in the onward march of political and social reform from Truman to Kennedy. They were a "postponement" (a term coined as early as 1958 by the columnist William Shannon) for which the nation paid dearly later on. Others, in a churning spectrum from liberalism to radicalism seem bent on making a case for the cultural innovations of the 1960s by casting them as a welcome liberation from the stuffy social authoritarianism of the 1950s. For conservatives it is by contrast precisely the strength of traditional institutions and lifestyles that lends a last "before the deluge" enchantment to the Eisenhower years. The challenge, then, is to cut through this tendentious decade-chopping and try to see the 1950s in its own terms.[2]

Eisenhower as President

One starts, inevitably given the power of the modern presidency, with Eisenhower himself. He came from much the same background as Truman. Both were farm-boys whose value structure reflected their beginnings in the semi-frontier Mid-West of the late nineteenth century. Each had a father who failed in business and by way of compensation a strong, motivating mother. Both had late-blooming careers that owed much to a single mentor. But there the paths diverge somewhat. Truman was eased into the US Senate by Boss Pendergast, made a middling record there, and was accepted without any real enthusiasm as the insiders' compromise candidate for vice-president in 1944. Eisenhower, whose interwar record was more impressive but little rewarded with promotions, was picked out over hundreds of senior officers by General Marshall to plan and then lead the victorious World War II campaigns in North Africa and Europe. He was always seen thereafter as a potential president. He was courted vigorously by both parties, won the office in a landslide in 1952, repeated the trick in 1956, and finally retired in 1961 as the most widely revered American president of the twentieth century.[3]

Military heroes do not, of course, necessarily make good presidents. Washington succeeded triumphantly; Grant failed miserably. Eisenhower's record remains, it seems fair to say, a matter for continuing historiographical debate. His approval ratings at the time were always high. They were sustained by persistent growth in the economy. The gross national product (in 1958 constant dollars) rose from $355.3 billion in 1950 to $452.5 billion in 1957 to $487.7 billion in 1960 – an overall increase for the decade of 37 percent. The historian James Patterson has estimated that median family incomes were 30 percent higher in 1960 than in 1950. And, a supreme illustration of social tranquillity, owner-occupied homes rose from 43.6 percent in 1940 to 55 percent in 1950 to 61.9 percent in 1960. Best of all there was very little inflation during the decade. The brief recessions of 1954 and 1958 dampened optimism for a time, the latter one dragging on and working to Democratic advantage in the lead-up to the 1960 elections, but for most Americans it was a time of prosperity and rising optimism.[4]

But Eisenhower's popularity was not simply a function of economic prosperity. His personality was warm and gregarious yet stamped with a self-confident authority he wore without affectation. Coming to the presidency at 62, with an awesome record, he functioned uniquely in modern history as a kind of father figure. More substantively it is clear, in retrospect at least, that he provided a widely desired breathing spell after two difficult decades of turbulent dislocation and heated politics. And while he did little to promote reform he indubitably reconciled the conservative opposition in national politics to the permanent existence of a welfare state. Most appreciated, perhaps, he ended the Korean War and, despite various frightening moments he kept the peace throughout his tenure.

This may seem, by any reasonable standard, a solid record of achievement. Eisenhower's problem was that, though not as passive as liberal critics have charged, he loathed conventional politics and, in domestic affairs at least, took a managerial rather than a programmatic view of his office. In an earlier time this would have been generally acceptable. But 20 years of socio-economic ups and downs, war, and modernization had intensified the pace of change in America and had transformed the presidency. The chief executive, whatever his party, was now inevitably the focal point of all the primary demands and tensions in American life. The issue-magnifying advent of mass-circulation television in the 1950s only further dramatized this development.

It is not clear that Eisenhower fully understood the implications of all this. What is clear is that, while he successfully distanced himself from right-wing Republican zealots who wanted to roll-back the New Deal, his political inappetence in the face of intensifying domestic problems, such as persisting segregation and urban poverty, helped the Democrats win back control of Congress in 1954. It also inspired such liberal critiques as economist John Kenneth Galbraith's *The Affluent Society* and columnist Marquis Childs' portrait of an ineffectual, indecisive leader in *Eisenhower: The Captive Hero*, both published in 1958.[5] That these charges expressed an increasingly widespread degree of public concern over drift and error in the late Eisenhower period can be seen in Senator John F. Kennedy's selection of the slogan, "Lets Get America Moving Again" during his successful 1960 presidential campaign.

Not everyone, then, was happy with the Eisenhower presidency. The evaluations of historians often seem to divide similarly along lines of party or ideological identification. Unsurprisingly, as the Democrats began a slow political

recovery a complementary liberal intellectual critique flourished. In the late 1950s and early 1960s, for instance, scholars
like Arthur M. Schlesinger Jr. and Eric Goldman portrayed a
stand-pat administration, a passive president content to delegate his powers to mediocrities or right-wing fanatics. Here
was a leader who had been unwilling to grapple with
McCarthyism or racial problems, was insensitive to modern
social problems, and much too attentive to the business elite
where he found friends and golfing partners. The liberal complaint extended to foreign affairs too. Townsend Hoopes and
other critics excoriated what they saw as Secretary of State
John Foster Dulles' dangerous adventurism in a global arena
that seemed to be becoming a nuclear tinderbox.[6]

But by the late 1960s and early 1970s the luster of the activist Kennedy–Johnson liberalism that had come bustling in
after Eisenhower had itself faded badly. The endless war in
Vietnam and the violent urban aftermath of the civil rights
movement, together with the fragmentation brought about by
the social radicalisms of the period, helped create a warmer
image of the Eisenhower years. Journalistic reappraisals began in 1968 with Murray Kempton's *Esquire* article "The
Underestimation of Dwight D. Eisenhower" and Garry Wills'
celebration of his "political genius." The new mood was soon
reinforced by the appearance of declassified documents at the
Eisenhower Presidential Library in the early 1970s. These
brought enhanced respect for what political scientist Fred I.
Greenstein memorably called "the hidden-hand presidency."
Eisenhower, it was now argued, had been much more active
than thought, pursuing his purposes shrewdly behind the
scenes. He even possessed, according to James Patterson, a
more or less consistent social philosophy, a kind of moderate
"middle way" emphasizing socio-managerial political values
in what that historian has described as a "cooperative commonwealth" conception.[7]

One thing that most commentators now accept is that Eisenhower was a gifted political leader. In 1983 one of his
strongest critics, Arthur M. Schlesinger Jr., conceded "that
Eisenhower showed much more energy, interest, self-confi-

dence, purpose, cunning, and command than many of us supposed in the 1950s."[8] In fact these qualities had been evident from the beginning of his political career. He hid his ambition well, letting himself be courted by both parties before 1948 (Truman had offered to stand aside for him in that campaign as early as 1945), before allowing Thomas Dewey to persuade him of the need to save America from the extremes of Democratic "socialism" and Taftian Republicanism and line up as a moderate Republican in 1952. He did so with great success, rallying the east-coast oriented Republican moderates against the Taftite right, capturing the nomination on the perception that he could win and then, having made peace with Taft, uniting the party for a "crusade" against the fading Democrats.

He then ran a very competent campaign flawed only by a failure to defend his mentor, George Marshall, against McCarthy's wild charges, and by his running mate, California Senator Richard M. Nixon's successfully surmounted funding scandal. Eisenhower took the high road while his associates blasted the Democrats over the Korean War and the issues of communists and corruption in government. As a personality he outshone the sophisticated Democratic candidate, former Illinois governor, Adlai Stevenson. At a deeper level though the perceptive contemporary analyst, Samuel Lubell, found Eisenhower benefiting from a "revolt of the moderates." Four years earlier, in what historian Robert Griffiths has aptly called "the last hurrah of the sometimes raw, class-conscious politics of the New Deal" Americans had voted, according to Lubell, to protect the New Deal reform system.[9] In 1952 they apparently saw in Eisenhower (who had carefully reassured voters that he would not attack Social Security or press a Cold War policy of "liberation" by force) a welcome political peacemaker who, unlike the right-wing Republicans, would not try to turn the clock back.

Once in power, as we have seen, Eisenhower showed a high degree of sophistication in his handling of the Republican right-wing, which was now in command of Congress again. His careful treatment of McCarthy, while hardly courageous, was a mixture of concession and resistance that helped avoid party divisions. There were difficulties with the budget, which Taft wanted reduced even more drastically than Eisenhower, himself an eager budget-cutter, was prepared to accept. Eisenhower neutralized his old rival effectively by making him a personal friend and golfing partner. This paid off in a number of ways until Taft's untimely death from cancer in July 1953. His relations with the new Republican Senate leader, William Knowland of California, a staunch China lobbyist and conservative, were more remote. But Eisenhower continued to divert or soften the right-wing domestic agenda until the 1954 congressional elections returned the Democrats to power in both houses of Congress. This development, together with the Korean settlement and McCarthy's fall effectively tamed the Republican extremists and left the "moderate" Eisenhower to preside amicably with two quintessential Texan, Democratic compromisers, Speaker Sam Rayburn and Senate Majority Leader Lyndon Johnson.[10]

Many of Eisenhower's Deweyite sponsors saw his success and the later retreat of the right-wing as opening the way to an ardently desired transformation of the Republican Party. Once again the elusive vision of a powerful centrist party presented itself. Earlier, it will be recalled, this impulse had tantalized Franklin D. Roosevelt and other Democratic liberals who were eager to disengage from southern conservatism. Now Republican moderates were thinking along similar lines. But the president did little to promote this. The memoirs of Emmet Hughes, one of his closest aides from the liberal wing of the party, testify to an acute sense of disappointment. Eisenhower made gestures in the direction of what he and the eastern wing often called "modern Republicanism." We see this in his administrative appointments and in some spasmodic efforts by means of party and judicial patronage in the South to form a progressive alternative to the conservative Democrats. But it became increasingly clear over time that Eisenhower was not prepared to waste his energy or his political capital in what he obviously saw as a hopeless quest.[11]

Clearly then, Eisenhower was in some ways a very competent political leader. Some scholars attribute his success to the orderly and efficient lines of authority he developed. Eisenhower, schooled in military hierarchies, delegated power freely. Historian H. W. Brands Jr. writes that "with the possible exception of Ronald Reagan, Eisenhower consciously apportioned responsibility to trusted subordinates to a greater degree than any other president in the last half-century." In a lively recent debate Fred I. Greenstein and Richard Immerman found much virtue in this approach. The ubiquitous Schlesinger, surely the quintessential Cold War liberal historian and watchful guardian of the faith, took the classic alternative view, arguing for the more flexible, informal structures favored by FDR, Kennedy, and many other modern presidents to facilitate the effective supervision of policy and the execution of direct executive power. This echoes the influential 1960 formulation of political scientist Richard Neustadt who, while acknowledging that the layered bureaucratic system may have suited Eisenhower, suggested that "its workings often were disastrous for his hold on personal power." Clearly, whatever its merits, and however dominant Eisenhower was behind the scenes, the dispersion of power implicit in his system helped create the image of passivity that his critics exploited effectively at the end of the decade.

A related question is the degree to which this very successful leader (whatever departures we find from conventional norms) was working from a coherent political philosophy. To get at this effectively we need to examine the record more closely. As we do we should avoid any partisan frame of reference. Democratic presidents typically come to power brandishing elaborate reform agendas and can be graded on their success in converting policy to law. Some liberal historians tend to treat Republican leaders in similar fashion, assuming a transcendent national interest in various forms of social advancement and faulting conservative politicians, explicitly or implicitly, for hindering or at least not furthering the cause.

It perhaps belabors the obvious to say that Republicans and conservatives have distinctive nonliberal values and priorities that deserve to be evaluated objectively. It is widely recognized, for example, that Eisenhower was eager to clear a path for American business. He appears to have seen this as simply a central part of an energetic, line-holding action against powerful forces in American life that were trying to subvert historical tradition and fundamental values by using government to force economic constraints, social dislocation, and unfair redistributions of hard-earned wealth. This battle, as Eisenhower conducted it, revolved as a practical matter around the size of the federal budget. It is not surprising then that, however lamentable this may seem from a liberal perspective, balancing the budget, rather than promoting civil rights or the relief of poverty, was his most passionate preoccupation, and that he saw this as a crucial precondition to the entrepreneurial vitality that must underpin a successful, free society.

With these cautionary thoughts in mind let us attempt a quick review of the Eisenhower administration's domestic record. The first point to make is that he never intended to break down the New Deal. As he sensibly wrote to his brother Edgar, "Should any political party attempt to abolish social security and eliminate labor laws and farm programs, you would not hear of that party again in our political history."[12] Eisenhower understood that he had to service the established social system. Hence he increased both Social Security benefits and the minimum wage. But he urged no social reforms himself. He did not favor the welfare ethos. And the two major socially oriented programs of his presidency were virtually unavoidable if his "commonwealth" ideal was to have any reality. One was the Education Act extending federal education aid to the states. This was prompted by the demands of the postwar baby-boomers whose presence overwhelmed local facilities. The only strong opposition came not from the Republican right but from Southern conservatives who percipiently saw the federal intrusion as an opening wedge for a similar intervention on civil rights issues, and from Roman Catholics who feared that their parochial system would be swamped by public school largesse for which they were constitutionally ineligible.

The second compelling issue was the pressure for civil rights legislation, a subject for closer examination later. Here too Eisenhower, without any enthusiasm, felt obliged to act. He was privately dismayed when Chief Justice Earl Warren (whose appointment he declared to have been his worst error as president) and his colleagues handed down the Supreme Court's landmark 1954 decision in *Brown* v. *Topeka Board of Education* outlawing segregation in education. But, always faithful to the constitution, he upheld it. In the same spirit he sent army detachments to Little Rock, Arkansas in 1957 to enforce the *Brown* principle against state authorities. In the same year he signed the Civil Rights Act (the first civil rights legislation from Congress since Reconstruction) which strengthened the Justice Department's powers to intervene to support voting rights in the South.[13]

The most creatively active law making in the Eisenhower years came in the old early nineteenth-century Henry Clay spirit of national improvements. Perhaps the education bill comes within this classification though, typically, Eisenhower was reluctant to face the cost. The two major projects were the St. Lawrence Seaway – linking the Great Lakes at last with the Atlantic – and the Interstate Highway Act of 1956 which, responding to vigorous lobbying from automobile, trucking, construction, and oil interests among many others, provided lavish subsidies for highway building. There was much hostility from social and cultural critics like Lewis Mumford who drew lurid but prescient scenarios of the transformative effect this would have on American life. But these massive projects symbolized the optimism of the 1950s, much as the space ventures did for the 1960s, and through user taxes and other means they were put on a self-funding basis that is another reminder of Eisenhower's prudent housekeeping.[14]

Is there then, a coherent pattern of thought and action in the Eisenhower record. Historian James Patterson identifies three complementary aspirations: "protecting his own standing, sustaining domestic tranquillity, and curbing the activity of the state."[15] His most passionate cause, as noted, was fiscal frugality. He saw sound economics as the basic foundation of both domestic tranquillity and a credible foreign policy. He was perhaps the last president to take budget balancing seriously. Truman, similarly marked by nineteenth-century values, had worried about the budget too, but the Korean War expenditures broke down his resolve and gave Eisenhower a 1952 target in the inflated defense budget. Despite ongoing Cold War tensions Eisenhower was determined to cut defense costs. This turned him, as we will see shortly, to the "New Look" strategy emphasizing nuclear weapons rather than a large military enrolment, by far the cheaper option. But he also worked in domestic politics, with varying success, to cut federal aid to agriculture and to return tidelands oil and other assets to the states.

Both Patterson and Robert Griffiths agree that behind Eisenhower's practical actions lay the larger conception of an ideal national community in which strongly organized groups – corporations, farmers, and labor pre-eminently – would collaborate effectively in what Griffiths has called a "corporate commonwealth" with the benevolent but distant guidance of the federal government. This conception, which Griffiths characterizes as "profoundly anti-democratic" was hardly new. Franklin Roosevelt, indeed, had tried to institutionalize it in a "broker state" during his first attempt in 1933 to revive American prosperity. Such scant credibility as Italy's Benito Mussolini enjoyed in the 1930s derived largely from his constant talk about "the corporate state," one of many such European visions; and economist John Kenneth Galbraith's 1953 *The Countervailing Society* had elaborated a more recent version in the United States. To Eisenhower these notions seem to have fused neatly with an essentially managerial approach to the presidency. Both his acceptance of New Deal structures and the "commonwealth" ideal (in whatever form) as well as his positive approach to at least some of the pressing problems in modern America, even if the social reform ethos was neglected, suggest "adaptation" and "continuity." Eisenhower liked to think in terms of equilibrium – in the budget of course; to moderate tensions in the Republican party; in executive–congressional relations; and, perhaps most profoundly, in the balance between domestic and foreign affairs so recently upset by McCarthyism. It was this last arena – international diplomacy – that, as we will now see, presented him with the most difficult challenges.[16]

Eisenhower and the World

We saw in the last chapter an Eisenhower apparently bent on fulfilling his election pledges to wage the Cold War with new vigor. His refusal to engage the post-Stalin Soviet leadership in a realistic attempt to find some sort of political accommodation, his championship of the new nuclear weapons, the aggressive CIA actions in Iran and Guatemala, the long stubborn resistance to international compromise over Vietnam in 1954 – all testify to a granitic hard-line. And we saw, moreover, evidence that this was not simply a calculated adjustment to McCarthy and the Republican right but an expression of Eisenhower's genuine, passionate anticommunism.

Yet, by the summer of 1955 we find him in Geneva with British and French colleagues holding a summit conference with the new Soviet leader Nikita Khrushchev. True, no agreements of substance were reached. But, in this first summit meeting since Potsdam in 1945, ideas and even practical scenarios for a more collaborative relationship were discussed, including the president's "Open Skies" arms control proposal. In all this Eisenhower was challenging right-wing sentiment at home. It was rumored that, fearing to inspire images of former Prime Minister Neville Chamberlain's appeasement at Munich in 1938 Vice-President Nixon had banned umbrellas at the welcome-home ceremony for Eisenhower at a rainy Washington airport. But everyone agreed that the tone of the conference was unexpectedly cordial. There was agreement on the desirability of further peace-seeking meetings and the leaders parted amid worldwide approval of what quickly came be known as "the spirit of Geneva."[17]

How does one explain this volte-face? The question leads us toward several crucial conundrums of the Eisenhower era. One is the much-debated question, already briefly canvassed, whether this stranger to politics was really in control of his foreign policy. For a long time the liberal view, spelled out by historians like Schlesinger and Townsend Hoopes, that Eisenhower was erratic, ineffectual, and dominated by his powerful but blundering Secretary of State, John Foster Dulles, was widely accepted.

But here too time and fresh evidence have forced a re-evaluation. In the 1980s fully researched portrayals of a more involved, even masterful chief executive began to appear. Historian Robert Divine emphasized Eisenhower's personal achievement in ending the Korean War, in working through several complex crises without direct military involvement, and in avoiding such subsequent liberal disasters as the Cuban imbroglio and Vietnam. Fred I. Greenstein found the "hidden hand" as vigorously active in foreign as in domestic affairs. From numerous diaries, memoirs, and other written records he concluded that Eisenhower, not Dulles, had made all the big decisions. Stephen Ambrose synthesized most of these positive assessments in a nuanced argument that faulted the president for his excessive distrust of communism and his failure to control the arms race, but insisted nonetheless that "he ran the show" and was "a great and good man."[18]

It is now increasingly accepted that Eisenhower was always in command and that Dulles' prominence and stridently anti-communist rhetoric had created a misleading impression at the time. A cautious politician who was often willing to let his subordinates make an elaborate showing in public, Eisenhower kept his options open and hoarded his political capital. His style was essentially managerial; his principal policy-making forum was the obscure but increasingly powerful National Security Council. He attended 339 of the Council's meetings and actively encouraged open debate. It seems likely that the Eisenhower–Dulles relationship was simply the most visible part of what was really a quite widely shared participation in policy formation and that historian Richard Immerman is right to characterize the two leaders as "in a real sense a team in almost continuous consultation." Each seems to have taken the lead in different spheres but with the president always the

final authority. Thus Eisenhower accepted with some reluctance Dulles' suggestion for a tougher line in his "Chance for
Peace" address after Stalin's death, but overruled the skeptical
secretary in deciding to meet the Soviet leader at Geneva in
July 1955.[19]

How then do we explain the Eisenhower administration's
apparent turn to conciliation after two years of Cold War
militance? Undoubtedly the end of the Korean War and the
fall of McCarthy had cleared the path for a new American
initiative. Clearly too, Eisenhower was concerned over the rising public impression that the primary American response to
the post-Stalin Soviet thaw had been little more than Dulles'
fiery talk of "brinksmanship" and "massive retaliation."
Moreover, Moscow had continued to present a softer image,
agreeing early in 1955 to accept a peace treaty freeing Austria
from postwar occupation controls. These attitudes encouraged
Eisenhower and Dulles to confound Republican die-hards and
release the diplomatic documents on the Yalta Conference of
1945 which, withheld for a decade of suspicious speculation,
now effectively demolished the popular right-wing notion that
Roosevelt had "betrayed" America's allies there. Washington
and Moscow were slowly but surely coming round to the convenient view that Stalin could be blamed for almost everything, a notion Khrushchev would put expressly in 1956.

Another prompt to warmer relations was a growing sense
of stability in the original European theater of the Cold War.
The tension over Germany, for instance, had apparently been
relieved in 1954 by the finally successful American effort to
weld the Federal Republic into NATO. Formerly the object of
Soviet bluster and threats the German issue was now (except,
as we will see, for a dangerous nuclear aspect) entering a
calmer, almost intellectual phase. During 1955 the Soviets
promoted Polish Foreign Minister Adam Rapacki's plan for
German neutralization, a theme echoed by George Kennan in
his influential Reith Lectures for the British Broadcasting Corporation. Significant too, perhaps, was an exchange between
the United States representative at the 1954 Geneva Conference on Indochina, Walter Bedell Smith (Eisenhower's chief

of staff during the war) and Soviet Foreign Minister Molotov. Smith stated his belief that their two countries could solve their problems peacefully, but expressed doubts about China. Molotov did not disagree, emphasized the distinctive character of China, and claimed that the Soviet Union had at times served as a restraining influence on Mao's regime.[20]

All this is more or less at the level of observable events. But we can also see deeper reasons for the new, accommodative spirit. For both countries were now independently taking a course that reflected economic rather than security priorities. In the United States Eisenhower, who often argued that a strong economy must be the basis of American diplomacy, had as early as 1953 proclaimed a "New Look" strategy that envisioned cuts in defense spending.[21] He reduced expensive, conventional forces and began to rely by way of compensation on the ability of the CIA to destabilize or overthrow fragile communist or radical regimes, and more visibly and alarmingly on a rapidly increasingly arsenal of nuclear weapons. Meanwhile, the post-Stalin Soviet leadership was emphasizing consumer over heavy industry and reducing the size of the Red Army while similarly relying on a rising, compensatory hoard of nuclear weapons. A root cause here, visible too in the only limited efforts the European powers were prepared to make to retain their imperial possessions in the early postwar years, was a sense of exhaustion throughout the industrial world after so many years of deprivation, war and tension, and a powerful desire to apply limited resources to economic growth and social purposes. Still it all conduced to a feeling of growing political stability, tempered by rising concerns over nuclear testing.

Why then, if it was indeed the logical outcome of a changing political context, did "the spirit of Geneva" not turn out to be a stepping stone to the end of the Cold War? For in fact it proved to be not much more than a brief moment of hope. New sharp tensions appeared in 1956, followed in 1958/59 by another promising collaborative episode that was itself confounded by renewed hostility in 1960/61. How does one explain the persisting tension and the confused seesaw quality of international diplomacy in the 1950s?

Much of the answer to this lies, I think, in two great structural factors that historians often treat as independent phenomena but which often operated together through the 1950s to frustrate the genuine accommodation that many seemed to want. The first was the enormous, seemingly uncontrolled enlargement of the nuclear arsenals on both sides. By stressing economy over conventional security, in the belief that nuclear weaponry could both save money and guarantee safety, the Americans and Soviets were each making a kind of Faustian bargain with their futures. The fantastic growth of nuclear stockpiles (the U.S. nuclear weaponry rose from approximately 800 to 8,000 warheads between 1953 and 1960; the Soviets appear to have made a comparable enlargement), together with the constant testing felt to be necessary in the inevitable arms race, repeatedly undermined the fragile spirit of accommodation and brought a destabilizing set of strategic calculations to every political crisis.[22]

One very visible crisis involved the Federal Republic of Germany which, historian Marc Trachtenberg has shown, Eisenhower was surprisingly eager to endow with an independent nuclear capacity. This is perhaps better characterized as a line of thought rather than an active policy. It was inspired seemingly by the president's deep desire to prepare the ground for an eventual American withdrawal from a Europe that could, if appropriately armed, stand on its own as an effective barrier to Soviet expansion. In deference to all the European powers (including a very anxious Soviet Union), who feared any German military revival and valued the American controlling presence, and out of concern too for opinion at home, this notion was pressed discreetly and was inevitably, one is inclined to think, unsuccessful.[23]

Just as disturbing as the nuclear cornucopia and much more visible during the 1950s, were the many crises that arose in the so-called "developing countries." These were largely the result of the second striking structural feature of the Eisenhower era: the epidemic appearance of new trouble spots caused by the rising tempo of European withdrawal and imperial devolution. As the exhausted imperialists gave up with varying degrees of reluctance, their grip on Asia, Africa, and other spheres, they left behind innumerable political problems and power vacuums in places like Indochina, North Africa, and the Middle East, which very soon became tense Cold War arenas. The nuclear arms race and the plethora of postcolonial political quagmires were distinct problems on their own with unrelated origins. But it was above all their combination that worked militantly against United States–Soviet accommodation. In the absence of large-scale, conventional forces every crisis now had nuclear implications, as Dulles' apocalyptic rhetoric (he repeatedly threatened "massive retaliation" – clearly meaning nuclear strikes – to chill communist expansionism) constantly reminded everyone. And the unavoidable association of nuclear weapons, either directly or as a background influence, with the recurrent crises thrown up by the general European retreat around the world, made real détente in the 1950s very unlikely.[24]

But even without these structural impediments, even if their difficulties had been confined to the slowly settling European theater, the United States and the Soviet Union would have had difficulty in unraveling the power systems that had now developed within their Cold War. This is shown vividly in the two overlapping crises that spelled the end of the benign Geneva impulse: the harsh Soviet reaction against the Hungarian revolt in October 1956; and the concurrent American humiliation of its two allies, Britain and France, in the Suez crisis. The interesting point is that each of the two primary powers acted in the first instance out of constructive motives that were, or should have been, designed to further rather than frustrate détente.

For the Soviets got into difficulties in Hungary because Khrushchev, in his famous speech to the 20th. Congress of the Communist Party of the Soviet Union, early in 1956, took a giant step toward loosening the Soviet system of coercion by exposing and condemning, in "secret" sessions but in conditions that were bound to become public, Stalin's brutal crimes and costly mistakes. This encouraging easement led within weeks to a political upheaval in Poland where eager reform

communists deposed the Stalinist leadership to general ap-
plause. Khrushchev reacted with threats but backed down
when the new leader in Warsaw, Wladyslaw Gomulka, threatened to call out the Polish people to resist coercion, and at the
same time temporized by assuring the Soviets that Poland
would remain in the Eastern bloc. But Moscow's backdown,
on the heels of Khrushchev's speech, induced a now highly
expectant combination of Hungarian workers and students to
topple their Stalinist bosses and install a Gomulka-style moderate leader, Imre Nagy. This situation quickly spun out of
control and turned violent. By the end of October Hungary
was intimating to a seemingly indecisive Moscow Politburo
that it might leave the Warsaw Pact.[25]

At this point the East European eruption coincided fate-
fully with events in the Middle East. The 1956 Suez crisis also
had its origins in a well-intentioned initiative: an American
offer to help finance the Aswan dam on Egypt's upper Nile.
But the Egyptian leader, Nasser, was a nationalist and socialist who constantly threatened the stability of the region in the
name of pan-Arab unity. When he purchased a shipment of
Czechoslovakian arms Dulles revoked the offer. Nasser responded by nationalizing the Anglo–French owned Suez Canal authority, thinking to finance the project himself from canal
dues. This led the British and French governments, deeply frustrated anyway over their long postwar political eclipse, to de-
vise with Israel a secret plan projecting an Israeli invasion across
the Sinai Desert upon which the two European powers would,
in the guise of a peace-keeping operation, move in to occupy
the Canal Zone. This was all too clever by half, especially as
the United States was not given any advance notice of the plot
(though British leaders of the intrigue always claimed later
that they had received implicit encouragement from Dulles),
and Eisenhower was deeply embarrassed both by the coinci-
dence of the affair with the culminating stages of his presidential re-election campaign and the general impression of
"gunboat diplomacy" surrounding the whole business. At the
end of October, as the Anglo–French forces took over the Canal
Zone while Khrushchev and his colleagues were deliberating

over Hungary, Eisenhower launched a series of ruthless, economic moves that forced London and Paris to a shamed withdrawal in favor of a United Nations force, and instructed his
Security Council representative to vote with the Soviet Union
in condemning his NATO allies.[26]

One historian has called Eisenhower's actions over Suez "his
most severe crisis." It was in large part a moral response, in
keeping with classic American anti-imperial principle, but it
undoubtedly had unfortunate results. For NATO's sudden
disarray encouraged Khrushchev and the Politburo, who up
to this point had seemed willing to let Hungary go its own
way, to send the Red Army into Budapest where it quickly
quelled the rebellion with much brutality and perhaps 40,000
deaths. Harsh communist rule was re-imposed and Hungary
was again imprisoned behind the Iron Curtain. The Geneva
goodwill evaporated immediately. There was also a heavy price
to pay in the Middle East where the rapid post-Suez erosion
of British and French influence thrust the United States forward into the labyrinth of Arab politics.[27]

We now have an overall perspective of the Cold War in the
1950s – a global power struggle with a dangerous nuclear
aspect from which neither of the two principals, despite brief
attempts at amelioration, seemed able to detach themselves –
to guide our examination of the various more localized crises
that Eisenhower faced. So far as Indochina is concerned we
have already noted the administration's two most important
decisions: the refusal to bail the French out at Dien Bien Phu
or to use nuclear weapons there as some wished; and the later
commitment to a "nation-building" enterprise under Diem.
The latter project seemed reasonably promising during 1955–
57 but the Diem refusal, immediately approved by the United
States, to allow the internationally supervised elections mandated by the 1954 Geneva Conference, led quickly to renewed
civil war. Diem now had the communist Viet Cong to deal
with as well as the recalcitrant Buddhists and a sullen army
leadership – burdens that increasing American economic and
military aid (approximately $1 billion between 1955 and 1961)
only marginally relieved.

The late 1950s, therefore, saw an increasingly oppressive Diem regime and a steady deepening of the crisis in Vietnam. But it was never given the close attention that, in retrospect, it deserved. Eisenhower himself talked in general terms about "a domino theory," which forced, he argued, a stand in Vietnam to prevent communist takeovers in nearby, vulnerable states, and he flattered Diem, as he did many other right-wing, anti-communist figures, with ample personal encouragement. But, as historian David Anderson has pointed out, he never re-examined basic assumptions or asked hard questions about the situation, which was not yet as important in the minds of American officials as more pressing difficulties in Europe and Latin America. Still, by 1961 South Vietnam was drifting toward disaster with on the one hand an intensifying communist insurgency now materially backed and directed by North Vietnam, and on the other an American "commitment" – manifest in a 1,500 strong American mission in Saigon, the largest such official representation in the world – that was steadily turning into a political trap.[28]

Meanwhile, a more immediately dangerous confrontation was being uncomfortably weathered in the narrow straits between communist China and Chiang Kai Shek's Taiwan nationalist remnant. This crisis also had real nuclear potential. It focused on the small, rocky island groups of Quemoy and Matsu some two miles or so off the mainland coast and still held tenaciously by Chiang's troops. According to historian Gordon Chang, the Eisenhower administration, which had committed itself in December 1954 to defend only Taiwan itself, secretly promised Chiang in January 1955 that it would also protect those islands, only to regret this geopolitical folly a few months later. Eisenhower now offered Chiang an American naval blockade of the whole 500 miles of the Taiwan Strait if he would withdraw from the dangerously exposed and worthless island outposts. Chiang refused. In April the crisis escalated with both Chinese regimes shelling each other and threatening invasion while Dulles, with Eisenhower's approval, announced that the United States might use tactical nuclear weapons if the communists tried to take the islands. The violence abated later in the year. But in 1958 the communists started again to shell this extraordinary Cold War flashpoint.

The basic problem here, as in so many Eisenhower-era crises, was not simply the communist threat but the relationship with a difficult, importunate ally. American leaders were well aware of Chiang's aim to entangle the United States in his aspiration to lead a victorious return to power. But they felt, and the China lobby and other conservatives constantly reminded them, that communist China was finally aligned with Moscow (an aspect explored by historian David Mayers) and was irremediably hostile. They therefore rejected several offers of negotiation and settlement from Mao's regime, lavished military and economic aid upon Chiang, and even installed intermediate range ballistic missiles on Taiwan.[29]

A characteristic combination of fears about communist intrusion and over-optimistic scenarios of effective "nation-building" led the Eisenhower administration deeply into the Middle Eastern power vacuum left by the humiliation of Britain and France in 1956. There was a lively concern in Washington with the politics of oil, but little knowledge of or interest in the deeper complexities of Arab politics. Nasser was widely viewed as a dangerous communist stooge with pan-Arabist ambitions that took on an added seriousness following a successful radical coup against the Iraqi royal family in early 1958. Conservatives like King Hussein of Jordan and Lebanon's president Camille Chamoun were seen as the exemplars of a desirable West-oriented alternative. In this cause Eisenhower landed 14,000 US Marines in Lebanon in 1957 to forestall any possibility of a pro-Soviet coup there. All this was done in the name first of the so-called "Eisenhower Doctrine," declaring an American interest in stability in the area, and designed, according to Robert D. Schulzinger, "to project the U.S. as the savior of conservative Arabs from Nasserism." This was shortly followed by the establishment of the Central Treaty Organization (CENTO) – the now familiar American collective security treaty covering, in this case, the vast area between member states Turkey and Pakistan, respectively the end of the line allies of NATO and SEATO. American guarantees against communist attack or subversion now ran from Japan in the North Pacific round to Norway in the North Atlantic.[30]

But what most contemporaries felt to be the most alarming crisis of the whole period came in the American backyard. Until 1959 policy-makers in Washington believed they had successfully protected the American hemisphere from communism, the CIA's Guatemala operation in 1954 being a kind of showpiece in this effort. But in January 1959 the sudden victory of radical guerilla forces in Cuba, led by Fidel Castro, set in motion a new disturbing political trend. Within a few months it became clear that, while Castro's personal political philosophy was still a matter of some speculation, he was a radical in temperament if not philosophy and was consorting with some highly influential communist associates. He was apparently intent on nationalizing, certainly without adequate or perhaps any compensation, the very substantial American investments on the island. Tensions grew as wealthy and middle-class Cuban refugees arrived with seemingly authenticated stories of confiscations and executions.

The most disturbing aspect of the developing crisis was the variety of long-term trade agreements the Castro government was now signing with Moscow and the increasing role of communists in the leader's immediate entourage. The Eisenhower administration, after a temperate early response to the situation, began in 1960 to tighten economic pressures culminating in the refusal to accept the importation of Cuba's sugar crop, upon which the island economy depended. The Soviets then pledged to buy the Cuban sugar, and to defend Cuba from American attack.

The significant issue here is whether, in this late-blooming forcefulness against Castro, the administration overreacted to the Soviet intrusion. These transitions from authoritarian, radical dictatorship to communist or near-communist rule have, after all, been a recurrent problem. Historians have even wondered whether a more patient if not sympathetic response to the new undoubtedly communist Chinese regime in 1949 might not have saved a lot of trouble later on. Similarly perhaps with Castro, and later with the Nicaraguan Sandinistas – both radical leftist movements in orientation but both much more broad-based successor governments than the Chinese revolutionaries. Viewing the American response to problems associated with the developing countries in these years historian Robert McMahon notes a frequent inability to distinguish nationalism from communism and concludes that, "the Eisenhower record appears one of consistent failure." Not that the administration's response to Castro in 1959–60 was unsophisticated. It had recognized from the moment the former Washington-supported dictator, Batista, had fallen from power, the danger Castroism presented of ideological contagion throughout central and southern America. Its first responsive impulse – to increase hemispheric economic aid for social purposes, heralding the Alliance for Progress of the Kennedy administration, was creative. But the full sugar embargo perhaps brought the crisis to a head prematurely. It was accompanied by a ban on all American exports to Cuba, by some encouragement for a government-in-exile now taking shape in Florida, and by active CIA involvement in training exiles in Guatemala for later military action. Historians Stephen Rabe, Richard E. Welch Jr. and others have pointed out that this first move toward intervention led directly toward the Bay of Pigs disaster in 1961.[31]

The Cuban crisis developed against a background of increasingly tense US–Soviet relations. A new phase opened in 1958 when Khrushchev, buoyed up by Soviet scientists' 1957 achievement in launching Sputnik, the first-ever space satellite, but fearful for the viability of his East German satellite, again challenged the Western presence in Berlin. He threatened to sign a treaty with the East Germans that would force the West to deal with that regime directly, thus surrendering the pledge Washington had given Adenauer not to recognize the communist government there. Eisenhower's response was characteristically calm and sensible. He made a variety of distracting arms control proposals and eventually Khrushchev backed off. In 1959 there was a dramatic improvement. The Soviet leader even made a successful visit to the United States, which culminated in cordial private meetings with Eisenhower and the so-called "spirit of Camp David."

But once again the thaw was short-lived. In 1960, on the eve of a new summit conference in Paris, the Soviets shot down an American U-2 reconnaissance plane. Khrushchev, under pressure from the Chinese (who were challenging for ideological paramountcy within the communist movement) and from his own hard-liners, set Eisenhower up by initially releasing only brief details. This induced the president to think the pilot had been killed. Anxious to save the summit meeting he therefore tried to pass off the flight as an off-course weather plane. Khrushchev then produced the fully confessing pilot and, after denouncing the hapless Eisenhower publicly left Paris for home. The dejected president told an adviser there was now "nothing worthwhile left for him to do until the end of his presidency."[32]

Much of the difficulty in the superpower relationship as the Eisenhower era wound down was due to vast nuclear overbuilding and atmospheric testing. Eisenhower was no doubt sincere in his frequently expressed desire to bring nuclear arms under control, and after 1956 even Dulles, historian Stephen Rabe notes, "saw greater danger in a spiraling arms race than in making a few concessions to the Russians." But the fact is that this administration raised the number of American nuclear warheads from under 1,000 to more than 18,000 during its tenure, with most of the growth coming in the last two years after the somewhat unfairly maligned Dulles had left the scene. The record, indeed, tends to support the suggestion of H. W. Brands Jr. that Eisenhower's celebrated Farewell Address lamenting the growing "military–industrial complex" was an admission of defeat rather than a warning to posterity.[33]

For in truth Eisenhower's arms control proposals, which had to be made acceptable to many skeptical hard-liners in the administration and which in many ways reflected the president's persisting distrust of the communists, were largely designed to please public opinion and were clearly seen by the Soviets as essentially self-serving. Thus the ostensibly reasonable 1955 "Open Skies" proposal would inevitably disadvantage the more "closed" Soviet sphere. And, as historian Thomas

Soapes and others have shown, the loudly proclaimed but uncoordinated US and Soviet test suspensions of 1958–59 invariably came immediately after the completion of a planned cycle of explosions and were understandably interpreted by the other side as propaganda gestures. It is true that each side showed some willingness in 1958 to compromise, the Soviets dropping demands for an immediate test-ban without a prior control system, the United States becoming less insistent that reductions in conventional arms, where the Soviets had the advantage, must precede a suspension of nuclear testing. But no meaningful negotiation ensued.[34]

In the last analysis the Eisenhower administration left many problems for its liberal Democratic successors. One wonders indeed whether Eisenhower's presently high reputation among historians (especially diplomatic historians) will endure. His admirers rightly emphasize the adroit ending of the Korean War and the fact that this president then kept a prospering America out of war for the next eight years. These were the impressive achievements of a competent chief executive. But he also made many decisions that turned into large, dangerous commitments which, ironically in so managerial a statesman, he would not or could not control effectively. Thus the "New Look" strategy heightened tensions (which Dulles' rhetoric undoubtedly magnified) and led to the rampant, virtually uncontrolled growth of the nuclear arsenal. It is remarkable, for example, that this prestigious military leader produced a cornucopia of nuclear weapons, only to suddenly blame the hitherto unchallenged "military–industrial complex" as he left office. It is remarkable too that he was not more sensitive to the emotions stirred up by the prospect of an independent German nuclear capacity, which he was in the end unable to bring about. His approach to the Cold War, recently illuminated by Marc Trachtenberg, had an enigmatic dimension. Even as, abetted by the incorrigible Khrushchev, he was converting the international arena into a potential cage of fire from which none were likely to escape, he was pressing a line in European affairs that would allow the United States to withdraw from political responsibility there, indicating in some respects a less than realistic kind of pre-1941 geopolitical sensibility.

Moreover, even as he seems to have taken a neo-isolationist (or "exit-strategy," as we would say today) view of America's ultimate NATO commitments, he was pushing the United States vigorously and without much political or intellectual preparation into a variety of smaller gluepot situations around the world. He failed, despite many warnings, to rein in a CIA whose budget he allowed to rise from $82 million in 1952 to $800 million in 1960, and whose uncontrolled activities grew from dubious intrigues in dusty Third World capitals in 1953 to assassination attempts in 1960.[35] He made an unnecessary and hazardous commitment of American power in Southeast Asia leaving his successor, George Herring reminds us, a stark choice between abandonment or substantial escalation. He pushed the United States into the Middle East arena without adequate preparation, while in the Eastern Pacific he allowed a weak ally to call the tune in an irrational, risky confrontation just off the China coast. All in all there were a good many contradictions, ironies, and loose ends in what appears to have been a rather dangerous legacy.

Society in the 1950s

We now move again from state to society. The 1950s were years of social transformation, especially prominent in American history because, while the Cold War remained a pervasive but nonviolent preoccupation, essentially domestic institutions like the suburbs, the corporation, and television made a striking impression, much as liberal reform and ideologically charged politics had done in the Roosevelt–Truman era. Now, with a Republican administration interested in reducing rather than enlarging the state's role, no fighting wars to distract attention, and a high degree of consensus in the nation generally, the private realm came more fully into its own.

As we explore these themes in necessarily abbreviated form we might remind ourselves first of the remarkable affluence that underlay this dynamic period. From figures given earlier let us simply recall that the inflation-adjusted Gross National Product grew from \$353.3 billion in 1950 to \$487.7 billion in 1960 – a rise of 37 percent for the decade. This prosperity was based, moreover, on a firm base. The American domination of the world economy continued; oil and other energy sources were still cheap; federal spending was robustly stimulative despite Eisenhower's frugal budgeting; productivity improved, fostered by many technological innovations; and the baby boom presented the promise and reality of a rapidly enlarging market.[36]

Not everyone did well of course. African-Americans, native Americans, and some regional groups hardly improved their lot at all. But even there we see a quickening of political consciousness that expressed itself in thought and action. Indeed, the rising tempo of black American activism, notably after a successful 1955 bus boycott in Montgomery, Alabama, was a feature of the decade. Up to that point the so-called "legal" strategy had governed the civil rights movement, culminating in the landmark 1954 Supreme Court decision in *Brown* v. *Board of Education of Topeka* outlawing racial discrimination in schooling.

The *Brown* case led to a rapidly growing spirit of resistance among white southerners anxious to defend the segregation system. Violent attacks on blacks became increasingly common in the region. But now blacks, led by church leaders and teachers were seizing the initiative. A charismatic young Atlanta Baptist minister, Martin Luther King Jr. came to the fore in 1955 and his Southern Christian Leadership Council provided an institutional focus for a growing number of peaceful protests in southern communities in the late 1950s.

The Eisenhower administration was broadly unsympathetic. The president had been shocked by Chief Justice Earl Warren's active promotion of the black cause among the hitherto divided justices. But, as we noted earlier, he upheld the law. Eisenhower sent troops to Little Rock, Arkansas in 1957 to enforce the registration of black students in the local high school. And in the same year he signed the first Civil Rights

Act since Reconstruction. It created a new Civil Rights Commission, established a civil rights division in the Justice Department, and authorized the Attorney General to seek legal remedy where voting rights were being denied. The reforms were less impressive than they seemed. A provision for jury rather than judge-alone trial in voting cases rendered that ostensible improvement a toothless reform in a hostile jurisdiction. Increasingly, blacks began to think in terms of self-help. Various individual initiatives paved the way for the celebrated "sit-in" movements of 1960, which saw groups of black students peacefully demanding service in segregated public restaurants. From this came the "jail-ins" and the "freedom riders" who carried the cause into the new decade.[37]

But for most white Americans the 1950s were a time of success and rising expectations. Much of the new prosperity poured into, and derived from, the burgeoning new suburbs. Before World War II suburbs were typically an attachment to, and barely separable from, the organic city. Afterwards they became a massive social reality on their own. There are perhaps two dates that stand out dramatically in American demographic history: 1910, when for the first time most Americans lived in communities of more than 10,000 inhabitants; and 1970, when the suburban population finally outstripped the urban. The move to the suburbs was especially dynamic in the 1950s, thanks in part to the continuing encouragement of the mortgage-granting resources of the Federal Housing Administration and the Veterans Administration, to the generous mortgage interest deduction against the income tax, and to enthusiastic developers like William Levitt who transformed Long Island and many other communities into what architectural critic Lewis Mumford called "a low-grade, uniform environment." A leading historian of the suburbs, Landon Jones, records that of the 13 million homes built between 1948 and 1958, 11 million were "suburban." By the end of the decade one-quarter of all existing homes in the United States had been built in the previous 10 years, and 83 percent of all population growth in the 1950s had been in the suburbs. These trends continued through the 1960s and beyond, though countered more recently by the progressive urbanization of the suburbs and a modest reverse flow back to gentrified areas of the inner cities.[38]

The suburb, then, is a classic 1950s' theme. But what was life like in these new societies? There has always been lively debate about this. The sternest critic was Mumford who in 1961 described a "Levittown" as follows:

> A multitude of uniform, unidentifiable houses, lined up inflexibly, at uniform distances on uniform roads, in a treeless command waste, inhabited by people of the same class, the same incomes, the same age group, witnessing the same television performances, eating the same tasteless, prefabricated foods, from the same freezers, conforming in every outward and inward respect to a common mold . . . [39]

An unappetizing picture to be sure. And it reappears in much of the social criticism of the period. Yet it seems overstated, as the sociologist Herbert Gans claimed in a later rejoinder. Gans trumped Mumford and other armchair cultural aesthetes by bravely going to live with his family in a Levittown for two years. He emerged, apparently no worse for wear, to write an upbeat account of his experience. He found life there richer and more diverse than expected and spiced by an unanticipated sense of adventure and excitement among the predominantly but not exclusively young families.[40]

Suburbanization brought many real benefits. Housing and space were widely affordable. Family life flourished. Marriage rates in the 1950s remained high, even after the record-breaking postwar years. Divorce rates dropped dramatically and the extraordinary "baby boom" clearly suggests a sense of contentment and optimism. Jones gives us the basic birth-rate figures: a total of 76.4 million babies born between 1946 and 1964, constituting nearly two-fifths of the population of 192 million in the latter year. Many have attempted to explain this remarkable and unpredicted fertility explosion. Applying Mumford-like rigor to the various theories we might say that Arlene Skolnik's notion that a desire for "normalcy" was the inspiring cause is rather too general. That Randall Collins and Scott Cottram's insistence that couples were responding in semi-Pavlovian fashion to wartime government propaganda

urging a built-up population is somewhat credulous if not un-
American. And that Elaine Tyler May's "containment" thesis
accusing men of an unacknowledged desire to trap women
securely in the suburban prison is an ingenious but improbable juxtaposition of Stone Age values and suburban realities.
Historian James Patterson gives a sensible explanation. He
notes the sudden convergence in child-bearing of two distinct
1950s' generations: older Americans who had put off having
children during the depression and war and were now rushing
to make up for lost time; and younger people in their late
teens or early twenties by the late 1940s who felt encouraged
by the rising affluence and general promise they felt about the
future to go ahead and raise a family unusually early. The
convergence produced the baby boom.[41]

But suburbanization had its dark side. It hurt the American
city badly, depriving it of industry, high quality commerce,
and much of its affluent tax base, thus strangling its increasingly cash-strapped cultural institutions and intensifying the
problems of crime, drugs, and poverty that afflicted the residual population – especially blacks who lived in wretched
ghetto conditions and found employment increasingly hard to
get. The overwhelmingly white move to the suburbs led directly to the crisis of the inner cities that became dramatically
visible in the 1960s.

The green, suburban sanctuaries bred their own inner tensions too. Many women clearly felt alienated by the daily routine. Unfortunately it is impossible to substantiate this with
any precision and historians often fall back on impressionistic
social evidence or on John Cheever and other novelists of the
suburban woman who, if she is not seen reaching desperately
for the gin bottle by mid-morning is portrayed as woefully
over-burdened with household chores, importunate children,
and an arsenal of failing appliances.

Female suburban angst was comparatively slow to break
into public awareness and only became a major theme in the
next decade. Much more overt was the so-called "youth" revolt, which appears to have developed most robustly in the
more affluent suburbs. Here there is both an abundance of

social science diagnosis and an exuberant cultural register in the Hollywood movies and rock music of the time. These agencies identified, reified, and certainly amplified the growing generational dissonance. Here too there is little hard data to anchor a comprehensive explanation. One can see that the fast-evolving youth economy of the decade stimulated a powerful sense of generational solidarity and self-importance and that, as sociologist Todd Gitlin's memoir of a Long Island childhood evocatively suggests, what parents and critics often called self-indulgence was really frustrated idealism. Both strains would attach themselves to political and cultural causes in the 1960s.[42]

One final point is worth stressing. We are often inclined to think (and the academic literature tends to encourage the thought) that these social phenomena are more or less exclusively American in character. In fact, they were present in most Western industrially developed countries. The common tie was the appearance at last of a general economic recovery. The decades of privation and austerity seemed over. The psychological overhang of World War II, never entirely surmounted, was nonetheless beginning to recede. We have already noted that the ostensibly militant Eisenhower administration now chose, in pursuit of the new prosperity, to entrust American security to cheaper nuclear weapons rather than expensive conventional forces. The NATO allies, perhaps even more eager to cut their costly military establishments as they moved away from the threadbare years, were making similar cheeseparing calculations of the minimum contribution they would have to make to retain the American protector's interest. The British military historian, Michael Howard, noting the gap between the alliance's generous force projections and its chronic shortfalls in actual strength, aptly commented that, "for the next forty years the states of Europe were to purchase military security by spending enough on their own armed forces to make them sufficiently fit... to obtain access to American military strength and to make nuclear deterrence credible."

Under this fragile nuclear shield the urge to a better life produced the aggressive suburbanization (especially in extra-

European open-space societies like the United States, Canada, Australia, and New Zealand) and high birthrates all commentators have noticed. An unabashed materialism flourished. Older social self-images that had softened the miseries of the recent past – the cult of the English gentleman for instance, and the ideal of the self-reliant, Emersonian American – seem to have declined, replaced by harder, more self-aggrandizing styles of behavior. The stridency of the rebellious young was also an international phenomenon. Iconoclastic American figures like the actor James Dean and the singer Elvis Presley had world-wide appeal. Alienation took different forms. In the more politicized culture of Britain the spectrum ran from dress-conscious "Teddy Boys" to the literary "Angry Young Men" and the "Kitchen Sink" dramatists, finding its emblematic moment in the lament of the fashionable London playwright John Osborne, that there were no great causes left to struggle for. American youth, resolutely apolitical (or anti-political) in the 1950s, would find causes aplenty in the next decade.[43]

We have touched on the experience of women and the young. What of the men, enduring the joys and strains of regular, bread-winning employment? This perspective brings us immediately to another great 1950s' theme: the American corporation. Here too we find an image ready-made for us by Hollywood screenwriters and other writers who have tended to link the suburb and the corporation as the primary institutional sources of a bland, deteriorating national character. Thus Sloan Wilson, in his 1957 novel *The Man in the Gray Flannel Suit*, attacked the shallow materialism of the anxious executive, shuttling daily from home to office and back. The movie *The Apartment* exposed the hypocrisy and dubious values supposedly associated with the corporate lifestyle, while W. H. Whyte's influential 1956 sociological study, *The Organization Man*, filled out the picture of a conforming, go-along team player in a systematic way, inspiring much anxious debate about the erosion of American individualism.[44]

We should not accept the validity of these images too easily. The alternative case, that the corporate career and the world of work generally were richly satisfying, or at least marginally

fulfilling, goes almost entirely by default in academic historical work. A review of historical textbooks over the last half-
century would reveal a very different set of preoccupations. A
few years ago the dominant concepts were politics, class, and
liberal reformism. More recently race and gender have been
principal themes. There has been a great deal of interest in the
play of morality and the advance of reform but very little in
the arena of daily employment where most Americans spend
the great preponderance of their waking lives. Yet the world
of work is in fact suffused with historical consciousness and
has its own largely autonomous cadre of professional historians who serve a vast audience. One important scholar in the
1950s, unusual in his ability to bridge the gap between academic and corporate America, was the economic historian
Alfred Chandler, who took the large corporation as his primary subject and devised a very influential "managerial" interpretation of American capitalism. But more typically the
business community has taken its sense of the past from a
strong business history tradition sustained by popular non-
academic writers like Peter Drucker and Tom Peters, by many
skilled biographers, and by a host of magazines and journals.[45]

Recently there have been promising signs of a more open-
minded attitude: a session at a leading historical convention
on Chandler's work, and Halberstam's elaborate emphasis on
the vitality of entrepreneurial innovation in his popular book
on the 1950s. An interesting re-evaluation of the 1950s' corporation is found in Robert Reich's *The Work of Nations*
(1991), which has become a popular college text. He finds
that it was a fabulously productive and successful entity. Noting the support given by the Eisenhower administration and
the attachment of a now domesticated labor movement, he
calls it the "National Champion" and postulates a "National
Bargain" by which, in return for prosperity, American society
accepted the legitimacy and permanence of the core corporation. Reich acknowledges and to some degree accepts the "conformity" critique popularized by Whyte and others. But he
points out that many other liberals in the 1950s not only accepted but also approved of these giant institutions. Thus the

former New Dealer, David Lilienthal wrote in 1953 that "Our productive and distributive superiority, our economic fruitfulness, rest upon Bigness." Historian Richard Hofstadter, often critical of business, nonetheless expressed admiration for the "enlightenment and urbanity of the occasional big-business leader compared to the parochialism of the typical small businessman." And Reich himself, while conceding that rugged individualism was rare at the lower levels of large companies, found plenty of creative endeavor at the higher levels, though it tended to come in dramatic leaps rather than incrementally.[46]

All this makes for a much more variegated picture of the Eisenhower-era corporation and the general work experience. Undoubtedly the social critics of the day were right to stress the increasing bureaucratization of life and the regrettable move away from individualism and the Emersonian tradition of self-reliance – already deeply undermined by the depression experience. But the 1950s were in many ways a creative period, not least in business practices and techniques. In any event most Americans at the time, glad to be free at last of depression, war, and reconversion, seem to have been more interested in success than in their immortal souls (even the much-noted religiosity of the decade had a distinct self-help, practical character). As *Fortune* magazine put it in 1955, "Corporate bigness is coming to be accepted as an integral part of a big economy. Whatever attacks may be made against them in theory, the large corporations have met the test of delivering the goods."[47]

Of all the major changes in American life during the 1950s none aroused as much excitement and anxiety as television. In 1948 only 172,000 homes had a set. By 1952 the figure was 15.3 million, rising to about three-quarters of all homes by 1955. Like suburbanization and the corporate grind television attracted a good deal of criticism. Yet its impact seems in some respects to have been broadly reconstitutive. The suburb tended to break up the large extended urban family, put a greater distance between work and home, and kept men and women apart during the day. The corporation brought its own kind of alienation and social disjunction. But in the evenings television bound up the wounds, brought the family together, and, in some seemingly magical way momentarily reduced this vast, complex society to the intimate dimensions of a seventeenth-century New England town meeting. The Canadian critic Marshall McLuhan later coined the resonant term "the global village" to convey the point.[48]

Television in the early 1950s was remarkably creative by later standards. For the sophisticated there were live dramas featuring distinguished actors and writers and a variety of hard-hitting documentaries and public interest shows. Cherished comedians like Milton Berle and Lucille Ball attracted millions, as did popular programs like *The Ed Sullivan Show*. Human interest family sagas like *Father Knows Best* and *Leave it to Beaver* were closely attuned to the new suburban audience, and by the mid-decade the cowboy, private detective, and hospital genres had all established themselves.

Despite the appearance of innocent entertainment there was from the start, however, a lively suspicion that the new medium was, at least potentially, an instrument of enormous mind-altering and therefore political power. To a generation of liberal intellectuals raised amidst concerns about the mass society, totalitarianism, and subversive propaganda, the growing power of the first national networks, with their dependent, nation-wide affiliates, seemed ominous. Recent studies have put these early fears in perspective. The cultural critic James Twitchell, for example, insists that commercial profit rather than political influence was always the main concern. And James Baughman's sober review of the business of television in relation to other media of the time confirms the point. There was real competition between the networks. Moreover, the new medium had to compete with newspapers, movies, radio, and magazines – all of which found ways to fight back for market share.[49]

But of course television was potential political dynamite all the same. Even Eisenhower, who professed contempt for the medium, found it useful to record campaign spots in the 1952 campaign. Television ruined McCarthy in 1954, as we have seen, and it was a big factor in 1956 (when it first covered the conventions) and even more so in 1960 when it probably determined the outcome of the presidential race by hosting the candidates' debate. By that time it was already revolutionizing and arguably corrupting the tone and character of political campaigns almost everywhere. It raised the cost of the effort beyond what all but a few could afford. Further, the triumph of celebrity politics and the virtual exclusion from high office of all but the rich and good-looking was implicit in television from the start.

This was only dimly understood in the 1950s, which explains the self-confidence of a saturnine Richard Nixon that he would win a televised debate with the more photogenic John F. Kennedy. Politics still seemed very much a left versus right affair and it was unclear which side the new medium would favor. Most of the network impresarios seemed reluctant to engage in conventional partisan politics. They felt obliged to show a respectable interest in public affairs. After the notorious quiz show scandals of 1959 (when the champion contestant, Charles van Doren, confessed to receiving answers in advance) they quickly increased coverage of public issues. They had to contend with conservatives who were offended by any attempt to go beyond the old limits of social convention, and liberals who complained about corporate domination through the advertising weapon and who felt that most of the programming was, as Kennedy's Federal Communication Commissioner Newton Minow put it in another classic formulation "a wasteland."[50]

Beyond television the 1950s was an extraordinarily creative period in many fields. There were striking innovations in architecture and automobile design. We have already noted the entrepreneurial successes cataloged by Halberstam and others. But what about Dr. Alfred Kinsey's quasi-scientific explorations of male and female sexuality between 1948 and 1953? Here was an exciting "new frontier" long before Kennedy popularized the phrase in his 1960 inaugural speech. *Playboy* with its glamorization of sophisticated sex first appeared in 1953 and was quickly followed by *Cosmopolitan*, a close equivalent for young single women. Explicit physicality in movies and novels increased at a steady pace through the decade. *Lady Chatterley's Lover* finally got into the bookstores in 1958 though Henry Miller's scabrous *Tropics* volumes were still banned. Meanwhile there was plenty of reassuring wholesome fare, much of it of high quality. This was a kind of golden age for the American musical, with Rodgers and Hammerstein especially prominent, and also for jazz which was now both a worldwide phenomenon and a source of national pride, and for rock and roll music which, combining African/American rhythm and blues with a variety of indigenous white music, captured the young and helped put older, big band styles to flight. Humor too had now evolved from the broad, much-loved humor of Laurel and Hardy and Will Rogers to the sophisticated wit of S. J. Perelman, Tom Lehrer, and Peter DeVries.[51]

There was a certain shortening of intellectual horizons in the 1950s. As we saw earlier the immediate postwar sensibility was understandably haunted by large dark subjects: war, totalitarianism, apocalyptic possibilities, and "man" in a profound way. It was influenced by deep-thinking authors like Ortega y Gasset, Arnold Toynbee, Reinhold Niebuhr, George Orwell, and Hannah Arendt, whose *Origins of Totalitarianism* (1951) properly belongs with this group. The main intellectual currents of the 1950s were quite different. This generation of social critics, historians, and novelists was perhaps the most self-conscious and self-critical in modern American history – surpassing in imaginative vigor and analytic penetration the mostly solitary efforts of the 1920s' expatriates and even the admittedly more impassioned productions of the 1930s' leftists. And while it is notoriously difficult in the mass and fluidity of the modern American experience to catch cultural authorities in transition we can recognize here, I think, something genuinely new. The old, unsystematic Anglo-hegemony in the nation's intellectual life persisted in many ways. But it was increasingly challenged through the decade by the exponents of a more pluralistic university-oriented set of values and interests.[52]

The new work was, except for important theoretical contributions from the so-called Frankfurt School of German social critics who came to the United States to escape Hitler in the 1930s, solidly rooted in America rather than Europe. Much of it was guided by the ideals and procedures of social science and practical academic inquiry rather than by the profound questions of human existence that had troubled intellectuals in the 1940s. Simply put, the governing interest was now "America" rather than "Man." Sociologists were especially prominent, people like C. Wright Mills, whose fierce attacks on the routine dullness and dissatisfaction of suburban and corporate life enlivened the decade, and David Riesman, whose 1950 book *The Lonely Crowd* (with Nathan Glazer) suggested that Americans, who had hitherto been "inner-directed" independent people, were in the new mass society becoming "other-directed" and highly susceptible to manipulation. This thesis became a kind of academic mantra for innumerable 1950s' social scientists and was complemented in 1960 by sociologist Daniel Bell's *The End of Ideology*, which suggested that the problems posed by affluence and manipulated mass taste had eclipsed Marxism and other idea-oriented polemics.[53]

These concerns were felt far beyond the academic world. We have already noted Sloan Wilson's unflattering portrait of suburbo-corporate man, and John Cheever's eviscerations of the suburban lifestyle. Both reflected an intensified interest among creative writers in social patterns. Sociology became a popular avocation. W. H. Whyte's best-selling *The Organization Man* was only one of several jeremiads deploring a transformation from the Protestant ethic to a "social" ethic. Some disturbing implications were presented in a number of books by Vance Packard whose *The Hidden Persuaders* exposed the subliminal tactics employed in advertising. The criticisms were serious and sharp. The intellectual historian Richard Pells points out that Whyte, Riesman, and others were "trying to re-define the meaning of individual freedom in a post-industrial society where psychological well-being was more important than economic reform."[54]

The 1950s also saw the emergence of a new school of American historians. To this point the so-called "Progressive" tradition – which saw modern American history as essentially a recurrent struggle between the people and powerful interests – had been dominant. In 1955, however, Louis Hartz in *The Liberal Tradition in America* and Richard Hofstadter in *The Age of Reform* presented what came to be called a "consensus" interpretation that played down conflict and emphasized instead the persistence of conformity and common values. Both took a negative view of this. Hartz stressed the dangerously doctrinaire tendencies of an unchecked liberalism that, without alternative philosophies to test and guide it, tended to degenerate into a form of moral absolutism. And Hofstadter, in several path-breaking books, employed insights from sociology, psychology, and anthropology to illuminate dark passages and tendencies in American history that, he insisted, suggested a long-standing vulnerability to intolerance, prejudice, and social breakdown.[55]

There was much that was new in this ferment, out of which a more vigorous pluralistic intellectual life seemed to be emerging. We see a certain premonition of imminent displacement in various quarters of the old literary establishment: in the mordant criticisms and gloom of Edmund Wilson and Dwight McDonald; among the old-stock social elites as they were still affectionately portrayed by mannerist writers like John P. Marquand and Louis Auchinloss; and in the writing of representative mainstream novelists like James Gould Cozzens. It contrasted quite unmistakably with the spirit of inquiry and broad social concern one finds in the new sociologists, historians, and novelists, many of whom were Jewish academics or intellectuals who were deeply influenced by European social criticism. Beyond this we see a number of other new individual thinkers from various backgrounds and especially a literature of eloquent and tightly controlled anger from emerging black writers such as James Baldwin.

An interesting feature of Eisenhower's last year or so in office is the sudden profusion of stock-taking and agenda-setting reviews of various aspects of American life, suggesting a widespread sense of the need to revive the moral resources of the nation and to set out compelling new objectives. There was a flurry of defense-oriented studies, notably the Science Advisory Council's "Gaither Report" pointing to a supposed Soviet superiority in nuclear missiles – later found to be erroneous – and calling for vast increases in defense spending. Several military commentators emphasized the need for a more flexible national security establishment, especially a build-up in conventional forces, which had languished during the Republican emphasis on nuclear weapons. More affirmingly, the Rockefeller brothers financed and published a series of inquiries in this period, published as a single volume in 1961 as *The National Prospect*. Journalist Godfrey Hodgson called this "a handbook of the shared assumptions of the American governmental and business elite." Its distinguished author-participants, in fact drawn from various sectors of American life, delivered an upbeat verdict on a successful and "responsive" economy and celebrated the "free" and spirited character of the American people. It did, however, stress the "critical situation" caused by the communist challenge. The Eisenhower administration also produced a report on national goals that projected much the same spirit – self-confidence bordering on complacency so far as the nation's domestic life was concerned; deep concern about the menace presented by world communism.[56]

One further group, though they functioned as individuals in different spheres, compels attention here. These were the heralds of what we might reasonably call liberal revivalism. Here the view of the home front was less sanguine. The end of the Roosevelt–Truman era had left, from a reform perspective, much unfinished business. And inevitably we see, slowly at first but much more energetically by the end of the decade, the intellectual groundwork being laid for a fresh start. A crucial pace-setting work here was John Kenneth Galbraith's *The Affluent Society* (1958). Acknowledging the new prosperity Galbraith's ironic critique contrasted private affluence with public squalor, and called for legislative reform and more spending on education, welfare, and infrastructure. Dean

Acheson and other Democratic Party leaders wrote thought-
ful books looking to further reform advances, and the old
Rooseveltian universalism found a typically systematic 1950s'
echo in Walt Rostow's *The Stages of Economic Growth* suggesting that any society could achieve affluence by moving
successfully through rational steps from "take-off" to growth
and beyond.[57]

At the deeper level, where issue politics dissolves into cultural consciousness, we find another prophetic figure pointing toward the 1960s. C. Wright Mills forecast, with unique
accuracy, the political radicalism of the next decade and gave
it, as will be seen, a certain intellectual rationale. He has a
claim to have coined the term "the New Left." In several 1950s'
publications he identified it as a constellation of approaching
issues and attitudes that were cultural and intellectual in character rather than class-based and economically focused in the
"Old Left" style. Halberstam calls him "the critical link" between the Old and New Lefts, and credits him with inspiring,
as Todd Gitlin and other 1960s' memoirists confirm, the new
decade's Students for a Democratic Society and other change-
oriented groups.[58] With the liberal revivalists we have an introduction to the reform politics of the mid-1960s, with Mills
we have, years before the event, a sense of connection to the
cultural radicalism that followed it.

4

The 1960s: The Triumph and Tragedy of American Liberalism

The 1960s is treacherous terrain for the historian. Only two generalizations may seem more or less safe. First, this was, it is widely agreed, a pivotal decade, the point perhaps upon which the whole postwar era in the United States turned. And second, it is broadly acknowledged that, for better or worse, a certain outlook and way of life came to grief in these years. Otherwise the period still glows with the fire of controversies passionately pursued and as yet unresolved: over the traumatic war experience in Vietnam, over the course and fate of the civil rights eruption, over the unprecedentedly unconstrained cultural rebellion, to name but a few.

Behind a turbulent historical scholarship, much of it produced by now graying academics drawing deeply on youthful memory, lies an intriguing question. Is it possible to identify in terms sufficiently precise to illuminate yet broad enough to encompass the principal developments, the fundamental drama of this fascinating period? Can we isolate anything resembling a root cause? It must be said that no historian has yet succeeded in reaching that level of conceptualization. But surely any answer that seeks to subsume the issues of race, war, and culture into some larger explanation will have to take certain primary facts into account. For example, the sudden acceleration, from whatever cause, in the tempo of national life; the ubiquity of radical change, and the clear and growing inability, as the decade proceeded, of traditional authorities to either predict or control these changes.

How much of any acceptable explanation is to be found, to cite one persisting theme, in the continuing struggle with communism abroad? Why, to mention one mystery, did the US government, having by 1963 surmounted a great crisis with the Soviet Union, and then embarked with it on a path of mutual reconciliation that seemingly carried some hope of ending the original Cold War, suddenly turn away and plunge headlong into a massive and costly confrontation with a remote Third World variant of communism that was deeply infused with anti-imperial nationalism? Do we find the master-key rather in the domestic arena, perhaps in the character and limitations of a liberal reform impulse which, emerging apparently refreshed from the Eisenhower interlude, flowered brilliantly for a time only to fade rapidly and find itself harassed by radicalism and then eclipsed by a resurgent conservatism. Liberalism did not die in the late 1960s, indeed it persisted with bursts of spasmodic vigor well into the 1970s and beyond. But its unforeseen decline, on the morrow of its remarkable success, is certainly one of the conundrums of the period.

Many historians, looking for more tangible causes, focus primarily on the revolution in civil rights as a dynamic of the time. It influenced most other spheres of public activity. And it was in the 1960s that race first supplanted class and region as the central issue in domestic politics. None of this was intended or expected at the outset. Nor did many contemporaries anticipate that racial violence, hitherto seen as essentially a southern problem, would become a familiar feature of urban life in the North. Or that powerful impulses in the African-American community would lead toward militance and separation.

And what of the transformations in cultural consciousness among many Americans? The so-called "youth rebellion" of the 1950s had been a broad, diffuse, but only marginally subversive impulse. But it now began to express itself in new life-styles and social behavior provocative enough to agitate and polarize various parts of the national community. As early as 1960 this began to take on a political form, joining with the civil rights surge and later with the anti-war movement. The "counter-culture" and "the movement" together had an immense and varied impact on American life, presenting many direct and subtle challenges to a surprised political and social establishment that searched desperately but unavailingly for a creative response.

This by no means exhausts the principal streams of causation. The whole question of generations obviously comes into play at numerous points, not least in the astringent revisionism of some younger, post baby-boom historians who profess to see a pretentious, self-dramatizing profundity in their elders' work. The role of the political parties was probably greater than many culturally oriented commentators have allowed. The economy (and the remarkable co-existence of affluence and cultural revolution) calls insistently for explanation. There is much to learn too from the diverse religious currents of the 1960s, so very different from the fidelity to mainline denominations that characterized the Eisenhower years. And then there is the rather neglected international dimension, reminding us that the turbulence of this period was a common experience in Europe and elsewhere – clearly leading back to the scarcely addressed importance of World War II and its aftermath as a crucial background to change.

On this note of epidemic ambiguity we begin our exploration of the 1960s.

Kennedy

The 1960s generated many myths, none more enduring than the "Camelot" image attached to John F. Kennedy's presidency. Even today, after many sobering revelations, the shining memory of that era, launched with Kennedy's inaugural invocation of a "new frontier," lingers on, summoning up for many Americans a moment of unique promise and brief transcendence, in which youth finally received its due and gave the United States a fresh invigoration of purpose and achievement.

Images of this kind do not last long unless they have some grounding in reality. The "Camelot" idea, to be sure, was pure hokum, conjured up by the journalist Theodore White after Jackie Kennedy's recollections, a few days after her husband's assassination, of the boyhood pleasure he had taken in reading about King Arthur and the Knights of the Round Table.[1] But it does reflect the genuine freshness of the new decade. It also reminds us of the sense of idealism felt by many Americans in the Kennedy years. The Peace Corps sent thousands of eager young people to help out in developing countries. The Alliance for Progress brought social and economic aid to Latin America. Kennedy's political style and inspiring rhetoric had enormous appeal. And it is entirely consonant with this favoring impression that, at least in the accounts of sympathetic biographers, each of his three years seems to have had a distinctive storybook flavor. There was a time of testing and momentary setback in 1961; a crisis of potentially catastrophic proportions brilliantly and victoriously surmounted in 1962; and a time of flowering maturity and productive achievement tragically cut short in 1963.

This celebratory interpretation, inaugurated by Schlesinger (who served in Kennedy's White House), and by speechwriter Theodore Sorensen in two indulgent memoir-histories published soon after the assassination, has been attacked with varying persuasiveness by later historians. Some have questioned the administration's pretensions to creative innovation. The "new frontier" call was lifted from the Rockefeller's recent *Prospect for America*; the Alliance for Progress was derived very largely from Eisenhower's earlier hemispheric initiatives; the Peace Corps concept originated with Kennedy's rival, Senator Hubert Humphery of Minnesota and Congressman Henry Reuss of Wisconsin. Others have stressed the president's early naiveté, his escalation of the nuclear and conventional arms race, the greatly enhanced commitment in

Vietnam perhaps foreclosing any real chance of extrication, an unhealthy preoccupation with Castro and Cuba, a lackluster domestic record, and an irresponsible private life of sexual adventuring beyond any known presidential precedent.[2]

Here is a distinct problem for the modern historian. He finds himself contemplating, on the one hand, a public life of gripping incident and apparent high purpose conducted by an unusually intelligent president; and on the other a turbid subculture of self-indulgence, mafia associations, and dangerous obsessions. From the dramatic viewpoint this is a fascinating contrast. But how important is the intriguing private life to the master narrative of American history? The old pre-Cold War historians handled these problems with impressive efficiency. The distinguished British scholar H. A. L. Fisher, for example, suddenly confronted during his serenely magisterial *History of Europe* by the unpleasant spectacle of a highly libidinous Louis XIV, skewered the wretched Sun King with the brisk observation that "the tide of his animal passions ran strong," and moved on quickly to the more congenial problems of the Spanish succession.[3] Obviously this minimalism won't do today. Human frailty is the gleaming coinage of modern history writing. Moreover, what historian William Chafe has called Kennedy's "macho values and sexual drives," perhaps inherited from his ambitious father, perhaps stimulated by pain-killing drugs taken for an ailing back, clearly have some intimate bearing on the political tone and practice of his administration: its combativeness, its emphasis on will, its insistence on the so-called "cult of toughness." As Schlesinger noted, the Kennedy presidency "put a premium on quick, tough, laconic, decided people."[4]

All these qualities, together with a remarkably sharp political instinct, are on display in Kennedy's pursuit of the White House. He had, we must remember, to win power in a society where Irish Catholics had long been mistrusted outsiders. His 1960 election campaign had many of the characteristics of a siege: of an Irish Catholic taking on an overwhelmingly old-stock, Protestant establishment; of a new generation challenging its fathers; of a highly organized political machine against the traditional jumble of the American political arena. Kennedy's race to the nomination is a fascinating story in itself, brilliantly described and anatomized by Theodore White in his *The Making of the President, 1960*, as compelling a portrait of America then as Gunther's is of the Truman era. White catches the American political system in a moment of transition. The old regional structures and variations are still much as they were in Woodrow Wilson's day. The big city machines that helped produce Franklin Roosevelt's and Harry Truman's urban majorities are still potent. But they are beginning to give way to the new homogenizing power of television and the manipulation of political specialists: pollsters, fundraisers, spin-doctors, and so on.

Here we also see laid out in fascinating detail, much elaborated on but not fundamentally improved by later historians, the inordinate ambitions of the candidate's father, Joseph Kennedy. Risen from Irish immigrant stock to Wall Street riches and service as FDR's ambassador to Britain, and now spreading his fortune liberally and exploiting his innumerable connections, Kennedy was determined to get his son into the White House. All this comes out in the victorious march through the primaries, through the thickets of suspicion in West Virginia, past the dubious southern Baptists with their fear that a Catholic president would be taking his orders from the Pope, and on to the San Francisco convention where the Stevenson liberals nearly derailed the juggernaut.

The national campaign was equally exciting. Despite Eisenhower's clearly hinted reservations Richard Nixon won the Republican nomination. There was little substantive difference between the two young candidates, both in their early 40s. Kennedy portrayed himself as a liberal in domestic matters; Nixon cultivated the image of a compassionate moderate. Both claimed to be supporters of civil rights for blacks, but Kennedy's sympathetic telephone call to Martin Luther King's wife after his arrest in rural Georgia just before the election finessed the Republican there. The principal arguments were over the Cold War, with Kennedy attacking the Eisenhower administration's supposedly ineffectual policies and its neglect in allowing a "missile gap" to develop, though in fact the United States was still vastly superior in this field. The crucial confrontations were in two very different arenas: on the television screen where in two debates the charismatic Kennedy seemingly bested a tired, poorly made-up Nixon, and in the South where Kennedy's surprising choice of Senate majority Leader Lyndon Johnson of Texas, helped bring most of the region back from its flirtation with the Republicans under Eisenhower. In a cliffhanger result Kennedy received 49.7 percent of the popular vote compared to Nixon's 49.6 percent, though the margin was greater in the electoral college. There were inevitable allegations of fraud from the Republicans but Nixon, in apparently statesmanlike fashion, refused to pursue them.[5]

Kennedy made a powerful impression in his inaugural address. Scarcely mentioning domestic affairs, he immediately established a new, more militant note in foreign policy. The famous promises "to bear any burden" and "meet any hardship" were, even favoring historians now agree, dangerously open-ended, and reminiscent, in their subsequent effects, of Truman's implicit promise in March 1947, to defend freedom everywhere. But they were in fact inspired by a typically truculent speech by Khrushchev only two weeks before asserting that communism was forcing capitalism into retreat. At the time, moreover, Kennedy's speech was generally viewed as inspirational and appropriate, all the more so because it was not simply an exercise in saber-rattling but a challenge to the American people to live up to their ideals and an eloquent expression of American mission with attractive promises of economic aid and assistance to weak, developing countries.[6]

The new administration mirrored the character of the campaign. Here and there Kennedy saluted experience and continuity with Republican Douglas Dillon as Secretary of the Treasury, Adlai Stevenson as United Nations Ambassador, and Averell Harriman in a high State Department role. And his Secretary of State, Dean Rusk, was a solid, establishment choice. But otherwise youth and vigor predominated. He appointed his brother and closest confidant, Robert, as

Attorney General. McGeorge Bundy, former Dean of Harvard College, became National Security Adviser and Robert McNamara came from the presidency of the Ford Motor Company to take charge of the Pentagon. Behind these major figures a host of intellectuals from the Ivy League and the University of California flooded into the capital.

This was immediately recognized as a new generation of leadership, known later, after the ironic title of David Halberstam's book about their Vietnam involvement, as "the best and the brightest." Coming, as Halberstam, Richard Barnet, and others have shown, from a remarkably similar white, mainly Anglo-Saxon background (leavened by a few Catholics) often with privileged upbringings and careers in law or some form of finance or banking they seemed, at least by comparison with the Eisenhower administration, youthful, irreverent, and iconoclastic. In fact, on fundamentals at least, they were remarkably conventional. Their close-cropped hair and buttoned-down clothing suggested purposefulness. They properly saw themselves as "the new generation of leadership" and as "the junior officers of World War II come to power." They seemed determined to "man the ramparts of freedom" (another Kennedy phrase), more vigorously, more competently, and more imaginatively than their predecessors. And, by enlarging the scope of American conventional military power they quickly set about fulfilling their promise to promote a strategy of "flexible response" to replace the Eisenhower–Dulles reliance on nuclear weaponry.[7]

Rarely has so much promise and euphoria been so quickly confounded. Kennedy almost immediately encountered a series of severe diplomatic setbacks. In retrospect these did little to dent his appeal. Indeed they deepened the drama of the young prince undergoing a series of trials before triumphing. The first was a botched operation against Castro. Ironically, for all the talk of fresh departures, the problem arose from the Eisenhower administration's plan, which Kennedy endorsed, to promote and aid the invasion by a CIA-trained émigré force of a Cuban region known as the Bay of Pigs. The landings took place on April 17, 1960. The area, swampy and far from any mountain sanctuaries, was poorly chosen. American air and other promised support did not materialize. Castro's intelligence sources had forewarned him and the 1,400 expeditionary invaders were all killed or captured almost immediately.

Kennedy immediately and gracefully accepted responsibility for the fiasco, and was much praised for doing so. Many contemporary commentators and the president's historian admirers later, blamed the previous administration for a faulty conception and the CIA (whose leaders Kennedy shortly fired) for mishandling the operation. An interesting analysis, by the psychologist Irving L. Janis, stresses that none of Kennedy's advisers raised questions about the plan and presents it as an example of the dangerous effects of "group-think" or peer group pressure – a tendency in government circles that became more pronounced as the 1960s advanced. But the basic decision to go ahead, and then at the crucial moment to withhold potentially decisive American air support, was Kennedy's alone.[8]

This very public humiliation was a sobering prelude to the president's hastily arranged and poorly prepared summit meeting with Khrushchev in Vienna in June. The volatile Soviet leader tried, in effect, to browbeat the chastened young American with a barrage of complaints and threats. The more urbane Kennedy found it difficult during their personal encounters over two days to adjust to this rough-house diplomacy. He was particularly alarmed by Khrushchev's renewed threat to sign a treaty with the East German government giving it control of East Berlin and access to West Berlin. This has been widely seen as an attempt to test the inexperienced president. But it is also true that Khrushchev was desperately concerned to enhance the authority of the weak Ulbricht communist regime. The exodus of trained people to the West through Berlin was an embarrassment and West Berlin was a provocative showpiece for anticommunists everywhere.[9]

Responding vigorously Kennedy, upon his return home, publicly announced significant increases in American defense spending. He then sent an armed convoy down the autobahn into Berlin to dramatize Allied rights, and dispatched Vice-President Johnson to reassure the beleaguered West Berliners that his commitment was steadfast. These actions inevitably brought a series of tense moments, including a United States–Soviet confrontation in the city that in the end passed off peacefully. In the event Kennedy's strong measures were successful. Khrushchev again failed to follow through completely and in August contented himself with the construction of the notorious Berlin Wall (which at least stopped the dangerous exodus to the West) and the face-saving detonation of a 100 megaton nuclear weapon.

This new Berlin crisis is fairly seen as a stand-off. If Kennedy's firmness prevented a Soviet diplomatic triumph and salvaged some of the prestige he had lost over Cuba and at the Vienna summit, the Wall, though widely trumpeted as a propaganda success for the West in its implicit admission that Soviet control rested on coercion rather than consent, was also a stark monument to the limits of American power. Many conservatives, and some West German leaders, blamed Kennedy for not challenging Khrushchev and forcing its demolition. This was unreasonable. From a different perspective Michael Beschloss argues that Kennedy should have been more sensitive to the pressures Khrushchev was facing within the communist bloc to solve the Berlin problem, which he had been presenting to Western leaders since 1958, and which arguably led him into the Cuban disaster in 1962. It is now accepted that the Soviet leader was indeed being pushed hard by the East Germans, the Chinese, and hawks in the Politburo. But it is hard to see how Kennedy could, in the inflamed atmosphere of 1961, largely created by Khrushchev's intimidationist diplomacy, have accommodated him.[10]

But it was Cuba, rather than Europe, that dominated the first two years of Kennedy's presidency. Many writers have emphasized his obsessive concern with the destruction of Castro. After the Bay of Pigs humiliation he launched Operation Mongoose, a CIA-directed campaign of political and economic destabilization on the island, including various attempts to assassinate Castro with the collaboration of the Mafia, which had been driven from its Havana rackets. Despite the absence of conclusive evidence most authorities on the subject assume Kennedy knew and approved of these plans. He also dramatized his commitment in 1962 by successfully prodding the Organization of American States to expel Cuba, by imposing a series of additional trade embargoes, by eye-catching meetings with anti-Castro émigrés and, most menacingly, with various military maneuvers in the Caribbean. And in October, only days before the missile crisis began, a variety of practical steps were taken, involving the movement of men, ships, supplies, and fighter planes to the area, that must have suggested the likelihood of invasion to the Cubans.

These facts offer a modified perspective on the origins of the crisis, long attributed to Khrushchev's opportunism. Certainly Castro and his Soviet allies had ample reason to expect an American attack. James Hershberg and several other historians, who have studied the subject, believe Khrushchev was sincere, therefore, in explaining his decision to send nuclear missiles to Cuba as an effort to protect it from the United States. At the same time it is widely and persuasively argued that the Soviet leader was tempted by the opportunity this offered both to win a spectacular political victory and to somewhat redress the unfavorable nuclear strategic balance. For by 1962 it was clear to all that the supposed Soviet missile superiority was a sham. It seems that the United States enjoyed a warhead superiority somewhere in a ratio variously estimated as nine or fourteen to one. Smarting from this setback, some argue, and from Kennedy's continued build-up of nuclear strength and public declarations that the United States might in certain circumstances make a first strike, and pressed also by domestic hawks to act more forcefully, the Soviets, in Thomas Paterson's estimation "hoped to enhance their much weaker deterrent power in the Cold War and (at the same time) save a threatened ally." This mixture of motives sounds reasonable enough but it seems now that there was a further less defensible impulse at work. For in 1990 Sergo Mikoyan, son of and secretary to Khrushchev's close associate, Anastas Mikoyan, revealed that the Soviet leaders had not been interested in negotiations but in seeing how far they could push Kennedy before he responded.[11]

If the origins of the crisis are still complex and controversial the actual course of events is now well established. The 1997 publication by Ernest R. May and Phillip D. Zelikow of *The Kennedy Tapes: Inside the White House During the Cuban Missile Crisis*, has given us an intimate view of what the book's *New York Times* reviewer aptly called "the single most dangerous episode in the history of mankind." The dynamic phase began on October 14 with the discovery by an American U-2 reconnaissance plane that Soviet missile sites in Cuba, hitherto thought to be for defensive weapons only, had an offensive capability of 2,000 miles. Kennedy immediately gathered a secret committee of advisers – the so-called Ex-Com. – to consider a response. The most favored early alternative was an air strike, fully accepting the risk of Soviet personnel being killed. Only slowly did a less drastic alternative scenario emerge – a blockade of the Soviet ships already en route for Cuba with missiles disconcertingly visible on their decks.[12]

In the middle of these deliberations, on October 17, Soviet Foreign Minister Gromyko visited Kennedy in the White House and gave assurances that the missiles were exclusively defensive in character. Kennedy knew better but chose not to reveal his hand. After much tense debate he opted for the naval blockade and appeared on national television on October 22 to describe the situation to the American people. There would be a strict quarantine on all offensive military equipment bound for Cuba. He called on Khrushchev to recall the weapons. Meanwhile, he warned, the United States would regard "any nuclear missile launched from Cuba against any nation in the Western hemisphere as an attack by the Soviet Union on the United States, requiring a full retaliatory response upon the Soviet Union."

Four indescribably tense days followed. The Soviet ships slowly approached the quarantine line and no word came from Moscow. Then, on October 26 Khrushchev replied privately offering, amidst much general rumination, to withdraw the missiles in return for an American pledge not to invade Cuba.

But within 24 hours he declared, in public this time, that the United States must also withdraw its Jupiter missiles from Turkey. On the suggestion of McGeorge Bundy (not Robert Kennedy, who claimed parenthood in his memoir) the president replied to the first letter and ignored the second, though he carefully had his brother secretly promise the Soviet ambassador in Washington that the Turkish missiles (which Kennedy had earlier wanted withdrawn anyway) would be removed. Khrushchev signified his acceptance on October 28 in a public declaration. The 16 Soviet ships turned for home. Shortly afterwards the missiles were withdrawn.[13]

Not surprisingly there has been an enormous literature on the Cuban missile crisis, with late-emerging revelations, especially from Soviet and Cuban sources, forcing some reconsiderations over time. The first almost unanimous assessment of Kennedy's conduct of the crisis reflected general public approbation. Schlesinger claimed that the event showed the world "the ripening of an American leadership unsurpassed in the responsible management of power." Most early historians and political scientists were impressed by the president's statesmanlike crisis management. And even recent critics, such as Mark White, have paid tribute to the cool, judicious skill with which he navigated through the options presented by hot-headed military and political advisers, the Khrushchev vacillations, and the various, intervening unforeseen events to a safe result.[14]

Inevitably, though, questions have been raised. Kennedy's insistence upon tightening the pressure on Cuba after the Bay of Pigs disaster is sometimes held to have been disproportionate and provocative in paving the way for some kind of unwelcome Soviet intrusion. It has been argued that, given the danger of nuclear war, he should have used the opportunity of Gromyko's visit to defuse the crisis with private diplomacy, an option he seems to have resisted from a determination not to have to negotiate on an issue of such surpassing importance. The Mikoyan explanation of Soviet motivation seems to justify that decision. The suspicion lingers in some accounts that Kennedy was thinking primarily of the looming congressional elections, and was resolved upon a firm demonstration of strength. But it must be said that there is no hint of such petty political calculations in the published record of Ex-Com deliberations. Much of the late-blooming criticism has sprung from a sense of the acute danger of full-scale war, and how easily the situation could have slipped out of control. What would have happened, for example, if Khrushchev had rejected Kennedy's decision to respond only to his first letter and had insisted on the removal of the Turkish missiles. For years it was thought that this might well have led to war. But here again more recent evidence puts Kennedy in a better light. At a 1987 conference on the crisis Dean Rusk let it be known that JFK had intended in that event to secretly draw in the United Nations as a face-saving intermediary, under whose aegis both the Cuban and Turkish missiles could be withdrawn without a direct American concession.[15]

There is, however, another set of disturbing issues, military rather than diplomatic in character, and hidden from the public at the time and for years afterwards, which dramatizes the profound dangers of the event. It is true that the records bear out Robert Kennedy's early account that the president, throughout the tense 13-day crisis and in the face of repeated calls for decisive action involving bombing the missile sites from military and other members of the Ex-Com, resolutely refused to order direct military action, even when a U-2 plane was shot down over Cuba at a crucial moment. But it became known in the 1970s and afterwards that the American military had been anything but the efficient and obedient instrument of Kennedy's clear-headed decision making. The political scientist, James Nathan, for example, has demonstrated that, despite the carefully fostered illusion of control, the president had only a very loose mastery of American action. Thus, at one point, Kennedy ordered the Navy to move the blockade from 800 to 500 miles from Cuba, desiring to give the Soviets more time to deliberate. The order was ignored and the blockade was enforced at 800 miles. When Secretary of Defense McNamara raised awkward questions about boarding procedures the Navy brass hustled him out of the Naval Operations Center insisting the "the Navy will run the blockade," though he claimed subsequently that he had established effective control. A little later an appalled Kennedy learned that the Navy had, without authorization, been forcing Soviet submarines to the surface in the waters round Cuba. Not to be outdone in hair-raising antics the Air Force, without any notice to the White House or to Moscow, sent a number of fighter-bombers over Soviet territory at the height of the crisis to escort out a U-2 pilot who through navigational error found himself returning from the North Pole to Alaska through Siberia, at that time off-limits by presidential direction.[16]

Most alarming of all have been recent revelations from Soviet and Cuban sources. They show that, contrary to American belief at the time, offensive missiles were already ashore in Cuba, and ready for action, and that the local Soviet commander had both the official authority and the capability to launch these missiles if the Americans invaded or attacked. In this context it is chilling to recall that Kennedy had publicly committed himself to action if it was found that Cuba had any offensive capacity against the United States, and also to see how nearly the Ex-Com (with military support) had come to recommending air strikes. The pressure was especially intense when the U-2 plane was shot down over Cuba. It seems likely that an American air strike on the missile sites at that point would have provoked a locally ordered Soviet attack on the eastern cities of the United States, forcing Kennedy to contemplate and almost certainly carry out, in some form, his promised retaliatory strike against the Soviet Union.[17]

All this seems from today's perspective to suggest a dangerous inadequacy in the political leadership of both antagonists in the early 1960s. Each displayed an imperfect understanding of the opponent's non-negotiable positions, a threat to which might well be expected to lead toward nuclear war, and also a failure to adopt policies to mitigate the consequences of the phenomenal build-up of nuclear weapon capability on both sides during the 1950s. Thus, Khrushchev should surely have realized that it was politically impossible for the West to abandon Berlin, and that it was dangerously provocative to arm Cuba, still in the turbulent aftermath of a violent revolution, with offensive missiles, a move that Kennedy had publicly warned would lead to a violent American response. By the same token Kennedy should have realized that his very menacing saber-rattling against Castro through 1961–62 was likely to inspire some Soviet response, and that his boastful revelations of American nuclear superiority, together with his large military build-up (ostentatiously set in motion in 1961) would tempt the risk-taking Khrushchev to seize the opportunity to convert Cuba into a Soviet nuclear base.

Many historians view the missile crisis as a climactic moment in the Cold War, creating by virtue of its universally perceived dangers a new atmosphere in which, having confronted each other so directly, the two superpowers could move more confidently toward a degree of co-existence if not détente. Kennedy himself began to lay the groundwork for a more collaborative approach to the Soviet Union. His Cold War rhetoric was now more subdued. And in June 1963, at American University, he urged the importance of improved relations and called for a nuclear test ban treaty. Khrushchev responded favorably and, though the president's forced compromise with the Pentagon and domestic hawks killed hopes of a comprehensive ban, the ensuing agreement – the Test-ban Treaty of 1963 – prohibited atmospheric testing. This popular achievement was followed by the establishment of a Washington–Moscow "hot-line" to ensure rapid communication in the event of another crisis. These initiatives, together with a few enigmatic public comments suggesting that the commitment to South Vietnam was not necessarily a sacred obligation, as well as his long-delayed but now forceful championship of a civil rights bill outlawing segregation at home, suggested to some contemporaries and many later commentators that the Kennedy administration was at last beginning to fulfil its promise.[18]

There are, however, various problems with that scenario. One is the president's continuing obsession with Castro, which led down several dark paths. Another is that Kennedy continued the arms build-up, partly to placate the military for the test-ban treaty, thus accelerating rather than trying to defuse an arms race which the Soviets, after their missile crisis humiliation, were only too likely to intensify. And he failed to find common ground with President Charles de Gaulle (perhaps impossible in the circumstances) on a range of European issues. The French leader, for instance, responded to Kennedy's rejection of his conception of a Western co-directorate in Cold War policy, and the American tendency to favor the British in nuclear and economic matters, by vetoing Britain's 1963 application to join the Common Market. Above all the "growth" argument is undermined by the invigorated but in retrospect unwise steps the administration took in 1963 to assert American control in South Vietnam.

In two powerful ways JFK escalated the American commitment in Vietnam. First, he accepted, without much careful evaluation, the advice of his Army Chief of Staff, General Maxwell Taylor and deputy national security adviser Walt Rostow, who after a brief visit in 1961 together urged a significant increase in troop levels. By November 1963 Eisenhower's 400 non-combat advisers had been transformed into 16,000 troops now authorized to join their South Vietnamese trainees on patrols involving combat potential. Second, when the view took hold in Washington during 1963 that even this was not enough to inspire the Diem regime to carry out what were regarded as necessary reforms, Kennedy approved plans for a coup that would bring a military government to power in Saigon. The coup, carried out only days before Kennedy himself was killed, turned out badly in that Diem was murdered by the successful military insurgents. The broader consequences were even worse. For the hapless generals produced a series of short-lived, ineffectual juntas that were only marginally responsive to American influence. Kennedy thus bequeathed to his successor a situation that was rapidly getting out of control and yet, by virtue of the enlarged military commitment, much more difficult to terminate than it had been in 1961.[19]

What, finally, of Kennedy's invariably overshadowed domestic policies? The conventional wisdom here is that he came to office as the standard-bearer of the New Deal tradition, promising medical care for the elderly, civil rights legislation, more educational funding, money for housing, and various other reforms. Very little was achieved, reflecting in some degree at least the fact that Kennedy was not a passionate liberal. Sympathetic writers have tried to explain the thin record of achievement. Schlesinger, who devoted only seven pages of his long book on the Kennedy years to his subject's domestic agenda in fields other than civil rights, blamed a recalcitrant Congress.[20] Similarly the journalist, Tom Wicker, in a sharp analysis of political reality in the early 1960s, argued that JFK was frustrated in his modest reform proposals by his wafer-thin mandate and, more particularly, by a Congress still effectively controlled by southern conservative chairmen and their Republican allies. The result was to make any legislation favoring blacks or union workers highly improbable, and to put a crimp in the reform agenda generally.[21]

Another partial explanation of Kennedy's thin legislative achievement is that he was focused primarily on reviving an ailing economy, a necessary precondition of any larger reform program. His instrument here was a stimulative tax cut, urged notably by his chief economic adviser, Walter Heller, an enthusiastic Keynesian who reassured the president that any revenue short-fall would soon be made good by returning prosperity. From a socio-economic point of view this would effectuate the classic purposes of postwar liberalism by enlarging the economic pie and easing the passage of reforms. Many students of this issue, including economic specialists like Edward Flash and Seymour Harris, have applauded the ensuing 1963 tax measures which, when in their final form pushed through by Johnson, they plausibly portrayed as the basis of the remarkable prosperity of the mid-1960s. But more leftish commentators like Bruce Miroff, who calls Kennedy "a corporate liberal," insist that most of the benefits went to the rich. Allen Matusow similarly laments Kennedy's "reactionary Keynesianism" and argues that the tax cut set the stage for inflation and unbalanced budgets later in the decade.[22]

This early pre-occupation with the faltering economy is part of the conventional explanation of Kennedy's seemingly tardy response to the civil rights movement. It is important to keep in mind here that, though increasingly insistent, this was not yet widely seen as the central national issue. Certainly, in Washington at least, it seemed less pressing than the Cold War that Kennedy himself always put first. He appears to have taken the view that there was little to be gained by confronting the conservative southern grandees prematurely, and much to be lost in the foreign policy area, where appropriations for foreign aid and such programs as the Alliance for Progress and the Peace Corps were always problematic. During his first two years, therefore, Kennedy made a number of gestures toward civil rights reform, but carefully avoided the full commitment he had promised during the campaign.

The result was that, as in the Eisenhower years, the main impetus came from civil rights activists, increasingly dominated now by black leaders, and from the still supportive Supreme Court. The process is well illustrated in the 1961 effort to desegregate interstate travel. Following the Court's decision in *Boynton* v. *Virginia* ruling such discrimination illegal, the celebrated Freedom Riders, organized mainly by the Council on Racial Equality (CORE) took Greyhound and other public transportation through various Deep South routes, encountering violent reaction from angry white groups in clashes that were widely covered for a shocked national television audience. This forced JFK and Attorney General Robert Kennedy into prolonged negotiations with several southern governors as they tried to protect the Freedom Riders without too much overt federal intervention. Eventually the administration found it politic to order the Interstate Commerce Commission to enforce the desegregation law in all interstate travel.

There was a good deal of black community action in southern cities during 1961. The results were mixed, with a notable setback in Albany, Georgia where the local authorities successfully resisted change by calmer, more sophisticated tactics that curbed white extremists. But the pace of the challenge to southern segregation quickened in 1962. When James Meredith tried to register as the first black student at the University of

Mississippi in September the Kennedys tried to manage the situation through private deals with the state's segregationist governor, Ross Barnett. But these broke down and, when violent clashes developed between an angry white crowd and federal marshals, involving two deaths and 160 injured, the president ordered army troops in to restore order and ensure Meredith's registration.

Historians have often been critical of the Kennedy record in this sphere. Always sensitive to the southern white establishment, he appointed well-known segregationists to the federal bench and carefully avoided a real commitment to civil rights. Martin Luther King's Pulitzer Prize winning biographer, Taylor Branch, faults him for a lamentable lack of political courage. Only when the pressure for commitment became irresistible, it is argued, did Kennedy act with any show of resolve. The real turning point came in 1963. The occasion was King's decision to challenge segregation in Birmingham, Alabama, notorious for systematic segregation under its racist police chief, Bull Connor. The developing boycotts, sit-ins, and public protests, many involving black children, soon provoked Connor, as intended, into violent excesses including the use of fire hoses, attack dogs, and beatings – all conveyed to a national television audience that also saw blacks fighting back as the violence quickly ran out of control. These events, James Patterson writes, were "pivotal" in forcing Americans nation-wide to confront the civil rights issue. Kennedy now ordered the preparation of a civil rights bill outlawing segregation. Yet, even as the bill entered the congressional arena, he showed caution. He tried to head off and then play down plans by King and other black leaders for a march on Washington for "Jobs and Freedom," scheduled for August 28. Compromises were made but the march went ahead essentially as designed, drawing 250,000 people and culminating in King's great peroration, looking to the day when all Americans could say "Free at last! Free at last! Thank God Almighty, we are free at last!"[23]

Kennedy gave the same cool, politically calculating, approach to virtually all domestic issues. There was a great deal of idealistic rhetoric, but little sustained effort to obtain reform legislation. There were, to be sure, small advances and larger promises toward women's rights in the job market, some improvements in education and environmental policy, an effort to rationalize agricultural policy and, after Kennedy read Michael Harrington's best-selling *The Other America*, some impressive first steps involving the federal government in what Lyndon Johnson would later call "The War on Poverty." These initiatives, mostly coming in Kennedy's last year, have been bracketed with his late-blooming commitment to comprehensive civil rights legislation to foster the notion, which we have just seen in the foreign policy area, of growth and/or fulfillment in his leadership, a view taken by in-house celebrants like Schlesinger and Sorensen, understandably enough, but also by some more recent historians such as Alonzo Hamby and James Giglio.[24]

Much of the resistance to this idea of eventual fulfillment has come from historians who have sensed a certain hollowness and moral vacuum in Kennedy. This is only partly to do with his serial womanizing, which by itself has had remarkably little adverse impact on his historical image. It comes rather from his authorization of widespread wire-tapping, his failure to rein in J. Edgar Hoover's erratic course as FBI director, and his presumed endorsement of assassination plots, together with his now well-documented association with Mafia elements. And behind this lies the conviction of many scholars that, whatever growth there was in the diplomatic area, he was not the kind of conviction politician the early 1960s needed. He was, rather, as historian Herbert Parmet put it in a well-received pioneering study drawing on the resources of the Kennedy library, "a moderate conservative and rational idealist." In November 1963 it fell to a very different kind of leader, a politician much more fully rooted in the New Deal tradition, to gather all Kennedy's tentative initiatives together and forge them into a wider program of truly remarkable reform.[25]

The Great Society

Lyndon Johnson, the architect of the self-described "Great Society" and the principal actor in the great Vietnam drama, is a massive, ostensibly transparent but actually rather mysterious figure in modern American history. Robert McNamara felt he would "never work with a more complicated man." He had many admirers, but few among his intimate associates, who often found him arrogant and intimidating. His press secretary, George Reedy, recalled that Johnson "as a human being was a miserable person – a bully, sadist, lout, and egoist" – a harsh judgment, but one now being documented in several volumes by his micro-biographer, Robert Caro.

How important is this kind of personal assessment? Surely a president should be judged on performance? This is more or less how historians and biographers have treated Truman and Eisenhower. And Robert Dallek, at least, while giving much attention to LBJ's psychological profile, has recently given him a full, achievement-oriented biography built round the thesis that, like his hero, Franklin D. Roosevelt, Johnson was a visionary "who helped advance the national well-being and fulfill the promise of American life." But with Johnson, and even more so with Kennedy and Nixon, personality often seems to lie at the heart of their place in the national memory. No doubt this is largely due to the generational change, to the suddenly more intrusive, psychologically oriented media led from the early 1950s on by the new theatrical techniques of television, and to the growing Cold War conception of an "imperial presidency" taking shape after Eisenhower. But it is also due to this fascinating, individually gifted but star-crossed trio themselves: Kennedy with his carefully nourished cinematic gloss; Johnson with his braggadocio and self-dramatizing flair; Nixon with his unappeasable paranoia and inability to find any fulfillment in success.[26]

But the performance is the real story here. Johnson made a brilliant start. In a moment of national trauma he presided over the memorial rituals and the whole difficult transition with reassuring dignity, competence, and firm purpose. He chose the members of the investigative Warren Commission on the principle of national reassurance, and was relieved when it concluded that the assassin, Lee Harvey Oswald, acted alone. This discredited speculation about a Soviet role that, if demonstrated, would have caused a profoundly dangerous foreign crisis. The Warren verdict has never been universally accepted. Don DeLillo's characterization of "history" in his novel *Libra* as "the sum total of all the things they aren't telling us" aptly reflects the suspicions of many Americans. Few were appeased by a generally confirming congressional review in 1979 (which did, however, concede the possibility that there had been a second gunman) and millions continue to believe that Oswald was part of a Cuban, mob-oriented or other conspiracy.

Addressing Congress five days after the assassination Johnson paid handsome tribute to his predecessor and, recalling Kennedy's inaugural proclamation "Let us begin!" he urged the legislators "to continue" by enacting the dead leader's domestic program. He proceeded over the next year to push most of that program through a suddenly more compliant Congress. He went on to a landslide re-election victory in 1964 and then inaugurated a massive reform program of his own. The "Great Society" accomplishments of 1964–66 were clearly, in some fundamental sense, a fulfillment of the New Deal liberal tradition and many historians, including those gathered by Steve Fraser and Gary Gerstle in their collection *The Rise and Fall of the New Deal Order, 1930–1980* display some kind of continuum from Roosevelt to Johnson, albeit one characterized by setbacks and disappointments as well as success. At the same time we might well ask whether the Johnson era activism was not, in its essential character, variety, and the general context of prosperity in which it developed, also descended in important ways from the great era of progressive reform in the early twentieth century – a conception that would ground 1960s' political liberalism even more firmly in a long-standing American tradition of reform.[27]

From the beginning Johnson imparted an immense charge

of energy to the political system. He rammed Kennedy's stalled tax cut through Congress after allowing only minimal spending cuts in the federal budget to placate the fiscal conservatives who had hitherto held it up. And he applied all his manipulative skills to get the greatest prize – Kennedy's civil rights law – past the seemingly implacable southern and Republican opposition in the Senate. In the end, ceaselessly pressing and flattering the legislators and constantly invoking the Kennedy legacy, he finally managed to outflank the southerners whose last effort was to filibuster the bill for three months. The key to Johnson's success was his assiduous courting of Senator Everett Dirksen of Illinois, the master of the Republican votes necessary to win a two-thirds majority that would close the endless debate. The act passed on July 2, 1964, a unique moment in American history. It finally outlawed racial discrimination in all accommodations for public use and looked to the cessation of federal funding for schools and other institutions that persisted in the practice. Attracting much less attention at the time, but highly significant in its eventual consequences, a Virginia committee chairman, thinking to make the civil rights provisions unpalatable to his fellow legislators, added sex to race and creed as forbidden categories in employment decisions. By this curious sidewind the road to gender as well as racial equality began to open up.[28]

Meanwhile, Johnson was moving ahead with what he dramatized as "the war against poverty." In its immediate origins this is usually traced to Michael Harrington's success in catching President Kennedy's eye with his *The Other America*. Harrington argued that up to 50 million Americans still lived in "invisible" poverty. In response Kennedy had encouraged administration liberals to define a "poverty line" that would clarify the situation. Settling at about $3,130 for a family of four this left around 40 million citizens in need. Kennedy took a few characteristically hesitant steps, mainly in the form of some legislative proposals addressing the problems of juvenile delinquency, but it fell to Johnson to draw together, add to, and amplify the disparate programs that had developed by early 1964 into a composite bill that was designed mainly to open up new opportunities for a wide range of poor people. Passed in August it included job-training and job-creation measures, work-study funding, loans for small businesses and rural development, a domestic peace corps, and other like-minded programs.[29]

There is an interesting relationship between these three legislative measures that transcends the link with John F. Kennedy and tells us something about 1960s' liberalism. The Civil Rights Act was unique in that it had been a long-gestating issue, so long indeed that some historians have called it and its follow-up legislation on voting rights in 1965, "a Second Reconstruction." But in important respects it resembled the anti-poverty legislation (the Economic Opportunity Act) which was also in large degree associated with the future prospects of African-Americans, though this was played down by the administration in favor of a more universalistic mission and image. This was tactically adept because the much-needed reform challenged another widely held American attitude – the faith in socio-economic self-reliance. Unquestionably Johnson's "War on Poverty" upset many conservatives who saw a potential undermining of the work ethic and a future costly mass of importunate dependents. At the same time, unfortunately, LBJ alienated some supporters on the left who welcomed anti-poverty action but lamented the haste and lack of planning in the specific programs.

In 1964, however, the self-confident Democratic administration brushed aside these objections. Johnson tried to reassure conservatives that the basic aim was "opportunity" not welfare, and Shriver described the programs as "a hand-up not a hand-out." To reformist liberals who had wanted a better-prepared, more measured, and therefore more enduring approach LBJ emphasized the importance of acting boldly and quickly during this brief (as he saw it) period of liberal ascendancy. Moreover, it would be wrong to assume from the haste with which the administration seized the opportunity proffered that there was no sense of an interrelationship between the various programs. Indeed there were linked assumptions here that reflected classic liberal optimism. Thus the tax cut was viewed in Keynesian terms as a measure that would extend and strengthen the emerging affluence which Johnson and his associates saw (very much in the Truman spirit) as the precondition of any successful social reform. The civil rights legislation, by removing legal and social impediments, would free blacks and other minorities to seize the opportunities offered by a rising economy, and the job-training and job-creation programs would provide all that was needed to help them make the transition to the mainstream.[30]

This seemed to many in 1964 to be a practical and politically viable vision. In retrospect it reflected the administration's rather shallow, over-optimistic understanding of the complex legacy of centuries of institutionalized racism and unaddressed poverty. There seems to have been a kind of time lag at work here. For even in the mid-1960s, David Burner has recently reminded us, "Liberals were coming to associate poverty with a social, mental, and cultural condition – with crime-ridden streets, with unemployment that saps the will of the victims, with drop-outs from school, with exclusion from the politics and economics and culture of the dominant sectors of society." By 1965, as we will see, the Johnson administration was catching up and engaging rather more fully with these deeper issues, especially in its appreciation of what Oscar Lewis had in 1961 called "the culture of poverty." But the adjustments were slow and the programs thinly funded. And, as we will see, just as the case for more vigorous action became more clearly persuasive the persisting reluctance in the higher reaches of the administration to carry out any fundamental socio-economic restructuring was strengthened by a series of unwelcome and unforeseen events at home and abroad.[31]

But for most contemporary observers these deeper problems were at first overshadowed by the pace and glamor of what seemed to many Americans to be far-reaching reforms. And in November 1964 Johnson was able to present himself credibly as not only the guardian of the Kennedy legacy, but also as the successful architect of a burgeoning new liberal reformism that rising prosperity made acceptable even where it was viewed with reserve. The Republicans, on the other hand, seemed to be going backwards, nominating for president an extreme conservative, Senator Barry Goldwater of Arizona. Goldwater's bluntly reactionary views – disapproving of social security and other well-entrenched welfare institutions as well as the new liberal programs, and apparently willing to use nuclear weapons in Southeast Asia – were out of tune with the national mood. Johnson won a landslide victory with 43.1 million votes to Goldwater's 27.2 million, and larger Democratic majorities in Congress where the party gained 37 new, mostly liberal seats in the House and one new Senate seat. The power of the conservative alliance in Congress was broken, at least for the moment, though Goldwater's capture of several southern states, together with Alabama Governor George Wallace's strong showing in the earlier primary campaigns in Wisconsin, Indiana, and Maryland, exposed widespread anger over liberal activism and revealed, we can see with hindsight, a potentially powerful base for a conservative revival.[32]

His 1964 victory is an apt moment to consider the scope and depth of Johnson's power as, having already enshrined Kennedy's main programs into law, he embarked on his own "Great Society" reforms. He now had an outstanding political mandate from the people. He had an enthusiastic, compliant liberal Congress. He could also rely, unlike Franklin Roosevelt in the 1930s, on a supportive Supreme Court that, led by Chief Justice Earl Warren, seems to have seen itself as a spearhead of liberal change. It was, throughout the 1960s, active in extending what later came to be called "the rights revolution" and in upholding many legislative reforms. It opened the way to more equitable voting rights in the landmark decision *Baker* v. *Carr* (1962) recognizing that reapportionment raised a constitutional issue. It established the one person, one vote rule the following year. leading to the redrawing of rurally favored congressional districts. It enlarged the rights of suspected criminals, loosened censorship laws, and cut back expressions of formal religion in schools – all highly controversial measures but all appealing to one liberal constituency or another.[33]

Just as important, but often neglected by historians exploring the roots of 1960s liberalism, was the flowering in the
early years of the decade of that liberal intellectual revival we
noticed getting under way in the late Eisenhower years, beginning with John Kenneth Galbraith's *The Affluent Society* in
1958. One must be careful, certainly, not to exaggerate this.
Johnson did not need a book to grasp that the moment had
arrived for fundamental civil rights legislation. And most of
the specific programs of the era can reasonably be seen as
emerging out of a long-developing political process shaped by
social change and a new moral consciousness.

Still, Kennedy–Johnson liberalism was not, like a good part
of Franklin D. Roosevelt's early New Deal, a hastily devised ad
hoc response to crisis wafting out to an uncomprehending popu-
lace. Many of its programs were, to be sure, put together quickly
and were improvisational in execution, but like many measures
in the Progressive era they tended to be the political expression
of long evolving ideas, often formulated by socially minded,
intellectual reformers and eased through by an expansive prosperity. Certain influential early 1960s' best sellers clearly had a
considerable impact. Galbraith's case for government activism,
economist Walter Heller's elaborations of the Keynesian gos-
pel, Walt Rostow's insistence in *The Stages of Economic Growth*
that any developing society could plan successfully for rapid
development – this kind of thinking was at the heart of many
policy initiatives. Paul Goodman's work emphasizing the social importance of more enlightened education for children was
very much a tract of the times, as was Jane Jacobs' 1961 book
The Death and Life of Great American Cities which emphasized the need for a sensible, human social perspective in urban
planning just as the federal government was coming forcefully
into this field. James Baldwin's passionate novel *Another Country* and his collection of essays *The Fire Next Time* illuminated
the human background to the civil rights upheavals for millions of readers. Rachel Carson's *Silent Spring* and Betty
Friedan's *The Feminine Mystique* were immensely influential
in presenting new perspectives – mobilizing support for environmental protection and women's rights, respectively.[34]

It was then with a favoring intellectual as well as a promising political context that LBJ bent his formidable energies toward a remarkable series of legislative triumphs in the 1965 congressional session. Each of the four major acts presented distinctive difficulties. Take, for example, the seemingly innocuous provision of federal aid to elementary and secondary education. Pioneered in the 1950s in response to the baby boom, it was now given a sharp, quality-oriented financial infusion, but only after a long, bitter struggle with Catholics, conservative states righters, and a variety of special interests. Johnson astutely tied it in with the general anti-poverty program, promised a high degree of local control, and found ways to allow parochial schools to share some of the benefits. The legislation was passed with a $1 billion appropriation for the first year.[35]

Medical care for the elderly had been on the agenda since Truman's bill for comprehensive national health insurance had fallen victim to the American Medical Association and other special interests. This opposition was as feisty as ever now and though LBJ pushed Medicare through (together with an aid program for the indigent called Medicaid) he had to agree not to impose any cost controls on doctors, hospitals, and insurance companies – a crippling, expensive concession as time would show. The president had an easier time with his immigration bill, pressed on him by congressional liberals intent on dismantling the "quota" system created in 1924 that restricted entry from Eastern Europe, Asia, and other unfavored areas. This act also had profound unintended consequences. Its framers had expected to attract more East European immigrants. In fact the large intakes during the next 30 years came from Latin America and Asia, ensuring that this would be a revolutionary instrument of demographic change in the ethnic make-up of the nation in the twenty-first century.[36]

The fourth eye-catching reform of this period was the Voting Rights Act which, inspired by Martin Luther King's concern over persisting denials of voting rights for blacks in the south, was in political terms a direct response to the brutality visited upon protesters in Selma, Alabama. This event early in

1965 forced the administration to recognize that outlawing segregation in the south was not enough, that some security for voting registration was necessary to achieve a full justice. Johnson again brought all his legislative skills to bear, outflanking the predictable southern filibuster and signing the bill into law on August 6. It gave the Justice Department extensive powers to intervene and itself effect, if necessary, the registration of eligible voters. Black voter registration surged, leading within a few years to a transformation in southern politics.[37]

These dramatic measures – an immense achievement despite the various expedient compromises – by no means exhaust the legislative accomplishment of the Great Society. There were, for example, a range of programs designed to regenerate the inner cities. This was fresh territory for the federal government and a new department headed by the nation's first black cabinet member, Robert Weaver, was established to lead and sustain the intervention. This dimension of Johnsonian liberalism is perhaps properly seen as part of the war on poverty. But it had aspirations that went beyond housing projects and rent subsidies for the poor to encompass large-scale inner-city job creation, urban rapid transit projects, a demonstration cities project, and a number of other general life enhancement measures. The environment was seriously addressed too, with the establishment of new national parks and, at a different but very important level, stronger codes of safety requirements in the work place. In the cultural field a National Endowments for the Arts and another for the Humanities were established. Overall, Johnson in 1965/66 presided over what William Chafe has called "the most extraordinary display of legislative action the country had ever seen." Even this was not the end. Among a number of smaller successes in the less ebullient years of his presidency, Johnson was able to push through a third Civil Rights Act in 1967 barring discrimination in housing.[38]

By 1967, however, despite these impressive legislative achievements, it was clear that the Great Society, especially that part of it concerned with social welfare, was running into deep trouble. Though still able to work the occasional legislative marvel in Congress LBJ gradually lost the mastery of his first years. Republican gains of 47 seats in the House in the 1966 elections made things much more difficult, though the swing was not unusual in such circumstances. His most serious problems can be traced to the impact of unanticipated events. One might begin here with the eruption of violence in August 1965 in the Los Angeles suburb of Watts – signifying both a new militant stage in black protest and its transmigration from the mainly rural south to the urban north – and also with LBJ's decision in early 1965 to send large contingents of combat troops to Vietnam. These were the first dramatic manifestations of two dynamic destabilizing forces – black militance leading to white alienation; and the rapidly accelerating and suddenly very costly commitment in Indochina – whose combined power would help undermine the whole liberal edifice. The Vietnam escalation, begun with enthusiastic support from most sections of American society, steadily became a profound problem. The enormous escalation to more than 500,000 troops by 1966, probably prevented a communist victory, but at a growing price in congressional and public criticism. There were more than 5,000 American deaths in 1966 with little to show for it. Draft protests grew, along with a general uneasiness and rising costs that led Johnson to scale back funding requests for Great Society programs for fear of alienating congressional support for the war.[39]

But it was probably events at home that took the most serious toll. The Watts riots upset the general public and seemed to carry the lesson that black America's problems could not, after all, be solved by legal desegregation and job training alone, even when the "empowering" aspects of community control were added. Johnson, slow to accept what he was first inclined to see as black ingratitude, sent aides to Los Angeles secretly to examine the causes of the disturbances. He was steadily forced to accept the unforeseen size and complexity of the issue, which presented itself again in the following summers with violent protests of various kinds in several northern inner-city communities. Most of the available evidence we have about white reaction to these annual urban eruptions is ambivalent. There was a chilling effect, certainly, but also, as general attention became focused on the inner cities, a new and widespread appreciation of the grievances felt by northern urban blacks. The really alienating impulse, it seems, was the concurrent prominence of a loud and, in the new television culture, highly publicized radical militance among younger blacks who, clearly not enraptured by the performance or promise of the Great Society, seemed to be abandoning the nonviolent, assimilationist approach symbolized by Martin Luther King Jr's evangelical style of leadership in favor of violence and separation.

There were several contributing streams here. In the South the Student Non-Violent Co-ordinating Committee (SNCC), in 1964 the leading element in the turbulent Mississippi voter registration drive, was by the time of the Selma demonstrations already expelling white members under the passionately exclusionist leadership of Stokely Carmichael, later the first protagonist of "Black Power." In the north and mid-west the highly disciplined Black Muslims, who had under Elijah Muhammed's leadership long proclaimed the separatist ideal, found themselves outpaced in the early 1960s by their charismatic, disaffected former member, Malcolm X, whose highly provocative anti-white rhetoric was accompanied by calls upon blacks to defend themselves as necessary with arms. Malcolm's murder by three Muslims in February 1965, moreover, reflected a growing brutality that also emerged in the California-based Black Panthers, group which, formed by Huey Newton and Bobby Seale, proclaimed Mao Tse-tung's doctrine that power grew from the barrel of a gun. They espoused a social mission in the Oakland area, but this was increasingly overshadowed by inflammatory language and violent infighting.[40]

These disturbing activities alienated many erstwhile white supporters. They also exposed the limitations of Johnson's Great Society as a medium for the peaceful assimilation of African-Americans into the mainstream. It took some time for this awareness to sink in. There was, to be sure, already a degree of visible success and black family incomes improved through the decade as 8 million Americans escaped the poverty rolls. But most of this was probably due to the general prosperity of the period. More immediately, the constant stream of new programs and wholesome laws, accompanied by much optimistic rhetoric, tended to obscure the Great Society's limitations, much as the officially stimulated good news from Vietnam hid the reality of that unstable situation.

For by 1966 the inadequacies of the programs were already becoming apparent. There were some regretful postmortems over the haste and only casual forethought with which many proposals had been pushed into law. The constant overselling of the programs as easy solutions to what were increasingly coming to be recognized as deep-rooted problems; the thin funding these programs received, inevitably confounding the exaggerated promise; and the careless administration of the funding, much of it placed in the hands of inexperienced and corruption-prone local groups whose failures gave conservatives the opportunity to claim that the wasteful liberals were simply "throwing money at problems." Perhaps the parsimonious funding was the greatest disappointment. James Patterson points out that Johnson, anxious not to confront powerful fiscal conservatives, consistently requested appropriations well below the level meaningful action seemed to require. He notes that Congress ordered only $800 million for the main "war on poverty" programs in 1964 – less than 1 per cent of the federal budget – and that when distributed among the 35 million designated poor this worked out at $200 per person per year even before administration expenses were deducted.[41]

As problems mounted there was also, as we have noted, a growing sense among more perceptive liberals that a bolder "cultural" rather than an inescapably rational approach was needed. This line of thought drew on Oscar Lewis' 1961 study of Mexican-American families, *The Children of Sanchez*, and on Harrington's characterization of a "culture of poverty" which could only be solved by some creative socio-economic restructuring that promised real advancement. In the White

House it came from Assistant Secretary of Labor Daniel Patrick Moynihan's 1965 report, *The Negro Family: The Case for National Action*, directing attention to the chronic unemployment, family breakdown, and welfare dependency of many black Americans. He traced the causation to slavery and called for national action leading from "equality of law" to "equality of condition."[42]

LBJ went a certain limited way in that direction. His decision to place some decision-making power and substantial funds in the hands of the communities receiving federal help (what the social scientists called "maximum feasible participation" by the poor) is surely to be seen as a psychologically as well as materially "empowering" action. Its widespread failure in much local waste and corruption was deeply destructive to the whole Great Society concept. Johnson also, impressed by Moynihan's report, spoke eloquently at Howard University in June 1965 of moving from equality of opportunity toward "equality as a fact," and later that year he issued an executive order requiring contractors with the federal government to take "affirmative action" in protecting individuals from discrimination. But this was mainly tokenism. It was left to the more conservative Nixon administration, strangely enough, to bring in a fuller concept of affirmative action.[43]

Johnson was well intentioned and, up to a point, willing to press on with new solutions to emerging problems. But he shrank from the full implications of the cultural thesis. He seems to have feared that corporate America, conservatives of every kind, and much of the middle class would oppose the substantial economic restructuring that alone promised full salvation for the poor. Once again James Patterson notes the significant equation: federal spending as a proportion of GNP was 18.3 percent in 1960; it was only 19.9 percent in 1970 after a decade of supposedly costly fundamental social reform. The fact is that Johnson carefully avoided extensive public works, higher taxes (until forced to a small increase by the Vietnam expenses), or any form of serious income redistribution. Instead he proclaimed large-sounding solutions like the "war on poverty" and the "revival of the inner city" in the hope that he could fund them out of economic growth alone. But growth began to slow in the late 1960s. Then the competing costs of the war began to rise rapidly. The Great Society inevitably began to founder.

It is not surprising then to find that by 1968 the "consensus" Johnson had called into being in 1964–65 was rapidly disintegrating. The high hopes had come resoundingly to earth. On the left, and among many blacks and other minorities, there was a sense of letdown. The civil rights revolution, in its legal and political dimension, was real enough and deeply appreciated. But in material terms the lack of a fuller financial commitment (especially to job creation) meant that few of its beneficiaries felt much better off. Meanwhile, the high rhetoric had bred even higher expectations and a resentful black militance. This in turn disappointed and frightened many white Americans who had been led to expect, as Shriver had promised, "the elimination of poverty in ten years" and also an easy cheap solution to racial division, surely the most complex and deep-rooted problem in American history. A growing conservatism was already apparent in the 1966 election, when the Republicans gained congressional strength, and in the rising volume of criticism now addressed to the faltering Great Society. When to this already combustible situation we add all the tensions of an increasingly unpopular and costly war abroad, we can see why the reactionary tide was beginning to run strongly by 1968.[44]

It would be premature to attempt a full judgment here on Johnson or the Great Society. LBJ had, in addition to his tangible accomplishments, created a new agenda (one centered on racial equality, minority rights, and a broader range of liberties) and a set of new institutions. Their impact and the debates they engendered would constitute much of the substance of America's future politics. It would also be ungenerous to withhold admiration for his solid achievements in civil rights, health care, the environment, and in other fields. Also his success in enlarging the scope of political possibility, in elevating the national vision, in temporarily taming if not entirely subduing many special interests, and in demonstrating the possibilities of vigorous political leadership should be noted. And if it is true that his reforms cured neither racism nor poverty (though they alleviated both) and that his programs were too quickly flung together and launched with excessively optimistic trumpeting, and then administered too cheaply and carelessly, it is also true that Johnson did more than any president before or since for African-Americans and the poor – the nation's two most vulnerable groups.[45]

We cannot, however, see this era simply in terms of its leading figures. American liberalism, destined now for a long political eclipse, is also necessarily under critical review here. Many historians have seen the Johnson era as a culmination if not as a vindication of the New Deal strong state, socio-economic reform tradition. But it steadily became clear to contemporary observers that the overoptimistic, systematizing, social engineering mentality was no match for the deep-seated problems and pathologies of America's poor. There had been too much faith in reason, in the belief that people's lives and thoughts could be decisively shaped by modest social tinkering, in the permanent validity of the new revealed wisdom of the Keynesian economy. Alonzo Hamby, noting the subsequent retreat to "a more cautious reformism" finds declining faith in the plasticity of human nature and institutions, in the classic American assumptions that people were fundamentally good and that social engineering was fundamentally beneficent. One may be tempted to think that the historical role of 1960s' liberalism was less to cure the nation's ills (though it certainly went some way in that direction) than to expose, by hesitant reformism and halfway-house measures, the deeper, hitherto largely unacknowledged problems behind the American promise.[46]

Finally, as we look beyond Lyndon Johnson and his compulsive activism to the limitations of liberal reason and virtue we might well push further back to some enduring realities about American society itself. The question then becomes, not so much why the Great Society did not more amply succeed, but rather how much real reform was ever really possible in the United States in the 1960s. Johnson's alleged "failures," seen from this perspective, may appear rather as noble cuts against the grain, not widely desired changes botched by clumsy politicians and subverted by atypical interest groups. For it is well to remind ourselves here that, by international standards America, so far as welfare reform is concerned, has been a very conservative country. Roosevelt in the 1930s was simply accomplishing a part of what Bismarck had achieved in Germany in the 1880s and Lloyd George in Britain in the early twentieth century. And even the Great Society's modest gains in welfare support were soon, as we will see, cut back sharply by President Ronald Reagan in the 1980s and then eviscerated by Bill Clinton, a Democrat, in the 1990s.

There is, however, one truly radical agency that has repeatedly shown a historical capacity to shake the traditional structures of American society profoundly and even effect some modest re-ordering of economic institutions. That agency is war. The nation's only significant though very modest redistribution of income in favor of the poorer elements in society came from Roosevelt's comparatively egalitarian tax policies during World War II.[47] Now once again, during 1965–69, war intruded sharply and affected the whole domestic scene. Its impact this time, however, was to work against rather than for poorer Americans. For the Vietnam War created a new bitter atmosphere that, together with the social turbulence stirred by Great Society programs at home, worked to bring the whole liberal ascendancy to a close.

Vietnam

One of the great ironies of the 1960s is that even as American liberalism seemed to be pressing vigorously toward a kind of long-delayed fulfillment at home, it was almost simultaneously coming to grief in the jungles and paddy-fields of Vietnam. Contemporaries found this contrast perplexing and historians too have had great difficulty explaining it. Clearly the Truman-era formula of domestic reform and robust containment abroad was undergoing a severe test here. But was it simply a matter of faulty statesmanship on the part of his successors? Or was it the consequence of profound political or cultural shortcomings in the American outlook upon an increasingly inhospitable world?[48]

Much of the problem here lies in the inordinate length of the American involvement, which ran for nearly 30 years from the Vietnamese Declaration of Independence proclaimed by the communist leader Ho Chi Minh in 1945 and self-consciously modeled on its American precedent, to the final South Vietnamese defeat in 1975. It has been hard, consequently, to see the story as a whole. It has been told, as Gary Hess aptly puts it, "more in fragments than in its entirety." Each presidential administration pressed the United States more deeply into what came to be widely seen by the 1960s as "a quagmire." Thus, as we have seen, Truman supported and heavily subsidized the French effort to restore its prewar rule. Eisenhower continued this and then, propounding a "domino" theory of successive collapses elsewhere in Southeast Asia if South Vietnam was not defended, took over and intensified the dominant anticommunist role after the French defeat and withdrawal. Kennedy increased the troop level to nearly 17,000 and sent them into battle though they were still officially only "support" units. And of course JFK promoted the coup against Diem in 1963 in the hope, soon falsified, of better local leadership.[49]

Each of these presidents has been held accountable in some degree for the eventual catastrophe. Each, to be sure, deepened the commitment and left a more difficult problem for his successor. But the chief opprobrium has been attached to Lyndon Johnson and his Kennedy-inherited advisers who, in 1965, effectively Americanized the struggle. In February he sent 3,000 Marine combat troops; in April 40,000 more troops were dispatched, and by December there were just under 200,000 American soldiers in Vietnam, a figure that would rise to more than 500,000 by 1967 with the military calling at the end of the year for an additional 200,000.[50] The dramatic escalation was carried through with public support. It did, most commentators agree, prevent an otherwise likely communist victory in 1965. But instead of the widely expected American success the intervention soon deteriorated into a long, increasingly costly, and savage war of attrition that steadily alienated many Americans. The growing sense of disillusionment was dramatically crystallized by the powerful communist Tet offensive in January 1968 – generally seen as a pivotal disillusionary moment – which obliged Johnson, and President Nixon later, to begin searching more imaginatively for an honorable extrication from a losing cause.

Why did the Johnson administration take those fateful steps in 1965? The short answer is that, as in the summer and fall of 1963, so in the winter of 1964–65, there suddenly developed in Washington a distinct sense of crisis about the situation in South Vietnam. In the Kennedy period it had been generally accepted that the communists controlled at least 60 percent of the countryside. Historian Stephen Pelz notes that by the summer of 1963 they were levying taxes in 42 of South Vietnam's 44 provinces, dramatizing the failure of the government's "strategic hamlet" program of rural defense. The impression of slippage was seen then to be compounded then by the insensitive leadership of Ngo Dinh Diem; and now, in 1965, by the chaotic rule of his military successors who seemed even less able to win the crucial battle for "hearts and minds" in the countryside.[51]

A key, often overlooked difference now was that while Kennedy believed he had in the military leadership a viable alternative to Diem waiting in the wings, Johnson, having seen seven inept military combinations come and go since Diem's demise, could have no such illusions. Who could he turn to? The political scientist historian George Kahin has suggested that the Buddhists were a usable "third force" and criticizes the United States for ignoring them. But this is probably a chimera. The Buddhists had long been hostile to the American intrusion and no one could see how their undeniable aptitude for the destruction of local political institutions could be converted into productive opposition to the Viet Cong. Johnson seems to have felt therefore that he had no local options to play now and that he would have to go ahead and take the hitherto carefully avoided decision to more fully Americanize the war.⁵²

Yet Johnson did in fact have other viable options. He had, after all, won re-election against a right-wing Republican in an unparalleled landslide only a few months before. He had, moreover, openly re-affirmed during the campaign that "Asian boys should fight Asian wars." He was therefore well protected politically if he had chosen to follow the course advocated by Senator Mike Mansfield of Montana, among other distinguished political figures, of funneling money and arms to the South Vietnamese but leaving them to do the fighting. It is also quite possible that Johnson could have covered himself politically by orchestrating an international settlement, somewhat on the Geneva 1954 line, looking to Vietnamese unity and neutralization though doubtless under North Vietnamese rule. Kennedy had considered this option and it was vigorously urged by America's European allies who, with their own abortive imperial rearguard actions still freshly in mind, were full of eloquently prophetic warnings. Certainly there was no desire to turn the South over to the communists but, if the "domino theory" was a concern would it not have been better to draw the line in Thailand, a much more reliable, culturally more homogenous ally, and use that as a base from which to harass the communists? And if troops must be sent, would it not have been wiser to send small detachments to simply secure certain strategic coastal areas in Vietnam while local troops came to grips with the communists inland?

Interestingly Johnson, though he asked his advisers for a full range of alternative possibilities, does not appear to have taken any of these options seriously. Each of them apparently seemed to him to invite congressional and media charges of weakness or appeasement. The lesson of "Munich" – the great symbol of democratic abdication in the face of totalitarian aggression – was still deeply felt. Yet in fact Johnson had already long since slipped the constitutional leads of Congress. For he had the previous summer persuaded it to give him almost unlimited power to act. This came in August 1964 after North Vietnamese gunboats apparently attacked (the nature

of the "attack" or whether it even took place remains mysterious and controversial) two American ships engaged in an
offshore intelligence-gathering operation. The resultant "Gulf
of Tonkin Resolution" authorizing the president to take all
necessary measures to "repel any armed attacks against the
forces of the United States and to prevent further aggression"
passed unanimously in the House and by 88 votes to 2 in the
Senate. This hastily devised formula (later widely seen as a
"blank check") became the constitutional basis for further
prosecution of the war. LBJ's own explanation, long afterwards, naturally emphasized the serious crisis in South Vietnam in 1964, but he usually stressed as a dominating motive a
deep solicitude for his Great Society programs. He feared that
inaction would arouse the American right-wing to attack (specifically to stop funding) his cherished domestic reforms.
McCarthyism was only a decade away and Johnson was always very sensitive to right-wing sentiment. But he had, in
effect, routed these elements in 1964 and the notion that he
intensified the war in Vietnam to save reform at home, accepted by Larry Berman and others, seems implausible.[53]

Further, the detailed exploration historians have made of
the confused if not chaotic decision-making process in 1964
suggests that, while Johnson did indeed express doubts and
fears on occasion, he made it abundantly clear to everyone
that he wanted victory. He was repeatedly insistent that he
would not be the first president to lose a war, and he constantly prodded his civilian and military advisers to promote
the war effort. Several historians of the issue have stressed
Johnson's characteristically intimidatory approach and the
effect this had of discouraging dissent, except from the institutionalized "devil's advocate," George Ball. When Vice-President Humphery, for example, noted the fresh diplomatic
possibilities opened up by the election triumph Johnson barred
him from the inner circle of Vietnam advisers for a year. As
for the vaunted policy review, Fred Greenstein and John Burke
have found that it was unsystematic and that "a great swirl of
policy recommendations and analyses simply floated past the
president."[54]

This line of thought, which seems to place most of the responsibility upon a leader who habitually masked his well-documented insecurities with a strongly machismo style, casts a rather softer light than earlier studies upon the foreign policy advisers Johnson inherited from Kennedy – the "best and the brightest" liberals so often blamed by Halberstam and others for leading the inexperienced president to disaster. Some, it turns out, had doubts and reservations, though few voiced them at the time. In any event, a hard inner core, including Rusk, McGeorge and William Bundy, McNamara, and Rostow were invariably encouraging and responded eagerly to Johnson's constant calls for support. Frederick Logevall has perceptively called this a "lethal combination" bringing together "a president lacking confidence in foreign affairs but vowing that he would not tolerate a loss in Vietnam, relying on advisers who by 1964–65 had a large personal stake in the outcome of the war."[55]

The effect was to promote that kind of strong "group-think" mentality that we have already seen at work among this generation of American leaders and which has been explained with skill and sensitivity by Richard Barnet, James Thompson, and others. It fortified itself with convictions of virtue and with deeply inspirational historical analogies such as the need to avoid another Munich and the supposedly encouraging examples of earlier successful counter-insurgencies in Malaya and the Philippines. And it led amongst this group to a solidarity that, as the situation in Vietnam deteriorated later on, developed into a siege outlook that became steadily less susceptible to second thoughts.[56]

At this point a cautionary note seems appropriate. Our discussion of the 1965 escalation, informed by hindsight, has doubtless conveyed an impression of American leaders entangled in a set of tragic dilemmas. At the time it looked very different. In fact, Johnson's escalation of the effort in Vietnam was popular, and was carried through with that pervasive sense of elan and virtuous mission that was characteristic of much American action in the early 1960s. There were very few premonitions, in public at least, of the ultimate disaster.

American self-confidence, brilliantly restored by Johnson's post-assassination leadership, was still very high in 1965, as any survey of the contemporary press and other media will amply show. The inspiring film of the first Marine detachments wading ashore purposefully at Danang, evoking memories of their World War II triumphs, reflected a general expectation of early success now that the United States was taking full charge. And at first all went well. The Viet Cong bid for power receded, the Saigon political scene briefly stabilized, and when the communists presented themselves for conventional battle in the Ia Drang Valley toward the end of the year they were defeated, though not without significant American casualties. Johnson now had some solid cause for optimism and, unworried as yet by the slowly developing student protest movement, he marked this apparent success in a speech at Johns Hopkins University in April 1966. He stressed not only his determination to prevail militarily but also the great work of physical and social engineering the United States would soon undertake to reconstruct and redeem the suffering Vietnamese.[57]

In fact, to summarize subsequent developments briefly, all this turned out to be a deceptively bright prelude to a long drawn-out disaster. After Ia Drang the communists, respectful of American firepower, avoided set-piece battles and returned to the persistent but smaller-scale guerilla warfare at which they excelled. This led the American military commander, General William Westmoreland, to persuade a reluctant Johnson to accept a war of attrition in which the enemy would be slowly but surely worn down by superior resources. Westmoreland's chosen instrument became the "search and destroy" operation, which proved increasingly costly in the communist-infested countryside. And, as Maxwell Taylor and others had predicted, the South Vietnamese military became depressingly passive as the American presence grew. By April 1966 more Americans were being killed in action than South Vietnamese troops. By this time many at home were protesting more vigorously against the war and this, together with the slow progress militarily and the lack of any encouraging

North Vietnamese response to American diplomatic overtures, led the increasingly anxious Johnson administration to mount a sustained and steadily less plausible public relations campaign picturing the war as a successful march toward inevitable victory. This house of cards collapsed dramatically in January 1968 when the communists surprised everyone with the massive Tet uprising, which saw them in action in almost every South Vietnamese city. This pivotal event, as we will shortly see, forced a fundamental change in American policy and foreshadowed the eventual communist success.[58]

Historians have inevitably found much to fault in the military, political, and social conduct of the war during this crucial middle phase. The most trenchant military critique, in its simplest form, holds that the United States could have won. It should have avoided the protracted war that played into the hands of the communists and steadily alienated public support at home. It should have gone all-out for a quick, decisive victory, mounting an invasion of the north and launching direct attacks on the Laotian and Cambodian sanctuaries. In these variants of the classic military commentary on the deficiencies of civilian leadership in war, little room is spared for a consideration of Johnson's anxieties about a wider war, with the Chinese probably coming in to protect a neighboring communist regime as they had done in Korea.

But criticism of the war effort ranges far beyond the traditional military complaints about civilian misjudgment. Much of it comes from generals, admirals, and other officers who served in Vietnam and have vivid memories of the various services' inadequacies. Several render a harsh judgment on Westmoreland. One distinguished veteran, David Hackworth, points out that his highly conventional "search and destroy" approach undermined pacification efforts and showed an "almost criminal" failure to understand guerilla warfare. A related argument, advanced by Larry Cable among others, is that only the Marines, with their long experience in Central America, understood counterinsurgency warfare. The army, he argues, insisted upon seeing North Vietnam rather than the Viet Cong guerillas, as the real enemy, and thus failed to grasp the need to secure and pacify the countryside.[59]

The most vivid illustration of the limitations of the conventional as opposed to a counterinsurgency military approach, was the increasing reliance on air power. Faith in air power was already, as it has been since World War II, the centerpiece of the American way of war. In some respects air power was effective in Vietnam. The use of helicopters was crucial to the "search and destroy" effort and probably saved many lives even as it prolonged this dubious strategy. The use of tactical air power, as in the Khe Sang campaign of 1968, clearly helped the cause. And it is often claimed that Nixon's even more extensive and intense bombing, especially in 1972, forced concessions. But most students of the "Rolling Thunder" bombing campaign against North Vietnam that began in 1965 have pointed, not only to the obvious fact that it failed to destroy the North's will to fight, but that it did little more than harass temporarily the steady infiltration of troops and supplies down the Ho Chi Minh trail on the Laotian and Cambodian borders and into South Vietnam. The much-criticized resort to defoliation of the jungle areas was, on the whole, ineffectual. What this effort did accomplish, complementing Westmoreland's socially insensitive attrition tactics on the ground, was the gradual estrangement of the remaining anticommunist elements in South Vietnam, the alienation of American allies around the world, and a growing feeling among Americans at home that the war was going badly and had lost its moral purpose.[60]

This feeling was only marginally and briefly tempered by Johnson's repeated offers of negotiations to the North Vietnamese. It is far from clear how sincere the American offers of negotiations were. In many respects they seem to have been largely a gesture to American and world opinion. Just as the politics of the war required a visible use of American technology, especially air power, to save American lives on the ground, so it required constant reaffirmations that the United States was as willing to achieve victory by diplomacy as by warfare. Beginning in 1965, therefore, and spasmodically through to 1968 when peace talks finally began, Johnson offered North

Vietnam peace talks characterized by an insistence that Hanoi withdraw the NLF guerillas and recognize the South Vietnamese government, whereupon an otherwise open-minded canvass of the issues would ensue against a background of lavish American promises of aid for reconstruction. The invariable reply from Hanoi was that the NLF was an indigenous South Vietnamese political movement and that the Saigon regime was an American-constructed sham. Its precondition was that the real intruder – the United States – should first withdraw from Vietnam and recognize the NLF as the legitimate authority. Given these stubborn bargaining postures it is hardly surprising that diplomacy was unproductive in these years.

Johnson's social policy – the loudly proclaimed effort to win "the hearts and minds" of the South Vietnamese people – was, if judged by results, another failure. It was a central feature of the "nation-building" side of the American effort and one that, it was hoped, would compensate for the socio-economic chaos in the cities. It involved spasmodic attempts to reassure the typical Vietnamese peasant by moving him and his family into fortified "strategic hamlets" where they would supposedly be safe from the ubiquitous communist intimidation. But these and other similar programs, which tore the reluctant villager from his fields and ancestral treasures, only aggravated the situation. True, communist coercion at the village level was often brutal, but the insurgents had been entrenching themselves in the rural infrastructure since the early 1950s. They were well organized and had a demonstrable hold on the loyalty if not always the affections of many of the most energetic village elements. The American effort, only fitfully supported by the Saigon military, relying excessively on often abstract counterinsurgency models and techniques accompanied by exhortatory leaflets and radio propaganda that was frequently culturally insensitive, and persistently undermined by Westmoreland's "search and destroy" intrusions, was demonstrably insufficient to win the crucial struggle in the Vietnamese countryside.[61]

Finally, and probably decisively so far as the failure of the American commitment is concerned, Johnson and his associates mismanaged the politics of the war. From the start his public statements were excessively optimistic, emphasizing the superior character, resources, and will power of the United States. He pursued, almost to the end of his tenure, a "guns and butter" political strategy that stressed the nation's ability to maintain its prosperity, carry through his expensive program of reforms, and wage war in Indochina, all without undue sacrifice. Only in late 1967 did he call for modest tax increases as war and domestic program costs shot up and inflation began to grow rapidly. Larry Berman, one of several critical scholars, faults Johnson for obscuring the implications of his policies by not calling for a national commitment.[62]

Having chosen to disturb the American people as little as possible Johnson found himself having to respond to rising criticism in 1966–67 with much resented and unprofitable attempts to control the growing media criticism with exaggerated false statistics of enemy losses and increasingly implausible rosy predictions of imminent success that events steadily belied. New phrases entered the public discourse: "body count," "light at the end of the tunnel," and, most famously, a "credibility gap" that developed as increasingly depressing news reports from American journalists in Vietnam, complemented by a growing protest movement led by draft-age students in the nation's large universities, fed a widening public skepticism. The impact of television was remarkable. At first it served the administration well, showing the Marines going ashore confidently at Danang in 1965 and dramatizing the early successes that followed. But over time, as the war deteriorated into costly search and destroy missions, as casualty lists grew, and an increasingly critical Saigon-based press corps began to expose the fragile and morally unappealing political realities of the South Vietnamese context, television became a serious problem. It tended to demythologize the war, revealing its ugliness and brutality far more immediately than government press releases or newspaper stories. It also tended to encourage, despite strenuous network efforts to avoid an anti-administration bias, the growth of dissent at home. From "teach-ins" to massive protest demonstrations the anti-war movement grew increasingly strong in this supportive media context.[63]

All these difficulties suddenly began to appear in stark relief with the climactic Tet offensive in January 1968. The communists launched an impressive, highly co-ordinated military campaign in virtually every urban part of the country at the beginning of January 1968. The military uprising was eventually repelled with severe communist losses. But Hanoi won the political battle. The communists showed that, far from defeated, they were much stronger than the American people had been led to believe. It is widely agreed that the Tet offensive broke the American will to win in Vietnam. Johnson rejected the military call for reinforcements, announced his intention not to run for re-election in 1968, stopped the bombing, and by the end of the year had engaged the North Vietnamese in talks looking toward peace rather than victory.[64]

Truly, as a lonely President Kennedy remarked after the Bay of Pigs fiasco, victory has a thousand fathers but defeat is an orphan. But there are commentators who look upon the embattled Johnson with sympathy. The journalist Leslie Gelb, for example, argues that the 1965 escalation was a sophisticated and valid strategy that looked not to victory but to a "designed stalemate" that failed only because public support collapsed after Tet. Guenter Lewy, Norman Podhoretz, and others stress the morality of the American quest for a free, noncommunist Vietnam. And R. B. Smith, in a multi-volume study of the international aspects of the war, emphasizes the Soviet and Chinese challenge in the region and argues that the real purpose of the American intervention was to buy time for the establishment of democracy – an objective achieved, at least partially, in neighboring Indonesia, Thailand, and elsewhere.[65]

Many of the critics have focused on shortcomings in decision making, faulting Eisenhower for not accepting the international compromise at Geneva in 1954, Kennedy for promoting the disastrous coup against Diem in 1963, Johnson for his ill-considered escalation in 1965. We can clearly see that American over-confidence, represented in 1966 by Senator Fulbright, Chairman of the Senate's Foreign Relations Committee as "the arrogance of power," was well entrenched, along with a range of misleading lessons from a very different past, in the early outlook of Johnson and his elite advisers. We recognize a characteristically American but perhaps inappropriate faith in arms technology and social engineering at work throughout the long crisis, and we can see the force of Frances Fitzgerald's demonstration of an unbridgeable cultural gulf between modern rational America and traditional, reverential Vietnam.[66]

The fact is, of course, that all these factors are relevant, even if their precise weight in the overall equation must inevitably be controversial. But they all relate, in one way or another, to the issue of American power. And here diplomatic historians have advanced a range of causes. The orthodox liberal explanation is that Vietnam was a blunder. John Lewis Gaddis calls it "the single greatest error the United States made in fighting the Cold War." It was, on this reading, an aberration involving a badly miscalculated exaggeration by successive leaders of the geopolitical significance of Vietnam. One balanced, influential thesis, advanced by George Herring, suggests that "Vietnam made clear the inherent unworkability of a policy of global containment" and dramatized the limits of American power. But Herring rejects the "aberration" thesis. In this he reflects a significant school of thought that developed out of the Vietnam experience itself. This came from scholars like Walter LaFeber, Lloyd Gardner, and Gabriel Kolko who, taking their cue from William Appleman Williams' 1959 book *The Tragedy of American Diplomacy*, looked back during the accelerating disaster in Indochina to the whole course of American diplomacy since World War II or beyond. They saw Vietnam not as an aberration but as a logical culmination of well-entrenched national tendencies. It was not the well-intentioned response of free men to totalitarian aggression but rather an expression of the hegemonic impulse governing a deeply capitalist society's relentless search for control as it sought foreign markets, access to raw materials, and opportunities for investment.[67]

The emergence and steady refinement of this revisionist interpretation was not simply an intellectual event. It was an active agent in dissolving the broad consensus in American foreign policy that had, arguably, carried the nation far too complacently into the Vietnamese imbroglio, and it also signified the arrival of a sharp new general critique of American political culture. For it represented one dimension (the accompanying critique of domestic liberalism was another) of that larger disillusionment with conventional and accepted views in American life that was so characteristic of the late 1960s. A primary effect was to bridge the gap between foreign policy and internal politics. For like McCarthyism the Vietnam War brought the external and domestic arenas into a passionate, direct, mutually interacting relationship. The outcome was profound in each case. For just as McCarthyism, in effect, set back the power of right-wing conservatism in American politics for nearly 30 years, so Vietnam appears, in retrospect, to have been a fundamental blow to American liberalism.

Radicals and 1968

It may seem to many readers, schooled to think of the 1960s largely in terms of turbulent change, that this is rather late in our discussion to be addressing the subject of radicalism. The rationale is that, at least for the historian attempting a short, politically oriented general synthesis, radicalism becomes a central preoccupation only when conventional authority begins to break down. And while we have already taken note of the youth rebellion of the 1950s and early 1960s, and the spasmodic civil rights eruptions from 1963 on, it was not really until the second part of the decade, when the classic liberal formula of diplomatic containment and domestic reform, inaugurated by Truman, began to falter, that political radicalism became a primary concern in American life, and only in 1968 that it seemed, briefly, to challenge the power structure itself.

What about cultural radicalism? That is a very different

story. The historian Arthur Marwick has recently argued in a densely packed book of just under a thousand pages that there was a cultural "revolution" in this period. He begins by describing what he considers some of the striking features of the 1950s. These include, inter alia, rigid social hierarchy, subordination of women to men and children to parents, repressed outlooks on sex, institutionalized racism, respect for the flag, government, and law, formal language and etiquette, melodic popular music, bland culture, and so on. The 1960s in Marwick's formulation exhibits itself rather more flamboyantly. Here we find black civil rights, youth culture, high ideals and loud protest, popular music from Afro-American origins, oriental mysticism, vast changes in sexual and personal behavior, openness to drugs, audacity in books and the media, optimism, and belief in a better world. One could go on. It is not difficult to see whose side Marwick is on. His encyclopedic discussion, which also usefully stresses the world-girdling scope of the new culture, is mirrored in the work of more issue-focused historians. Among the most recent are Maurice Isserman and Michael Kazin who, while mainly concerned with socio-political themes, insist upon the lasting significance of the sea-change in consciousness, the new toleration of divergent lifestyles, and the new humanism that emerged from what Allen Matusow has memorably if exaggeratedly called "the unraveling of America."[68]

The most visible roots of this cultural radicalism lie in the basic statistics of the postwar baby boom. In 1960 there were 24 million Americans in the 15–24 age bracket; by 1970 the number was 35 million, a rise of nearly 50 percent.[69] An unprecedentedly high proportion found themselves in the rapidly enlarging college–university system. And they came, for the most part, with vivid memories of the generational solidarity and self-conscious antimaterialism fostered by the youth culture of the 1950s and the idealism of the early 1960s. They had their own essentially nonpolitical heroes: the radical poets and the Beats; the rock musicians; and surly but compelling anti-establishment Hollywood figures like Marlon Brando and James Dean. And at an even deeper instinctual level this already pulsating demographic cohort was grappling restlessly with the dionysian temptations presented by the birth control pill and newly accessible drugs.

This is fascinating but frustratingly elusive cultural material. One is always necessarily conscious in modern American history of public feeling, even if one cannot easily define it. But for the most part the cultural flux seems to lie safely beneath the level of significant events and formal convention – a congenial subject for life-style columnists and quiet academic analysis, but often consigned by historians to the role of social embroidery. Much depends on the temper of the times. Thus we found Dwight MacDonald and other social critics in the comparatively serene 1950s sorting out various cultural expressions into hierarchies and categories. We see little of that detachment in the mid- to late 1960s. By then the "culture" seemed to many observers to have broken through the conventional crust, affecting all kinds of behavior and finally reaching into the political arena in an unprecedentedly direct way.

Few historians have been fully successful in integrating culture, society, and politics in their accounts of the 1960s. This reflects both the difficulty of the task and the confusion of the period. The result, from a historiographical viewpoint, is that each field has attracted its own often very astute specialists. Thus we read Greil Marcus to learn about the rock scene; Pauline Kael to understand films; and James Twitchell to come to grips with aggression in popular culture. These writers are, on the whole, admirably unpretentious, as the title of Marcus' most recent book, *The Dustbin of History*, eloquently suggests. But they make little effort to connect with what we might call mainstream scholarship.[70] Nor, on the other hand, do conventional historians show much interest in the cultural primordium. As a consequence the relationships between politics and culture – except for the occasional academic social science study, which tends to be normative rather than historically focused – are often left in a kind of hazy, intellectual limbo. We still lack a fully persuasive synthesis of all the politico-cultural impulses at work in the late 1960s.

But one pertinent question seems reasonably accessible. Why and how did demographically and culturally driven radicalism find its way into the political process? A conventional short answer is that John F. Kennedy's example and rhetoric (themselves "radical" in their self-conscious break with Eisenhower-era traditionalism) inspired a widespread idealism in the youthful, impressionable stratum that first made its voice heard in the 1950s. And that this in turn became attached to, and in various ways transformed by, the subsequent dramas of civil rights agitation and the Vietnam escalation. As both these problems became more profoundly unsettling, partly due to the errors of overconfident liberal politicians, youthful idealism in many cases, even as it was concurrently caught up in the seductive culture of social innovation, turned sharply to political involvement, passionate protest, and a general taste for the notion of rebellion against the establishment.

But this hardly does justice to the complexity of the process. It is helpful first to realize that there was some significant self-mobilization of American youth before civil rights and Vietnam became effective rallying points. Consider, for instance, the appearance in the early 1960s of three small but highly significant institutions representing three very different ideological tendencies. One was the Student Non-Violent Coordinating Committee (SNCC) which was established in 1960 by black college students with a commitment not just to civil rights but to independence from Martin Luther King's broader, more formalized, more traditionally church and teacher-based organization. Another, started in June 1960, was the Students for a Democratic Society (SDS) – the important "New Left" group that would also go on to a prominent role in the decade's agitational politics. The third, founded in 1962, was Young Americans for Freedom, a conservative group that received even less initial attention but actually attracted about the same-sized membership as SDS and became more prominent in 1968 and thereafter. Its activities, long neglected by commentators on the 1960s, are now coming into sharper focus as historians search for the roots of Reagan era conservatism.[71] The story of 1960s' conservatism is at once fascinating and multi-faceted, a subject for further discussion later. But after the Goldwater debacle in 1964 it was eclipsed by the mid-decade liberal surge and its confused aftermath.

The left, on the other hand, has from the start been subjected to searching scrutiny. We have already encountered the SNCC briefly in its central organizational role in the Mississippi Freedom Summer of 1964 and in the Selma registration crisis of 1965. But black student activism is generally held to have begun with the February 1960 "sit-ins" at segregated lunch counters in Greensboro, North Carolina. The tactic spread across the south and about 70,000 blacks participated with varying success in 1960/61. The SNCC came out of that campaign, and several of its members participated in the 1961 "freedom rides." It was a prime mover in many southern protest campaigns in those years. It forged links with white student activists in the Mississippi voter drives of 1963–64. For a brief moment, black and white students worked together in what historian Edward Bacciocco has called "the maximum community organizing effort of the New Left." But the unity was short-lived. By 1965 the young student leaders in SNCC had become disenchanted with their would-be supporters. They resented the fact that King and the older figures in the movement monopolized the decision making and received most of the credit for the great public confrontations while leaving the grass-roots preparations and the often violent aftermath to them. More deeply they thought King's whole Gandhian, non-violent, redemptive approach was too temporizing and unproductive. They also came to resent what some of them regarded as the patronizing participation of well-meaning, white students who similarly tended to assume leadership roles in situations calling, psychologically and in practical terms, for black direction. By this time they had also learned that Attorney-General Robert F. Kennedy's promises of federal protection in the Deep South, if they would focus on voter registration rather than protest, were hollow. Many also took the Democratic Party's compromise decision in 1964, allowing only minimal token representation for the mostly black Mississippi Democratic Freedom Party, as a betrayal by the administration that had gathered plaudits for pushing through a Civil Rights Act banning segregation but was not protecting crucial voting rights either by law or in practice. They therefore took on a new radical leadership under Stokely Carmichael and expelled their remaining white members.[72]

These attitudes go far to explain the tension between the SNCC and King's Southern Christian Leadership Council at Selma in early 1965 and also the electrifying proclamation of "Black Power" by Carmichael in a Mississippi appearance the following year. By this time the radical impulse had emerged violently in the Watts riots and in the sudden appearance in California of the new Black Panther Party, which openly proclaimed a revolutionary and separatist mission very much in the spirit of Malcolm X, whose assassination by similarly exclusionist Black Muslims in 1964 had left a charismatic martyr. Meanwhile, the frightening inner-city summer riots continued. At Watts in 1965 the death toll had been 34. In 1966 riots in Cleveland, Dayton, Milwaukee, and San Francisco left 400 injured and seven dead; a year later violence escalated again with 25 fatalities in Newark and 43 in Detroit.[73]

These years also saw a rising tide of disaffection among young whites, driven mainly by resistance to the escalating war in Vietnam. Here, as we have seen, the contributing impulses were more variegated than those prompting the more highly politicized, more purposeful black student radicals. Steadily adhering to a more or less common sensibility and life-style that was eventually given the description "counterculture" by Charles Reich in his 1968 book *The Greening of America*, many young white, middle-class students had by 1967 also acquired a distinctive political persona.

This collective outlook is usually dated from the SDS 1962 meeting in Michigan that produced *The Port Huron Statement* – a strongly reformist manifesto written mainly by the young activist Tom Hayden. It contained a long litany of perceived imperfections in the contemporary, allegedly materialistic, Cold War-oriented American way of life. It called for higher ideals, a more humane economic system, and "participatory democracy." An eloquent statement, written very much in the critical New Left spirit of C. Wright Mills, it served thereafter as a primary reference point for student radicals of many types. In many ways a generationally oriented echo of Kennedy's rhetoric, it led easily to various kinds of specific and general support for the civil rights movement and later to the indictment of American foreign policy.[74]

The university campus became the principal arena of protest and confrontation. The great set-piece general demonstrations in Washington and elsewhere, and most memorably in Chicago in 1968, had a thousand rehearsals in noisy protest meetings within the comparative safety of an academic environment with often supportive professors and easily intimidated administrators. But not always. Indeed, the famous Free Speech movement at the University of California's Berkeley campus, in 1964, widely agreed to have inaugurated the student protest phenomenon, was characterized by police intervention and violent scenes later repeated at the University of Wisconsin, Columbia University, and elsewhere. By the late 1960s the violent campus disruption was as regular an annual visitation as the ghetto riot. It is not too much to say that the university soon became to the 1960s what the corporation had been to the 1950s – the central shaping institution of the decade. In the new television-fixated culture of permanent expectancy it provided a dramatic spectacle, a tense generational clash, and yet at the same time a conveniently confined forcing ground for debate and confrontation. And just as the social critics had focused on the corporation and the business executive in the 1950s as guides to contemporary meaning and future trends in American life, so many academics and journalists – led by sociologists like Kenneth Keniston and Seymour Martin Lipset – set out to understand and explain the young student radical in terms of his nurturing opinion-shaping institution.[75]

There was in the early 1960s a good deal of white involvement in the civil rights movement in the south. Many of the traditional organizations, especially the venerable NAACP (National Association for Advancement of Colored People) had been bi-racially led and King had always cultivated and welcomed white liberal supporters. White students had participated in specific campaigns such as the "Freedom Rides." In 1963 students from Yale and Stanford Universities had helped with the election "rehearsals" carried out in Mississippi and many more had joined the great vote mobilization campaign there the following year when the murder of two white and one black rights workers had dramatized the problem for a national audience. But this effort tailed off when the SNCC elected to pursue an all-black strategy and the main focus of the struggle moved to the urban north. Nevertheless a vast groundswell of sympathy and support for the civil rights cause progressively widened to embrace Hispanics, native Americans, and poor people generally.

From 1965 onwards, however, the dynamic mobilizing cause for white students was the Vietnam War. Sentiment moved in close relation to the deterioration of American military prospects. In 1965, with an American death toll of 1,400 there was widespread support for the enterprise tempered only by occasional mild protests and "teach-ins." But in 1966 the number of American dead exceeded 5,000, rising to 9,000 in 1967. By this time the rapidly rising number of draft calls on American youth, and the expansion of the full troop level in Vietnam to more than 525,000, had helped produce a growing volume of student protest. In October 1967 a nationwide "Stop the Draft Week" brought a rash of tumultuous demonstrations at Berkeley, Wisconsin, and other major campuses and a dramatic, culminating "March on the Pentagon," where police battled protesters, many of whom burnt their draft cards.[76] As Terry Anderson and other historians have shown, these developments, together with the accumulating opposition of Senate Foreign Relations Chairman William J. Fulbright and other influential congressional figures, church leaders, press columnists, and many more in what was rapidly becoming a broad-based movement, greatly disturbed President Johnson and the military leaders. The official response was a barrage of optimistic reports and uplifting scenarios designed to reassure and rally an increasingly divided and confused public opinion.⁷⁷

The first overt sign of fundamental change came on March 12, 1968 with the New Hampshire Democratic primary. The anti-war candidate, Senator Eugene McCarthy of Minnesota, won an astonishing 40 percent of the vote, a humiliation for Johnson who eked out a narrow win. This led Robert Kennedy, now a senator from New York, to declare his candidacy. Johnson, dismayed by the collapse of support, discouraged also by the advice he received from most of a panel of past and present high officials (the so-called "Wise Men") not to send more troops to Vietnam, announced to the nation on March 31 that he would devote all his remaining time to settling the war and would not run for re-election. A turbulent race quickly got under way for the Democratic nomination.

During the campaign, on April 4, Martin Luther King Jr. was assassinated in Memphis where he was supporting a strike by sanitation workers. This set off violent riots in more than 100 cities, leaving a casualty toll of 3,000 hurt and 46 dead, nearly all of them black. Once again Americans were forced to accept the loss of a seemingly indispensable leader, as King was buried amidst emotional scenes in Atlanta. Then in June, on the evening of his victory in the California primary, Robert Kennedy was gunned down by a deranged Jordanian. His death, another moment of depressed national mourning, left Vice-President Hubert Humphrey, the favorite of the party regulars, well placed to win the Democratic nomination at the Chicago convention in late August.⁷⁸

This event was the setting for some of the most memorable scenes of this dramatic year. More than 10,000 anti-war activists – students, liberals, and radicals of various kinds – showed up in Chicago to protest. Horrified viewers were treated to scenes which suggested that the nation's politics was spinning out of control. While Humphrey cruised to victory in the convention hall, which was itself convulsed with spasmodic fighting as delegates clashed over support for Johnson's Vietnam policy, Mayor Richard Daley's police, inflamed by various rumors (that pot-crazed subversives planned to poison the water supply, that Humphrey delegates were to

be kidnapped, etc.) reacted to harmless but taunting provoca-
tion in the streets outside with unjustified violence. On successive nights they clubbed and beat up demonstrators and
innocent bystanders alike. It was all captured on nationwide
television, deeply upsetting mainstream Americans and giving
the impression that the Democratic Party was coming apart.
As the civil rights activist, Allard Lowenstein, put it on the
night of the worst scenes, "This convention elected Richard
Nixon President of the United States tonight."[79]

Meanwhile the Republicans were resting complacently after a tranquil convention in Miami that nominated Nixon following spirited but finally ineffectual challenges from Governor
Nelson Rockefeller of New York on the left and Governor
Ronald Reagan of California on the right. The Republicans
seemed set to make a remarkable recovery from the 1964
Goldwater debacle, basing their case on Nixon's vague promises to restore "law and order," opposition to "wasteful spending" on programs that were failing, and a promise to bring
"peace with honor" in Vietnam.[80]

This strategy nearly failed, for at least three reasons. The
first is that Governor George Wallace of Alabama, running
again on a program of unabashed commitment to victory in
Vietnam and opposition to civil rights (especially school integration and fair housing laws) drew millions of votes from
disaffected southern and border state Democrats who would
almost certainly have voted for Nixon. The second is that
Nixon squandered a large lead in the post-convention polls
and waged a lackluster campaign, notably refusing to elaborate upon his plans to end the war satisfactorily. And the third
is that Humphrey, always a feisty and well-liked liberal campaigner, fought back well, stitching up various traditional
Democratic constituencies, gaining support from labor, and
almost catching Nixon at the end. The Republicans finished
with a thin margin of a half million votes.[81]

In retrospect it seems that the strain of the 1968 political
process, memorable for its assassinations and raw violence,
overmastered the moral resources of the various principal parties. It has been suggested in recent years, by historian Robert

Dallek and others, that Humphrey was denied victory by Nixon's deceit in privately assuring President Thieu of South Vietnam that he would receive full support from a Nixon administration, thus sabotaging Johnson's last-minute effort to make a peace agreement with the communists at the ongoing Paris discussions. It has also been alleged that Johnson secretly worked for a Nixon victory, believing that his vice-president would tarnish the Johnsonian legacy by settling too easily with Hanoi. And Seymour Hersh, an unsympathetic biographer of Nixon's principal future colleague, has charged that the political academic Henry Kissinger played a shadowy opportunistic role, using private knowledge gained as a trusted Democratic insider to send secret word to Nixon about Johnson's last-minute peace efforts, valuable intelligence which inspired the Republican's deal-killing assurances to Saigon of unqualified future support.[82]

There have been many attempts to explain this crucial Republican victory in deeper terms, especially as it turned out to be the beginning of a new conservative swing in American politics that, with brief interruptions, has continued to the present day. A significant contemporary interpretation was Kevin Phillips' *The Emerging Republican Majority*. Written essentially as a campaign guide for Nixon, in whose campaign Phillips served as a strategist, it argued that the balance of power in American elections was now in the south and west – the sunbelt states – rather than in the traditionally decisive north-east and mid-west. Phillips cited sunbelt population increases that far outpaced those in the east and stressed that the Johnsonian reforms had alienated both the South and millions of working class whites elsewhere. He pointed out too the still growing affluence of the Catholic and broader ethnic groups traditionally beholden to the Democrats but now increasingly attracted by more conservative impulses. Another crucial factor, now much more pervasive and central to political campaigning than ever before, was the role of television. Joe McGinniss' study of Nixon's success with this medium, *The Selling of the President* together with Phillips' anatomy of the new battleground, registers significant changes from the more variegated political landscape mapped out by Theodore White a decade earlier.[83]

Much of this was plausible at the time and has since become a part of the conventional wisdom. But the Republicans in 1968 had to ask themselves whether their victory meant a general repudiation of liberal reformism. Ostensibly it may have seemed so. In the four years since Johnson's great political landslide certain basic liberal assumptions had clearly been undermined. The basic equation that saw economic growth encouraging a progressive reform agenda and leading to a harmoniously united society no longer seemed, to many Americans, a universally viable proposition. By 1968 economic growth was faltering as inflation rose; the reform programs were languishing, either for lack of funds or because they had been too carelessly conceived; and the "consensus" society proclaimed by Johnson was now bitterly divided along political, ideological, and generational lines. And the apparent failure of the complementary liberal design abroad – successful resistance to communism, "nation-building," the strengthening of international peace – only aggravated the growing malaise that lay behind the Republican resurgence.

But it was not altogether clear that liberalism – though evidently in eclipse – was finished. The 1968 election brought more conservatives to the House of Representatives but actually added to the liberal ranks in the Senate. Democrats remained in control of Congress. Many liberals clung to the belief that Robert Kennedy, had he survived, would have gone on to win the nomination and the presidency – perhaps a last Kennedy myth to close a decade that began with "Camelot," but a durable one as Ronald Steel's recent *In Love with Night: The American Romance with Robert Kennedy* suggests. Steel's analysis debunks the notion that Kennedy could have brought the blacks and other outside groups he had been cultivating together with the rightward-drifting white working class. Still, there were other reassuring thoughts. In many ways Humphrey's last-minute recovery was the surprise of the campaign and offered hope for the future. And while Nixon found the Johnson administration an easy target he was careful to make only generalized and subtle attacks on the Great Society, clearly uncertain where public sentiment really stood. As we will see the new president's ambivalence over the Johnson reforms, and his own leaning toward a degree of social change, would prolong the question about liberalism's place in American life well into the 1970s.[84]

The election was undeniably a judgment upon the Democrats. It is doubtful whether it should be seen as a verdict upon "the 1960s" in the broader sense. For that complex, richly generative phase in post-1945 American history arguably projected well into the next decade. The wild ride of 1968 allowed neither a searching inquest nor a sober review. The war still raged. The Great Society was still working itself out. Public life seemed ever more intense; the counter-culture daily noisier and more insistent. The great era of liberal hegemony seemed to be receding. But a full conservative triumph was by no means assured. It would fall now to the enigmatic Richard Nixon to try and fashion, from a fragmenting polity, a new Republican coalition and a fresh sense of direction.

5

America at Bay: The Enigmatic 1970s

Nixon and America

It was widely anticipated that the absorbing issue of the post-1968 years, in domestic politics at least, would be a confrontation between Richard Nixon and American liberalism. The new president had long been the object of a liberal hostility that began as a response to his office seeking in California, which seemed largely founded on the ruthless exploitation of his various opponents' alleged softness toward communism, and was consolidated with his leading role in pressing the 1948 charges against Alger Hiss. He had himself been savaged for decades by liberal cartoonists, led by the *Washington Post*'s durable Herblock, and by columnists like Murray Kempton, who once remarked condescendingly that Nixon was "the President of every place in this country which does not have a bookstore." There is no reason to doubt historian Samuel Walker's conclusion that his 1968 election "sent a shiver through the civil rights and anti-war movements."[1]

But in January 1969 this liberal critique was temporarily muted. There was talk of "a new Nixon" – less aggressive, more mature, broader in outlook. Joe McGinniss' 1969 book *The Selling of the President*, an analysis of Republican campaign manipulation through television imagery, expressed a continuing liberal suspicion after the election. But it was soon overshadowed by Garry Wills' brilliant 1970 biography *Nixon Agonistes*, which broke down the theatrical image of Nixon and gave him a resonant "place" by depicting his southern California small-town early life as a paradigmatic American experience. It portrayed a "rootlessness" that fostered an intense ambition for success and led to "the crisis of the self-made man." According to Wills this crisis was founded in a marketplace conception of liberalism. Thus Nixon himself could now be seen as a "liberal" – a characterization many later historians would go on to accept as this protean American philosophy took on new forms after 1968.[2]

Part of the difficulty in coming to grips with Nixon's place in American history has to do with his elusive personality. His formal outward appearance was a Main Street white shirt, a dark suit, an American flag ostentatiously in the lapel. All this masked a bundle of complexes, insecurities, and resentments that was far too much for the early practitioners of psycho-history, a subdiscipline that flashed briefly across the historiographical scene in the 1970s. Even his close associates felt defeated by the inner man. Bob Haldeman, his long-time political confidant, called him "very complex." Henry Kissinger recalled his "complex psychological make-up." The historian Stephen Ambrose, after a three-volume biography, still found him "a most complex man."[3]

An antidote to this confusion comes from the traditional approach of historian Herbert Parmet. The real significance of Richard Nixon, he argues, lies not in his personality but in the leadership he provided, in both foreign and domestic policies, "for a wide variety of second- and third-generation ethnic groups and older line Republican stalwarts in protecting their interests from the excesses and abuses of welfare state liberalism." The significant clues are to be found, accordingly, in the context and the record.[4] But here too there is a good deal of ambiguity. No one expected Nixon to behave like a Great Society liberal. Some degree of reactionary politics was universally expected. The very conservative John Roy Price triumphantly proclaimed "The New Deal is dead." Patrick Buchanan, a Nixon speechwriter, talked of "a counter-revolution." And when the president tried to consolidate his election success among white southerners with equivocal approaches to civil rights and provocatively conservative nominations to the Supreme Court, he was widely stamped as a right-wing reactionary by liberal columnists. There was indeed a cold-eyed review of the Great Society's approximately 400 programs. A few were scrapped. Others found their appropriations cut. And when the Democratic Congress allocated funds for favored agencies the president responded in a few notorious cases by impounding the funds until forced by the Supreme Court to release them. An anguished Lyndon Johnson told a biographer in 1971, "It's a terrible thing for me to sit by and watch someone else starve my Great Society to death."[5]

Nevertheless, when we look beyond these more or less predictable actions to Nixon's social policies a rather different picture emerges. Observers noted, for example, early signs of moderation. The tone of his inaugural speech was not unduly partisan and many were moved by Nixon's evocation of his boyhood yearnings for a fuller life and reassured by his vision of a unified society serving "black and white together." His cabinet, seemingly intended to avoid both hard-right Goldwaterites and sophisticated eastern progressives of the Rockefeller type, was made up mostly of rather gray but apparently moderate and managerially oriented personalities. His appointment of two Harvard professors – Henry Kissinger as National Security Adviser and Daniel Patrick Moynihan as a domestic adviser – struck an unexpectedly creative note. Many were impressed both by Nixon's early intimations of a desire for settlement in Vietnam and by his apparent receptivity to Moynihan's suggestion that he model himself upon the nineteenth-century British Prime Minister Benjamin Disraeli - famed as a conservative who finessed the liberals by attracting the lower classes with a "one nation" vision of unity, patriotism, and social harmony.

Soon there were more substantive signs of the Disraeli spirit. Nixon embraced Moynihan's Family Assistance Program (FAP), which was intended to replace the Johnson-era AFDC program of various services with a guaranteed annual income of $1,600 (together with food stamps) for all poor families. This failed in Congress, basically because liberals thought it offered too little and conservatives considered it too much. Once he saw this Nixon's own enthusiasm flagged. Ostensibly a barebones solution to poverty it has been praised by some social analysts as, in principle at least, a sophisticated fair alternative both to the heterogeneous system that it was designed to replace and to the administrative nightmare that came afterwards and helped make welfare the subject of acrimonious debate for three more decades.

Most dramatically, working with Labor Secretary George Schultz, Nixon approved the so-called "Philadelphia Program," which evolved into a powerful affirmative action policy. This required construction firms with federal contracts to hire more black apprentices. It became the pace-setter for regulations imposing "goals and timetables" for hiring minorities and women upon all corporations doing business with the federal government, rules eventually affecting over a third of the work force. Local governments, universities, and unions also found themselves increasingly obliged to set quotas. All this reflects a high degree of continuity between the late 1960s and the early 1970s – another caution against rigid periodization.[6]

Nixon's primary gesture to Republican orthodoxy, reflecting old concerns about the drift of power to Washington, was revenue sharing. He persuaded Congress to pass legislation leading to the transfer of block grants of about $16 billion for the states and localities between 1973 and 1975. Otherwise there was a good deal more liberally oriented activity in Nixon's first term. The Democratic-led Congress generated most of it. But in general Nixon cooperated, sometimes enthusiastically, sometimes with a show of reluctance. Thus in 1970, after opposing it initially, he signed a five-year extension of the important Voting Rights Act. He approved a large appropriation for medical education and the "war on cancer." He signed a bill establishing the landmark Occupational Safety and Health Administration (OSHA). And, in the reformist spirit of the FAP, he took the initiative in calling for a national health insurance plan providing universal coverage. He worked with Democratic leaders to enlarge Social Security payments, indexed them to inflation, and created a supplemental program for the indigent and disabled. He federalized and enlarged the food stamp program. In this, and in his support for higher student loans, he showed, as Carl Lieberman has pointed out, a certain "redistributive" instinct. And, again colluding with the Democrats, he allowed spending limits on social programs to rise far above 1960s' levels. During his administration means-tested federal spending per person rose by 50 percent, much of the increase going to female single parents.[7]

Hardly the actions of a conservative reactionary. Historian Joan Hoff concludes in a recent study that Nixon exceeded the accomplishments of the New Deal and the Great Society in several spheres including civil rights, social welfare spending, economic restructuring, revenue sharing, government reorganization, and funds for culture. This rehabilitative note appeared even more recently in a feature essay by Michael Barone in *U.S. News and World Report* emphasizing both Nixon's achievement in curbing the turmoil of 1968 and "the variety and scope of his legacy," which the author found to have been constructive. Even Arthur M. Schlesinger Jr. has conceded that while Nixon was "not a man of profound convictions," but rather one who "rolled with the punches and went along with a reform-minded Congress" his domestic record had been "underrated."[8]

A growing awareness of all this has led to some interesting attempts to pin Nixon down ideologically. Recent historians, with the intervening and markedly more anti-liberal Reagan era freshly in mind, tend to avoid conservative characterizations. Many, like Hoff and Barone, see him as some kind of liberal. Herbert Parmet has drawn attention to his "practical liberalism." James Patterson describes him as "easily the most liberal Republican American President, excepting Theodore Roosevelt, in the 20th century." He has frequently been called "a centrist" or "a moderate" and has been linked with the emerging "neoconservatives," a group of mostly chastened "Vital Center" liberals who, in commentator Kevin Phillips' words, wanted "to preserve the intellectual and institutional structure liberalism built," but found the new Great Society approach too wasteful, incoherent, and anti-meritocratic. Alonzo Hamby similarly views him as a "neoconservative" president.[9]

But, as so often with Nixon, this kind of ideological definition, especially the effort to present him as a liberal, seems incomplete without a crucial psychological gloss. It is true that, deeply resentful from various slights at the hands of the wealthy elite, he showed a spasmodic, probably sincere reformist impulse. The key points, though, seem to be that he was an ambitious loner, an unsentimental political realist, and, unlike Taft and the Republican Old Guard, a post-World War II man who understood the indispensable role of the state in harnessing and shaping American power for world leadership, and who therefore recognized the inevitability in the United States of that late-blooming governmental interventionism associated with Franklin Roosevelt and the New Deal. In short, he was a modern man, thoroughly at home with the reality of a large federal establishment even as he labored to curb its excesses under the liberal Democrats and to reduce its vast range of activities to his own personal control.

The image of Nixon as a progressive reformer, therefore, is only partly convincing. It is important to remember that he was always preoccupied with foreign policy (Haldeman later recalled that in the early years Vietnam "overshadowed everything") and he tended to lose interest in the complexities of domestic issues.[10] Close examination, furthermore, often reveals a self-serving political calculation behind the ostensibly progressive performance. His affirmative action initiatives, for example, may well have been inspired by a determination to punish labor for its opposition to one of his Supreme Court nominations. And his lavish spending on Social Security and student loans in the run-up to 1972, were clearly aimed a capturing the two fastest-growing segments of American society – the elderly and the young voters – whose numbers were now swelled by a constitutional amendment lowering the voting age to 18.

This leads us to what is, perhaps, the crucial point. Nixon's reform impulse, however strong or feeble, was fundamentally incompatible with, and demonstrably subordinated to, his governing political concern. This was, quite simply, to ensure his re-election by consolidating and strengthening the tenuous combination (hardly a "coalition" as yet) that had brought him to power in 1968. Here the "southern strategy" was a central concern. Nixon had done well with disaffected white southerners on the earlier occasion but could not take them for granted. The overtly segregationist George Wallace had captured the Deep South and had also shown the ability to appeal to a blue-collar constituency in the north. He was expected to run again in 1972. On the other hand, as Schlesinger has remarked, "the liberal tide was still running strong." Nixon had won election with only 43 percent of the popular vote. The administration therefore felt obliged to play both sides of the street. Thus, while quietly helping in various ways to ease the progress of school desegregation and allowing progressive officials in the Health, Education and Welfare and Housing and Urban Development departments to press modest reform agendas, he both sanctioned Attorney General John Mitchell's covert encouragement of segregationist elements by deferring the cut-off of federal funding where progress was slow, and consistently deprecated the busing of students as a remedy.[11]

The principal focus of the southern strategy was the Supreme Court. By 1969 the forceful approach of the Warren Court on civil rights was at last bringing results in the form of more unified schools and significantly higher mixed student enrolments. Against this current Nixon now played to his expectant southern audience by nominating Clement Haynsworth, a South Carolina federal judge with respectable professional qualifications. But congressional liberals, citing Haynsworth's demonstrable earlier antipathy to civil rights and unions, rejected him. The president then nominated G. Harrold Carswell, a Florida judge with a segregationist past and unimpressive legal credentials who suffered the same fate. Nixon had to be content with a Minnesota moderate, Harry Blackmun. But with Warren retiring in 1969, to be replaced by another supposedly conservative Minnesotan, Warren Burger, and with two other retirements, he was finally able to give the Court a more conservative cast. By 1974 we find the Burger Court allowing local districts more flexibility in their desegregation plans and chipping away at the 1960s' decisions favoring the rights of those suspected of crimes. Yet this supposedly conservative court exhibited a very typical 1970s' ambivalence in stigmatizing the death penalty (as it was then imposed) as "cruel and unusual punishment" in 1972 and then going on the following year to deliver the famous *Roe* v. *Wade* decision approving women's right to abortion.[12]

The "southern strategy" was only one wing of Nixon's political plan. The other was, as in 1968, an appeal to ethnic and other voters in the north and west involving the exploitation of the perceived excesses of war protesters and the counter-culture. Growing doubts over Nixon's promise to end the Vietnam War led to massive protests in November 1969, and the American invasion of Cambodia the following spring led to an epidemic of campus eruptions and six student deaths at the hands of the National Guard. But significantly, polls showed that most people blamed "student radicals" for the disturbances, and a mob of construction workers sharpened the point by attacking and bloodying peaceful anti-war demonstrators in New York. The counter-culture – a potent political conceptualization through the 1970s – developed in ever more striking, new ways during the early years of the decade. We should perhaps think of it as an umbrella term covering a vast variety of new kinds of unconventional, sometimes radical, social behavior. It had by now shed most of its institutional political character. The SDS broke up in 1969 with extreme factions like the Weathermen playing the wreckers' role. Cultural radicalism, however, flourished. The great August 1969 gathering at Woodstock, New York saw about half a million young people celebrating with rock music, drugs, and some public love-making. Iconic figures like the singers Janis Joplin, Jimi Hendrix, and the Rolling Stones ostentatiously defied social convention. Sexual experimentalists, gay activists, pro-abortion advocates, and a vast range of food faddists, environmental crusaders, sectarian, and communal organizers of various kinds agitated an already frazzled society. Many middle-class Americans increasingly felt themselves caught between the provocative excesses of the rebellious young and the fevered jeremiads of the rising cultural conservatives. Institutions were questioned, family authority was challenged, formalities were cast impatiently aside. Old pillars of public decency, literary censorship for instance, broke down as the champions of permissiveness advanced behind the banner of a judicially liberalized First Amendment. And in public and private speech, as well as in the public media, traditional euphemisms gave way before a swelling volume of scatological and verbal abuse.

In the 1970 mid-term elections, therefore, Nixon exploited the anti-war protests and counter-cultural excesses against the ostensibly complaisant Democratic liberals, appealing to southern whites and northern ethnic voters with invocations of "patriotism" and attacks on "violence, lawlessness, and permissiveness." The results gave Nixon little cause for satisfaction. The Democrats increased their House majority. The Republicans gained two Senate seats but fell far short of a majority. More alarmingly, the House Democrats received a markedly higher vote count than they had in 1968, and also gained 11 governships while losing only two. In the process, moreover, Nixon seemed to have alienated many liberal-to-moderate voters by his sharp-edged campaigning. A leading Democratic presidential prospect, Senator Edmund Muskie of Maine, gained attention by delivering a well-received "Lincolnesque" rebuke to the president. A *Time* columnist called Nixon's efforts "an appeal to narrowness and selfishness" and "a disgrace to the presidency," a judgment echoed by historian Alonzo Hamby who writes that Nixon "somehow had failed to learn that Presidents were not supposed to resemble alley fighters."[13]

The 1970 election deserves more attention from historians, particularly those eager to close the gap between political and socio-cultural history. It was, arguably, the first modern national election driven almost entirely by divisive cultural dynamics. All American politics is, of course, permeated by cultural and emotional factors: race, social philosophies, national pride, prejudice, and so on. But since 1933, in domestic politics at least, socio-economic and class issues had normally been paramount and constituted the principal rallying points. Now we see an aggressive politics of cultural division and, correspondingly, a much-diminished emphasis on the common values that had been stressed even in the heat of conventional political struggle. It may be tempting to ascribe this to a new viciousness in politics. But at a deeper level it was the product of logical calculation. For the class–economic issue invariably favored the more mass-oriented Democrats. In 1970, if the Republicans were to consolidate their new opportunity and create an effective coalition they could not hope at this stage of the conservative revival to win by ostentatiously favoring the affluent, as Ronald Reagan would do to advantage in 1980 when the need to create wealth was more widely accepted. At this earlier stage, with New Deal liberalism still apparently powerful, a cultural strategy was clearly the safer course. In pressing it aggressively Nixon inaugurated a new phase in national politics that saw both parties stressing resonant cultural themes, the Democrats emphasizing expanded rights, the Republicans calling for a return to basic values.

All this would become clearer in the longer term. More immediately an economic downturn following the 1970 election seemed to herald a return to traditional bread and butter politics. Since 1967 the combination of Great Society and Vietnam War spending, without significant tax increases, had set off a dangerous wage–price spiral whose effects were only partly tempered by slowing general growth. The consumer price index rose about 11 percent between 1968–70. Even more alarmingly, in an apparent confutation of the Keynesian scenario, unemployment rose along with inflation from 3.6 percent to nearly 5 percent overall. Nixon responded boldly. In August 1971 he issued an executive order imposing a 90-day freeze on wages and prices. Even more shockingly, in an effort to aid American exporters and free the United States from restrictive international obligations, he twice devalued the dollar, effectively removing the United States from its Bretton Woods role as, in effect, the guardian and guarantor of the postwar monetary system.[14]

These were dramatic and far-reaching initiatives with significant domestic and international repercussions. More to the point, so far as Nixon was concerned, they temporarily arrested the growth of inflation and restored some jobs. But, determined to avoid an election year recession, he suddenly lifted the controls as the primary season approached. At the same time his complaisant Federal Reserve Board chairman, Arthur Burns, began to increase the money supply. The economy boomed through 1972, reviving the inflationary trend but encouraging in the short term the more upbeat outlook Nixon needed for the campaign.

His re-election was widely seen as problematic well into 1972. Nixon therefore raised a vast sum of campaign finance from large corporations and radicalized his immediate entourage by demanding a very aggressive approach that led eventually, probably without the president's direct knowledge, to the June 1972 burglary of the Democratic National Chairman's office at the Watergate complex in Washington D.C. He also demonstrated impressive political skill in overcoming a number of problems. Confronted with a faltering economy he had professed allegiance both to Keynes and Republican orthodoxy while in fact master-minding the most direct, socialistic intervention of the postwar era, only to emerge with a sharp investment and consumption recovery just before election day. His stage-setting in foreign policy was also skilful, as we will shortly see. Facing the reality that he had not fulfilled his promise to end the Vietnam war, he astutely managed to subordinate it in many minds to the popular and glamorous statesmanship of a thaw in the over-arching Cold War that was dramatized by his visits to both Beijing and Moscow early in the election year. Meanwhile, he played the domestic political game with professional shrewdness. While proclaiming loyalty at least to the principle of progressive reform, he again decided to rely on the provocative excesses of racial, counter-cultural, and left-wing political publicists to consolidate his new conservatively oriented "silent majority" coalition, shoring it up with closely focused new spending for the elderly and education.

Democrats and liberals approached the election in an optimistic spirit. They had long seen the 1968 reverse as an aberration, a view at least partially vindicated by the 1970 results. They had seen American opinion turn against the war and most of them were now on the right side of that issue. They had a number of potentially attractive candidates, the continuing Kennedy legacy (only partially dimmed by Senator Edward Kennedy's conduct in the 1969 Chappaquidick accident involving the drowning death of his companion), and they had high hopes that young voters, their ranks now swelled by the lowering of the voting age to 18, would turn their way. They were demonstrably superior grass-roots campaigners. Black leaders, women's rights activists, and minority conscious voters would doubtless perform effectively, labor was still at least nominally loyal, though more subdued than usual, and Catholics were expected to return to the fold. The emergence of new moderate southern governors like Jimmy Carter of Georgia and Reubin Askew of Florida kindled expectations of a recovery in that crucial region. There was even, at a more rarified level, a revival of liberal philosophy, increasingly defined in terms of an ongoing "rights revolution" and finding impressive expression in John Rawls' 1971 *A Theory of Justice*, perhaps the most authoritative intellectual exploration of liberalism since World War II. Ominously though, there was little of that practical reformism and sense of unfinished business that, in the prescriptions of progressives like John Kenneth Galbraith and Michael Harrington, had produced the promising liberal intellectual renaissance in the late Eisenhower era. In 1970, for instance, change-minded readers could choose between Charles Reich's rather precious *The Greening of America* and Philip Slater's gloomy *The Pursuit of Loneliness: American Culture at the Breaking Point*. There was little in the way of practical analysis to stimulate the reform impulse.[15]

As the campaign developed it became clear that the Republicans had made the right choices. Nixon, whose whole career had been driven by a keen sense of resentment, must have been surprised to find that fate had at last dealt him an unbeatable hand. He was fortunate in that George Wallace was shot in Maryland on May 15 by a deranged young man, Arthur Bremer, and had to withdraw. Then the Democrats, rejecting the advice of two perceptive commentators, Richard Scammon and Ben Wattenberg, to focus on restoring the old New Deal coalition, chose as their candidate one of the architects of the new, radical party rules that gave activist minorities (blacks, women reformers, gays etc.) a potentially decisive prominence. The very liberal George McGovern, a genuine war hero, was in some respects one of the most attractive candidates of the postwar era. But he owed his nomination largely to an unruly coalition of noisily provocative minority leaders and anti-war activists who, by insisting on their command of the podium, delayed his convention acceptance speech, which finally floated out uselessly to millions of sleeping Americans in the early hours of the morning. McGovern's initial choice as running mate, Senator Thomas Eagleton of Missouri, was forced to withdraw after revelations that he had received shock treatment in the past for depression. The nominee's passion for civil rights upset the white south. And his primary anti-war focus, compressed into the cry "Come Home, America" alienated many old Democrats including Lyndon Johnson, organized labor, and many Catholic and ethnic Americans. In the end Nixon won a landslide victory, receiving 60.7 percent of the total vote and carrying every state except Massachusetts and the District of Columbia. A distraught McGovern was widely reported to be contemplating emigration to Britain.[16]

Yet this was not a decisive Republican triumph. The Democrats retained Congress, losing only 12 seats in the House and actually gaining a seat in the Senate. Thus the conservative reaction to Johnsonian liberalism was still somewhat halting and tentative, arguably the product of events rather than a sea change in American politics. Republican euphoria was further tempered by Nixon's emphasis upon his own rather than the party's significance during the campaign, and his call immediately after it for the resignation of his Cabinet officers, a chilling denouement he later tried to justify as part of a plan for more effective government organization. But the tightly self-controlled president had neither the taste, nor as it turned out the time, for much celebration. He was almost immediately overtaken by two profound developments. One was the rapid decline of the American economy as the election-focused boom evaporated and inflation soared again. The other was the fast-growing press eruption over the 1972 Watergate burglary. Nixon and the media steadily became locked in an all-consuming confrontation that allowed the crucial economic problem to slip out of effective control.

This was deeply unfortunate. 1973 was arguably a pivotal year for the economy, marking both the end of the post-1945 boom and the onset, as Nixon's stoked-up election year prosperity quickly petered out, of inflation (the rate doubled in 1973), declining productivity, and growing unemployment. A major catalyst here was the Arab oil producers' embargo after that year's Middle East war, followed by dramatically higher prices that presented the United States, which with 6 percent of the world's population was now consuming about 33 percent of its oil, with a serious crisis. At the same time a world-wide grain shortage developed. Nixon, distracted and increasingly preoccupied with his own political survival, offered no solution. Neither the controls of 1971 nor the stimuli of 1972 seemed appropriate in the new situation. Many economists were also baffled as it became clear that contrary to postwar experience both inflation and unemployment could operate concurrently.

No one seems to have foreseen in 1972 that the Watergate burglary of the Democratic Party chairman's office that May would turn into a unique constitutional crisis. Though the burglars were indicted in September, and links were established with the president's re-election campaign, the trials were postponed until after the election. McGovern tried but failed to make it a prominent issue. The media showed little interest. All this changed in January 1973 when Judge John Sirica threatened the convicted burglars with long sentences. This led one of them to implicate members of the campaign committee. From there the path led into the administration, setting off several ill-fated attempts at self-preservation. Leading the stampede was John Dean, Nixon's own White House counsel, who, fearing the president was setting him up to take full responsibility, came before a grand jury and claimed that the latter had orchestrated the post-burglary cover-up. The result was a series of forced resignations (eventually including Haldeman and Erlichman) and intense preparations for televised summer hearings before a Senate investigating committee chaired by Senator Sam Ervin of North Carolina.

It was never established, and it seems unlikely, that Nixon directly authorized or even knew of the projected break-in in advance. But it appeared increasingly probable, from the Senate's committee hearings and relentless press investigations, notably by the *Washington Post*, that Nixon had become aware of it within hours and had thereafter master-minded a cover-up that involved lying and illegal attempts to use the CIA to frustrate further inquiries. A crucial development here was the unexpected appearance of tapes made by Nixon in the Oval Office. He released a selection, which contained a suspicious 18-and-a-half minute gap at a crucial point. He withheld the rest on ground of "executive privilege" but was ultimately forced by the Supreme Court, in a July 24, 1974 decision, to release them. They demonstrated his deep intensive involvement in the post-burglary machinations. Worse, they exposed both the president's vulgar and profane language, which affronted a vast number of Americans, and his unmistakable preoccupation with his own self-preservation.[17]

Meanwhile, there had been other damaging revelations. On October 10, 1973, Vice President Agnew had resigned in disgrace, having secured immunity after conceding that he had continued to receive illegal kickbacks in Washington for favors given while he had been Governor of Maryland. Nixon, with congressional approval, replaced him with the Republican House leader, Gerald R. Ford of Michigan. It then transpired that the president's lawyer had improperly back-dated papers allowing him to claim a hefty tax deduction for his vice-presidential papers – leading Nixon to proclaim publicly "I am not a crook." It was also shown that he had paid no income tax in some years of his presidential term. The excesses of his money-shaking re-election campaign were now publicly documented. There were damaging disclosures of sums of public money paid to beautify Nixon's Florida and California properties, and even worse, of his harassment of political "enemies" through illegal use of the Internal Revenue Service.[18]

It is hardly to be wondered at, then, that on July 30 the House Judiciary Committee voted, with many Republicans joining a unanimous Democratic majority, to impeach the president for obstruction of justice pertaining to the Watergate investigation, for constitutional violation in the use of wiretaps and federal agencies, and for resisting congressional subpoenas. Republican leaders quickly urged Nixon to resign, which he did on August 8, 1974. Much of the immediate press and public reaction was upbeat, even euphoric in some quarters. While worldly European savants claimed to be baffled by this exhibition of moralistic puritanism, Chief Justice Burger doubtless spoke for many if not most Americans in claiming that the nation's constitutional system had been vindicated, a judgment *Time* echoed in hailing an "extraordinary triumph of the American system." There is surely much to be said for this view. The crimes and misdemeanors – 14 top officials were imprisoned or fined – were clear enough. There was a general feeling that justice had been done, reflecting, many thought, the maturity of a mass electorate that had re-elected Nixon by a landslide majority less than two years before and now saw his departure without rancorous divisions.[19]

There is little historiographical controversy about Watergate. Some sympathetic writers have amplified Nixon's own resentful declarations that in his use of wiretaps and electronic surveillance he was only doing what most presidents since FDR had done. A few old associates like Elliott Richardson, and biographers like Stephen Ambrose, have expressed regret that he was prevented from carrying out a desirable governmental re-organization and other reforms. But it is generally accepted that Nixon brought his tragedy upon himself and that he was forced out by properly observed legal and constitutional processes. The principal dynamic in the whole affair was the steadily growing public conviction that he had in several ways violated the shared values that most Americans believe to be indispensable to the functioning of modern democracy. Here the epitaph pronounced by liberal historian Arthur Schlesinger Jr., "In a democracy policy can succeed only if it is based upon consent," can be seen as an echo of the very conservative *Chicago Tribune*'s editorial comment on May 9, 1974 after perusing Nixon's released tapes. "The ultimate arbiter in this matter must be the public, and the public reaction today is clearly one of revulsion."[20]

Watergate did, of course, have a long ripple effect. It distracted attention from growing economic problems. It is sometimes claimed to have been fatal to the cause of détente because the Soviets saw Richard Nixon as the indispensable partner. Historian James Patterson, on the other hand, sees little enduring impact and believes détente was in any event "oversold" by Nixon to help his re-election in 1972. The affair clearly did have a profound effect on national politics. It greatly diminished the presidency. From our long perspective we can also see that it operated as a great distortion, creating as journalist Thomas Edsall and others have shown, a political situation that was uncoupled from general trends that were pushing America in a more conservative direction.[21]

All this will become clearer when we examine the perhaps inevitably turbulent years between Watergate and the full conservative triumph of 1980. Meanwhile, for a fuller understanding of the Nixon era we must briefly retrace our steps and examine the great foreign policy issues of the early 1970s, particularly the painful extrication from Vietnam and then the appearance of détente, the first real change in the great Cold War confrontation.

From Vietnam to Détente

Richard Nixon's primary interests were always in foreign policy. As he put it, "I've always thought this country could run itself, without a president. All you need is a competent Cabinet to run the country at home." In his purposeful post-Watergate campaign for rehabilitation he rarely featured his arguably progressive domestic accomplishments, and showed little interest in academic attempts to brand him a liberal. The stress was always on diplomacy: the opening to China, détente with the Soviets and the arms control agreements. His reputation was only partially restored. Many commentators were dismissive. Henry Kissinger took much of the credit with his better-written and more widely read (at least among intellectuals) memoirs.[22]

The Nixon–Kissinger relationship is fascinating. The impact upon academic commentators of Nixon's post-Watergate eclipse can be seen in political scientist John Stoessinger's 1981 references to "secretary Kissinger's détente policy" and "Henry Kissinger's triangular policy". This may be a misleading emphasis. In fact, Nixon was the prime mover, Kissinger the instrument and facilitator. It was Nixon who, in a 1968 *Foreign Affairs* article, first hinted at the later approach to Beijing. And on the campaign trail that year he talked freely, according to Garry Wills, of a post-Johnson period in which "a man who knows the world will be able to forge a whole new set of alliances, with America taking the lead in solving the big problems." George Herring has succinctly captured the essence of their relationship as one based on "mutual dependence" with "Kissinger viewing Nixon as a means to prominence and power, Nixon relying on Kissinger to shape and implement his broad designs."[23]

One thing Nixon and Kissinger had in common was an intuitive sense of power – where it lay, how to gain and use it, above all how to deny it to others. Both acquired early on a keen sense of life's hard side – Nixon through his bleak early experiences in California and his disappointments as a young lawyer; Kissinger from boyhood memories of anti-semitism in Germany. Each found later developments, a harsh political arena for Nixon, a distant but anguished view of the Holocaust for Kissinger, strengthening an essentially Darwinian outlook.

It is hardly surprising then that they were determined from the outset to try and concentrate power in their own hands. The historical trend encouraged this. FDR had effectively created the primacy of the presidency within the constitutional trinity and also showed the way to the next centralizing step: securing presidential authority over the executive bureaucracy. Truman consolidated the trend by setting up the National Security Council and the Council of Economic Advisers; Kennedy and Johnson created ad hoc groups of advisers outside formal bureaucratic lines. Nixon and Kissinger took the process even further by systematically neutralizing and outflanking other foreign policy elements in the administration such as the State Department, the arms control advisers, the CIA, and the economic departments. Working through a number of key committees, which Kissinger staffed and chaired, they gathered power ever more tightly in their own hands. Their passion for total control fostered a paranoiac spirit and led to wire-tapping and other excesses which, with the creation of the White House "plumbers' group of Watergate fame, led finally to disaster.

Vietnam was Nixon's principal and most urgent problem. There was a brief "honeymoon" period: a temporary lull in the fighting, the fitful continuation of the Paris peace talks, and an encouraging feeling that Thieu's Saigon government was becoming a little stronger. Nixon began in quasi-conciliatory fashion, sending word to Hanoi through French intermediaries of his desire for peace and proposing the mutual withdrawal of American and North Vietnamese forces. There was widespread gratification following his announcement in June that 25,000 American troops were being withdrawn, and his declaration of a "Nixon Doctrine' limiting American post-Vietnam military involvement in Asia to air and sea forces.

But hopes soon faded. Ho Chi Minh, as before, would

settle only on the basis of an immediate unconditional withdrawal by the United States and the deposition of the Thieu
government. The effect of this intransigence was to incline
Nixon to tougher measures. As early as July he laid plans envisioning "savage, punishing blows" by American bombers
upon North Vietnam's cities and ports, and apparently even
contemplated a possible nuclear attack. An ultimatum was
sent to Hanoi. But the communists again stood firm, forcing
Nixon, like Johnson earlier, to chose between escalation and
retreat. The president, listening to his anxious advisers, reluctantly backed down.[24] He was now ensnared in what we might
call "the Johnsonian trap." The unyielding North Vietnamese
would settle only for absolute victory and were apparently
susceptible only to force not persuasion. But any show of force
by the United States was judged likely to arouse intense anti-
war protest at home and inspire suspicions that Nixon, far
from wanting to end the war, was going for victory much as
Johnson was generally believed to have done. In fact Nixon
recognized, unlike his predecessor before 1968, that he did
not have the necessary public support to persist indefinitely.
His policy, therefore, designed essentially to end the American involvement with some show of success (if possible the
preservation of a non-communist South Vietnam), seems to
have developed along four main lines. First, to defuse domestic opposition, he steadily reduced American troop numbers
from 550,000 when he took office to fewer than 50,000 by
election day 1972. Second, he lavished aid and intensified training upon the fragile ally in Saigon in a compensatory policy of
"Vietnamization." Third, he tried to force the Hanoi regime
to the desired settlement, or at least buy time for Vietnamization to work by intensifying the military pressure through
heavier bombing and bold, spasmodic ground operations. And
fourth, in a slower developing stratagem that became more
important as the others seemed unproductive, he tried to undermine support for Hanoi in the Soviet Union and later China,
both thought now to be interested in better relations with the
United States.

   In some respects this was a rational, sophisticated scenario.

It was confounded by the tenacity of the North Vietnamese, the political limitations upon the use of American power and, fatally, the chronic inability of the South Vietnamese, even with vast American aid, to take up the slack as the United States forces withdrew. Time was on Hanoi's side. In the spring of 1970, therefore, a frustrated Nixon gave rein to his penchant for dramatic action. He sent troops into eastern Cambodia (which the United States had been secretly bombing since 1969) to clear out the communist border sanctuaries and operational "nerve center."

The ensuing Cambodian tragedy has inspired some of the most acrimonious historiography of the war. It was not, as Herring correctly points out, entirely due to American actions. The North Vietnamese had, after all, been using the Cambodian border areas with South Vietnam as sanctuaries for years. Some were only 60 miles from Saigon itself. Earlier bombing had been ineffectual. However, in March 1970 a coup in Phnom Penh, the Cambodian capital, had ousted the ruler, Prince Sihanouk, who had hitherto tried with some success to protect his state by a show of neutrality, and brought a pro-American, right-wing group to power. American complicity was widely suspected but never proved. Nevertheless, the event undoubtedly helped inspire Nixon's decision to send troops in. The operation was only partially successful and the forces were soon withdrawn. The unfortunate and unforeseen result was to push the North Vietnamese units deeper into the country where they linked up effectively with the now-burgeoning local Khmer Rouge communists and eventually helped them win power in 1975. This led to a communist reign of terror and upwards of two million Cambodian deaths over the next few years. A bitter intellectual clash followed in 1979 when the British author, William Shawcross, in his book *Sideshow: Kissinger, Nixon and the Destruction of Cambodia*, blamed the Nixon administration for the whole disaster even as Kissinger's best-selling *White House Years* was presenting a justification based on the need to strengthen the threatened Saigon government. What is clear is that no one in the administration anticipated or was concerned with the possible implications of this operation for the fragile Cambodian state and population.[25]

One immediate result of the Cambodian venture was, as Nixon had expected, the eruption of the anti-war movement. Campus disturbances proliferated and at Kent State University and Jackson State College National Guardsmen and police shot and killed a total of six students and injured several others. These dramatic events affected the 1970 election as we have seen. The inconclusive results there, and the rapidly growing disillusionment with the war – with 71 percent of a respected national poll feeling by summer 1971 that the American military intervention had been a mistake – obliged the administration to revitalize the diplomatic search for peace. In May 1971, therefore, after the humiliating rout of two South Vietnamese divisions that had been sent into Laos as a test of Vietnamization, Kissinger secretly presented an amended plan to the North Vietnamese in Paris abandoning the mutual withdrawal concept. The United States would withdraw within seven months, the North Vietnamese would return American prisoners of war and simply agree not to move beyond their existing positions in the south.[26]

This concession of their right to retain their southern enclaves, though not yet made public, was a political triumph for Hanoi. Typically, they were unappeased, demanding in addition the ouster of the Thieu regime pending a final settlement. The United States was now fast running out of options. Vietnamization, despite enormous American material aid, seemed ever less likely to compensate for Nixon's accelerating troop withdrawals. Other initiatives like the Phoenix program, a CIA-led effort to purge the rural communities of communist sympathizers, normally by education but probably with a considerable degree of coercion, were only partly successful. Enormous American spending had by 1971 gravely distorted the local economy and brought rampant inflation and endemic social breakdown. Meanwhile, events like the infamous 1968 My Lai massacre of Vietnamese civilians by American troops, the subject of a sensational court-martial in 1971, symbolized the growing distance between teacher and student.

The denouement came, not coincidentally, in the 1972 American presidential year. Nixon needed to show results. Two developments now worked in favor of a settlement. The first was Kissinger's dramatic high-level diplomacy culminating in presidential visits to China in February and the Soviet Union in May. These events seemed to many to transcend the crisis in Southeast Asia and clearly warned the Hanoi regime that it risked isolation. The second was a sudden demonstration of military gridlock that appears to have sobered both sides. In March, the North Vietnamese, aware that American ground combat strength was now fewer than 10,000, had launched a massive invasion of the south with 120,000 troops reinforced by Soviet tanks. Initially they routed the South Vietnamese forces in several engagements, but were checked when Nixon ordered a new round of intensified bombing.

These violent but finally inconclusive military exchanges, together with the great power summitry, had a galvanizing effect on the diplomatic side of the war. Thereafter, historian George Herring believes, each side "found compelling reasons to attempt to break the military deadlock by diplomacy." Nixon was understandably nervous about his as yet unfulfilled 1968 promise to the American people to end the war, and Hanoi, pressed to settle by China and the Soviets both of whom were now eager to please the Nixon administration, grievously hurt also by the long war and contemplating the likelihood of Nixon's re-election, was at last ready to deal. By October, Kissinger and his North Vietnamese counterpart in Paris, Le Duc Tho, had worked out a basis for settlement. Following the cease-fire the United States would withdraw its troops within 60 days. The North Vietnamese would remain in existing positions in the south but would not seek to enlarge them, and they would return American prisoners of war. A tripartite commission, including nationalists, communists, and "neutralists" would organize and supervise elections in South Vietnam.[27]

But now Nixon, scenting easy victory at the polls as the McGovern-led Democrats vigorously self-destructed, felt stronger. He therefore supported President Thieu, who characterized Kissinger's Paris deal as a betrayal and refused to accept either the legitimized presence of North Vietnamese troops in the south or any form of Viet Cong representation. A disappointed Kissinger was therefore sent back to Paris. Now it was the communists' turn to feel cheated and by mid-December the whole settlement had broken down. Nixon, triumphantly re-elected, decided to force the issue. He launched the most punishing raids of the whole war on the Hanoi area, including its port of Haiphong where there was Soviet shipping, gambling that the Chinese and Soviets would protest but not intervene. The attacks indeed provoked harsh criticism at home and around the world. But when he indicated that he would desist if the communists resumed the talks, the North Vietnamese, perhaps impressed by the president's re-election and self-styled "mad dog" resolution, returned to the table. In January 1973 a compromise embodying most of the original December terms was signed. Thieu, softened if not reassured by Nixon's large military shipments over the past year and expansive promises of future aid, and perhaps by the president's written undertaking to "respond with full force" if the North Vietnamese violated the treaty and moved out of their agreed enclaves, sobered also no doubt by Nixon's warnings that he would settle without him if necessary, finally acceded.

Was this, as Nixon and Kissinger claimed, "peace with honor?' George Herring is doubtful. He points out that the basic issue – the future of South Vietnam – was left unresolved. Kissinger's 1999 book, however, revives the claim that the settlement was a success and that, but for the refusal of the Democratic-controlled Congress to continue aiding the South between 1973 and 1975 and then to respond vigorously in 1975 when the North clearly violated the treaty and commenced their final, victorious drive south, the United States could have preserved a free South Vietnam. Similarly, though more cautiously, Elliot Richardson, Nixon's one-time Attorney General, has suggested that had Nixon remained in power, "It's arguable, I think, that North Vietnam might not have dared to breach the treaty reached in 1972–1973."[28]

Few scholars seem to agree. To the extent that the argument depends on Vietnamization historian Jeffrey Clark concludes that no one believed ARVN (the South Vietnamese army) could withstand an assault from the North on its own. So far as American public opinion and the Congress are concerned, Arnold Isaac writes that in the final stages of the 1972 negotiations Nixon and Kissinger treated their South Vietnamese allies with "contemptuous disregard" and their North Vietnamese enemies with "bad faith and brutality." He concludes that, "in doing so, they had almost certainly magnified the enormous difficulties of enforcing the peace they had finally succeeded in negotiating." Similarly, political scientist Gareth Porter characterizes Nixon's final air assault on Hanoi as "the most important defeat suffered by the United States in the whole war because by arousing great public opposition and provoking Congress to cut off further funds for Saigon, it made any American re-intervention very unlikely."[29]

This seems to touch the heart of the matter, for it was widely appreciated in 1973 that Nixon's "return" pledges were conditional on a public and congressional support that was simply not there. Historians have, in general, also been critical of Nixon's four-year conduct of the war. Stephen Ambrose, in many ways a sympathetic biographer, has said that, "he mishandled the retreat." He should have followed Eisenhower's Korea model and liquidated the wasting commitment in 1969. Ambrose believes Nixon could have had the same terms then that he accepted in 1973. This seems doubtful in view of Hanoi's granitic intransigence. Even William Shawcross now concedes that in his criticisms of Nixon and Kissinger he gave too little attention to communist obduracy and cynicism.

But few historians today would disagree with Herring's bleak balance sheet on the Nixon phase of the war. A further 20,553 Americans died for a full wartime total of over 58,000. The South Vietnamese lost about 107,504 more battlefield dead, while the combined communist casualties were probably well over half a million. Beyond that there were millions of civilian dead in Indochina, a devastated economy throughout the region, a ruined environment in many areas, and a disoriented, often homeless population. The long-term consequences for the United States were less drastic in human terms but still profound. In time they could be seen as an epidemic inflation, a deep political polarization unparalleled since the Civil War, a people disenchanted with international engagement, and a tarnished image in much of the world. And in geopolitical terms the war distorted the central strategy of containment, shifting attention from the European center to the Southeast Asian periphery, draining energy and resources.[30]

Much of this was, of course, still hidden or unknown as Nixon began his second term. The prevailing emotion at the beginning of 1973 was one of relief that the business was finally finished. There was also a widespread desire to avoid undue recriminations, helped along by the new positive feeling engendered by the president's dramatic successes during 1972 with the two main communist powers. This did indeed seem to be ushering in what Nixon liked to call "an era of peace," characterized by negotiation rather than confrontation. In the event détente was short-lived – flaring brightly at first, deteriorating slowly, and finally ending acrimoniously. But in 1972–73 it inspired considerable optimism, suggesting to many a path to stable, evolutionary international conditions. It is still the object of some interesting historical questioning. What were the origins of détente? How well or badly was it managed? Why, in the end, did it fail?

We might first ask, however, why détente did not appear earlier. We have already taken notice of three moments which historians have marked as carrying the potential of a thaw. The first came with the death of Stalin in 1953. It seems likely that the new Soviet collective leadership wanted some kind of settlement, but the timing was off for the United States which was then pledged under a newly elected McCarthy era administration to a more robust anti-Soviet policy, and was also especially anxious to complete the full politico-military integration of western Germany – a development that depended for its success upon a lively apprehension of Soviet aggression. Another possibility opened up in 1959, but fell victim to events within the communist bloc and Khrushchev's anxieties over Eastern Europe. And after the Cuban missile crisis there was a flutter of concord with the 1963 nuclear test-ban treaty. However, the American diversion into Southeast Asia on the one hand, and the Soviet arms build-up together with Moscow's brutal repression of Czechoslovakia's "Prague Spring" in 1968 on the other, kept the Cold War pot boiling.

Each of these missed opportunities can, therefore, be explained in its own terms. But perhaps there was a deeper impediment? For one is constantly struck, when contemplating Cold War history, by the great difficulty these two great systems of power had in even considering the possibility of fundamental change. Each political elite seems to have felt locked into a confrontation that was also, at some mostly unacknowledged level, a congenial risk-minimizing bondage. It is true that the Soviet Union, as a totalitarian state, was at least potentially freer to make a dramatic move, as indeed it finally did with astonishing speed under Mikhail Gorbachev. Thus Stalin had found it possible to personally transform his foreign policy virtually overnight, apparently without feeling it necessary even to consult the Politburo, when he made the Nazi–Soviet treaty with Hitler in August 1939. His successors, however, deriving their thin legitimacy from an essentially combative ideology, encumbered too with an increasingly complex society and a more assertive range of vested special interests, and watched closely by an increasing number of fired-up allies in the new, turbulent de-colonizing world arena, must have found this kind of flexibility much more problematic.

It was even more difficult for the United States to move away from the Cold War once the postwar alliance system had been laboriously put together in the late 1940s. The Truman era posture, presided over by a resolutely anti-communist, anti-Soviet, bipartisan foreign policy elite, and energized at lower levels by the Red Scare and a mission-driven media, became steadily more entrenched politically thanks in part to the constant drumbeat of elections. It developed economic roots too as Eisenhower's "military–industrial complex" took shape, and flourished philosophically as the supposed best hope of morality and freedom. Here too, then, it was by the 1950s much easier to stay on the familiar track than to seek vigorously for changes whose consequences were at best unpredictable.

It is not surprising then to find that, contrary to the impression given by much of the historical literature, in certain crucial respects the impetus to détente came from outside the United States and even outside the United States–Soviet relationship. This is less obviously true of the American "opening" to China, which was nonetheless inspired in large part by the Chinese desire to wrong-foot the Soviets whom they saw as a mortal threat. But it is clearly true of détente in Europe, where there was still, despite the rigidities of the Cold War, a tradition of diplomatic maneuver. As early as 1967 the NATO powers had officially made détente with the Soviet Union in Europe an accepted objective. Here the main prompt came specifically from West Germany. Under Adenauer and his Christian Democratic successors, the German government had stuck closely to the United States and a firm anti-Soviet line. But in 1969 a new Social Democratic government under Willy Brandt committed itself to *Ostpolitik*, essentially a concerted human effort to reconcile with Moscow and the East European governments. And it was Brandt who blazed the trail for Nixon and Kissinger in 1970 with a much-publicized trip to Moscow and Warsaw (where he fell on his knees before a memorial in the wartime Jewish ghetto). This initiative culminated in formal German acceptance of the loss of its eastern territories to Poland after the war (hitherto withheld), and the conclusion of various political, humanitarian, and economic agreements that remained subject, however, to a ratification process in the German Bundestag that was considered problematic.

This more complex view of détente's origins has been advanced most recently by William Bundy. He challenges the Nixon–Kissinger line, accepted by most scholars, that détente was the outcome of a purposeful American diplomacy culminating in "a magnificent 1972 sequence" leading from the opening to Beijing through the détente with Moscow and on to the first Paris peace agreement over Vietnam in October.

Bundy sees, rather, a much less structured, more opportunistic set of initiatives and responses. He views détente, in the broad sense, as the outcome of actions taken by five strong-minded individuals – Willy Brandt, Zhou Enlai, Nixon (advised by Kissinger), and Brezhnev – each having a general sense of the need for international amelioration but each governed essentially by his own national or other interests. He persuasively stresses, above all, the primacy of a Vietnam settlement in Nixon's approach to détente. The evidence does suggest that the two communist great powers did urge Hanoi to settle at various times but that their role in the crucial last stages of negotiation was a minor factor. As Bundy puts it, after about July 1972 they "simply stood aside," wishing to offend neither their Vietnamese ally nor their new American partner in détente.[31]

When all this is taken into account, however, and American policy is properly seen as part of a broader international transformation of attitudes, it is nevertheless clear, as we have already noted, that Nixon was eager from the beginning of his presidency to effect fundamental changes and was receptive to opportunities as they presented themselves. Most historians stress, in addition to Vietnam, a growing recognition that American power in the world was declining. In the immediate postwar world American political and economic dominance, in the so-called "free world" at least, had been recognized and acknowledged. But by the late 1960s the recovery of Germany and Japan, vigorously promoted by the United States, had created more assertive political partners and unexpectedly robust economic competitors. It was in recognition of this that Nixon in 1971 devalued the dollar and broke up the Bretton Woods system. American power also seemed to be lessening in relation to the Soviet Union, which was widely thought by 1970 to have achieved a position of parity, if not superiority, in some nuclear weapon categories. At the same time the unmistakable breakdown of Sino–Soviet solidarity presented tempting diplomatic opportunities.[32]

In his approach to détente, however, Nixon was inspired by the Churchillian maxim that one should always try to deal with the communists from a position of strength. His starting point was the relationship with China. There had been no formal diplomatic link between the two countries since the 1949 revolution. But in 1970, after Sino–Soviet border clashes along the Ussuri river had dramatized the rift between the two communist powers, Nixon successfully initiated secret preliminary talks with Beijing through the two countries' diplomatic representatives in Warsaw. He certainly saw better relations with China both as a desirable end in itself, and as a way to bring pressure to bear on North Vietnam. But he also saw them as a way of pressuring the Soviets toward a similar accommodation. In the same spirit he gave notice to the Soviet side of the developing triangular diplomacy that he was contemplating the creation of a domestic anti-ballistic missile system, an inevitably provocative break with the existing concept of mutual assured destruction. In fact Nixon was self-consciously creating bargaining leverage for the future. Much the same coercive instinct was at work in the massive arming of Iran, which was still, under the Shah, a staunch American ally, strategically placed along the Soviets' southern border.

By 1971 Nixon was ready to move. The turn toward China came first. Out of the tentative Warsaw talks came a sudden Chinese invitation in March to the United States' table tennis authorities to participate in a tournament. Next came Kissinger's secret visit to Beijing in July, made while he was said to be ill during a visit to Pakistan. Kissinger met Mao Tse-tung and foreign minister Zhou Enlai, reaching with them the outlines of a new "normalization" and leaving with an invitation for a presidential visit. This took place in February 1972, with Nixon's plane touching down in Beijing during television prime time on the American east coast. The well-orchestrated visit was aglow with dramatic television images: Nixon shaking hands with Mao; Nixon visiting the Great Wall; Nixon struggling with chopsticks. More substantively, there were mutual pledges to end the long hostility and create a "normal" relationship. In the Shanghai communiqué the United States conceded that Mao's regime was sovereign in China, and promised to try and resolve the Taiwan issue peacefully. All this inevitably caused alarm among American conservatives, sharp anxiety in Taiwan, and also in Japan, which had with American encouragement forged strong economic ties with the Chiang regime in the contested island state. Neither had been given any detailed forewarning from Washington of the planned initiatives.[33]

But most American and world opinion was enthusiastic. And Nixon's gamble that the Soviet Union would be alarmed by the developing United States–China accommodation, yet all the more anxious to improve ties with his administration because of it, proved well founded. In late May, therefore, just three months after his China trip, we find Nixon on the way to Moscow for another summit spectacular. Here there were even more remarkable achievements. For where the Beijing meeting had produced, understandably given the parties' long separation, mainly general and symbolic accords, the Moscow summit resulted in major, tangible agreements. The most significant was the first strategic arms limitation treaty (SALT I). Agreeing to scrap the destabilizing construction of ABM systems (except for two allowed each side) Nixon and Brezhnev went on to establish ceilings on the number of missiles permitted to each nation. In the "apples and oranges" negotiation the Soviet Union was allowed 1,600 offensive missiles to the United States' 1,054, but the latter had the overall advantage because it was ahead in the multiple independently targeted re-entry vehicles (MIRVs) now attachable to conventional missiles.

There were other important agreements in Moscow. A general trade deal, giving the Soviets access to the American market on most-favored nation terms, was approved in principle. A wheat agreement, later known as "the great grain robbery" pleased mid-western farmers but led to shrewd Soviet purchases at low prices and a significant increase in the cost of American bread and cereal. There were treaties envisioning cooperation in space, measures to avoid sea and airspace accidents, and various scientific, environmental, and health accords. More politically sensitive was a declaration of "Basic Principles of Mutual Relations" that, affirming openly that

differences of ideology were no bar to normal relations, looked
to "peaceful co-existence." This language was much cited in
later American complaints about active Soviet political conduct in Africa and Europe. In fact, as William Bundy points
out, the words used were ambiguous. At the time, however,
they seemed to symbolize a new mutuality in international
affairs that many contemporaries found encouraging.

Nixon's long career was now at its highest point of achievement. His landslide election victory seemingly left him free to
develop the promising new relationships fruitfully. The troops
and prisoners of war came home from Vietnam and the president stepped up aid to the Thieu government and resumed the
bombing of Cambodia in February to demonstrate a continuing if radically diminished American commitment. Meanwhile,
Kissinger rather patronizingly proclaimed a "Year of Europe"
(inspiring President Pompidou of France to declare tartly that,
for Europeans, every year was a "Year of Europe"), to indi-
cate that the United States would in 1973 focus upon shoring
up its long-neglected relations with its closest allies.

Events soon shattered this vision. The administration's general freedom of action was sharply curtailed by a new assertive mood in Congress, still ruled by the Democrats and eager,
after the shock of Nixon's final bombing extravaganza over
Hanoi in January, to rein in the presidency. In April it qualified Nixon's earlier promises of reconstruction aid for North
Vietnam - crucial in his view to the preservation of the Paris
agreements and a source of leverage in Hanoi - by declaring
that funds for this purpose could not be advanced without
congressional approval that, it was clear, was unlikely to be
given. In late June both the House and Senate voted to stop
funding future military operations in Cambodia, Vietnam, and
Laos. Nixon, after some attempt at delay, accepted the ban in
August and American air activity there finally ended. These
actions, opening shots in Congress' general campaign to re-
assert its constitutional powers, reflected the decline of Nixon's
political position as the Watergate investigation gathered steam
through the summer of 1973.

Meanwhile, both détente and the "Year of Europe" conception were undermined by the president's growing preoccupation with his political survival, and by unforeseen crises in Latin America and the Middle East. In September, Chilean President Salvador Allende Gossens was murdered in a military coup and replaced by General Augusto Pinochet's military regime. This was the drastic culmination of a process that had begun with Allende's legitimate, democratic election in 1970. A pronounced left-wing populist, easily but dubiously stigmatized as a Moscow-leaning Marxist, Allende began by nationalizing the property of two major American copper corporations and, perhaps fatally, showed little interest in paying any sort of compensation. The corporations, in traditional fashion, complained to Washington. The Nixon administration, while maintaining ostensibly correct relations with Allende, now began a concerted campaign of subversion involving coercive economic pressures (notably by discouraging international credits) and the encouragement of right-wing military elements who shared the rising anger of many better-off Chileans over their leader's increasingly left-wing course. These events have been seen by many liberal commentators and historians as emblematic of a certain taste for intrigue and ruthlessness in the Nixon–Kissinger diplomacy. Bundy calls the American role in Chile "deplorable." Kissinger later admitted the economic pressures but denied any involvement in the Pinochet coup. Paul E. Sigmund in *The United States and Democracy in Chile*, a dispassionate account based on the available evidence, found no evidence of direct American involvement but amply documented a major indirect role (through the CIA, the embassy and the economic agencies) in creating the conditions that led to the coup.[34]

Within weeks of the Allende murder the Middle East erupted. Egypt and Syria launched surprise attacks on Israel on Yom Kippur, the holiest Jewish holiday. Initially successful in the Sinai and elsewhere, the Arabs were nonetheless soon in retreat. Egypt's President Anwar Sadat called on Brezhnev for assistance and Soviet preparations to send military help raised the stakes and made the issue a sharp test of détente. Nixon warned the Soviets not to intervene and tried to defuse the situation by obliging the Israelis to halt their advance toward Egypt. He took the dangerous step of putting the United States' nuclear forces on world alert. It was not at all clear that the Soviets would back off. Fortunately common sense prevailed and a cease-fire was arranged.

The Middle East crisis had two important consequences for the United States. The first arose from Sadat's displeasure with the low level of Soviet support. He now cut his ties with Moscow and began to collaborate with Kissinger's "shuttle diplomacy" between Israel and Egypt. This formalized the cease-fire and the status quo, though without settling any of the basic issues. The second outcome was global and profound in its effects. This was the decision of the Arab members of the Organization of Petroleum Exporting Countries (OPEC) to withhold oil shipments to the United States and the almost completely oil-dependent countries of Western Europe and Japan. By 1974 the price of a barrel of oil had quadrupled. This had the effect of dividing a pro-Israeli United States from its European allies, several of whom felt bound to take a more pro-Arab policy line. The "Year of Europe" was in ruins.[35]

United States–Soviet détente, however, continued notwithstanding the dangerous Middle East confrontation. Each power showed some early consideration for the other – the Soviets reacting calmly to Nixon's Christmas bombing of Hanoi, the United States accepting the presence of a Soviet submarine base in Cuba. Brezhnev came to the United States in June 1973 on his reciprocal visit and, although there was little substantive achievement there was a further flourish of minor political and cultural agreements. But it was already clear that there might be difficulties with Congress over the trade legislation. Further, the Kremlin seems to have associated the new relationship with Nixon and Kissinger personally, and ostentatiously helped the president by inviting him for a third showy summit spectacular in Moscow in the summer of 1974, just before his resignation.

It fell to President Gerald R. Ford and Kissinger (continuing as Secretary of State and now given a much freer hand under his new, diplomatically inexperienced leader) to face the final act of the Indochina drama. During 1974 the Thieu government and the communists had launched small-scale, mostly unsuccessful attacks upon each other. At the beginning of 1975, however, the North Vietnamese and their allies advanced in full force, pushing south as South Vietnamese resistance broke down. Ford, hobbled by congressional restraints, could not respond to Thieu's entreaties to honor Nixon's pledge to return "in full force." Americans watched with mixed emotions as their remaining compatriots and a small number of compromised Vietnamese associates were evacuated as Saigon finally fell in April. In the ensuing gloom Ford gained some credit for an apparently daring operation by the Marines rescuing crew members of an American ship, the *Mayaguez*, which had been seized by hostile Cambodian forces. After a brief, bloody operation in which 40 marines died, it transpired that the crew members had been released earlier. On this emblematic note of costly futility the American engagement in Indochina came to an end.

Détente continued its increasingly fitful course. Ford and Kissinger met with Brezhnev in late 1974 and agreed to a preliminary framework for a SALT II treaty. As historian David Reynolds explains "Both governments . . . saw détente as a continuation of the Cold War by safer means." But there was rising concern about the continuing Soviet arms build-up. On the Soviet side enthusiasm was dampened by the success of Democratic Senator Henry Jackson of Washington in securing congressional passage of the so-called Jackson–Vanik amendment tying any extension of most-favored nation treatment to an express number of exit visas for Soviet Jews. The Kremlin was not willing to accept this public humiliation. The effect, as Kissinger repeatedly warned, was to remove much of the incentive for Soviet adherence to détente.[36]

The Soviets were eager, however, to seal their central European settlement with the West Germans by securing American acceptance of the arrangements they had made with Brandt. After 30 years they still relied in Eastern Europe almost entirely on force, symbolized by the so-called Brezhnev "doctrine" whereby they assumed, following their 1968 intervention against reformers in Czechoslovakia, the right to protect any "fraternal" regime in the region. But revolts against communist rule had continued, most recently a Polish workers' rising in 1970. In 1975 Ford and Kissinger joined the leaders of 34 countries in Helsinki for a basic compromise accepting the postwar boundaries in Eastern Europe in return for Soviet undertakings to pursue a more tolerant human rights policy.

The arms control accommodations at Vladivostok and the Helsinki deal inspired Republican concern and right-wing charges of a new "Yalta." With the 1976 presidential election looming up Ford found it necessary to strip Kissinger of his National Security Adviser role (he remained Secretary of State) and to ban the use of the word "détente." Meanwhile, Kissinger began to speak out against Soviet policy, criticizing it for promoting "Eurocommunism" (a term inspired by the surprising rise of the French and Italian communist parties in this period) and for violating in Angola and Ethiopia a supposed "linkage" pledge they had given at Moscow in 1972 to refrain from political action in Africa. The Kremlin protested, with some justice, that it had given no such undertaking. But human rights became the policy touchstone of the Carter administration that took office early in 1977, and their Helsinki commitments in that sphere put the Soviets on the defensive thereafter. Détente continued in a fashion, and indeed in the summer of 1979 President Jimmy Carter and Brezhnev met at Vienna to sign the long-gestating SALT II agreement. But by the end of that year, with the Soviet invasion of Afghanistan in December marking a clear transition, détente had finally run its course.

Détente has had a very mixed evaluation from historians of American foreign policy. John Lewis Gaddis characterizes it as "a new kind of containment" that, for all its disappointments and limitations, maintained stability between the superpowers and represented progress toward the goal of "graduated reciprocation in tension resolution." Raymond Garthoff, on the other hand, views the process negatively, seeing it as vague and disarmingly illusory in its promise. He faults Nixon and Kissinger for failing to define détente clearly enough. He notes that while the need for some adjustment in political posture was recognized in Washington and Moscow, each side "saw itself as the manager of the transition of the other." There was no real meeting of minds and the protagonists failed to find a "common political standard to govern their competitive actions in the world."[37]

The Hollow Years, 1974–80?

The title, even with the evasive question mark, is undeniably provocative. Yet one feels, with the Vietnam and Watergate disasters just past and the arguably regenerative 1980s still ahead, we are, in some respects at least, at the bottom of some sort of trough. It is hard to think of any profound accomplishments in this period. It was a time of strident complaint, confused paths, and hazy perspectives. The Johnsonian ideal of "consensus" was now seen as hopelessly illusory. The nation was led by two eminently decent but vulnerable presidents, neither able to offer a compelling vision, each obliged to fight off a debilitating challenge from within his own party when he sought a second term. Each was tormented by economic challenges few understood and no one could master. And neither could turn confidently for support to a society that, still grappling with the socially subversive life-styles left by the 1960s, seemed disenchanted with politics (only 53 percent of those eligible voted in 1980) and, as the most casual glance at the newspapers and magazines of the day will attest, inclined to a divisive irritability.

So much for the mood or social tone. The challenge is to identify its deeper causes, beyond the obvious emotional catalysts of Vietnam and Watergate. One starts instinctively with the economy. The postwar "golden age" had rested on a steady economic growth that paid for the Cold War commitment, made profound domestic reforms possible without unmanageable social upset, and maintained an optimistic spirit. But, as already indicated, the growth peaked in 1973. GNP declined 2.5 percent in the first three-quarters of 1974, 3.2 percent more in the winter of 1974–75. Meanwhile, inflation grew rapidly in the new "stagflation" tandem that saw price levels rise by 11 percent in 1975 as unemployment reached 9 percent. Hourly wages declined for the first time since 1945: by 0.1 percent in 1973, 2.8 percent in 1974, and 0.7 percent in 1975. Median family income, adjusted for inflation, fell from $29,172 in 1973 to $28,145 in 1974, to $27,421 in 1975. Particularly affected were blacks who, encouraged by Great Society reforms to join the mainstream, now found good jobs hard to find in the private sector and were thrown back on public institutional employment, affirmative action, or the various welfare benefits whose rapidly rising costs (Food Stamps served 400,000 in 1965 but 17.4 million people in 1975) steadily alienated many white Americans. Journalist Thomas Edsall draws the obvious conclusion and identifies a central problem of political leadership in the later 1970s: "Family income after 1973 abruptly stopped growing, cutting off what was left of popular support for government-led redistributional economic politics."[38]

The economic decline produced an increasingly divisive politics. We can get a sense of the significant political changes in this period by focusing on the state. Like the economy the state had prospered since World War II. Now it was put to the test. The most noticeable development was the decline of the "imperial presidency." The economic deterioration left little room for the costly programmatic agendas that had sustained its power. And now foreign policy, where earlier presidents had eagerly sought an arena for dramatic action, was heavily constrained. After Vietnam the public mood, as in the similar immediate postwar contexts of 1919 and 1945, was inclined to turn inward following strenuous military exertions. And a responsive and newly assertive Congress now passed the War Powers Act of 1973, limiting the president's power to send troops overseas without congressional approval to 60 days. It also reined in the hitherto largely autonomous CIA. All this signified a degree of neo-isolationism that soon came to be called the "Vietnam syndrome."[39]

But it was not only the presidency that was losing power

now. The whole political system and its surrounding political culture was undergoing a sea change. Congress, while successfully reasserting itself against the long executive tyranny, was simultaneously losing the crucial cohesiveness needed for effective action. For the seniority system, with its all-powerful committee chairmen, was giving way in this rapidly democratizing era to a looser power-sharing system that inevitably encouraged further fragmentation and various forms of politically sectarian contention. The decentralizing tendency can be seen too in the political parties, increasingly broken down now into passionate, latently rebellious groups that had to be bribed and bullied toward some sort of common outlook every election year. In all these developments, as well as in the growing power of the states, cities, and localities as Nixon's revenue-sharing took hold, we see clearly the drift of power from the center to the periphery, a trend that often led to legislative gridlock and gave an enhanced role to the Supreme Court as a focus of cultural politics, and to the Federal Reserve Bank as a more dynamic actor in economic decision making.

This tendency – the draining of power from a long-established center toward a broader constellation of forces – can also be seen at work beyond the formal constitutional system in the changing character of the wider political establishment. The old white, Anglo-Saxon, Protestant hegemony was not fully eclipsed. Indeed, with Carter's election it could be held to be reformulating itself in a "New South" form that was, however, markedly different from the old, cohesive "governing class" defined by Richard Barnet as drawn in the main from offices "within fifteen city blocks in New York, Boston, and Detroit." The most dramatic change lay elsewhere. Richard Polenberg notes "Evidence of a new ethnic awareness could be found everywhere in the late 1960s and early 1970s." After the Vietnam disaster, especially, we see a much more heterogeneous grouping in the higher reaches – political, socio-economic, and cultural – of American life.[40]

John F. Kennedy's victory in 1960 signified the full emergence of Irish, and more generally Catholic Americans. Kissinger's prominence in the 1970s and Washington's post-1973 solicitude for Israel symbolized the remarkable rise of American Jews to positions of prominence in politics, academia, and the media, complementing their longer-rooted influence in finance. Italian film makers, actors, and writers proliferated. The election of the Greek-American Spiro Agnew as vice-president was notable in 1968, and the sudden simultaneous appearance of two Polish-Americans as Secretary of State (Edmund Muskie) and National Security adviser (Zbigniew Brzezinski) in the late 1970s doubtless fluttered the Kremlin's dovecotes. And in a more general way the large number of African-Americans and women in the Carter administration dramatized the new, more representative character of the political establishment.

In the media also the fragmenting, variegating trend, so characteristic of the decade, was evident though slower to develop. The power of the three dominant television networks, supportive pillars of the Cold War consensus since the 1950s, was still clearly evident in the 1970s. There is an echo of the old 1950 debates about "alienation" and the "mass society" in the widely expressed fears in the 1970s about the moral impact of this now omnipresent medium. Some of these alarms were perhaps exaggerated. Parents were shocked to read social critics' estimates that many children were watching for around 30 or more hours a week. The British historian G. M. Young, who calculated in his 1936 classic, *Victorian England: Portrait of an Age*, that a typical young man in Victorian England may have heard 1,000 sermons, might have been less impressed.[41]

But decentralization was coming in here too, and by the end of the decade the proliferation of public television, cable, the revival of radio, and a resurgent press of aggressive newspapers and special interest magazines sustain the impression of a widening arena of power sharing and media decision making. Three striking 1970s' developments stand out. First, officials were no longer treated with deference. Media historian James Baughman notes that the office of the presidency "had become open game." Indeed the journalistic profession generally became much more intensely aggressive toward public officials after the press triumph over the Watergate exposés.

Secondly, there was, despite the Republican setback, a less liberal, more conservative tone after 1976. The newspaper scene until then was full of syndicated liberal columnists like Nicholas von Hoffman, Murray Kempton, and Jack Anderson. Afterwards their constituencies dwindled while hitherto lonely right-wing writers like James Kilpatrick found themselves joined by a host of new, acerbic conservatives like William Safire and George Will. And thirdly, there was an explosion of lifestyle-oriented journalism that, in a society where the voices of socially emancipated women, vociferous minorities, and born-again life enhancers of every description rang ever louder, reflected the felt need for shared experiences and new codes of behavior.[42]

One would like to be able to explain the deeper socio-cultural currents in this decade more fully. Some scholars – for instance Christopher Lasch whose *The Culture of Narcissism* is often cited as a classic portrait of a paradoxical culture suddenly transfixed with new cults and behavioral models yet turning in on itself – have grappled bravely with the subject.[43] But much remains beyond our reach. Take, for example, the astonishing comeback of business values. Many commentators (including Lasch) have remarked the takeover of the 1960s' "counter-culture" by the "consumer-culture." The trend toward a rapidly permeating commercialism accelerated sharply in the 1970s. There were numerous tokens of this. Traditionally Americans had maintained a fastidious line between advertising and normal life. Suddenly, and epidemically, this inhibition vanished. Clothes and hats festooned with commercial logos and business labels proliferated. As commercial display advanced reverence for tradition declined. It was in this era that entertainers acquired the habit of torturously putting an individual spin upon the presentation of the national anthem. Many attending sporting events doubtless squirmed helplessly in the stands, but the subversive practice went essentially unchallenged and is now itself an established tradition.

To mention such changes is simply to scratch selectively the surface of a broadening transformation in habits and outlooks. Two further changes, among many, seem noteworthy. One was the tendency of older institutions to bend acquiescently before the winds of change. The adaptations of the nation's governmental establishment were highly visible. Similarly, venerable religious denominations, fearful of losing adherents in the new hedonistic atmosphere, embraced what James Twitchell has called "a glad-handling Christianity." Schools started to inflate grades and focus upon their students' self-esteem. Family solidarity was undermined by liberalized divorce laws from the 1960s, which were now producing what one writer has called "a divorce culture" favoring adult self-fulfillment at the expense of their children. It was estimated that by the end of the 1970s a child had about one chance in two of ending his youth in a home with his parents. Soaring illegitimacy rates, especially in the African-American community, were encouraged, it was argued by conservative critics, by 1960s' welfare laws. Many contemporaries saw in these crumbling institutions and broken hierarchies a marked departure from traditional American codes. Lawyers debated the societal consequences of the widespread change from personal to absolute liability in tort law (which watered down or removed entirely the principle of accountability in personal injury and other claims). Philosophers worried that "rights" were increasingly replacing "responsibilities."[44]

These political and socio-cultural transformations are sometimes overshadowed in accounts of the 1970s by the conventional heavy focus on two indubitably dynamic social groups of the period: blacks and women. African-American civil rights leaders had been the pacesetters of reform in the 1960s. Now the later-developing women's movement was the locomotive of change, pulling behind it a long train of aspiring minority groups, gay liberationists, mental patients representatives, illegal aliens, and many others. All actively engaged, typically through the courts now rather than in street agitation, in what some scholars have called a "rights revolution." Here there was much success. The rising career woman was a conspicuous emblem of the decade. William Chafe cites evidence showing that while in 1970 college men outnumbered women students in expressing an interest in business, engineering, medicine, or law by eight to one, by 1975 the ratio was down to three to one. Female enrolment in many law and medical schools hovered around 50 percent. And there is abundant, if rather impressionistic evidence from polls, surveys, and interviews suggesting that the subsequent entry of legions of women into the higher professions was accompanied by increasingly supportive public attitudes.

But the advance of individual women, and the impressive cooperation of millions of others who organized effectively in innumerable communities for practical reforms, working together to break down deep-rooted unfairness in traditional society, came at a price. Even successful women often encountered a "glass ceiling" as they sought promotion, and female pay rates lagged behind, a primary motive behind the movement for an Equal Rights Amendment (passed overwhelmingly by Congress in 1972 but finally falling just short in the prescribed state votes) to the constitution. More generally, Chafe notes that the composition of the typical family changed drastically. In the 1950s over 70 percent of American families possessed a working father and a homemaking mother. By 1980 only 15 percent showed that profile. The divorce rate rose almost 100 percent in the 1960s, and then another 82 percent by 1980. Getting toward half of 1970s' marriages would end in divorce. Single households proliferated: only 10.9 percent in 1964, but 23 percent in 1980. Clearly the more liberated sexuality introduced in the 1960s was now bringing both enhanced pleasure and unforeseen misery – nirvana and nemesis – in very large measures.[45]

Much the same mixture of success and frustration is found in the black experience of the 1970s. With the great legislative reforms in place the emphasis was now on socio-economic progress. Nixon's affirmative action program was widely welcomed. And there was heartening success as many more blacks now graduated from high school, went on to college, and found good jobs that moved them into the middle-class mainstream. The success of two-income black families outside the South in earning 88 percent of the money earned by white, two-income families, was encouraging. Black political power grew in the

1970s too, with black mayors in Los Angeles, Detroit, and Atlanta, and several other cities, as well as a congressional representation of 18 by 1980.

But here too there were many setbacks. The timing of the early 1970s' economic downturn, just as black Americans were poised to advance, was tragic in its implications. Just as calamitous was a post-1960s' schism that divided the black community. The smaller, relatively successful group tended to move out to less depressed locations, leaving behind a leaderless vulnerable society of the underprivileged, the uneducated, and the unemployed. The urban ghetto, universally seen now as America's most visible failure, was a desperate crime-ridden arena whose inhabitants functioned less as a community than as ravaged clusters of individuals, human testimony to the gap between high social ideals and poor planning. These problems, especially the absence of work, placed enormous pressure on the welfare system, which steadily produced what came to be called a "welfare mentality." There were vigorous liberal defenses of the Great Society in the mid-1970s, notably by social scientists Sar Levitan and Robert Taggart, who praised Johnson for his commitment and found much to welcome in the new federal social activism. But many took a more critical view, arguing that the system tended to degrade its recipients, breaking down family life by refusing benefits where an employed male was present, encouraging an epidemic of illegitimacy with benefits for single mothers, and inhibiting the development of healthy social or work ethics. The consequences from this perspective were perhaps inevitable: a drift toward crime and drugs among young black males; and a growing reactionary critique that focused on the vivid symptoms of social disintegration in a way that steadily eroded public support for the reform cause.[46]

One final point. Our theme in this introduction to the Ford–Carter years has been the growing fragmentation of American life and the drift of power away from traditional institutions. Our attempt has been to refine and substantiate the acknowledged but vague "unraveling" concept often applied to the 1960s but actually more significant in the following decade.

But our final emphasis on the limits of women's and blacks' success in the 1970s should remind us that new structures were appearing. Some were constructive, like the fresh communitarian enterprises identified by Peter M. Carroll. But others were depressingly negative, notably the growth of a wider division between rich and poor. This bifurcation, so visible now after two decades of market-driven economics and a politics that was less and less engaged with finding solutions for deep social issues, can already be seen in the growing divisions in the 1970s between career and uneducated women, between rising and falling blacks. William Chafe, noting the minimal education, non-existent health care, and inadequate nutrition of the poor, identifies welfare mothers, ex-drug addicts, and various societal drop-outs as members of a bottom group that Senator Edward Kennedy strikingly described as "a permanent underclass in our society." Chafe, struck by what he calls "the feminization of poverty" sees in all this "the ultimate intersection of race, class, and gender." In other times this intersection might have been the basis of a new reformist solidarity. But in the late 1970s and even more in the 1980s, conservative politicians found it easy to play these three potentially radicalizing impulses off against each other, inhibiting the development of an effective political front on the left.[47]

Gerald R. Ford, never viewed beyond his intimate circle as a presidential prospect, was a moderately conservative Republican stalwart known mainly for his dogged attempt years before to press the impeachment of Supreme Court Justice William O. Douglas. His administration seems to have been only dimly aware of, and minimally interested in, the trends we have just noted and which seem so clear to us with a quarter-century's hindsight. This is surely understandable. Ford came to office without any preparation and no programmatic agenda. He began well, conducting the transition of power smoothly and taking particular care to separate himself symbolically from the "imperial presidency." Much was made of his daily struggle to prepare the family breakfast. He was clearly solid and likeable. But within weeks he lost his grip on a large part of the public by issuing a pardon for his predecessor.

Many had dreaded seeing Nixon on trial and he was now reportedly ill. But others were outraged that the supposed architect of the crime should escape while so many of his associates were serving prison terms for carrying out his orders. There was immediate speculation, never substantiated and resolutely denied, that Ford was fulfilling his side of a deal that had brought him unexpectedly to the White House.

Despite this public letdown Ford persisted stubbornly. He seems to have taken a compartmentalized view of his task. He left foreign affairs almost entirely to Kissinger, whom he retained as both Secretary of State and National Security adviser. He grappled more vigorously with the economy for inflation, neglected during the long Watergate distraction, was still accelerating. But he shrank from Nixon's bold interventionism and relied without much success on rhetoric, conferences, and media pressures to persuade corporations to lower prices and labor to accept lower wages. He found it easier to curb federal spending. His brief presidency is notable for the combination of deepening recession (with attendant unemployment) and the 39 vetoes he was able to impose on legislation the Democratic Congress sent him. Liberal and Keynesian critics pointed out that the spending bills would have produced some economic stimulation and found Ford's policies reminiscent of the Hoover era. All this signified the continuing confusion created by the "stagflation" mixture of recession and inflation. But the president's main interest lay in the political realm he knew best. He campaigned energetically in the 1974 congressional elections; inevitably a setback for the Republicans who lost 48 seats in the House. From then on he devoted himself to forging party unity for 1976 in the face of rising right-wing disaffection.

Foreign affairs offered some distraction from the growing domestic woes. As we have seen it fell to Ford and Kissinger to preside over the last phase of America's long Indochina involvement, trying unsuccessfully to persuade an obdurate Congress to provide last-moment succor for the Thieu regime, then playing up the *Mayaguez* incident as a consoling display of continuing American vitality, and going on to press a still resistant legislature to provide support for Angolan elements eager to resist Soviet–Cuban advances in Southwest Africa. But the anti-interventionist tide, especially after the influx of liberal Democrats in 1974, was far too strong. Much of the Ford–Kissinger effort seems, in retrospect, inspired less by a hopeless quest for a vigorously engaged activism than by the need to rally support for the 1976 presidential campaign from the Republican right-wing. This group, threatening to divide an already weakened party, was increasingly suspicious of Kissinger's continuing dealings with the communist powers, especially the Vladivostok and Helsinki compromises.[48]

The basic problem lay with détente. Defeat in Vietnam had so far produced neither a bloodbath nor a rampant domino effect, but there was plenty of totalitarian activity to worry about and Laos and Cambodia were obviously lost to communism. The Soviets were politically aggressive in northeast as well as southwest Africa. In Europe the rising popularity of the French and Italian communist parties seemed to many to threaten NATO and Western solidarity. Further, the Soviets continued to oppress domestic dissidents, whose travails were widely publicized, and, most alarmingly, there was growing concern about the apparent disparity between Moscow's arms spending and an American defense budget that was now in post-Vietnam decline. We know now that much of this concern was justified, for the Brezhnev regime's build-up was bringing it to a position of nuclear parity (perhaps superiority in some categories) and they were indeed violating pledges not to develop further their biochemical weaponry. Politically, the odium fell directly on Kissinger, who now frequently found it necessary to chastise the Soviets publicly. Ford, keenly aware of the looming conservative challenge of former California governor Ronald Reagan, reshuffled his Cabinet in a rightward direction, stripped Kissinger of his National Security adviser role, and ostentatiously banned use of the word "détente."

The Democrats, after their 1974 mid-term success had reason to expect victory. Significantly, however, the nomination went not to liberal contenders but to an outsider. Jimmy Carter, a one-term former governor of Georgia, campaigned long and relentlessly against "Washington politics" and the evident moral and political imperfections of the "imperial presidency." Carter was liberal in his commitment to the civil rights cause. For the rest he was essentially a "managerial" progressive, the first in a long line of post-Johnson Democrats who, adjusting to the new conservative mood, cultivated the art of presenting themselves as both warm-hearted heirs of the Great Society and waste-conscious custodians of the national interest.

Carter eked out a narrow victory over Ford, who had barely won his party's nomination. He owed his success to several factors: the continuing public anger with the Republican party over Watergate; the Republican split made worse by Ronald Reagan's refusal to campaign vigorously for the ticket; foreign policy reverses and the waning of Kissinger's star; the continuing economic woes, which Ford's "jawboning" approach failed to address effectively; Ford's gaffe in a debate with Carter in which he claimed that Poland was not dominated by the Soviet Union; the unattractively aggressive campaigning of the president's running mate, Senator Robert Dole of Kansas. And behind this lay a profound regional factor. It is no accident that the only successful Democratic presidential aspirants since 1964 have been southern politicians, the only candidates able to counter the drift of the white South – reacting variously to the civil rights revolution, the increasing secularity of the American middle class, and the new prosperity – to the Republican party.[49]

Still, it is hard to see how Carter could have produced a successful presidency. In a structural sense the Democratic mishaps of the late 1960s and the early 1970s had changed the rules of the game. The old unifying liberal unity, founded since Truman's day on the containment of communism and the promotion of reforms that were funded comfortably out of steady economic growth, was now shattered. Carter had to face the complex enigmas of détente in an atmosphere approaching neo-isolationism, and a diminished reform prospect that was deeply undermined by a declining economy. This was bound to exacerbate the divisions already threatening the Democratic Party.

And the corollary of this liberal decline, conservative reaction and Republican recovery, was only momentarily checked by the Nixon collapse. As Thomas Edsall has pointed out, the Watergate affair "resulted in a political system out of sync with larger trends." He identified a number of active leftish groups – Democratic prosecutors, some media, junior congressional Democrats, new reform organizations, and traditional liberal interest groups – who after 1974 "gained control over the political agenda just when a variety of developments and changing attitudes, mostly associated with a declining economy and a growing disenchantment with welfare and social policy generally suggested the revival of a powerful right-wing."[50]

We will examine these developments in a moment. First, let us see how Carter approached his task. Like Ford he set himself to downplay what was left of the "imperial presidency," presenting himself with ingratiating modesty. In a number of early symbolic gestures – walking down Pennsylvania Avenue after his inaugural, addressing the nation in a cardigan, carrying his own suitcase – he soon outpaced his predecessor in the humble-pie competition. When it came to serious matters his fundamental touchstone here was a belief in reason. For the new president, shaped as much by his training in engineering and his disciplined service in the Navy as by his rural Georgia background, was a practical, intelligent man who saw himself as a problem solver. Morally self-confident, technologically proficient, and business-like in his approach, he saw what needed to be done. It quickly became apparent, however, that for all his attention to American moral concerns on the campaign trail, when it came to high-level politics Carter lacked sensitivity. His first act in domestic politics was to veto expensive water projects that he considered wasteful, ignoring the anguish of the many powerful senators who would never forgive him. His first major step in diplomacy was to send Secretary of State Cyrus Vance to Moscow with sensible proposals designed to cut through years of laborious arms control negotiation, failing to anticipate the outrage of the Soviets at these suspicious simplifications which quickly led to Vance's embarrassed early return empty-handed.

These early setbacks in the face of stubborn realities go a long way to explain one of the most common criticisms of the Carter administration: that for all the protestations of rationality, its general course was "incoherent." The president was, of course, keenly aware that inflation was the most serious economic problem. Yet he began with expansionary measures designed to alleviate unemployment. This was good Democratic politics, and was justified by the administration as a necessary stimulus to recovery from "the Ford recession" whose miseries Carter had naturally trumpeted during the campaign. But as he stepped up public works and public service jobs and pushed through a modest tax cut Carter was not only aggravating inflation but also flouting the conventional wisdom, recently demonstrated by Nixon, that a new president is wise to pursue contractionary policies early in his term so that he could expand the economy later when facing re-election.

At the same time the effect of these stimulative measures in an inflationary context meant that Carter had to take a very cost-conscious line with the two major programmatic reforms cherished by liberal Democrats. Thus he instructed his Health, Education, and Welfare Secretary, Joseph Califano, to come up with a low-cost welfare reform. The result was a minimal expansion that failed in Congress after disappointing liberals and enraging conservatives. National health insurance suffered a similar fate. Carter's bill, hailed by domestic adviser Stuart Eisenstat as "the greatest step towards universal coverage since the passage of Medicare," envisioned $17 billion for a wide-ranging first stage and included coverage against catastrophe for the elderly and full coverage for low-income children. But liberals, led by Kennedy, who had hoped for immediate full coverage for all, were again disappointed. Southern Democrats, who wanted an even more limited system than Carter's, were also upset. The scheme was a failure.[51]

In all this Carter, who was under constant pressure to increase social spending from congressional liberals, union officials, and black leaders like Jesse Jackson and Vernon Jordan, tried to maintain a moderate middle position between liberal and conservative extremists who, in an era of rising social tension amid dwindling resources, persistently frustrated rational change. His problems with Congress were intensified by an epidemic of special interest lobbyists in these years and by the breakdown of the seniority system which complicated the legislative process. As Carter noted later, House Speaker Thomas O'Neill, "had a nearly impossible job trying to deal with a rambunctious Democratic majority that had been reformed out of almost any semblance of discipline or loyalty." But the president was also to blame. O'Neill records that after three years of this administration he had not yet met Carter's chief of staff, Hamilton Jordan. The lack of coordination led to confusion, misunderstanding, and a growing liberal upset, grounded in a perception that the president and his Georgian advisers were arrogant, provincial, and unsympathetic. This finally produced the Kennedy insurgency in 1980. The administration's memoirs bristle with a keenly felt reciprocal resentment.[52]

These destructive cross-currents complicated Carter's basic struggle to bring down inflation and solve the stagflation problem. Moving beyond both Nixon's direct but dislocating interventionism and Ford's ineffectual rhetoric, he focused on the post-1973 explosion in energy costs (the cost of a barrel of oil was still four times above the 1972 level in 1977) as the heart of the issue. His solution, hammered out within the administration, reflected the many interests at stake and seems to have been a good faith attempt to encourage economic adjustments, soften dislocations, reform some old inequities, and foster domestic energy production and independence. The result was an energy bill with over 100 separate parts. Carter insisted that it be passed in full or not at all. It was an unproductive approach that underestimated the complexity of the issue and the political power of the oil, coal, and labor forces involved, as well as a vast range of broader economic interests affected by the ripple impact of rising energy costs and an army of disparate consumer groups reflecting the concerns of ordinary Americans. In the end he was able to please the oil companies by effecting the decontrol of oil prices, securing by

compensation the end of the infamous oil depletion allow-
ance, and to get from Congress a number of incentives for
coal production and alternative energy sources. These gestures
to business were balanced by an excess profits tax to placate
liberal critics of what was seen by many as a pro-business
boondoggle.

In the long run, as Carter predicted at the time, his bill helped
lead to the break-up of the OPEC cartel and to lower oil prices.
But its immediate consequences were even higher prices and a
strong sense of public dissatisfaction. It was, therefore, in a
pre-existing context of public upset that the administration
had to accept, in June 1979, a further 50 percent price rise
from OPEC, an event that, combined with rising difficulties
in foreign policy, precipitated what Eisenstat aptly calls a "deep
crisis" in the administration. Faced with crumbling policies at
home and abroad, with a re-election campaign looming and
an insurgency brewing on the left-wing of his own party, Carter
withdrew in biblical fashion for a wrenching 10-day period of
contemplation and review with an assortment of "wise men"
to his mountain-top retreat at Camp David.[53]

This was a good time for a presidential review because the
immediate effect of the new OPEC initiative, which was inspired partly by an intensification of the Iran crisis, was to
bring domestic issues and foreign policy problems together.
Before examining Carter's response, therefore it may be well
to trace briefly the evolution of his diplomacy up to June 1979.
Though inexperienced in international relations Carter brought
to this arena the same rationalizing, problem-solving spirit,
energized by moral fervor, we have observed in domestic affairs. Eager to get away from what he and many Democrats
regarded as the excessively cynical power politics and spurious "realism" of Kissingerian diplomacy, Carter had promised to "replace balance of power politics with world order
politics." He put the emphasis on "human rights" and the
wholesome, mission-oriented aspects of the American diplomatic tradition. Much of this recalled Woodrow Wilson, a
predecessor Carter somewhat resembled in his southern origins, his emphasis upon reason, his religiosity, and his ini-

tially veiled but steadily more visible sense of self-righteousness.[54]

This meant a very different approach to the Soviet Union. Carter shared the characteristic American suspicion of the Soviet Union in a general way, but seems to have taken the view that after four years of détente the United States could look upon the world in broader, more creative terms than the Cold War and Kissinger's realpolitik had allowed. He sought almost from the start to move his Soviet policy beyond détente to a kind of fastidious disengagement. Thus in May 1977 he told a Notre Dame University audience that "an inordinate fear of communism has led us to embrace any dictator who joined in our fear." He wanted to free himself to address wider, morally charged issues such as human rights abuses in Latin America and the whole question of relations between the rich industrialized "north" and the poor, undeveloped "south."[55]

By this time he had already alienated the Brezhnev regime by sending Vance on his ill-fated arms control mission. This angered the Soviets, always in the pre-Gorbachev era more comfortable with long, drawn-out diplomatic wrangles, and always fearful of being finessed by the technologically superior Americans. Vance had embarrassed them too by revealing his new proposals publicly. Meanwhile, throughout his first year Carter made repeated public statements of support for Soviet dissidents, further infuriating the Kremlin and perhaps, as Walter LaFeber argues, giving the impression that he saw human rights abuses as, in the Nixon style, a bargaining chip in the arms control negotiations.

In this they undoubtedly misread the new president. Carter disliked the subtle but laborious preparation of negotiating strategies and the working out of dubious compromises. As with complex domestic issues like the energy bill he preferred to study a problem from all sides and emerge with a rational solution which he could then persuade the parties to accept. At the "studying" stage he was open to, indeed wished for, discordant views. Thus he encouraged a fundamental fissure between Vance and his National Security adviser Zbigniew Brzezinski. Essentially Vance and the State Department wished to keep United States–Soviet détente on track, especially in the crucial arms control negotiations. And they tended to see Third-World problems as a consequence of local nationalistic assertion rather than the Kremlin's hidden hand. The deeply anti-Soviet Brzezinski, on the other hand, favored closer relations with China and encouraged Carter in his calls for human rights in Eastern Europe. He saw Soviet manipulations behind many of the world's trouble spots, and urged closer relations with China as a means of pressing Moscow. These divided counsels produced what political scientist Stanley Hoffman has called an "incoherent" diplomacy in an administration that seemed to speak with two voices.[56]

None of this is to suggest that the Carter administration was solely responsible for the slow death of détente. That is a complex issue. Détente was declining rapidly in Kissinger's last years as Soviet enthusiasm flagged with the disappointments over economic benefits and conservative Republicans forced a sharper American response to Soviet actions in Africa and elsewhere. There was further aggravation for Moscow in Carter's 1978 decision, breaking a previous undertaking to work together, to cut the Soviets out of the Middle East diplomacy that culminated in the Camp David accords later that year. Only arms control issues, already jeopardized by Vance's importunate 1977 initiative, kept détente going. Then the president allowed Brzezinski to travel to Beijing to revitalize that connection. The outcome was formal US recognition of the People's Republic of China in January 1979, and the subsequent visit to this country of the Chinese leader Deng Xiaoping, giving a powerful impression that the two countries were now ganging up on the Soviets. By mid-1979 there was little substance or feeling left in the 1972 "spirit of Moscow."

Elsewhere, especially in discrete situations which lent themselves to practical outcomes, there were more positive results. Carter was notably successful in bringing about a treaty with Panama over the Canal Zone. Here was a powerful symbol of American strength, established dubiously by Theodore Roosevelt early in the century. But modern presidents from

Lyndon Johnson onwards had wrestled with this issue know-
ing that American control of the Canal was no longer essential for security or economic needs, and that it provoked
anti-American feeling in Panama and throughout the hemisphere. Carter grasped the nettle, negotiated tenaciously with
the Panamanian leader, General Torrijos, and lobbied reluctant senators to support the treaty which gave Panama sovereignty and control in 2000 subject to the right of the United
States to return if it believed its own security threatened. Carter's success was costly, passing the Senate by only one vote
and using up much of his political capital on a controversial
issue that promoted the mobilization of a fierce right-wing
resistance in which Ronald Reagan was active.[57]

Carter scored another diplomatic success with the Camp
David accords in 1978. Here too he intervened creatively after others had taken the initiative, in this case Egyptian president Anwar Sadat who in 1977 flew to Israel and made a
dramatic call for peace in the Middle East. Carter promptly
dropped the pre-existing United States–Soviet negotiating
framework and entered the faltering Egypt–Israeli deliberations, bringing Sadat and Israeli premier Menachem Begin to
Camp David for 13 days of intense, uncomfortable dealing.
The three men finally emerged with a compromise accord that,
following improvements during a subsequent Carter trip to
the Middle East, effectively ended the long Egypt–Israeli confrontation. Egypt got back the Sinai territories (held by Israel
since its victory in 1967) in return for its recognition of the
Jewish state. The United States sweetened the deal by promising $3 billion of annual military aid to Israel and $2 billion to
Egypt – commitments that continue to this day. The settlement is widely regarded as Carter's finest hour as president. It
did bring a new stability to the region, for only Egypt of the
Arab powers could then pose a credible threat to Israel's security. But like détente, the *Mayaguez* affair, and much else in
1970s' diplomacy, it was oversold. The great flaw lay in the
failure to deal conclusively with the Palestinian issue – still the
central problem in the area.[58]

Carter's foreign policies were suffused with a kind of

practical moralism. He wanted to redress the imbalance between the prosperous, industrialized world and the impoverished Third World, though little could be achieved in this era
of domestic economic preoccupation and general anxiety. He
was deeply sympathetic to the cause of black Africa, rejecting
Brzezinski's advice to treat the various crises there as commu-
nist-inspired and accepting instead his United Nations Ambassador Andrew Young's call of "African solutions for
Africa." He championed human rights effectively in Latin
America and cut aid to offending military regimes in Argen-
tina, Brazil, and Chile. Sensitive to Central American populism,
he welcomed the victory of the leftist Sandinista front against
the long-entrenched and thoroughly corrupt Somoza family,
and secured some aid for their initial period in power.

But this approach was repeatedly confounded by grim international realities and, like all idealistic statesmen, Carter
was often charged with hypocrisy. It was noticed, for example, that while he vigorously criticized the Soviets for human
rights abuses, he passed little comment upon similar, arguably much worse Chinese failings. It was seen too that long-
term American allies like President Mobutu of Zaire and King
Hassan of Morocco got off very lightly. Most egregiously, the
Shah of Iran, a durable ally, was fulsomely courted and publicly praised by Carter, who was certainly aware of that government's dismal record of domestic oppression. This was
quickly seen as a mistake when, in February 1979, the funda-
mentalist Muslim, Ayatollah Ruhollah Khomeini, toppled the
Shah and inaugurated a long politico-cultural confrontation
with the United States. Thus a new Middle Eastern crisis was
already simmering dangerously when the OPEC states, including Iran, raised oil prices a further 50 percent in June.[59]

This brings us back to Carter's mountain-top inquest into
the nation's infirmities. A wide assortment of prominent 1970s'
figures – social critics, academic gurus, a sprinkling of politicians, business people – talked in relays as Carter and his wife
dutifully took notes. The country watched suspensefully for a
week. Finally the president returned to Washington and delivered a solemn address on national television. Citing "a crisis

that strikes at the very heart and soul and spirit of our nation" he described a threat to the social and political fabric of America, manifest in the observable decline of hard work, strong families and close communities and the eroding faith in God and other traditional values. Government and legislatures, he insisted, were unable to solve the problem by themselves. The situation demanded a sense of redemption and renewal and above all a self-willed faith in America. He then went on, rather anti-climactically, to call for yet another energy program, the first battlefield, he suggested, in the struggle for active renewal.

Carter's boldly homiletic address, intended to unify, struck an immediately positive public response. He quickly squandered it, however, by firing four senior cabinet secretaries, shocking the public, and reinforcing the growing impression of governmental incompetence. His approval rating sank to its dismal pre-speech level of 25 percent. Commentators took up Senator Kennedy's destructive "malaise" characterization of the speech, though Carter had never used the word. The sociologist of religion, Robert Bellah, one of those consulted at Camp David, thought the speech "pathetic." He had wanted "a serious consideration of what the options are as we move into a different world." Some thought on the other hand that the president had been right in resisting the temptation to rummage profitlessly through failed programs and lost causes. But many found the reduction of modern America's complex problems to an issue of faith very thin gruel. Some remembered unkindly that Carter had toured the country only three years earlier proclaiming, in effect, that America was good but its leaders were bad. Now he was the leader, but the country was apparently going to the dogs.[60]

Time was running out for the Carter administration. In October 1979 the president acceded to a request from the Shah's American friends that he be admitted to the United States for medical treatment. An infuriated mob in Teheran, with Khomeini's approval, seized the American embassy and 69 hostages. Carter thus had to run for re-election while his inability to secure the release of these Americans gave a daily impression of impotence and failure. Only when power was passing to Ronald Reagan in 1981 were the hostages released.

Meanwhile, the Cold War, suddenly returned to unwelcome vigor, was proving itself another hard teacher for the administration. The president's hopes for a transcending, progressively internationalist diplomacy came sharply to grief in December 1979 with Brezhnev's sudden and unforeseen invasion of neighboring Afghanistan. Carter was criticized at the time politically and later by historians for failing to anticipate this event, which was seen on the left as a failure to nourish détente carefully and on the right as irresponsible naivete, an impression heightened by his unwise public complaint that the Soviets had lied to him. In fact the disjunction was less sharp or shocking than it appeared. Carter had been made aware of the conservative opposition when his SALT II treaty, a last flourish of détente signed by he and Brezhnev together in Vienna the previous summer, struck trouble not only in the Senate itself but from outspoken members of the foreign policy establishment. Many of them were now gathered in the Committee on the Present Danger, formed by Paul Nitze and Eugene Rostow in 1976 to rally domestic opposition to what they saw as an increasingly dangerous coddling of the Soviets.[61]

The president was sensitive to this growing body of critical anti-Soviet opinion and in mid-1979 he had begun a large-scale military re-armament program, including a build-up in the Persian Gulf area and the creation of a Rapid Deployment Force for quick action in dangerous Middle Eastern and other trouble spots. The Soviet move into Afghanistan therefore, which seems to have been prompted mainly by fears of internal turbulence in the country's Moslem south, and which was no longer inhibited by a détente in which the Politburo now saw little profit, came after, not before, the reappearance of a new militant impulse in Washington.[62]

Carter nonetheless found it necessary to respond vigorously and publicly. He took a number of radical steps, proclaiming a "Carter Doctrine" promising defense of threatened regimes in the Persian Gulf, the entrance to which was only a few miles from southern Afghanistan, imposing an embargo on wheat and technology exports to the Soviet Union, and declaring that the United States would not participate in the 1980 Moscow Olympic Games. The Cold War was very much alive again.

The economic crisis also deepened in this period. Faced with sharply rising inflation during 1979, Carter called ineffectually, as Ford had before, for voluntary restraints on prices and wages. In part the inflation was due to agricultural price supports, minimum wage increases, industrial benefits, and other structural cost-push factors. As noted, the OPEC price increases made things much worse. With inflation soaring to nearly 13 percent and the dollar declining in a now very competitive international arena, Carter found it necessary to reassure world markets by appointing a Republican financier, Paul Volcker, as Federal Reserve Bank chairman. In a last, almost abdicatory gesture he encouraged Volcker, who needed no prompting, to raise interest rates to an unprecedented 15 percent in late 1979, thus, in historian Peter Carroll's words "virtually ensuring a recession in the coming election year."[63]

The logical political consequences of all these unwelcome developments, especially the economic woes, were a long-building liberal insurgency whose leading figure, Senator Edward Kennedy, announced his campaign for the Democratic nomination late in 1979, and a rapidly growing tide of conservative Republican mobilization as the president's vulnerability became ever more clear. In the gathering gloom the Carter White House could, however, see a gleam of hope. This was the prospect that Ronald Reagan, now 69, might win the GOP nomination. The conventional belief on the American left had long been that Reagan, a second-tier movie star and former Goldwaterite whose polished communicative skills had propelled him into the California governorship in 1966, was an extremist of limited intellectual capacity who, despite his near success in 1976, would be unpalatable to the national electorate. In domestic affairs, Hubert Humphrey sniffed, Reagan was simply "George Wallace sprinkled with eau de cologne." As to his foreign policy credentials Democrats happily disinterred a fear-mongering slogan conjured up by the Ford campaign during the presidential primary campaign in 1976, "Governor Reagan can't start a war. President Reagan could." As they watched Reagan surge ahead of George Bush, Robert Dole, and other presumably more widely appealing GOP contenders, gathering what they complacently saw as a shaky coalition of right-wing zealots, Christian fundamentalists, and economic radicals, the Carter administration began to sense the possibility of an unexpected deliverance.

These attitudes look deeply wrong-headed in retrospect. But, contrary to legend, the 1980 election seems to have been, in Carter biographer Kenneth Morris' words "anybody's race" up to the weekend preceding the vote. Pre-election polls showed that voters favored Reagan on economic issues and as a promoter of "strength," but preferred Carter for "the preservation of peace" and for "character." *Newsweek*'s poll a few days before the vote showed Carter ahead, the Gallup and ABC/Harris tabulations had Reagan leading by a slight margin. The independent candidacy of John Anderson, a Republican liberal, was an unpredictable factor. Exit polls later showed that fully 17 percent of voters waited until the last two weeks before deciding. Carter's own pollster, Patrick Caddell, caught the last-minute swing, predicting on election eve that, "A lot of working Democrats are going to wake up tomorrow and for the first time in their lives vote Republican." In the event Reagan won in a landslide with 489 electoral votes to Carter's 49, drawing sufficiently to bring the Republicans to a Senate majority for the first time since 1953 and an increase of 33 seats in the House of Representatives.[64]

Some commentators have rightly stressed that the Republican victory was not quite as remarkable as this suggests. Reagan's popular vote was smaller than those of Eisenhower, Johnson, and Nixon in his 1972 triumph. The impressive Anderson campaign hurt Carter far more than Reagan. And the late swing suggests the importance of immediately pressing issues: the disenchantment with Carter, especially after his poor debate performance; Reagan's poise and self-confidence; the shocking election day "misery index" of 12 percent inflation and over 15 percent interest rates together with the blight of eight million unemployed; and the on-going hostage crisis in Iran.

It would be unfair, however, to leave this period without noting a remarkable recovery in Jimmy Carter's historiographical image in recent years. The general view through the 1980s and early 1990s was that his had been a failed presidency. A representative critic, historian Burton I. Kaufman, cited the runaway inflation, high interest rates, the energy crisis, the Iranian hostage fiasco, and the failure to delegate effectively among other imperfections. But in the last few years Carter revisionism has produced a much more favorable picture. Notable in this cause have been historians Douglas Brinkley and John Dumbrell and the journalist Martin Walker. They stress variously such neglected accomplishments as Carter's enduringly effective human rights policies, his consistently strong defense program (contrary to the impression of a weak posture before the Soviets pushed into Afghanistan), his successes in environmental and energy policies, and of course his bad luck, recognized by critics and sympathizers alike.[65]

The title of Peter Carroll's book about the 1970s, *It Seemed Like Nothing Happened*, conveys something of the emotional let-down many felt after the excitements of the previous decade. Yet there was more real change in the latter years. Nixon took office in 1969 after a year of violence and theatrical political display. But he was still able to preside over a solidly united governmental establishment, firmly led by a powerful executive, and a society that was disturbed and confused but structurally and functionally much as it had been since World War II. Ten years later this was not the case. In politics there had been a powerful shift in authority from the executive to Congress and in some degree from both to the judiciary, and more broadly from Washington to the states and localities. Central control of the economy – increasingly plagued by inflation, unemployment, and declining productivity – was moving toward the Federal Reserve leadership. In the business world the corporate "national champion" of the 1950s had typically merged, reorganized, or dissolved into a wide variety of multinational or domestic units that were less responsive to government guidance. Socially and culturally the old authoritative WASP hegemony had declined sharply as a pluralistic combination of minority and ethnic groups claimed a long-deferred place in the sun, a reminder that there were positive aspects in all this reshuffling. By the late 1970s it was no longer possible to celebrate the American family as a redoubt of security and tranquility. Many religious denominations alarmed their followers by throwing doctrine to the winds in an unnerving show of spiritual and organizational reinvention. The media in general were more powerful than ever and aggressively intrusive, though the television networks themselves were now confronting fragmentation thanks to the threat of cable. Perhaps most dramatic in all this spiraling downwind was the decline of American power in world affairs. A decade that began with Nixon's bleak recognition that he confronted a multi-polar rather than the congenial, post-Hiroshima bi-polar world order, proceeded with a galling demonstration by the Middle East oil producers of the nation's inability to respond effectively to politico-economic pressure, and ended with an even greater humiliation at the hands of Iran, as a well as a chilling rejection of détente by the Soviet Union.

It is hardly surprising then that historians often take a dim view of the 1970s, though David Frum's recent "slum of a decade" characterization seems excessive. For the positive, counter-balancing aspects of this period are also striking. As old hierarchies faltered there was an enormous if finally unmeasurable accession of openness, tolerance, and public consideration for others in almost every sphere of American life. We see this in the increasingly confident assertiveness and self-empowerment of women, of ethnic Americans, of racial minorities, gays, the handicapped, and many others. There was inevitably a degree of resulting tension and discomfort. Once established the emergent groups soon showed that they could effectively promote their interests and defend themselves. A new range of social taboos and an inhibiting "political correctness" came in with the new pluralism. But on balance the level of human dignity and group respect was substantially improved and the various transformations reflected the resilience and moral vitality of American society. There were also specific reassurances. The Watergate outcome, for instance, demonstrated that the United States was indeed governed by law and could survive the most insidious of threats. One can cite too the sophistication of a mass electorate that could overwhelmingly endorse Richard Nixon in 1972 and equally approve his dislodgment in 1974. The success in 1976 of Jimmy Carter, virtually unknown to Washington insiders hitherto, similarly challenged cynicism about the openness of American politics.[66]

One thing was as clear to contemporaries as it is to us. Ronald Reagan's victory in 1980 marked what seems to have been the most profound impulse at work: the return, after a brief Watergate-induced Democratic recovery, to the conservative trend in American politics. This had been driven mainly since 1968 by the reaction of white southerners to the civil rights revolution and by the new affluence and social conservatism of millions of Catholic and ethnic voters who were now inclined to consider voting Republican. But one has only to compare Nixon's 1968 and 1972 campaigns with Reagan's more broadly ecumenical approach in 1980, to see that the range of so-called "conservative opinion" was now much more varied, more closely refined politically into distinct groups or voting blocs, and much more self-conscious and confident than it had been earlier. It was largely his skill in appealing to and uniting this wider range of conservatives (especially former Democratic voters of working class origins like himself) that brought Reagan his victory. And it is to this conservative triumph, and the transformations it brought in both the domestic and international realms, that we now turn.

6

Ronald Reagan and the End of the Cold War Era

Conservatism on the Threshold

There is, as yet, little authoritative scholarly guidance to the 1980s. Historiographically speaking it is a kind of frontier experience. Still, the definitional phrases we find in the scant literature are suggestive. The widely remarked purposefulness and linearity of the Reagan–Bush era does seem distinctive in retrospect. We might not wish to go as far as the editors of one widely read anthology who insist that "When Ronald Reagan assumed office in January of 1981, an epoch in the nation's political history came to an end. The New Deal, as a dominant order of ideas, public policies, and political alliances, died, however much its ghost still hovers over a troubled polity."[1] For one of the great emerging questions is whether the Reagan era was "revolutionary" or simply a continuation, in sharply modified form to be sure, of earlier trends.

Certain broad issues call for preliminary comment. One is the character of 1980s' conservatism. Like its liberal foil, which it resembled in several respects, it was not a coherent set of interrelated doctrines. Insofar as it was a political philosophy it served to express and rationalize its adherents' interests and emotions. It derived, like liberalism, from a venerable and heterogeneous collection of Anglo-American intellectual sources including, variously, Adam Smith's laissez-faire economic doctrines, John Stuart Mill's libertarian ethics, and Ralph Waldo Emerson's notions of self-reliance and independence, augmented in the Reagan era by daring appropriations of fashionable modern thinkers like Frederic Hayek, George Orwell, and many others.

The fact that most of these iconic figures were also in some sense "liberal" is a conundrum that perhaps reflects a certain lack of intellectual rigor in American public life. Historian Gary Gerstle, noting "the protean character of American liberalism" attributes this in part to its role as a surrogate socialism. But this hardly accommodates the conservative "liberals" who were in no way left-wing, nor does it do justice to what Leo Ribuffo reminds us was the persisting strength in American conservatism. The essential point seems to be the adaptability of liberalism as a centering political philosophy to which both left and right found it tempting to lay claim. Just as liberalism evolved in American conditions from nineteenth-century small-government individualism to the vast Rooseveltian collectivist/welfare state, so modern conservatism, while aggressively appropriating as opportunity offered the old liberal verities abandoned by the New Deal, went on in enterprising fashion to embrace new or reinvigorated causes – anti-communism, fierce resistance to modernist culture, monetarist economics – that enhanced its political appeal. Yet its devotees remained, again resembling their liberal antagonists, wedded to clusters of beliefs and impulses that were structurally loose and coalitional in their political expression.[2]

This sense of intellectual diffusion is amply reflected in the variety of strains in Reagan-era conservatism. They included, for instance, not only the residues of late nineteenth-century laissez-faire individualism and the anti-statism of Mill, but uneasily co-existing corporate and small-business sectors, a passionate claque of free market economic reformers of monetarist, anti-Keynesian views, a long-rooted intellectual right-wing perspective claiming descent from the Anglo-Irish sage Edmund Burke and epitomized by William F. Buckley's *National Review*, a strident new group of neo-conservative apostates from liberalism, foreign policy hawks from the

Kennedy–Johnson administrations and, bringing a dose of populist political realism to all this heady jostling, a mass of newly affluent Catholics (among them, as historian Patrick Allitt has shown, some influential intellectuals) and freshly mobilized southern Protestant activists with a very clear conservative cultural agenda. Not, one might think, a group instinctively susceptible to a call for unity. Yet hardly less so, surely, than the southerners, urban immigrants, union bosses, and intellectuals who had underpinned Truman era liberalism.

What brought these only marginally akin conservatives together in the 1980s? Historian Alan Brinkley draws attention to the pent-up "frustrations of political exile in the 1930s and 1940s, the passion of the anti-communist crusades of the late 1940s and early 1950s, and perhaps above all the political and cultural upheavals of the 1960s and 1970s."[3] More specifically we can identify three powerfully compelling unifying forces. The first, which virtually all historians have noticed, was a widespread sense of decline in the material conditions of American life, which most conservatives attributed mainly to liberal Democratic excess and incompetence. This manifested itself most obviously in the ailing economy of the 1970s, especially in the disturbing phenomenon of stagflation and the felt oppression of a tax code that persistently carried politically sensitive middle-class Americans into higher tax brackets. The standard of living was felt to be deteriorating. People were working harder – the two-income family was now ubiquitous – yet falling behind. Secondly, a decline was also widely sensed in the advance of the new permissive culture that threatened family structures, violated traditional religious teaching, and seemed to undermine civic virtue. The passionate campaign against abortion after the 1973 *Roe* v. *Wade* decision was a powerful conservative mobilizing cause.

There was also, thirdly, an almost universal feeling that American power and prestige in the world was diminishing. In large part this impulse was economic, a sense of quickening displacement in world markets as German and Japanese competition grew rapidly. The international character of the 1970s' economic crisis is worth emphasizing for it marks a transformation in American history. In 1945 the US economy had still been remarkably self-contained and American life moved largely to its own self-generated rhythm. In 1979/80, however, the changes in economic direction, tentatively initiated by President Carter and accelerated by Ronald Reagan, were very clearly part of a broad international movement away from state-directed, collectivist postwar liberalism toward a more open, entrepreneurial, individualistic 'growth' scenario. Two dates stand out. In 1973 the unforeseen Arab oil embargo, appearing in a pre-existing context of apparently uncontrollable inflation and rising unemployment, set off a global crisis. In 1979 Margaret Thatcher's British Conservative government came to power pledged to growth rather than equitable distribution, to the partial destruction of the welfare state, and to whatever stimulation could be produced by the deregulation of a stagnant economy. This set the stage for Reagan's very similar measures in 1981.

But the revival of Cold War passions is even more striking. Here once again, seemingly, was a menacing Soviet Union and expansionary communism in all its treacherously concealed forms. And here the Reagan right-wing found its primary mission. For decades New Deal liberals and Eisenhower moderates in their vigorous Cold War activism had systematically stolen the conservative thunder. Now the diplomatic failure of both Nixonian détente and Carter's international humanism, together with a growing public conviction that the Soviets had never really changed, indeed had deceitfully used the 1970s lull to get ahead in the arms race while post-Vietnam America rested on its oars, helped create the conservative revival that led to Reagan's presidency. And now, along a spectrum that ran from the Committee on the Present Danger through the various layers of the foreign policy establishment and media to the easily roused masses of the ethnic urban communities and the country-oriented religious right, there was a pervasive sense of the need to catch up.

The crucial element that brought the right-wing to power was the national emergence of Ronald Reagan. Erratic or ineffectual leadership had been the right's chronic problem.

Robert Taft had lacked charisma, McCarthy had been an eccentric crusading loner, in no sense a political organizer, Goldwater seemed to have unavailingly pushed western, cowboy-boot libertarianism to its limits in 1964. The unfair but pervasive liberal caricature of the American right-wing as an assortment of tub-thumpers, bible-bangers, and carpet-chewers had been a staple of political cartoon imagery up to the late 1970s. And Ronald Reagan, another passionate conservative apparently far removed from the moderate, successful Eisenhower/Nixon strain of Republicanism, seemed to many observers unelectable.

But Reagan turned out to be a skilful political leader with a clear understanding of the distinctive aims of the disparate groups in play on the American right. He took full advantage of the new corporate and foundation funding now available and of the sophisticated networking and direct-mailing techniques that cultural conservatives had been perfecting for years before 1980. To these elements he added both a Hollywood actor's professional gift for televisual communication and an appealing personality.

Yet he was always, despite what historian Paul Boyer has aptly described as "an almost mesmeric" hold on public affection during his presidency, a controversial leader. Liberal media criticism was relentless. *The New York Times'* James Reston ridiculed "his amiable incompetence, his tolerance of dubs and sleaze, his cronyism, his preoccupation with stars, his indifference to facts and convenient forgetfulness." Historian Arthur Schlesinger Jr. similarly found his administration "incoherent, incompetent, duplicitous and dedicated to rash, mindless policy." Such comment was common on the liberal left throughout the Reagan years. Even when he confounded expectations in his second term by apparently collaborating in the dismantlement of the Cold War he gained no real purchase on the left. The indictment simply shifted from charges of warmongering to allegations of irresponsible detachment from policy in general. In 1989 the *New Republic's* leading columnist scoffed at the notion that so limited a leader could leave "a Reagan legacy." Academics showed little respect. *The*

End of the Cold War: Its Meaning and Implications, a book published in 1992 featuring the views of 22 scholars, contains only three personal references to Ronald Reagan. In retrospect this air of contempt and casual dismissal can be seen as an invitational overture to the limited labors of official biographer, Edmund Morris, who, given the unparalleled advantage of highly paid close observation in the White House, emerged after a decade of rumination with nothing more than an abdicatory semi-fictional, "hollow man" portrait of his subject.[4]

But there were always staunch defenders of Reagan and his administration on the increasingly assertive intellectual right-wing, which was fortified from the mid-1970s by a profusion of conservative think tanks and journals. A 1993 retrospective conference at Hofstra University brought a strongly argued defense of Reagan's presidency. Many participants – former administration officials and independent outsiders – credited him with a considerable degree of insight and political skill. Several argued that he had shown an astute understanding of Soviet strengths and weaknesses, and that his powerful military build-up had been decisive in causing them to throw in the towel. Among professional historians John Lewis Gaddis has been prominent in applauding Reagan for a modulated performance – focus on American strength in the first term, willingness to deal constructively with Soviet leader Mikhail Gorbachev in the second – that was a crucial element in preparing the final unraveling of the Cold War. And a recent study by Frances Fitzgerald, though critical in several respects, reveals a talented politician with a rare and instinctive understanding of his constituency's deepest impulses.[5]

A more definitive judgment, one suspects, will come from a much fuller exploration of the two great concerns that clearly preoccupied Reagan during his presidency. One was the role of the state. Reagan showed a visceral dislike of what he saw as the bloated postwar American federal establishment with its tendency to inhibit the American economy by constant intrusion and officious regulation and the ever-lengthening tail of importunate dependents fastened upon it by the liberal

Democratic establishment. In practice, as we will shortly see, this mostly meant war on excessive controls and taxation. His other great cause, which will claim our first attention, was Soviet communism. Reagan's long battle against the radical left on the domestic front had begun with his successful campaign to keep communists and radicals out of the Screen Actors Guild, of which he was president for several years in the late 1940s and early 1950s. It intensified with his outspoken support for Goldwater in 1964 and then as a conservative television celebrant for General Electric. Later he attracted much attention during his governorship as the hammer of student radicalism on the University of California's Berkeley campus. Now, brought to power on a tide of suddenly renewed mass concern about the Soviet threat, he was in a position to wage the Cold War in earnest.

Renewal: Containment with Teeth

The Reagan administration quickly changed the tone of American foreign policy. President Carter's approach was essentially universalistic and rights-oriented. His decision to refurbish the military and renew confrontational diplomacy with the Soviet Union was a reluctant response to an unanticipated threat. It was a legacy that Reagan nevertheless took up eagerly and turned to his own purposes. Human rights was immediately superseded by national security as the diplomatic mantra. International law was subordinated to national interest. World trade and north/south economic global issues, often prominent in the 1970s and again in the 1990s, faded in this more geopolitically focused decade. The Middle East continued to force attention sporadically – notably with the hostage crises in Lebanon and later the Iran–Iraqi war – but the new administration showed much less taste for involvement with Israel's problems. Nor was there much sustained interest in relations with China. The Asian theater of the Cold War was comparatively quiet during the Reagan years, and China was still seen, as it had been through the 1970s, as a kind of partner against the Soviet Union. For this was now the principal concern. The focus was on two contested arenas: Europe, where Soviet power was once again seriously menacing; and a long chain of peripheral trouble spots – especially Afghanistan, Cambodia, and Central America – where the possibility of low-cost but dramatic success was alluring.

Reagan led an administration that has been variously described as remarkable for its "ideological purity" and, conversely, "a coalition" representing "almost every range of thought in the Republican Party."[6] It is not likely, however, that Robert Taft, Dwight Eisenhower, or representatives of the old east coast elite would have felt comfortable here. There were, certainly, some prominent old Nixon hands, comparative moderates like the two successive Secretaries of State: Alexander Haig and George Schultz. But the more doctrinaire Goldwater strain was uppermost, represented by Reagan himself, CIA Director William Casey, the devoutly hard-line National Security Advisers Richard Allen and William Clark, Secretary of Defense Caspar Weinberger (once a Nixonian pragmatist but now a fanatical anti-communist), and United Nations Ambassador Jeanne Kirkpatrick. And at a second level, where the staffing was rigidly controlled for ideological consistency by a tiny coterie of White House Reaganites – notably Michael Deaver and Edwin Meese III – we find an energetic group of young State and Defense Department conservatives including Richard Perle, Kenneth Adelman, and Elliot Abrams, all skilled in polemics and the trench warfare of political Washington.

The left-liberal critique of Reagan's foreign policy holds, alternatively, that he was either a doctrinaire anti-communist who exaggerated the Soviet menace and pursued politically and economically irresponsible counter-measures – a portrait drawn mainly from his first term – or an ignorant and personally detached president who was little more than an accomplished front man for the purposeful group he nominally led, an assessment focused principally on the later years. Neither view seems intellectually satisfying today. While there is undoubtedly much to question in the Reagan record the image of fecklessness, at least, is confuted by the remarkably systematic course he followed between 1979 and 1984. For when a full defense of his presidency is mounted it will surely identify three successive, highly purposeful stages. In the first phase, from 1979 through 1980, he concentrated upon making the case that the Soviet Union had become dangerously stronger, thus upsetting the balance of power. In the second, 1981–84, his effort was directed to the actual rebuilding of American military strength. And in the third, from 1984 onwards, apparently satisfied that he could now negotiate from the classic position of strength advocated by western anti-Soviet statesmen from Churchill to Nixon, he reached out to the pre-Gorbachev Soviet leadership, tentatively but perhaps sincerely, for more productive high level meetings and arms control negotiations.

Reagan had used the 1980 election to make the case that while post-Vietnam America had become weak under a naïve, incompetent Democratic leadership, the Soviets had moved ahead both in nuclear weaponry and in the apparently successful sponsorship of several new communist or proto-communist regimes in Asia, Africa, and Central America. The core of his case was that while U.S. defense spending had declined the Soviets had developed sufficient nuclear striking power to achieve a potentially successful offensive capacity. Nor were the Soviets to be trusted. Reagan went out of his way to express publicly his contempt for the Soviet system. He accused its leaders of deceit in his first presidential press conference and went on to tell the British House of Commons that communism was destined to end on the scrap heap. Most famously, in a 1983 speech, he characterized the Soviet Union as "an evil empire."

It was therefore from an established basis in public support that Reagan was able to prepare and then push through Congress a 1981 defense budget that came in at $184 billion (compared to Carter's last budget of $134 billion) and was declared to be the beginning of a massive five-year build-up to cost $1.6 trillion. This inevitably became a central aspect of the general Reagan economic policy that will concern us later.

For the moment the noteworthy features are the enormous increase in funding; the absolute refusal of Reagan to compromise on his defense estimates ("Whatever you need," he told Weinberger) even when errors in administration accounting forced some budgetary adjustments; and the sheer material scope of a program that was intended to create a 600-ship navy, a new nuclear submarine, the B-I bomber (shelved by Carter earlier), a new tank for the army, and up to 17,000 new nuclear missiles.

Critics then and since have indicted this as a grossly excessive and economically self-wounding response to an exaggerated Soviet threat. One historian, noting that Reagan's last defense budget was $298 billion, estimates that the administration's real increase over Carter's spending, allowing for inflation, was 71 percent. As economist Anne Markusen remarks, "During the Reagan years the United States went on the biggest peacetime splurge in its history."[7] However, it looks a little different in comparative perspective. Carter's Defense Secretary, Harold Brown, for instance, estimated in 1980 that, in terms of relative defense spending, the Soviet advantage over the United States was between 25 and 45 percent. Another estimate has the Soviets spending between 15 and 20 percent of its GNP on defense in the 1980s – a significant clue to its accelerating internal crisis. Moreover, political scientist Dennis Ippolito has demonstrated that in the Reagan years military spending never rose beyond 6.5 percent of GNP. This compares eloquently with Eisenhower's 1954–59 average level of 10.4 percent and the Kennedy–Johnson level in 1960–64 of 9.3 percent – both peacetime periods.[8]

Further, the military build-up was widely supported because of the apparent reappearance of Soviet expansionary tendencies, directly in Afghanistan and indirectly in Africa, Asia, and Central America. Most alarming was the growing crisis in Europe inspired by the Kremlin's installation during Carter's last months of intermediate range missiles targeting principal European cities. A complement to their strategic missile strength aimed at the United States, these shorter range weapons inevitably revived in acute form the old West European fear that they might be decoupled from their American guarantor. Would an American president, following a perhaps "limited" Soviet strike upon a European target, honor the NATO pledge and launch an almost certainly suicidal retaliatory blow upon the Soviet Union? No one really knew. In political terms the situation, if unaddressed, seemed likely to lead to "Finlandization," a scenario in which West European governments might well shrink from actions unpalatable to the Soviets.

The developing crisis of confidence called for some bold reaffirmation of NATO solidarity and American credibility. Consequently, in 1979, President Carter and the NATO allies had agreed that the United States would respond by installing its own intermediate range Pershing and cruise missiles on European soil. To placate European public opinion, where there were intense forebodings about the growing nuclearization of the continent, the allies agreed to pursue a "dual track" process of arms control negotiations with Moscow. As the negotiations developed in 1981–82 Reagan contributed what came to be known as the "zero-option." If the Soviets would dismantle their missiles the American ones would not be installed. At the time few expected the Soviets to accept this and even the president's principal arms control delegate, Paul Nitze, considered it an unduly hard-nosed approach that lessened any chance of agreement.

Here again we find the Reagan administration following the Carter footprints, but with a much firmer tread. Two problems quickly emerged. The first was the anticipated refusal of the Soviets to back down. This forced the United States to go ahead with the installations in 1983, which prompted a breakdown in the talks. The second was a remarkable eruption, in the United States as well as in Europe, of popular anti-nuclear protest. This phenomenon was familiar enough in Europe. There had been large spasmodic demonstrations there since the 1950s. But this one was more widespread, passionate, and better organized, mobilizing many in Britain, Germany, and France who considered Reagan a "warmonger" and wished devoutly to return to détente. Some governments felt threatened. Communist agitators were blamed, of course, but it was clear that the sense of alarm was general. Many Europeans read a 1978 book by Sir John Hackett, a former NATO general, ominously titled *The Third World War: August 1985*. It demonstrated with authoritative plausibility how easily nuclear war might come in Europe, and how devastating it might be in densely populated areas.[9]

A similarly hostile public reaction in the United States seems to have surprised the Reagan administration. Here too there were dramatically frightening literary scenarios including astronomer Carl Sagan's vivid portrayal of a "nuclear winter" and journalist Jonathan Schell's 1982 book *The Fate of the Earth*, which envisioned the total destruction of all human life by nuclear war.[10] A television documentary in 1983 called *The Day After* gave a mass audience a horrific yet credible sense of the likely aftermath of a Soviet missile attack on an American city. Meanwhile, a strong public campaign came together around the call for a "nuclear freeze" that would outlaw any further testing or deployment by either side. This became, briefly, a major force in national politics and a "freeze" resolution in the House of Representatives lost by only two votes.

In a March 23, 1983 speech Reagan warned that "A freeze now would make us less, not more secure and would raise, not reduce, the risks of war." He then went on to launch his famous Strategic Defense Initiative (SDI). "Let me share with you a vision of the future which offers hope," he told the American people. "It is that we embark on a program to counter the awesome Soviet missile threat with measures that are defensive." He described a system that could destroy incoming missiles, holding out the promise of a return to pre-1945 immunity and security, "An effort which holds the purpose of changing the course of human history."[11] The origins of Reagan's dramatic proposal (soon branded "Star Wars" by Senator Edward Kennedy) have received the attention appropriate to a project that was greeted by many with skepticism and by some with ridicule but has nevertheless survived to this day having run up thus far a research and development bill of about $60 billion. Some thought it was simply an attempt to defuse the nuclear freeze clamor. Others suspected that the bitterly anti-communist nuclear physicist Edward Teller, who championed it passionately, had got to Reagan in an intellectually unguarded moment. Most recently Frances Fitzgerald has argued that a 1979 visit to the North American Command base inside Cheyenne Mountain, Colorado – a surreal, Strangelovian nuclear nerve center with computers and radar detectors that could track incoming Soviet missiles and sound the alert – marked the epiphanic moment for the horrified presidential candidate. Perhaps more weight should be given to the steady accumulation of evidence that Ronald Reagan genuinely hated nuclear weapons. Lou Cannon, generally recognized as the Washington journalist who knew him best, insists that he was "a nuclear abolitionist from day one." He seems to have seen his "zero-option" in this light rather than as a political ploy, and as early as May 1982 he had laid out in a speech at Eureka College plans for bilateral nuclear reductions that later reappeared as the basis of the Strategic Arms Reduction Treaty proposals put to the Soviets.[12]

However that may be the SDI speech was not very well received. Few thought the project was technologically feasible. And it clearly jeopardized the fragile balance of terror maintained by the formal 1972 commitment by the two superpowers not to defend themselves, thus rendering a surprise first strike by either of them suicidal because it was bound to trigger a retaliatory blow that would fall on undefended targets. Since the Nixon–Kissinger era each side had professed to be observing this, agreeing to build only two (later only one) anti-ballistic systems (ABMs) to protect the decision-making centers. Reagan's threat (as Moscow was bound to see it) to build a comprehensive defensive system raised the prospect of an American first strike, upsetting many in the United States and around the world as well as the Soviet leadership. Further, the obvious high cost of the proposed system challenged the Soviets to a new arms race for which, we see more clearly now, they had neither the technology nor the money.

In retrospect, then, the nuclear protesters of the early 1980s had much to worry about. In general the two superpowers seemed to be creating an ever-more nuclearized world, with an expected extension into space and the emergence of a new generation of missiles and satellites. Both seemed to millions of watching Americans (and many others) to be behaving irresponsibly: the Soviets by trying through their intermediate range missile siting to decouple Western Europe from its American ally; the United States by threatening through the SDI to subvert Soviet confidence in a reasonably safe nuclear balance. It is hardly surprising that the public was unusually deeply engaged in the Cold War politics of these years.

On the other main front of the renewed Cold War we can see the persistence of the inhibiting "Vietnam syndrome" in the similar press and public questioning of the Reagan administration's vigorous opposition to Soviet and communist (or radical) activities in peripheral Cold War arenas. Carter had inaugurated aid programs to the Afghan resistance and to anti-Marxist elements in Angola. Reagan accelerated these and started others, notably in Central America. His policies were alternately bold and cautious. Thus, while focusing obsessively upon the downfall of the relatively strong Sandinista regime in Nicaragua he nevertheless refrained from direct military action. But he seized the chance, in October 1983, to send troops to topple the Marxist rulers of the tiny Caribbean island of Grenada who were close to Castro and looking for Soviet military aid. He was almost as quick, in February 1984, to withdraw US forces from Lebanon after 230 Marines were killed by a suicide truck-bomber. In April 1986, however, there was another brief flash of the sword as the Air Force was sent to bomb Libyan targets after its government had seemingly sponsored terrorist attacks upon American citizens in Berlin. Later President George Bush would send troops in a similarly rapid invasion strike against the dictatorship in Panama. The emphasis throughout was upon vivid but politically economic displays of renewed American power and resolve.

In reluctant recognition of widespread skepticism about its motives the administration devoted some effort to the conceptual dimension. CIA Director William Casey, for example, often urged the importance of geopolitical thinking, especially in resisting communist threats to the world's sea-lanes. More concrete was Jeanne Kirkpatrick's much-publicized distinction between Soviet and associated "totalitarian" enemies, who were beyond redemption and must be resisted, and "authoritarian" regimes that might with support evolve toward democracy and should be helped when menaced by communism. This became a foundation of the so-called "Reagan Doctrine" which was distilled from the president's second inaugural speech in 1985 in which he justified American support for robust anti-communist "roll-back" efforts round the world.[13]

The principal non-European theater of action was the very traditional one of Central America. There were two main related problems: in Nicaragua a radical left if not fully communist regime; and a vicious civil war in neighboring Salvador where the Sandinistas were supporting the leftist guerillas. The American response called for free elections and moderate solutions but in practice favored, not always approvingly, the right-wing elements in each country. Policy was officially justified, in the main, by reference to two prior decades of confrontation with Castro's Cuba and fears of Soviet penetration and communist contagion throughout the region. But the roots of American involvement are, of course, much deeper, going back at least to the casual, self-willed, finally chronic intrusions of the Theodore Roosevelt/Woodrow Wilson era. Then too the principal justification for American action was usually the danger of European interference. But now, in the more socially conscious 1980s, many saw American interventions as prolonging tragic social inequities and economic dependency. "Radical takeovers were hardly surprising," comments historian David Reynolds, "given the dominance of the region by repressive elites that were sustained by the United States."[14] It is hardly remarkable, perhaps, that while the orthodox, affirming historiography of American diplomacy tends to dwell congenially upon Europe and the scarcely impeachable record of constructive American expeditionary military and economic efforts there, the principal focus of critical revisionist historians is often upon the effect of Washington's policies in and around Central America, where the record is much more difficult to defend, being little distinguishable in some respects from European imperialism.

Nevertheless, if we are to understand the problem fully, it is important not to overstate this or to take an excessively moralistic view. Three points can be made in defense of Reagan-era policies in this region. First, there was then more reason to be concerned about the consequences of radical turbulence in Central America than in prior decades. A Marxist might well think, and many did, that the revolutionary denouement was at hand in the early 1980s, with the Sandinistas, the Salvadoran rebels, and the Grenada Marxists setting the pace with Cuban and Soviet support. The fate of Mexico, viewed as unstable in Washington at the best of times, was now seen by many officials as being at stake. In this situation no American administration was likely to take a detached view. Second, the Caribbean/Central American region is, quite apart from its Cold War aspect, a primary and legitimate US interest. As the revisionist scholar Walter LaFeber has pointed out nearly two-thirds of American trade flows through the Caribbean. The Panama Canal was another concern. And third, while its efforts often seem to have been inspired by nothing more elevated than a desire to aid self-interested American corporations or forestall desirable reforms, the US government from FDR to Carter had spasmodically provided a degree of social and economic aid. The Reagan administration's contribution, the 1983 Caribbean Basin Initiative, offered trade benefits and incentives together with plans for long-term development.[15]

Still, the Reagan record in Nicaragua is hard to defend. For here we find disturbing conduct stubbornly persisted in long after public support had faded. As the Sandinista leftist (never explicitly communist) core became dominant and began to carry out some radical social reforms, Reagan, with military action politically impossible, set the CIA to aid and train a local opposition which was itself increasingly governed by a rightist group whose guerilla fighting force (the so-called "contras") was composed largely of former Somozaist

National Guardsmen. CIA operatives tutored the contras in tactics, including, lamentably, brutal methods of interrogation. They inspired them to bomb oil storage and other government facilities and to place mines in the country's Atlantic ports, which damaged several Soviet ships. This led the International Court of Justice, upon Nicaraguan petition, to declare the United States in violation of international law. Much of this was fully exposed in the American press, leading to a rapid decline in public and congressional support for the activism of the Reagan administration, which consequently began a dangerous lurch toward covert action.

As the 1984 election drew closer Reagan's prospects looked mixed. The economy was only now beginning to emerge from the worst postwar recession. Critics suggested that his enormous budget deficits and continuing high interest rates might chill the recovery. He had united his party effectively and in foreign policy he had established a clear image as a purposeful, resolute national leader. Millions were glad to see America, in the contemporary idiom, "standing tall" again; an impression of renewed strength enhanced by the success of American athletes at the summer Olympic Games in Los Angeles. But here too there was criticism: of policy in Central America, which did not seem to be working; and of the president's apparent lack of interest in any sort of negotiation with the Soviet Union.

This last consideration was viewed by many commentators as the explanation of a surprisingly conciliatory speech Reagan gave on January 16, 1984. Instead of his more familiar anti-Soviet theme he pointed in more general terms to the threat of war created by "vast stockpiles" of nuclear weapons. He repeated his call for the zero-option in Europe. But he emphasized that reducing the risk of nuclear war was "priority number one," and suggested that the United States and the Soviet Union faced the same common perils: "poverty, disease, and above all, war." He called for reduced nuclear arsenals and the removal of "misunderstandings" associated with the "gap in Soviet and American perceptions" in world affairs. Most strongly he urged a rapprochement with Moscow.

"We must establish a better working relationship, one marked by greater cooperation and understanding."[16]

Since the unraveling of the Cold War some historians have attributed great importance to this speech. Beth Fischer, for example, sees it as "the first step toward defusing superpower hostilities even before Moscow showed signs of change." This tallies with Reagan biographer Lou Cannon's belief that the president always intended to negotiate with Moscow over nuclear weapon reduction and had simply delayed until the American arms build-up was in place. Similarly, his first and very conservative National Security Adviser, Richard Allen, notes that Reagan was "always a disarmer at heart.' And as early as 1983 he had only at the last minute been dissuaded by Allen's equally hawkish successor, William Clark, from writing to Soviet leader Andropov that he believed reduction of nuclear weapons should be "a first step toward the elimination of all such weapons." In the same spirit he told a news conference in June 1984 that he was not in fact against summit meetings and was "willing to meet and talk anytime."[17]

These do not appear to have been politically inspired impulses. On the very day of the election he told an interviewer that he was indeed committed to "peace and disarmament." A few days later, encouraged by Secretary of State Schultz, he wrote to the new Soviet leader, Konstantin Chernenko, proposing comprehensive talks covering offensive and space weaponry and including strategic and intermediate range missiles. Chernenko accepted and Schultz and Gromyko planned a meeting for January 1985.

In retrospect all this looks portentous, and when we examine the remarkable post-1984 phase of Reagan's diplomacy we must consider the extent to which these early green shoots of reconciliation deserve recognition as causative factors in the eventual winding up of the Cold War. To be sure no one was expecting so profound an outcome in 1984. If Ronald Reagan in the allegedly unfathomable recesses of his mind believed he might be instrumental in bringing about the end of the Cold War he gave no sign of it. To this point we might be justified in seeing him as neither the warmonger of left-wing imagery nor the far-seeing visionary of today's right-wing memory, but rather a conventional American Cold War statesman following the Churchill–Nixon adage that one can only deal with the Soviets from a position of strength. The expectations were, at best, for some modest degree of arms control. Even this was problematic given both persisting Soviet sullenness on the one hand and the influence of the administration's hard-line majority (which was already beginning to mobilize against any further relaxation) on the other. Indeed, as tensions with the Soviets began to abate during 1985 and then move rapidly toward a new détente, so in proportion deep fissures began to open up within the hitherto united Reagan administration.

The Domestic Re-Ordering

Ronald Reagan was unusual among modern presidents in that he came to office calling for fundamental change in both foreign policy and domestic priorities. To some extent this was deceptive for, as we have seen, his much-maligned predecessor had already laid some of the crucial groundwork. But the change of emphasis was sharp nonetheless – a move from human rights and universalism to national interests and security in diplomacy, and from equitable distribution to growth at home.

This sounds simple enough but the desired transformation presented problems of leadership. Reagan certainly came in with a strong, clear mandate. But the coalition he led was heterogeneous. The vigorously stoked renewal of anti-Soviet emotion, the enhanced military, and the active, not to say aggressive diplomacy proved to be excellent unifying elements. But domestic change would inevitably be more challenging with the potential to expose divisions in the disparate web of assertive, expectant groups, movements, and opinions that lay behind the impressive front of Republican solidarity.

There was, for instance, the Republican bedrock of small town America where Reagan's own roots lay and which historian Lisle Rose has persuasively placed at the heart of 1950s' conservatism. Then its center had been the Taftite mid-west. Now it took in an infinity of like communities all over the country. Here there was a ready response to Reagan's efforts to restore American prestige in the world and a fresh, optimistic spirit in the national life. But there was still, as sociologist Jonathan Rieder reminds us, a deep suspicion of Wall Street and the large corporations that must surely be the primary instruments and first beneficiaries of any economic stimulus. And there was division in the business world itself. Recent work by Kim McQuaid has recently put several stereotypes in question by demonstrating the persistence of another old fault line in American politics, the gulf in 1979/80 between the many large corporations, which were actually comfortable with their federal connections (and had not favored Reagan for the Republican nomination) and the more populist, small business, individualistic, entrepreneurial line associated with his successful campaign. Further, many business people of all kinds were deeply skeptical about the supply-side innovators who seemed to have the new president's ear. Then there were the "cultural conservatives" – an umbrella term that variously covered Protestant fundamentalists, observant Catholics, and other improbable bedfellows including a tiny but influential ginger group of ardent Jewish neo-conservatives who co-existed uneasily with the more traditional right-wing gurus grouped around William Buckley's *National Review*.[18]

Reagan appears to have set certain priorities. Diplomatic and domestic renewal were in large measure interrelated, for the rebuilding of the American military was in essence a legislative, budgetary issue. Still, he clearly decided to put his economic package ahead of cultural issues, a choice the parlous stagflation would have forced upon any president. But the charge made then and later, by conservative columnists like Jeffrey Hart and George Will, that he either abandoned or at least failed to press the cultural agenda – anti-abortion, anti-busing and an end to affirmative action, endorsement of school prayer, and other causes – does not really stand up as we will see later. From the start, and throughout his presidency, he consistently applied his rhetorical skills to the propagation of traditional American family and moral precepts. He filled his administration with conservatives who worked away at different parts of the liberal Washington edifice with termitic vigor. He flooded the judiciary, seen on the right as a primary instrument of cultural regeneration, with right-wing appointees. And he worked throughout to create a politically conservative mood and context, not least at the very beginning of his tenure when he was confronted with a general strike by the air traffic controllers union. He dismissed the strikers, called in substitutes from the military and other sources, and survived the dangerous transition without accidents. The effect was to establish his image as a courageous, fortunate leader. He had little trouble with the labor movement thereafter.[19]

But the principal early focus was economic. Here too he acted boldly from the start. While aides prepared legislative proposals for lower taxes, enhanced military appropriations, and cuts in social spending, Reagan pushed Carter's comparably modest deregulation drive (confined to transportation and a few other industries) into high gear. The war on red tape and federal supervision culminated in the notorious license given to savings and loan institutions in 1982, allowing them to expand credit facilities with federal guarantees, a fateful measure generally seen at the time as a desirable loan-enhancing mechanism for an economy in recession. Where regulation remained, in the supposedly sacrosanct anti-trust sphere for instance, pro-business appointees quickly made a virtue of studious inaction. Like Eisenhower and Nixon before him Reagan was a skilful practitioner of this kind of administrative sabotage, which he took to new lengths. His Environment Secretary James Watt was as efficient in opening up federal lands to business interests as his colleague Anne Burford, entrusted with the Environmental Protection Agency, was tardy in penalizing chemical companies violating toxic waste rules.

All these signature initiatives were soon overshadowed by the congressional drama early in 1981 as Reagan presented his tax cuts, military appropriations, and welfare reductions.

The country wanted action of some sort against the stagflation and high taxation that was an omnipresent background to all these events. But the Reagan administration had reason to expect considerable difficulty in getting its program into law. There was, for one thing, a general skepticism, widely expressed in the media, about its viability in economic terms. The sums clearly did not add up. His own vice-president, George Bush, had talked loudly of "voodoo economics" during the primaries. There would, admittedly, be an enormous early deficit which the president's supply-side advisers dismissed as a temporary condition that would pass quickly as the tax cut stimulus produced a greatly enlarged revenue. They predicted a balanced budget by 1984. Few were convinced. Moreover, the House of Representatives was still controlled by the Democrats with a mainly liberal leadership. When Reagan made a courtesy call on Capitol Hill upon his arrival in Washington the Speaker, Thomas P. O'Neill condescendingly told him "You're in the big leagues now." Many liberals thought he would produce a more moderate compromise plan now he was safely elected.

They were soon disabused. Reagan's proposals, reflecting his campaign promises faithfully, sailed through. He had called inter alia for a 30 percent tax cut over three years and for defense appropriations totaling $184 billion. To help bridge the anticipated deficit he called for immediate cuts in federal social spending amounting to about $40 billion, with further unspecified cuts to be requested later. The tax cuts proved almost universally popular, the spending cuts, after more than a decade of systematic criticism of Lyndon Johnson's Great Society for its tendency to "throw money at problems," scarcely less so. Liberals tried to resist the welfare reductions. But a host of southern and moderate Democrats (immediately dubbed "boll weevils") joined the triumphant Republicans in voting the program through. The whole business was marked by confusion, vivid scenes in both chambers of Congress, and much bidding and counter-bidding as the tax-cutting frenzy intensified.

When the dust cleared Congress had passed a 25 percent

tax cut over three years (cooler heads at the last minute effecting a small abridgment); tax brackets, the source of much public anger, had been indexed to inflation; and business had received an accelerated tax credit for investment. The enormous military appropriation was passed virtually as asked. And $39 billion in spending cuts had been accepted. These were almost entirely at the expense of Great Society programs. Food stamps, AFDC grants, and other family benefits for the poor felt the axe. Several programs were abolished including the CETA job-training agency, which lost 300,000 positions. It all added up to a remarkable political victory for Reagan and his allies. The conservative columnist James Kilpatrick exulted, "If this was not a revolution it was something very close to it." And the president himself, in his 1989 Farewell Address, was obviously thinking of this accomplishment when he referred proudly to "the Reagan revolution."[20]

How valid is this characterization? It must be acknowledged that in addition to his political achievement Reagan had here gone a long way toward redefining both the contemporary agenda and the prevailing consciousness – from redistribution to growth, from collectivism (with its powerful directing federal state) toward a more entrepreneurial, free enterprise context. The way ahead would be marked by a weaker government, a freer business culture, and a smaller welfare component – though he promised throughout to maintain a "safety net" for the truly needy. Still, "revolution" is a term that comes rather unconvincingly from American public figures at any time, given the narrow constitutional and attitudinal channels within which political action moves. And it falls with some incongruity from the lips of self-described conservatives – another example of the confusion we get into if we take protestations of ideological or philosophical consistency by politicians at face value.

In retrospect it is the limits rather than the reach of the "Reagan revolution" that are striking. The tax cuts, for example, were a logical stimulus in the stagnant conditions of the time. *Fortune* magazine noted that "any president would have had to cut taxes in 1981." The military appropriations were certainly impressive, but they came with the 1980 mandate and were not all that much in advance of Carter's in the early stages (and, as we have seen, well below the proportion of GNP taken by Eisenhower, Kennedy, and Johnson).

The spending cuts were more significant for here there was genuine political innovation rather than simple adjustment, and here the spirit of the new conservatism, as opposed say to Cold War liberalism, showed itself more clearly. At last conservatives had the satisfaction of seeing an unprecedented, direct, and at least marginally effective attack upon the liberal Democratic welfare state. But for all the right-wing triumphalism of 1981 there is less here than meets the eye. The New Deal structure (social security, union rights, the principle of governmental intervention where necessary) was untouched. The blows fell only on some of its Great Society extensions, and even there the check was, except for a few closures, to the rate of growth in federal spending rather than the programs themselves. The politically untouchable middle-class entitlements – social security, Medicare, veterans benefits – were not challenged, though there were some hints of future reductions. And even the poorest Americans could look to a continuing basic welfare provision.

In one sense there was a genuinely revolutionary atmosphere in 1981. The speed with which important processes like the budget preparation and the congressional deliberations were rushed through; the pace of events generally and the almost universal urge for action, whatever it might be, to deal with the worsening economy; the lack of interest, either within the administration or in Congress, in close analytic examination of proposals, in careful oversight or in counting the cost; the confusion among the principal participants – all testify to a heady feeling of momentum and a generalized willingness to contemplate bold measures.

There was, for instance, behind the show of unity and self-confidence in the administration, a chaotic decision-making process that had important consequences. The central figure was David Stockman, a young former right-wing congressman and ardent supply-sider who was now the overworked

Director of the Budget. Trying desperately to complete the administration's legislative proposals within tight deadlines, he made two egregious mistakes. The first involved the military spending increases. He predicated these on Carter's 1980 defense budget but rashly agreed to start the planned 7 percent annual increases in 1982. "What he had forgotten" Frances Fitzgerald explains, "was that the Congress had raised the 1981 budget by 9 percent and the Reagan administration had already plugged in an additional $32.6 billion increase for 1981 and 1982, so the baseline started at $222 billion – not $142 billion as he had assumed." Stockman was aghast but powerless to change the figures, which were already in the public domain.[21]

This disaster was compounded by the hapless Budget Director's assumption, not cleared with the president, that the inevitable gap between spending and revenue would be made up by later cuts in social security and Medicare as well as welfare. He soon realized that this would be politically impossible for both the administration and the Congress. Yet some action was needed and, having gathered support from a number of key officials, he urged Reagan to compensate with new taxes and lower defense expenditures. But the president, firmly committed to both military enhancement and lower taxes, flatly refused. A vast annual deficit inevitably followed rising, William Chafe notes, to $100 billion in 1982 and finally to $300 billion – three times the largest Carter deficit. "No one imagined how bad the outcome would be," Stockman reminisced after his 1984 resignation. "It got away from us."[22]

As a consequence two distinct lines of criticism plagued the Reagan administration. One, emanating mainly from the left, focused on social issues; the other, which also preoccupied much moderate opinion, was the apparent irresponsibility of its economic management. The two were related for the mounting deficits inevitably limited the ability of the federal government to deal with social problems, even if it had wanted to. Stockman came to the view, which became a staple of liberal media criticism, that this had been Reagan's aim all along.

Thus the president looked on the deficits with equanimity because they precluded future spending sprees. This was never proven, and it ignores the defense realm where Reagan was a remarkably heavy spender.

In the early years, although they were on the defensive, liberals and Democrats, who never accepted the argument that the wealthy would invest tax largesse productively, consoled themselves with the belief that the administration's reckless giveaways would exacerbate rather than cure the gathering recession and lead to its political rejection. At first this seemed correct. For in 1982 the worst recession since the 1930s presented itself. Unemployment rose to nearly 11 percent. Inflation continued to fall as Volcker persisted stubbornly in his high-interest policy, but real incomes were down. Worst of all there was no sign of the promised growth as, contrary to Reagan's assurances and supply-side dogma, the tax breaks seemed to spur not healthy investment but a riot of conspicuous and provocative consumption among the rich, evidenced in rocketing sales of fur coats, yachts, and other delights. It looked like "trickle down" economics to the critics who pointed out that the $100 billion deficit in 1982 was a drag on any recovery because it drove the government into the capital markets, squeezing the funds available to the private sector. Meanwhile the strong dollar created by the high interest rates (which could now be blamed on Reagan rather than Volcker because they were needed to attract the foreign capital that was necessary to cover the deficit) hurt exports and produced a flood of cheap imports. Many businesses were now relocating overseas, aggravating the employment problem. A conservative commentator, reviewing the overall record, lamented that, "The operation was a success but the patient hasn't recovered." Reagan's approval rate was now lower than that of any president – except Ford – since Truman. In the 1982 elections the Republicans paid the price, losing 25 seats to the Democrats.

But during 1983 the situation improved and by 1984 a full recovery was in train. How did this occur? Any explanation must take account of the enduring figure of Paul Volcker.

Throughout the difficult 1981–82 period. with the tacit approval of the president, he had maintained his high-interest, inflation-fighting policy. This contributed to the recessionary tendencies of the early 1980s. But it also had two powerful constructive effects that served the administration's political needs. First, it softened the impact of the deficit by attracting a large compensating volume of foreign investment. Second, much more important, it was slowly but surely squeezing the decade-long inflation out of the economy.

Volcker's progress was impressive. By 1984 inflation was down to 4.3 percent, less than half what it had been in the later Carter years. To many critics at the time this seemed inconsequential. Kennedy's former economic adviser, Walter Heller, for example, saw the combination of Reagan's supposedly stimulative spending and Volcker's contractionary fight for low inflation as futile and contradictory, with high interest rates obviously discouraging any revival in consumer spending. Some modern historians seem to agree, with William Chafe commenting "It was simply not possible to have a government both tighten and loosen the purse strings simultaneously."[23]

But over the longer run it *was* possible, and constructive. For it seems clear now that the full explanation of the surprising rebound in 1983 was largely the consequence of two separate but suddenly converging policies. One was the Federal Reserves' tight money policy, which cleared the way for a healthy recovery (if other factors prompted it) with low inflation. The other was the Reagan administration's mixture of lavish military spending and generous staggered tax cuts which were now, in their third year, applying a classic Keynesian stimulus to an economy primed for inflation-free growth. Interestingly, it appears that this was not simply the lucky intersection of two independent lines of action. For, as economist Robert Samuelson has pointed out, even as Volcker kept interest rates high during the recession Reagan, apparently eager to keep up the anti-inflation drive, never criticized him publicly or attempted to rein him in. In effect they collaborated. The results (helped by cheaper oil) were impressive.

Unemployment fell back to 7.5 percent (the 1980 figure). People felt the warmth of extra cash in their pockets after three years of tax relief. Their spending revived the crucial automobile and housing industries, and gradually the whole retail economy.[24]

The Democrats nevertheless approached the 1984 election optimistically. They had not yet come to grips with their post-1968 problems. The continuing influence of strident minorities still limited their appeal to the broader public. The Carter years were still widely associated with economic stagflation and diplomatic decline. Nevertheless, the early 1980s' recession had left scars, and many appeared to believe, pointing to the alarming deficits, that the recovery had been purchased at the expense of the nation's deeper interests. The party nominated Carter's vice-president, Walter Mondale, a respected Minnesota liberal, electrified his convention by choosing New York Congresswoman Geraldine Ferraro, as his running mate. He then went on to remind the American people that the deficits had created a dangerous situation and promised to rectify it with increased taxes.

"I will raise taxes" has never been a compelling cry in American politics. In the quickening prosperity of 1984 few were eager to don the hairshirt. Reagan's more pleasing slogan "America is Back," drawing attention both to the returning prosperity and the rising power and prestige of the United States in world affairs, better caught the public mood. He won a stunning landslide victory.

Reagan's second term, though full of incident, was dominated by the dramatic events that heralded the end of the Cold War. At home the economic expansion grew steadily, confounding the jeremiahs who persisted in viewing the rapidly accumulating overall deficit as a harbinger of imminent disaster. The president's radicalism was now spent, his only major initiative being a popular tax reform bill that rationalized the code, closed loopholes, and systematized the hitherto haphazard collection method while further reducing the highest income tax rate from 50 percent to 33 percent. Characterized by one observer as "a small step back toward progressivity" it passed easily.[25]

But these were difficult years for Reagan. He had to endure the extraordinary Iran–contra crisis which, as we will see later, nearly brought his impeachment, and the sudden October 1987 stock market crash that, though quickly brought under control, was seen by many as an indication of the fragility of an economy that he seemed to be monitoring in disturbingly distant fashion. In many ways he appeared even more removed from daily control of his office than his management style had earlier suggested, an impression fostered by confidence-betraying memoirs published by Stockman, who threw doubt upon his ability to grasp basic economics, and by former chief of staff Donald Regan, who unkindly revealed that the president's daily schedule was organized in strict conformity with the calculations of his wife's astrologer.[26]

More substantively there was a steady stream of criticism from socio-cultural conservatives who felt short-changed by the emphasis on economic restructuring. George Will, looking back in 1989, thought Reagan had neglected the social agenda, as did columnist Jeffrey Hart who also blamed the administration for failing to cut farm and Amtrak subsidies and grants to small business. Such charges, reminiscent of conservative disillusionment at the close of Eisenhower's presidency, certainly put the "revolutionary" characterization of the 1980s in question. They are reinforced by other observers like Frances Fitzgerald, who was struck by Reagan's careful avoidance of the social preoccupations of the religious right in the 1984 campaign, and Paul Berman who found his commitment in that area to have been full of "ambiguities."[27] But perhaps he had done as much as could reasonably have been expected. He had to deal with a Democratically controlled House of Representatives throughout his term. Every social program was protected by vested interests and even the dubious ones often received support from a fiercely custodial liberal press. And in fact he did cut into the Great Society welfare system and often came close to achieving much the same purpose by appointing conservative militants to administer vulnerable liberal institutions like the Civil Rights Commission and the anti-trust division of the Justice Department.

So far as abortion, school prayer, and minority and family issues are concerned Reagan could hardly expect to overturn the "rights revolution" of preceding decades overnight. But he took advantage of his long tenure to successfully nominate three conservatives (Justices O'Connor, Scalia, and Kennedy) to the Supreme Court. Walter Murphy, a Princeton University law professor, points out that by 1989 his almost exclusively conservative nominees held nearly half the federal district and appellate appointments in the country, their "unifying feature" being support for Reagan's public policies. And in his brilliantly effective persona as "the Great Communicator," Alonzo Hamby suggests that "he expressed the values of culturally conservative working and middle classes who resented the new permissive morality."[28] These periodic brickbats from ungrateful social conservatives probably hurt more than the constant drumbeat of liberal criticism. Much of the latter was personal and dismissive. From Lewis Lapham's patronizing 1981 impression in *Harpers* "of a man . . . accustomed to the safer suburbs, expensive cars, the scent of jasmine on a golf course, Bob Hope's geopolitics, and the smiling camaraderie of Frank Sinatra" to TRB's *New Republic* 1989 farewell to a man who "was virtually brain dead," there was an unceasing parade of ridicule and condescension.[29]

But there were more substantive liberal indictments. In addition to their principal charges – social injustice restored and seemingly entrenched, the deficit diminishing any prospect of further reform – Reagan's critics on the left were alienated by the general atmosphere of materialism, vulgar consumption, and financial corruption that was undeniably part of the 1980s' reality. Wall Street seemed to many liberals to have regained its historic primacy as the epicenter of American vice, temporarily displacing Hollywood and Las Vegas. As the economy recovered many easy fortunes were made. Young financial professionals ("Yuppies") became rich overnight. Unscrupulous moneymen like Ivan Boesky (known for his "greed is good" axiom) and Michael Millken, the creator of "junk bonds" that seemed designed only to facilitate dubious takeovers and corporate power struggles but later revealed a constructive side in also forcing new efficiencies and higher productivity, typified a new era that many viewed as immoral. Boesky and Millken both went to prison, emerging ostentatiously penitent but still mysteriously rich. The taint of sleaze and corruption was also felt in Washington. Remarkably, over 100 Reagan administration officials, including Cabinet members, were indicted or forced to resign for corruption of one sort or another. Meanwhile liberal critics were uncovering other blemishes. A 1988 anthology entitled *Freedom at Risk: Secrecy, Censorship and Repression in the 1980s* showed the administration, citing the national interest, trying to restrict and manage the flow of information, prevent the declassification of documents unreasonably withheld, exclude aliens on flimsy ideological grounds, and carry out illegal forms of domestic surveillance.[30]

But the most passionately voiced charge by left-liberal critics during the 1980s was that the Reagan campaign against welfare, affirmative action, busing, and other Great Society programs was deepening the gulf between white and black and leading inexorably, in social critic Andrew Hacker's later phrase, to "two nations." It expressed the continuing liberal conviction, stressed by Gunnar Myrdal in 1963, that the effective emancipation of an oppressed people could not succeed without a rational vision and plan for their rapid integration into the larger society. Now Reagan was kicking away the thin Johnsonian supports long before their work was done. Many pointed to the tribulations of the typically fragmented black family, the black illegitimacy rate of more than 60 percent, the fact that half the nation's prison population was black, and all the continuing problems of the ghetto, drug addiction, and, worst of all because it foreclosed any prospect of progress, low employment rates. The Urban League's leader, Roy Wilkins, normally a comparatively mild-mannered man, expressed the bitterness of many African-Americans when he openly branded Reagan a "racist." Social scientists like Frances Fox Piven and Richard A. Cloward made a powerful case for continued state responsibility for vulnerable Americans. They broadened the issue toward the form it increasingly took in the less racially charged 1990s by emphasizing the growing divide between "rich and poor," interpreting the Reagan spending cuts as essentially class-focused and intended to force the poor and unemployed into low wage, poor quality service jobs.[31]

These views were fiercely contested. The conservative commentator Michael Novak, for example, suggested in 1983 that overall spending on social programs had risen in the two previous years (presumably due to the intensified recession) while the cuts had not hurt the really poor. Novak put forward a statistically founded case and concluded that, "As Roosevelt is sometimes referred to as the liberal who saved capitalism, Reagan may someday be known as the conservative who saved the welfare state intact for the very poor." Sociologist Charles Murray built on this work in his controversial 1984 book *Losing Ground,* which argued that the "War on Poverty" had not only failed to erase poverty but had actually helped prolong it. Other right-wing critics elaborated the point. At a more philosophical level sociologist Stephen Steinberg maintained a running critique of the excessively optimistic and idealized view of human nature implicit in the well-intentioned liberal Myrdal tradition, which ignored, he argued, "the depth of American racism."[32]

This debate, pitting liberal and conservative positions against each other with unprecedented sharpness and clarity, developed, nonetheless, in an atmosphere of lessening racial tension. In 1980, for example, we find George Wallace, now retired from national affairs, ostentatiously courting black support in Alabama politics, reflecting the growing leverage of black Americans since the Voting Rights Act of 1965. Race-baiting, in its extreme form, was quickly becoming a thing of the past in the South. Yet the racial issue was still potentially divisive. The 1988 presidential election, for instance, presented on the one hand the remarkably successful campaign of the African-American, Jesse Jackson, the former aide of Martin Luther King, whose "Rainbow Coalition" won him Democratic primary votes in the north and south as he pursued the nomination, and on the other the successful presidential campaign of Republican George Bush, which ruthlessly and probably effectively played up fears of increased black criminality if the Democrats won.

Over time scholars have taken a calmer view of President Reagan's social policies. Alonzo Hamby, for example, refers to "a few cuts" and notes the survival of a largely intact safety net. To the surprise of many a severe critique of the welfare system developed among conservative black intellectuals like Thomas Sowell and Glen C. Loury who characterized it as socially destructive, especially of the black family. And Democratic President Bill Clinton's welfare initiative of 1996, which led to severe reductions in eligibility and benefits, puts the Reagan program in a less apocalyptic light.[33]

The other great source of concern – to moderate and even some right-wing as well as liberal opinion – was the astonishing deficits of the Reagan years. He and Volcker had by 1984 done much to bring the economy back to life. But the deficits were alarming and the president, apparently relished his annual increasingly ritualized stand-off battle with Congress, in which he repeatedly and unavailingly called for further spending cuts but made no serious effort to force them down. Indeed he increased them drastically. His first (fiscal 1982) budget had a deficit of $127.9 billion (Carter's last was $78.9 billion) and forced the overall national debt over $1 trillion. His last (fiscal 1989) was $152 billion and carried the full figure to nearly $3 trillion. All Americans learned the resulting shorthand mantra: the United States had been the world's greatest creditor in 1981: by 1989 it was the world's greatest debtor.

Critics saw two main issues here. One was the drag on the economy. The vast debt forced continuing high interest rates to attract the compensating foreign investment (mainly Japanese) that was necessary to maintain current viability. This strengthened the dollar and encouraged corporate flight to more hospitable, cheaper overseas locations with consequent loss of jobs at home. It meant a weakened federal government and a diminished source of investment capital at home (by 1989 interest payable by the government on the national debt was over 20 percent of the budget). And it meant increasing foreign ownership of American assets, which was politically provocative. Still, by the end of the decade, after more than five years of rising prosperity, all this looked a little less frightening. Liberal economist Robert Samuelson called the deficit "serious but not calamitous," and suggested its consequences had been exaggerated politically to discredit the president. The real problem, he urged, was the productivity rate, which had doubled in the 1980s over the 1970s, but was still only about half the 1945–70 average. This temperate view gained adherents during the 1990s as the long boom developed and Washington found itself, by 1999, handling unanticipated surpluses.[34]

More passionately condemned and more lasting were the apparent social consequences. One aspect of this, as we have seen, was the Stockman thesis that Reagan was willing to put the government in debt in order to force future cuts in social spending. Another loudly voiced complaint was that the deficit was eating up the nation's "seed corn," portending a bleak future for the next generation. More immediately the persisting high interest rates seemed to be diminishing the quality of American life. The dynamic here was the incentive given to American industrial corporations to relocate overseas. For the resulting strong dollar hurt exports and brought a flood of competing cheap imports, which did help keep inflation low but further dried up jobs at home. All this was described in lofty terms as a more or less pre-ordained transformation from an "industrial" to a "service" economy. In fact, from the viewpoint of the average American worker and his rapidly fading union support structure, it was an unwelcome, sometimes devastating transition from well-paid stability to precarious volatility.

The liberal/conservative divide, which the advent of Ronald Reagan intensified, also had a lively intellectual/cultural dimension during the 1980s. There was, for instance, what we might call a "high conservatism" inspired by claims to descent from such supposedly legitimate luminaries as Adam Smith, Edmund Burke, Frederic Hayek, and Ayn Rand. The new mood produced several analyses of American life, such as Allan Bloom's best-selling *The Closing of the American Mind*, a 1987 condemnation of the course taken by American higher education since the permissive 1960s. There were also many expressions of deeply felt satisfaction that classic American values – patriotism, family solidarity, church, self-reliance, and so on – were being reaffirmed. Beneath this we often see a rougher kind of populistic, aggressive conservatism reflected both in the pell-mell materialism, urban glitz, and unscrupulous financial hustle captured memorably by novelist Tom Wolfe in his evisceration of 1980s' New York, *The Bonfire of the Vanities*, and in the combative activism of some pro-life advocates, religious fundamentalists, and, at a much lower level, white supremacists.[35]

Similar fissures are observable in the competing left-liberal culture. Enduring New Dealers and New Frontiersmen like Arthur Schlesinger Jr. hoped the "cycle" of American politics later would soon bring a reforming administration back to power. The serious, idealistic impulse of 1960s' radicalism and concern for social justice was still active, though much attenuated, beating visibly in the progressive media, in the universities, and among historians like Maurice Isserman and sociologists like Todd Gitlin whose published work kept the flame alive. Later historian Lawrence Levine would produce the left-liberal answer to Bloom in *The Opening of the American Mind*, arguing that, far from being the preserve of politically correct radicals American universities were both intellectually creative and socially dynamic, reflecting the new multiculturalism certainly, but in ways that were essentially democratic and progressive.[36] And, as noted, there was an abundance of serious critical analysis of the Republican administration and the allegedly bad values it was encouraging. But just as pretensions to conservative respectability were subverted by scandalous behavior, so liberal piety was undermined by the permissive 1960s' life-style culture that continued to develop with scant regard for the political changes in Washington, generating social innovation, new modes of self-realization and self-satisfaction (self-indulgence in traditional eyes), sexual freedoms, unconventional approaches to education and child-rearing, and much more that seems to have been beyond the reach of the conventional political culture but posed a continuing challenge to hierarchy, reverence, and respectability.

The journalist Thomas B. Edsall, noting its persisting influence in American life, called this counter-cultural projection into the Reagan era "an insurgency." Similarly, the neo-conservative Irving Kristol saw "a culture at odds with civilization." And the sociologist Gilbert T. Sewall, assessing the 1980s as a whole, aptly concluded "The great contradiction of the decade remains the consolidation of progressive power in culture and society despite the solid Reagan majority."[37] There was, therefore, in this decade of ostensibly clear political and social division, a much more complex socio-cultural reality, juxtaposing not only conservative and liberal intellectual outlooks, but also conservative political and radical social mores. All this played out later in the "culture wars" of the 1990s when the respectable high priests on each side of the ideological fence labored prodigiously to define the other by accusing reference to its noisy, loose instinctual outriders, thus mixing up high and low culture in rather confusing fashion.

It seems, in retrospect then, that if there was a revolutionary experience in Reagan's America it was, as in the 1960s, at the cultural level – a matter of consciousness rather than policy. For while he had undeniably lowered taxes, made a dent in the welfare state, and brought about (with Volcker's help, a rising curve in the business cycle and cheap oil) a significant economic recovery, he was unable, and perhaps did not really try, to effect any major institutional change. The federal government was as large and imposing a presence in 1989 as it had been at the outset. He had cut into Lyndon Johnson's civil rights edifice, but it had been strongly defended and in the end its principal features – affirmative action, busing, voting rights, and a large degree of social protection – were still in place. By contrast, as we have just seen, his cultural call for stronger families and traditional values had made little impact on the increasingly hedonistic, celebrity-fetishing, consumption-satiated, urban American life-style.

Recent analysis conveys a strong sense of the limits of Reagan's impact. Robert Reich, in his treatment of modern American economic history, finds most of the roots of change in the 1980s in long-developing, private sector trends and the international milieu. Reagan's name appears, mainly without consequence, on only six of his pages. Similarly Stanford Lyman's more recent review of civil rights history virtually ignores the rollback efforts attempted in the 1980s. And Allan Bloom's lengthy discussion of the alleged degradation of American cultural and educational standards has much to say about Socrates and Nietzsche but mentions Reagan only four times. General historians too, while acknowledging his persuasive powers and sometimes remarkable political leadership, have been reluctant to ascribe any transformative outcomes to Reagan. William Chafe writes that "To a degree unmatched in any era since Franklin Roosevelt's New Deal, Ronald Reagan imprinted his personal brand on the decade of the 1980s." But he shows little in the way of legislative substance, let alone a revolutionary legacy. Alonzo Hamby is also struck by the Roosevelt analogy but finds a large measure of continuity in parallels with Eisenhower, Nixon, Carter, and John Maynard Keynes. He absolves Reagan of any blame for the "decade of greed," which he finds no worse than any other, and credits him with the revival of a sagging economy, a triumphant foreign policy, and the restoration of public confidence. But unlike Roosevelt, Reagan failed to create a new enduring political realignment.[38]

Yet there had been a real change. People felt it. Reagan had done things hitherto thought politically impossible. He had shown that a right-wing conservative in the modern age could win the White House. He had demonstrated that an attack on the outer, poverty-oriented reaches of the welfare system could be at least partly successful. And he had established the point that the New Deal/Great Society order – the political juggernaut of the postwar years – had real limits. Above all he had shown that America was, at least by comparison with other countries, a more conservative, market-driven society than the liberals had allowed.

But while the drama of all this was keenly felt at the time by an American society that was still, for all its global activism, remarkably introspective, it is lessened for us in retrospect by the realization that much the same sort of thing was going on more or less contemporaneously in other industrialized societies. For in the 1980s, wherever one looks – at Margaret Thatcher's Britain, at Germany and socialist France, at Scandinavia, Australia and New Zealand with their social democratic traditions, even at the increasingly restless communist states – one finds a decisive move away from the post-World War II model of the strong central state, with its more or less collectivist, redistributional ethic, toward growth economics, laissez-faire techniques, privatization, and market impulses generally. Perhaps Reagan and his times were more fully in harmony with each other than his critics thought.

Cold War Finale

It is widely agreed that in the wake of Ronald Reagan's 1984 re-election there was what political scientist Condoleeza Rice calls "an about face" in US diplomacy.[39] The first term seems dominated by the arms build-up and a militant confrontational approach to the Soviet Union and other left-wing antagonists; the second by the remarkable and unanticipated unraveling of the Cold War. In fact the dichotomy is not as stark as it seems. We have already noted that Reagan was interested in negotiation with Moscow, albeit from a position of strength, as early as 1981. On the other hand he was still issuing warnings about Soviet duplicity in 1988. Further, while acknowledging the very distinct difference between the two periods we might well interpose a third, transitional phase – say between early 1984 and the first Reagan–Gorbachev summit in November 1985 – during which there was a discernible struggle within the administration over future policy as the president began moving with growing vigor toward summit meetings and negotiations.

The new dispensation emerged with increasing clarity through 1985. Fresh arms control talks at the beginning of the year were disappointingly unproductive. Administration hard-liners argued that the Soviets had violated existing agreements, notably by constructing a radar defense system at Krasnoyarsk in Siberia. Still, a second round began in March 1985. On the morning of the first session Konstantin Chernenko, last of the post-Stalin generation with any memory of the Bolshevik revolution, died. Mikhail Gorbachev succeeded him as Soviet leader. This was well received in Europe for Gorbachev had already established an image of youthful energy apparently directed to some degree of reform. Reagan responded positively too, declaring that the Russians were now "in a different frame of mind than they've been in the past." After a few months of mutual assessment a Reagan–Gorbachev summit was announced.[40]

This meeting was arranged, on the American side, by Secretary of State Schultz and his ally, Paul Nitze. There was considerable opposition from CIA Director Casey, Defense Secretary Weinberger, and many others. The bitter infighting has been illuminated by historian Frances Fitzgerald who shows Weinberger passionately lecturing the president, of all people, on the theme of "the evil empire" and the dangers of any negotiations with the Kremlin.[41] A group of Reagan's most committed conservative political supporters told him that Schultz had gone soft on the Russians and should be dismissed. Schultz, who was now able to rely on Nancy Reagan's desire to see her husband's militant image softened, tried with equal force to push Weinberger, Perle, and other hard-liners out of the nest. In the event there were no resignations or dismissals. But the moderates prevailed and Reagan decided to meet Gorbachev, setting in motion the diplomatic process that led finally to the end of the Cold War. It is doubtful whether the president foresaw this. Some historians see his decision in conventional political terms. Alan Brinkley, for instance, writes "Reagan never took sides consistently in the battle between Schultz and Weinberger until he realized that siding with Schultz was the course most likely to benefit him politically." This is in line with the growing tendency, which Fitzgerald's work to some extent reinforces, to view Reagan as a skilful, calculating politician. It cuts across the more familiar perception of him as, in Arthur Schlesinger Jr.'s phrase, "a conviction politician," driven by a few simple but deeply felt beliefs, one of which was his increasingly well-documented desire to cut down if not abolish nuclear weapons.[42]

The Geneva summit produced no substantive agreements. But it broke the ice and set the stage for later accords. The two leaders got on well personally. They discussed the possibility of deep cuts in strategic level weaponry, the prospects for improved verification, and the controversial Strategic Defense Initiative, which Reagan refused to abandon. This would be the principal sticking point in subsequent United States–Soviet talks, but it was not a fatal impediment. Meanwhile, they agreed to meet again, and Gorbachev felt emboldened to produce, in January 1986, his own initiative, a proposal that both sides agree to abolish nuclear weapons altogether by 2000.

They met again in Reykjavik, Iceland in October 1986. Since Geneva some momentum had been lost and various diplomatic squabbles had intervened. But here, after Gorbachev led off with proposals for a 50 percent cut in both sides' strategic arsenals, the two slipped away from their respective advisers and, attended only by interpreters, came to the verge of agreeing to demolish all their nuclear weapons. Gorbachev enthusiastically, and characteristically, quickly pushed on to suggest that this be done by 1996 rather than his earlier 2000 deadline. Reagan was eager but insisted on retaining the SDI concept. To his surprise Gorbachev balked. The meeting broke up with some mutual resentment and without tangible result.[43]

This extraordinary meeting was the antithesis of the conventional modern Cold War summit, typically a carefully planned, politically dressed up register of decisions laboriously hammered out in advance by self-effacing officials. Many commentators found the casual handling of nuclear issues – so vital to American and West European security – disconcerting or dangerous. For the historically conscious it may have awakened memories of the famous 1905 summit between Kaiser Wilhelm II and Tsar Nicholas II – a lost opportunity before

World War I – where, in similar isolation from their advisers, the two constitutionally potent monarchs personally settled a range of persisting differences between their states, but were obliged or persuaded to repudiate the settlement once their horrified entourages got wind of it. Reykjavik had a very different sequel. Despite the setback, evident in the strained faces of the two leaders at the time, both governments put a positive spin on the meeting and sanctioned continuing lower-level talks.[44]

How can we explain this? We might begin by recalling the extraordinary impact of Gorbachev. It had long been expected that his generation, when it finally came to power, would be even more ruthless, aggressive, and self-serving than its geriatric predecessors who had at least been through the perhaps humanizing trauma of World War II. There was little in the way of warning from the nation's Sovietlogists who, after decades of self-confident pontification on a status quo they seem to have regarded as unchangeable, in general failed to predict the transformation. There had been an awareness that the Soviet economy was in deep trouble, that there were serious social problems such as declining birth and life expectancy rates, epidemic absenteeism and alcoholism, and chronic inefficiency throughout the system.[45] But as late as 1988 the regime seemed as strong as ever at home and demonstrably able to project power overseas.

Today, after a decade of revelation and study, we can see the unfolding Kremlin picture more clearly. At its heart was the increasingly urgent realization that the inefficient command economy, with its lock-step plans and managerial rigidities, lacked both the expertise and technology to keep up with the West. The death of Brezhnev in 1982, after nearly two decades of economic stagnation, brought some fresh thinking. The new leader, Yuri Andropov, wedded according to Soviet specialist Archie Brown to "Discipline and Reform" brought new progressives into the higher levels of government, including Gorbachev who, after Chernenko's shortly following death, took the lead with the same formula and no generational inhibitions.[46]

Gorbachev remains a somewhat enigmatic figure. The evidence suggests an initially limited aim. "Back to Lenin" was one much publicized slogan. But the reforming trends he set in motion took him far beyond Lenin's prescriptions. He consistently managed to give the impression, accurate or not, that he was leading the transformation rather than being driven by it. He certainly wanted change, remarking to his wife before accepting the leadership, "We can't go on living like this." Believing that reform was dependent on public support he conceptualized his program in terms of *glasnost* (openness and free expression) leading to *perestroika* (restructuring.) But to succeed he knew he had to divert resources from the military sector (then absorbing perhaps 20 percent of Soviet GNP) to the civilian economy. And to do that he had to conclude arms control agreements with the United States that would allow the necessary military spending cuts. He was therefore eager to persevere despite the Reykjavik failure.[47]

President Reagan also had compelling, mainly political reasons to keep pressing for reductions. By late 1986 his presidency seemed suddenly to be in steep decline. The economy was still buoyant but his political mastery in Washington was now a receding memory. Despite his re-election success he appeared to have lost his clout in Congress. His SDI proposals were skeptically viewed and minimally funded. He, rather than Congress, was blamed for the vast deficits with their shaming, highly publicized consequence of national relegation to debtor status. His administration was rocked by numerous scandals. Worst of all was the sudden eruption in November 1986 of the notorious Iran–Contra affair.

This scandal, which for a time threatened the president with impeachment, had its origin in three deep American frustrations: an inability to stop the periodic seizures of American hostages by Islamic fundamentalists in the Middle East; the continuing hostility of the Ayatollah Khomeini's Iran, which seemingly promoted and supported such acts; and the impressive ability of the Nicaraguan Sandinistas to resist American-supported efforts to dislodge them. In 1985 American and Israeli intelligence operatives, working with shadowy Middle

Eastern arms dealers, suggested that Israel furnish supposedly moderate Iranians with American arms. In return they would facilitate the release of several hostages in Lebanon. Meanwhile, the United States would replace the Israeli arms. The net effect, American arms in exchange for hostages, violated the administration's public pledges not to negotiate their release and the covert arms dealing was of dubious legality. Then, in January 1986, a clique of White House insiders, perhaps inspired by CIA Director Casey, but led in fact by NSC staffer Oliver North, saw a further opportunity. They overcharged the Iranians and used the profits to sustain the increasingly desperate contras. This was clearly illegal. Congress, through the 1984 Boland Amendment, had expressly forbidden any further aid to the contras by the CIA or any other intelligence or military agency.

In another time or place this might have been hailed as creative policy. North made a vivid case for it before the ensuing congressional inquiry. But many Americans were shocked by the full story, which first broke in a Beirut newspaper and quickly moved – in Watergate fashion – to target the White House. In the event the current National Security Adviser Admiral John Poindexter and Oliver North (Casey having died before he could be examined) were judged responsible. Poindexter later served a prison term while the more adroit North was acquitted and began a well-publicized political career. Secretaries Schultz and Weinberger, both of whom had approved the Middle Eastern aspect but denied any knowledge of the Nicaraguan connection, were exonerated.

Reagan himself was generally suspected of being privy to the whole process. He certainly knew about the Iranian part, which he had authorized in writing. He admitted this "mistake" but denied any knowledge of the more serious contra dimension. Poindexter, North, and others sustained him in this (his reputation as a distant manager also helped for once) and the danger of another impeachment soon faded. It had never been popular and his presidency was nearing its end. But his prestige and approval rate declined precipitously. As Theodore Draper's close analysis shows many Americans were upset that he had been so easily bypassed by his own intimate advisers, and alarmed at the ease with which a tiny group of highly placed officials had been able to function beyond the law. There was much talk in the media of "a secret government" and "the usurpation of power."[48]

The net result of all this was that Reagan, no less than Gorbachev, had compelling reasons to look for a restorative diplomatic triumph in the always-sensitive sphere of arms control. It came, most conveniently, in December 1987 when Gorbachev visited Washington and the two leaders, capitalizing on their officials' long negotiations, signed the Intermediate Range Nuclear Forces treaty effectively eliminating the whole class of Soviet SS-20 and American Pershing and cruise missiles then confronting each other in Europe. This was historic – all earlier agreements had looked merely to control of the growth in nuclear armaments. Here at last was some real disarmament. It was also an unambiguous triumph for Reagan for it essentially embodied his Europe-focused zero-option of 1981. Further, the Soviets agreed for the first time to on-site verification. There was also some advance toward a START treaty emphasizing the desire for more reductions, and a decision to hold another summit in Moscow the following spring.

This took place in May 1988. Reagan strolled amiably with Gorbachev through Red Square and made friendly speeches about freedom in his characteristically skilful way. In December it was Gorbachev's turn. During a similarly triumphant visit to New York to address the United Nations General Assembly, he announced a unilateral Soviet reduction of 500,000 ground troops. This put a seal of credibility upon his statesmanship for millions of hitherto skeptical observers, the more so because it moved the arms control process from nuclear to conventional forces and thus held out encouragement for East Europeans and for the reduction of tensions in other trouble spots. Thus, even as the Reagan–Gorbachev phase was winding down there was a sense of new beginnings with the focus now increasingly on the crucial political issues of Europe.

Still, Reagan clearly believed he and Gorbachev had orchestrated the decisive breakthrough. In four summit meetings they

had together gone a long way toward alleviating United States–
Soviet tensions and diminishing fears of nuclear war. They
had eliminated a dangerously provocative class of missiles and
had begun to work toward more general reductions.
Gorbachev, whom *Time* magazine named "Man of the Decade" in 1990 received more plaudits. But historian John Lewis
Gaddis, noting several points "where one can see that the President himself had a decisive impact upon the course of events"
gave Reagan "a great deal of credit, both for his early renewal
of American strength and his subsequent willingness to negotiate with the new Soviet leadership." British historian David
Reynolds goes even further, suggesting that without the
Reagan–Gorbachev change in the international climate,
"Gorbachev would not have sanctioned the European revolutions of 1989. Nor would he have felt able to embark on radical repairs at home." Certainly Reagan thought he had played
a shaping role. Leaving for California after Bush's inaugura-
tion in January 1989 he clearly felt that "the Cold War was
winding down."[49]

This, however, was a little premature. As with the Cold
War's origins we do best to think of its ending in terms of
distinct stages. The first phase of the Cold War's unraveling
was over; the second, Europe-oriented phase was about to
begin. Reagan's attitude shows a representative American
outlook that the post-1962 Cold War was dominated by the
nuclear confrontation and the struggle for the so-called Third
World. It neglected the European dimension. Europe was still
the geopolitical heart of the whole struggle, the original arena,
now expectant and turbulent as Gorbachev's ameliorative leadership unnerved communist regimes and opened up fresh hopes
of liberation in the East. Europe was just as important to
Gorbachev as nuclear weaponry and for the same reason –
the need for money. He needed understandings with and over
Germany and cuts in the cost of the expensive, unpopular
Soviet empire in the East. In early 1989, therefore, he moved
to this second phase, signaling the new approach by repudiat-
ing the Brezhnev doctrine and withdrawing Soviet troops from
Afghanistan, and at the same time warning the communist

regimes in Eastern Europe, first privately then publicly, that he was not prepared to uphold them against popular pressure.

Gorbachev set a cracking pace. In January 1989, building on his United Nations initiative, he called for substantial conventional force reductions in Europe even as he unilaterally reduced Soviet troop levels by 14 percent. In February he withdrew the last divisions from Afghanistan. In April the Polish communist regime reached agreement with the vigorously democratic Solidarity union, legalizing it and setting elections for June. In May the Hungarian government dismantled its 150-mile fortified border with Austria, inducing tens of thousands of East Germans to flee by this route to the West. June produced an overwhelming election victory for Solidarity and a democratic prime minister took office in Poland.

As the democratic momentum accelerated all eyes turned to Moscow. But during much of 1989 the Soviet government was distracted. Ethnic riots, independence movements in several republics, a rising tide of popular complaint and resentment as *glasnost* flourished, and much new questioning of communist legitimacy – all these domestic problems kept Gorbachev busy. His response was an uneasy mixture of firmness and appeasement. The East European regimes were chilled by the Kremlin's apparent irresolution. They were disconcerted by the new penchant in Moscow for confessions of past errors. Foreign Minister Shevardnarze publicly acknowledged that the invasion of Afghanistan had violated Soviet and international law, and went on to admit that the controversial radar complex in Siberia had indeed been contrary to the ABM treaty with the United States. Meanwhile, Gorbachev seemed focused on political and economic retrenchment. In Germany in May, where he was rapturously received, he held out the prospect of the Wall's demolition. In Paris in June he told inquiring reporters that the political future of Poland and Hungary was "their affair."

This was the death-knell for East European communism which basically collapsed in late 1989. In September democratic elements in Hungary forced agreement for free elections in the spring. In November, in the so-called "velvet revolution" democracy came to Prague. Meanwhile the East German government, until now the most strenuous supplicant for a tougher Soviet line, threw in the towel. It declared its citizens free to leave. Immediately thousands of East Berliners came through the Wall and rushed into the arms of their long separated neighbors. The Berlin Wall's human dismantlement became the most vivid image of the Cold War's demise. In a final plunge south the new passion for liberty swept into Bucharest where, in the only real violence of the whole sequence, the Ceausescu dictatorship was toppled. Rumania now joined the democratic parade and Bulgaria, somewhat more tentatively, soon followed.[50]

In all this the United States took a generally supportive but only marginally significant part. This "passive" approach as one historian calls it, may seem surprising, but it reflects the distinction made earlier between a nuclear/Third World set of issues in which the United States was crucially engaged as a principal, and a European arena where it was but one of several vitally interested parties. Also, there was unreserved support for *perestroika* because, as Secretary of State James Baker put it rather bleakly, improvements at home would lead to "Soviet actions more advantageous to our interests." But there was much suspicion in the Bush administration of Gorbachev's sincerity. They did not respond enthusiastically to his early 1989 call for further arms reductions. Defense Secretary Dick Cheney warned darkly of "a dangerous trap." Bush did meet Gorbachev in December at Malta, but there was little discussion of European issues.[51]

The United States could hardly avoid the now looming issues of East Germany and German reunification. For many Europeans the prospective revival of German power put an awkward crimp in the general euphoria generated by the 1989 communist retreat. The Polish, British, and French governments were particularly worried. They initially put their faith in Gorbachev. Surely no Russian leader would allow German reunification? And indeed Gorbachev had begun with the expectation that a free East German people would elect to remain socialist and independent. As late as October 1989 he reassured East German leaders that unification was "not a problem in current politics." But public demonstrations in East German cities favoring a joinder with the Bonn republic soon exposed these illusions and any residual enthusiasm for independence withered as the regime's luxurious life-style and the pervasive excesses of the secret police were exposed.

As the socialist state crumbled West German chancellor Helmut Kohl seized the initiative, offering the impoverished Easterners an attractive currency union and then flying to meet Gorbachev in early February 1990 to make the crucial deal. . By this time Gorbachev, now anxious about rising turmoil in the Soviet Union, was ready to put economics ahead of politics. Kohl promised not to acquire nuclear weaponry and to cap the German military at 370,000. He promised a loan of $20 billion and undertook to pay the Soviets' military repatriation costs. In return Gorbachev declared that "it was up to the two Germanies to decide on unification." Sensitive issues were quickly resolved. The post-1945 border between East Germany and Poland, for instance, was confirmed "in perpetuity." And it was agreed that the united Germany could remain in NATO – another surprise but seen in Moscow, and soon in other Western capitals, as an assurance that, as Kohl constantly stressed, there would be a European Germany, not a Germanized Europe. On October 2, 1990, amid celebrations in Berlin, the new Germany came officially to life.[52]

By the end of 1990 then the Cold War was indeed over. The two sides continued to tie up loose ends. In November NATO and the now hollow Warsaw Pact agreed to much reduced force levels in Europe. By March 1991, however, the Warsaw Pact had collapsed with its East European members now deeply engaged in assisting the repatriation of their Soviet garrisons. The Western response was to offer the Soviets and their former satellites a face-saving membership in a new North Atlantic Cooperation Council.

Here too the American role may seem, to those accustomed to stress the power of the United States and its primary influence in all aspects of the Western alliance, surprisingly marginal. By this time Bush and Baker were active supporters of Gorbachev and Shevardnadze, with whom they formed warm personal relationships. But their interventions, though sometimes potent, notably in supporting German reunification in the teeth of British and French reservations, were spasmodic. And a certain suspicion continued, sustained by the undeniable fact that, as historian Stephen Ambrose puts it, "The Red Army, although retreating from Eastern Europe, remained the largest in the world. The strategic forces were still there – the navy, the missiles, the nuclear warheads – and the Soviets remained capable of destroying the world in a flash."[53]

But this relative American detachment should not surprise us. It was consistent with the character of United States–European relations as we have seen them ebb and flow through the Cold War era. For the tendency of those relationships, and the determinedly cohesive alliance systems they produced on each side, was to mask the continuing historical gulf between the United States and Europe which we saw more clearly in the earlier years of the Cold War, in the convoluted alliance politics of the 1950s, in the move toward détente inaugurated by Willy Brandt, and now in the Europe-focused geopolitical initiatives of Gorbachev, Kohl, and others in 1989–90. There were, to be sure, occasional tension-reducing moves by the United States during the long struggle, but not many. The character of American diplomacy, in the service of containment (an inherently standstill concept) was essentially managerial – designed to maintain strength, predictability, and stability. The Russian dissident writer Alexander Solzhenitsyn noted approvingly, "The United States was like granite." This was very different from the European diplomatic tradition with its inbuilt tendency to flux, volatility, and opportunism.

In one respect, however, the American contribution to the European unraveling was profound. If it did not initiate or even vigorously promote the process its tacit approval was indispensable. The Bush administration maintained contact with all the parties involved, and played a calming reassuring part as the final, most unexpected denouement took place: the dissolution of the Soviet Union itself. This took everyone by surprise. But as 1990 progressed the illusion that had sustained Gorbachev's vision of reformed socialism in a more humane, modern Soviet Union was brutally exposed. The economy was spinning out of control, a consequence of deep budget deficits, shortages of all kinds, especially machine tools and other technology, revenue shortfalls, and the emergence of rampant inflation as the desperate government printed money to pay the bills and maintain the impression of stability. The resources necessary to carry through a viable transformation to a market economy were lacking. There was virtually no commercial infrastructure. Each "reform" seemed to uncover another deficiency. And the Russian people, encouraged to purchase in the Western consumerist style, often chose to stockpile their goods and put any money that came their way under the mattress.[54]

These problems and privations produced growing turmoil. New political parties formed through 1990 and the privileged place of the Communist Party quickly eroded. Noisy extremes – radical reformers calling for privatization and market capitalism on one side, enraged reactionary conservatives urging a restoration of coercive controls on the other – created an impression of failing authority that Gorbachev encouraged by favoring each side in turn. Several of the nation's 15 republics threatened secession. This in turn stimulated Russian nationalism, soon personified in the figure of the popular ex-communist Boris Yeltsin, who made the independence of Russia his cause and, having won a democratic election for the presidency, his power base. Gorbachev tried to maintain the Union. But the system was now under enormous pressure. Historian David Reynolds notes, "Plan versus market; party versus state; authority versus democracy; center versus republic; Union versus Russia; Gorbachev versus Yeltsin: such were the multiple fractures opening up in the USSR by 1990."[55]

The constitutional crisis grew through 1991. A treaty looking to a loose federal structure angered conservatives and produced an attempted coup led by high-placed communist diehards including the heads of the KGB and the Defense and Interior ministries. This failed, thanks largely to Yeltsin's leadership, popular Moscow resistance, and the impact of immediate worldwide publicity that apparently unnerved the conspirators. Gorbachev was publicly humiliated by the disloyalty of his associates. He briefly remained as Union president but resigned as general secretary of the Communist Party on August 20. Yeltsin, and other republic leaders round the nation seized the opportunity to declare their independence. Some formalities remained for adjustment. But on December 25 the Soviet Union ceased to exist.

It will be many years before historians feel confident enough to render a comprehensive account of the ending of the Cold War. The subject may turn out to be as complex and controversial as the debates about its origins. Much attention will be devoted to the search for a decisive turning point, and to the elaboration of a satisfactory reconstructive pattern somewhere between the now discredited determinism of the Marxists and the pessimism of philosophers like Paul Feyerabend who insist upon the unbridgeable gulf between the views people have before and after a revolutionary transformation.[56]

One fundamental issue is already on the table: Was the outcome produced essentially by the persistent and finally overwhelming pressure generated during the Cold War (especially in the 1980s) by the United States? Or was it rather due to the more or less autonomous judgment of the Soviet leadership in the mid-1980s that the communist venture could not proceed without a radical internal overhaul that was bound, once it got under way, to put their authority at risk? Around this central conundrum there are a host of ancillary questions. What were the relationships between purposeful individuals and the structures and institutions they were entangled with? What weight should be given to the contributions of individual leaders like Gorbachev, Reagan, Kohl, Pope John-Paul II, Yeltsin, and others? Were the principal dynamics political or economic, and how were these spheres interwoven? What common features or significant distinctions do we find in what appear to have been the three phases of the process – the agreements over nuclear arms, the liberation of Eastern Europe, and the dissolution of the Soviet Union?

Three general perspectives seem to be emerging among diplomatic historians. The first emphasizes the American role and especially the decisive influence of the containment policy and of President Reagan's policies. There is very widespread recognition of the long-term efficacy of containment and the finally intolerable burden it imposed upon the Soviets. Even conservative historians like Walter McDougall, who tend to emphasize liberal soft-headedness, acknowledge that all post-1947 presidents from Truman to Reagan adhered faithfully to this central geopolitical strategy.[57]   *containment*

A more liberal celebrant of containment, historian John Lewis Gaddis, in similarly ecumenical fashion, gives much credit to Reagan, as does Samuel Wells who finds the basic cause of the Soviet retreat in the impressive restoration of visible American power. Former administration stalwarts make this point too with Kenneth Adelman stressing the impact of Reagan's "delegitimation" of the Soviet Union with his tough, first-term rhetoric. Interestingly, a number of Russian historians, especially Gorbachev's critics, take the view that, in Genrikh Trofimenko's words, "Ronald Reagan won the Cold War." Other Americans are beginning to share the limelight, notably Secretary of State George Schultz, whom journalist Don Oberdorfer and historian Frances Fitzgerald both portray as a creative statesman.[58]

The clear alternative view emphasizes neither the intensifying force of containment nor any other form of American pressure, but rather the parlous internal conditions of the Soviet Union and the political conclusions Gorbachev and his fellow reformers drew from them. This is the perspective from which most European commentators proceed. They see the Reagan–Gorbachev arms negotiations as only one aspect of a complex issue. They also emphasize the active influence of purely European impulses such as the election of the resolutely anti-Soviet John-Paul II to the papacy in 1979, the highly significant Polish revolt led through the 1980s by Solidarity, and the creative opportunism of Helmut Kohl. But Gorbachev is inevitably the dominating figure here, as he is for many American commentators including George Kennan, who had from the

parlous – perilous or dangerous

start argued that the Soviet Union contained "the seeds of its own destruction" (as had Churchill) and now insisted that its leaders were acting autonomously and not in response to American pressure. Similar views are expressed by historians John Ullman and Thomas Paterson (who scoffs at "the Reagan victory school") and journalist Strobe Talbott who wrote an admiring article about Gorbachev when *Time* made him "Man of the Decade."[59]

On both sides of this divide, which is as yet far from having crystallized into the rigidity that long characterized writing about the Cold War's origins, one finds a welcome acknowledgement of multiple causation that seems to herald a third, more balanced outlook. Thus one of Reagan's champions, Peter Rodman, concedes that there was a powerful, at least partly autonomous European dimension. And from the other side historians like Raymond Garthoff and Richard Barnet, while stressing the primacy of the Soviet Union's internal dynamics and Gorbachev's responses to them, admit that American containment hastened if it did not cause the Soviet collapse. This seems to accord more or less with the view I have advanced here, that the process developed at two distinct levels, in two distinct phases, and with two separate arenas – a United States–Soviet geostrategic evolution and a Europe–Soviet geopolitical development in which the United States was only marginally involved – each crucial to the final outcome.[60]

In the search for more general causes of the Cold War's unexpected end historians may focus eventually on the clearly discernible realization of many governments and peoples from the 1960s onward that the widespread democratic and totalitarian post-World War II commitment to state-directed, industry-focused collectivism – itself the consequence of economic breakdown in the 1930s and political trauma in the early 1940s – could not produce the plenty and fuller life that consumers everywhere now wanted. Slowly, delayed through the confused 1970s, but quickening in the early 1980s, and bursting out more vigorously from around 1985, the call for a market-driven, consumer-oriented economics that could only flourish in a context of widened freedom (from economic controls as well as political oppression) captured first the easily persuaded Anglo-American capitalist stronghold, moved rapidly on to the European, Scandinavian, and Australasian social democracies, and finally, against all expectations, inspired that self-willed transformation of the once potent communist world that Gorbachev began and others are continuing.

The resulting process of integrating internationalism may indeed turn out to be the key that unlocks the full history of the Cold War era. We are certainly a long way from any confident assertions about this. History today is still dominated by the national outlook. And the subject is both too large in scope and too close to us in time to permit any but the most superficial generalizations, even if we confine ourselves to the United States.

But one can at least try to predict some of the themes that may engage future historians. Many will, of course, continue, as multitudes of scholars have always done, to emphasize the enormous range of 1945–90 experience that lies quite outside the Cold War's ambit. The period we call "the Cold War era" can be presented with equal validity from a variety of perspectives. We can anticipate conceptually oriented books with titles like *The Age of Plenty* (focusing on the extraordinary economic developments) or *The Coming of Multi-national (or Multi-cultural) America*, emphasizing the large-scale Hispanic and Asian migrations of recent years, the rise of African-Americans to prominence, and the dramatic fulfillment of the ambitions of millions of descendants of the great eastern and southern European infusions of the late nineteenth century. For there are great areas of modern experience – social mobility, urban history, private intimacy in all its forms, the world of work, much of popular mass culture – that the Cold War touched only very tangentially, if at all.

Even diplomatic historians, no longer trapped within the subject they are trying to understand, will doubtless question the Cold War's historiographical hegemony. Here they will be following the path cleared by Geoffrey Barraclough, whose 1964 *An Introduction to Contemporary History* downplayed the Western view of world politics and asserted that neglected

hegemony – leadership dominance

factors like science, non-Western ideologies, and Third World cultures were powerful agents of historical change.[61] More recently E. J. Hobsbawm has argued the legitimacy of a "short 20th century" (1914–90), effectively subsuming the Cold War within a broader interpretation featuring three related world struggles. And already one sees signs, tentative as yet, of two other subversive lines of thought. One is that World War II, with its incalculable moral and emotional hangover and, in the West at least, the combination of pent-up wartime savings and the intellectual triumph of Keynesian economics it produced, was, certainly in the early years, at least as powerful a causative factor in shaping the postwar as the Cold War itself; a second is that the great struggle with Soviet communism, serious as it was, should be seen as essentially an episode in an enduring and profound series of competitive relations between the United States and Europe.

Still, when all alternative avenues have been explored and all proper qualifications made, it is likely that the impact of the Cold War (however we define it) will continue to impress. Taken in its most familiar forms – as a political–military struggle, as a contest between market capitalism and totalitarian socialism, as a clash of ideologies, as the instrument of the full emergence of the United States as the dominant world power – its effect has to be seen as genuinely transforming. There are certainly many paradoxes. The Cold War was always controversial. At home it fostered even as it distorted economic growth. It diverted resources from social needs. Yet it surely facilitated the development of world trade, the recovery of Western Europe, and the emergence of modern Asian capitalism. Politically, it strengthened the power of the state and the military in the United States and elsewhere. It created a durable system of international order that, even as it led to coercive tendencies that limited individual freedom, proved strong enough to avoid a full-scale superpower military confrontation and to maintain control over the nuclear arsenal. This was an achievement, though the "long peace" perspective has to be balanced against the casualties of the Cold War, calculated by David Reynolds at around 18 million deaths. In the more autonomous socio-cultural sphere, in America and its Western allies at least, the Cold War promoted a variety of progressive impulses, such as an increasing freedom for minorities, even as it inspired fear, especially fear of nuclear war, a solidarity that too often calcified into unimaginative or even coercive conformity, and a masculine tone to public life that provoked at least half the population.

Future historians of the United States, grappling with the domestic and foreign issues of the Cold War era, will therefore find paradoxes, unresolved issues, and a robust historiographical tradition. Some areas seem likely to remain comparatively uncontroversial. The outline of economic developments, for instance, registered in the ostensibly hard evidence of statistics and accounts, is widely accepted: impressive growth until the early 1970s; inflation, stagnation, and foreign competition thereafter; a measure of recovery from 1983. The decline of Marxism, and indeed of collectivist thinking generally, has exalted market capitalism. Academics are still interested in the clashing ideas of Keynes, the monetarists, and others. But they argue much less about fundamentals today than about growth strategies, administration, and, of course, social consequences.

In political and social history, however, controversy will doubtless persist. It comes not only from the intense moral concern naturally aroused by accessible issues of power and societal organization, but also from the endlessly invitational character of those issues. For while the evidence in economic studies is mostly encased in forbiddingly machine-like formulas, the materials available to political and social historians are incorrigibly human, endlessly abundant, and softly responsive to authorial ingenuity. It is therefore not simply from the spur of moral or ethical preference, but also from a professional desire to bring order to potentially unstable fields of study, that historians have devised strong explanatory categories that tend, however, to narrow as much as they encourage debate. In political history the liberal/conservative dichotomy, though persistently buffeted by radical revisionism, has long been a cherished prop to mainstream scholarship. In social

history, where the left has been more influential, most thinking seems to be channeled through the prisms of class, race, or gender. Taken together all these compelling formulas, while conveying the pleasing image of a stable polity and an imperfect but morally informed society capable of producing desired change without severe dislocation, encompass most of what the historical profession regards as fundamental in post-1945 American history.

Will future historians accept these familiar categories as a legacy or a burden? Let us assume for a moment a fresh generation of boldly questioning young intellectuals eager to challenge the conventional wisdom. Some may wish to revive the flagging momentum of left-wing revisionism. Radical critics have often, since the 1960s, depicted liberalism as a hypocritical and sometimes oppressive political force, able very occasionally to effect reforms but unable to address social inequities effectively. It is on this view essentially a sham counterforce to a system dominated by corporate and conservative special interests. A more innovative and perhaps more likely point of attack in these blander post-Cold War years, however, may emerge from a cold-eyed realism that, bypassing old ideological battles, exposes the chameleonic character of political and intellectual liberalism. It may be asked whether this notoriously baggy concept, or indeed the similarly loose collection of nostrums that constitute modern American conservatism, has any residual validity. The critique might go on to examine the constitution, often (and rightly) seen as a pillar of the modern liberal/conservative order, manifest for example in the practical bias against third parties. It might be argued that the constitution was gravely distorted during the Cold War era and that serious scholars, instead of writing unthreatening books about the excesses of the imperial presidency or the legislative usurpations of the Supreme Court, would be better employed looking beyond the sacred texts and institutions with a view to exposing the "invisible" and arguably more coercive "outside constitution" governed by an all-powerful media, by overmighty corporations, and by a host of affluent manipulators who enjoy immense power and are largely unaccountable.

Similarly provocative questions may be put to historians who have focused more or less exclusively on class, race, or gender as primary generative impulses in social as well as political history. These are unquestionably central and profound preoccupations. They all, perhaps especially the civil rights advances of the mid-1960s, contributed to that enlargement of human freedom which was the most strikingly progressive feature of American life during the Cold War era. But the notion of evolutionary reform is certainly open to question. Change often came in fits and starts, with surprising reversals and unexpected renewals in the flux of American public life. Class was a primary rallying cause in the 1940s. It returned in attenuated form in the 1970s and 1980s. Race claims our attention in the 1960s, but it is also crucial to our understanding of the 1950s and arguably has remained central ever since. The women's movement has over time taken many forms, its victories half-won, its supporters often divided. Another range of queries – going to proportion rather than substantive relevance – might arise from the suspicion that these main causes have operated somewhat imperialistically to crowd out a host of other potentially illuminative issues such as the wide implications of the immigration experience, career patterns, the world of work, urban/suburban tensions, and many intriguing aspects of American cultural life.

Cultural history, at least in the broad sense, often seems to function as a kind of no-man's land. Always inescapably in the foreground, open to the quick exploratory foray, but far too risky for sustained inspection. Yet there are great opportunities here for a future historian with a synthesizing bent. One task is to define cultural phenomena more closely. Another is to examine their elusive relationships to politics and social behavior. A series of efforts were made in this cause during the 1950s as we have seen. But Dwight McDonald's mid-cult and mass-cult classifications look very old-fashioned now. And W.H. Whyte's "organization man," John Kenneth Galbraith's portraits of a controlled economy, and Daniel Bell's "farewell to ideology" were all more or less confounded in the turbulent 1960s. The taste for bold prediction faded as the exploding cultural firmament produced a heterogeneous collection of iconoclastic youth cultures, new musical and literary genres, a widening range of permissive and soon commercialized lifestyles, a rising flurry of minority and ethnic solidarity and sensitivity campaigns, and finally a burst of increasingly organized reaction which included the neo-conservative intellectuals and religious fundamentalists who played a significant part in Reagan's 1980 victory and opened the way for the "culture wars" of more recent years. The main problem here seems to be the constantly changing context. The 1950s' social theorists, whose schematizing approach still appeals as a model, were inspired by sharp memories of recent totalitarianism. They feared overt or hidden control. In the 1980s and since the critics have been moved by fears of lost control and have expressed their concerns emotionally rather than systematically in anguished jeremiads. Thus historian Gertrude Himmelfarb laments the "demoralization" of society, while the philosopher Richard Rorty calls, in an echo of the Cold War consensus-building Truman–Eisenhower years, for a reinvigorated patriotism as the healing social bond.

So we come back finally to foreign relations and to the Cold War itself. Here too we can anticipate interest in a basic question. Was the Cold War, on the whole, a positive event for the United States? To be sure the United States "won" by any reasonable definition. Looking at it simply as a power struggle we can see that the persistent application (even in the 1970s) of the containment strategy – the steady, highly pressured politico-economic isolation of the Soviet Union, which was in effect subjected to the modern equivalent of a long medieval siege – was a productive formula. It faltered only when the United States allowed itself, in the mid-1960s, to focus obsessively on the Cold War's periphery – notably in Vietnam, the most profound error of the period – rather than on its European center.

But the Cold War has typically been viewed by its historians as essentially a moral issue and here, as we have repeatedly seen, there are two diverging lines of thought. The affirming mainstream will doubtless continue to consider the

American struggle with communism as the culminating act in its defense since 1917 of freedom and the open society against various authoritarian and totalitarian threats. The United States from this perspective has been the decisive military and moral agent in each of the last century's three great world-wide struggles. It was responding to felt necessity certainly, but also to a tradition that can be traced to the Puritan sense of mission, which evolved more tangibly through the elevation of reason in the late eighteenth century and the enthusiasm for international law 100 years later, found its highest practical expression in the political and economic management that brought the impressive victories of the twentieth century, and eventually received a strong measure of vindication in the eagerness with which, at least initially and admittedly with many local variations and some reservations, much of the post-communist world embraced representative democracy, market capitalism, and a degree of American political leadership.

The critique of American Cold War policies, it will be remembered, has been equally persistent and has taken several forms. There have always been isolationists on the American right, though their influence has waxed and waned. Many on the left still trace the Cold War to aggressive and/or insensitive American policies. Their indictment has broadened over time to assert the United States' economic ruthlessness, its alleged exploitation of the post-colonial world, and its self-serving political and military support for the corrupt dictators and elites that resisted the legitimate struggles of their oppressed peoples. Stress has been laid too on state coercion and the pervasive militarization of Cold War America, not least upon a rampant arms technology which produced a dangerous nuclear arms race but which has also, from Hiroshima through the incontinent air assault on Indochina and on to the attacks on Iraq and Serbia allowed the United States to inflict heavy casualties upon its enemies at comparatively little cost to itself.

We can hardly hope to harmonize these contrasting attitudes (admittedly stated here only in outline) which have long given a disconcertingly Jekyll and Hyde image to American foreign initiatives. Two partial explanations help understanding. One, frequently remarked, is that the two approaches spring not only from the analysis of international reality but from very different and passionately held views about what the United States is and should be. This is perhaps why periodic attempts at reconciliation are rarely fruitful. The old attitudes tend to reappear promptly, sometimes under modified labels.

The other explanation emerges from the often-overlooked fact that the United States operated during the Cold War in two very different arenas. As a great power leading alliances of like-minded nations in the politico-military defense of Europe and Japan and the developed world, it arguably functioned virtuously and successfully. In the more volatile "Third World" arena it clearly did somewhat less well. The associative, managerial ethos that served so creatively in defense of the West was often ineffectual in the post-colonial gluepots that emerged almost everywhere after 1950. The new societies were typically poor, dictator-ridden, and racked with social inequities. Here the representative American nostrums of evolutionary reform, necessarily based on a middle class that was fragile if it existed at all, were repeatedly challenged and sometimes trumped by ardent nationalists or radical revolutionaries inspired by iconic figures like Lenin, Mao, and Castro. Their resistance led to a long series of controversial American interventions, often in league with badly compromised local despots, and sometimes in remote areas where there was no obvious national interest.

A large part of the problem was that in "world communism" American leaders thought they possessed the master-concept that linked these otherwise distinctive theaters. Seen in the early Cold War as centrally directed from Moscow, later as a hydra-headed but still united threat, the image of a monolithic antagonist gripped American official and much public thought through most of the long struggle. Such thinking is now recognized as simplistic. Along with a number of related facile assumptions and false historical analogies it took little account of the backwash of European imperialism, of nationalism, or of local variations that seem so obvious in hindsight.

The error was tragic. But it becomes understandable when we remember that most Americans, still preoccupied in their daily lives with their own affairs, experienced the Cold War as a succession of crises and unpleasant surprises, some of them admittedly drawn out in time. The unifying idea of a generalized communist threat was all too effective in retrospective explanation and also in inhibiting fresh thought or subtle policy discrimination. Moreover, as a predictive instrument it was often blunt and unfocused. It could not foretell where, how, and in what form the next problem would emerge. Thus the Cold War, let us remember, unfolded in distinct, unanticipated stages: first in Europe; then in northeastern Asia; finally somewhat more incrementally in the rest of the world. The containment approach, vitalized by the Munich analogy with its compelling stress on quick, resolute resistance, was therefore given an unintended universal application, often in unlikely places. During the whole period furthermore, sudden confrontations, frequent public alarms, and the spiraling nuclear arms race discouraged risk-taking reconsiderations. Powerful vested interests – most obviously Eisenhower's military–industrial complex – were similarly inhibiting. And there was throughout the political leadership a reluctance to change course for fear of jeopardizing the hard-won Cold War consensus built up so arduously in the Truman years. In the later stages of the conflict, from about 1972, we do see some reevaluation and more sophisticated approaches: détente, arms control, human rights concern. Yet it still took nearly two more decades to end the confrontation.

The Cold War then was a complex struggle, not an easy or unblemished American triumph. It is not altogether clear why it lasted so long, a question historians are now beginning to address. There is, however, one further feature of the American role that seems finally noteworthy, especially when we contemplate the remarkably rapid transition from the state-focused Cold War to the interdependent and globally integrating political and economic tendencies of the 1990s. This is the persisting notion of American universalism. The United States played its part in the Cold War as a nation state, but also very self-consciously as a model for the fulfillment of supposedly universal aspirations – of democracy, of freedom, of opportunity. There was a feeling, long-rooted in American self-perceptions, that as the nineteenth-century novelist Herman Melville put it "We are not a nation so much as a world."

This sense of transcendent American significance, viewed with skepticism in some overseas circles, is also perhaps a clue to what might be regarded as the most profound impact of the Cold War upon the United States. It is surely no less than the full engagement, after centuries of fitful isolationism and po-litical inappetence, of this country with the outside world. The process was long in the making. It may have come about with-out the Cold War, but one suspects that it would then have been a more drawn out, halting, and less spectacular develop-ment. The Cold War, with its nuclear arms dimension and rapidly globalizing tendency, ensured that it would be sud-den, sometimes violent, and quite transformative, both in its effects at home and its impact on the world. That it turned out to be, in the end, a mostly successful emergence, was the achievement of the generations we have followed in this book.

Notes

Notes to Chapter 1

1 William E. Leuchtenburg, *In the Shadow of FDR: From Harry Truman to Bill Clinton* (Ithaca and London, 1985), p. ix.
2 David McCullough, *Truman* (New York, 1992); Alonzo Hamby, *Man of the People: A Life of Harry S. Truman* (New York, 1995), p. 635.
3 For general historiographical surveys see Richard Kirkendall, *The Truman Era as a Research Field: A Re-Appraisal, 1972* (New York, 1974) and more recently Michael J. Lacey (ed.), *The Truman Presidency* (Cambridge, 1989). See also Geoffrey Smith, "Harry, We Hardly Know You: Revisionism, Politics and Diplomacy, 1945–1953," *American Political Science Review,* 70 (1976), pp. 560–82.
4 Steve Fraser and Gary Gerstle, eds., *The Rise and Fall of the New Deal Order, 1930–1980* (Princeton, 1989); Leuchtenburg, *In the Shadow of FDR.*
5 For wartime business–labor tensions see Richard Polenberg, *War and Society: The United States, 1941–1945* (New York, 1972), chapter 6.
6 Gary Gerstle, "The Protean Character of American Liberalism," *American Historical Review* (October, 1994), pp. 1043–5; Henry Wallace, *The Century of the Common Man* (New York, 1943); Henry Luce, "The American Century," *Life* (February, 1941); F. A. Hayek, *The Road to Serfdom* (Chicago, 1944).
7 Polenberg, *War and Society,* chapter 5; John Blum, *V Was For Victory: American Politics and Culture During World War II* (New York, 1976). See also James T. Patterson, *Grand Expectations: The United States, 1945–1974* (New York, 1996), p. 13.
8 Alan Brinkley, *The End of Reform: New Deal Liberalism in Recession and War* (New York, 1995), pp. 251–8.

9   Alonzo Hamby, *Liberalism and its Challengers from Roosevelt to Bush*, 2nd edn. (New York, 1992), pp. 48–51; James Gilbert, *Another Chance: Postwar America, 1945–1985* (Chicago, 1986), p. 11; Brinkley, *The End of Reform*, pp. 265–71.

10 Leuchtenburg, *In the Shadow of FDR*, p. 12.

11 Arthur S. Link and B. Catton, *American Epoch: A History of the United States since 1900 Vol. II, 1921--1945* (New York, 1973), p. 299; William H. Chafe, *The Unfinished Journey: America since 1945* (New York, 1999), p. 28.

12 James McGregor Burns, *The Lion and the Fox* (New York, 1956); Warren F.Kimball, *The Juggler: Franklin Roosevelt as Wartime States-man* (Princeton, 1991).

13 John Lamberton Harper, *American Visions of Europe: Franklin D. Roosevelt, George F. Kennan, and Dean G. Acheson* (Cambridge, Massachusetts, 1994), pp. 7–131.

14 This argument is elaborated in Fraser J. Harbutt, *Yalta's Shadow: The Decline and Fall of Traditional Diplomacy* (forthcoming). See also Geir Lundestad, *The American Non-Policy Toward Eastern Europe, 1943–1947* (New York, 1978).

15 Robert M. Hathaway, *Ambiguous Partnership: Britain and America, 1944–1947* (New York, 1981). For Yalta see John Snell (ed.), *The Meaning of Yalta: Big Three Diplomacy and the New Balance of Power* (Baton Rouge, 1956); Diane Clemens, *Yalta* (New York, 1970); and Russell Buhite, *Decision at Yalta: An Appraisal of Summit Diplomacy* (Wilmington, Delaware, 1986).

16 For Teheran see Bohlen Minutes, Roosevelt–Stalin meeting December 1, 1943, *Foreign Relations of the United States* (hereafter *FRUS*), *Cairo and Teheran*, pp. 594–6.

17 Plenary meeting, February 9, 1945, *FRUS, Yalta*, pp. 971–3. For elaboration see Fraser J. Harbutt, *The Iron Curtain: Churchill, America, and the Origins of the Cold War* (New York, 1986), pp. 87–90.

18 Ibid., pp. 91–9.

19 Leuchtenburg, *In the Shadow of FDR*, p. 40.

20 Merle Miller, *Plain Speaking: An Oral Biography of Harry S. Truman* (New York, 1973), pp. 408–9. *Public Papers of the Presidents: Harry S. Truman (1952–1953)*, p. 1201.

21 See Arthur M. Schlesinger, Jr., "Origins of the Cold War," *Foreign Affairs*, 46 (October, 1967), pp. 22–52.

22 Felix Willmer, *Betrayal* (New York, 1950); George F. Kennan, *American Diplomacy, 1900–1950* (Chicago, 1951) pp. v–vi, 65–6, 95–101; Hans J. Morgenthau, *Politics Among Nations: The Struggle for Power and Peace* (New York, 1948). For early left critiques see *PM, Nation, Monthly Review* among other newspapers and journals published in 1945–1948.

23 William Appleman Williams, *The Tragedy of American Diplomacy*

(New York, 1959). For a range of revisionist and other historiography see Thomas G. Paterson and Robert McMahon (eds), *The Origins of the Cold War*, 3rd edn (Lexington, Massachusetts, 1991).

24 Vladislav Zubok and Constantine Pleshakov, *Inside the Kremlin's Cold War: From Stalin to Khrushchev* (Cambridge, Massachusetts, 1996).

25 Robert Hathaway, *Ambiguous Partnership*; Randall Bennett Woods, *A Changing of the Guard: Anglo–American Relations, 1941–1946* (Chapel Hill, 1990); Harbutt, *The Iron Curtain*, pp. 117–50; Geir Lundestad, "Empire By Invitation: The United States and Western Europe, 1945–1952," *Journal of Peace Research*, 23, (September, 1986), pp. 263–77; Odd Arne Westad, Bernath Lecture, Organization of American Historians Convention, St. Louis, June 2000; Marc Trachtenberg, *A Constructed Peace: The Making of the European Settlement, 1945–1963* (Princeton, 1999).

26 See, for example, Clemens, *Yalta*, pp. 267–91.

27 Bruce Kuklick, *American Policy and the Division of Germany: The Clash with Russia over Reparations* (New York, 1972). See also Marc Trachtenberg, *A Constructed Peace: The Making of the European Settlement, 1945–1963* (Princeton, 1999), pp. 18–33.

28 The most balanced view of the events leading to Hiroshima is Martin J. Sherwin, *A World Destroyed: The Atomic Bomb and the Grand Alliance* (New York, 1975).

29 Gar Alperovitz, *Atomic Diplomacy: Hiroshima and Potsdam* (New York, 1965); Sherwin, *A World Destroyed*; Barton J. Bernstein, "Roosevelt, Truman, and the Atomic Bomb, 1941–1945: A Reinterpretation," *Political Science Quarterly*, 90 (Spring, 1975) pp. 23–69.

30 J. Samuel Walker, "The Decision to Use the Bomb: A Historiographical Update" in Michael J. Hogan (ed.), *Hiroshima: In History and Memory* (Cambridge, 1996), pp. 13–37.

31 For Smithsonian controversy see Michael J. Hogan, "The Enola Gay Controversy: History, Memory and the Politics of Presentation," Ibid., pp. 200–32. For harshness of the Pacific War's latter stages see John Dower, *War Without Mercy: Race and Power in the Pacific War* (New York, 1986).

32 David Holloway, *Stalin, and the Bomb: The Soviet Union and Atomic Energy, 1939–1956* (New Haven, 1994).

33 Schlesinger, "Origins of the Cold War," pp. 22–52.

34 Robert L. Messer, *The End of an Alliance: James F. Byrnes, Roosevelt, Truman, and the Origins of the Cold War* (Chapel Hill, 1982), pp. 156–80.

35 Harbutt, *The Iron Curtain*, pp. 151–266.

36 For the concept of a first Anglo–Soviet "Cold War" see Ibid., pp. 117–50. See also Henry B. Ryan, *The Vision of Anglo–America: The US–UK Alliance and the Emerging Cold War* (Cambridge, UK, 1987).

37 Kennan to Byrnes, February 22, 1946, *FRUS*, 1946, II, pp. 696–709.

38 *Vital Speeches*, 12 (March 15, 1946), pp. 329–32.
39 John Lewis Gaddis, *The United States and the Origins of the Cold War, 1941–1947* (New York, 1972); Harbutt, *The Iron Curtain*, pp. 180–1; *New York Times*, March 7, 1946; *Washington Star*, March 7, 1946.
40 For geopolitical context see Bruce R. Kuniholm, *The Origins of the Cold War in the Near East: Great Power Conflict and Diplomacy in Iran, Turkey, and Greece* (Princeton, 1980).
41 Isaac Deutscher, *Stalin*, revised edn. (Middlesex, UK, 1966), p. 565; Strobe Talbott (ed.), *Khrushchev Remembers* (Boston, 1970), pp. 361, 393.
42 For Paris Peace Conference see Patricia Dawson Ward, *The Threat of Peace: James F. Byrnes and the Council of Foreign Ministers 1945–1946* (Kent, Ohio, 1979). For Wallace see Hamby, *Man of the People*, pp. 355–9.
43 John Lewis Gaddis, *The Long Peace: Inquiries into the History of the Cold War* (New York, 1987); Ward, *The Threat of Peace, passim*.
44 Joseph M. Jones, *The Fifteen Weeks: An Inside Account of the Genesis of the Marshall Plan* (New York, 1955). For Vandenberg see Dean Acheson, *Present at the Creation: My Years at the State Department* (New York, 1969), pp. 218–19. For Truman speech see *Public Papers of the Presidents: Harry S. Truman (1947)*, pp. 176–80.
45 Gabriel Almond, *The American People and Foreign Policy* (New York, 1960), p. 73; Walter Lippman, *The Cold War: A Study in U.S. Foreign Policy* (New York, 1947); Arthur M. Schlesinger, Jr., *The Vital Center: The Politics of Freedom* (New York, 1949), p. 224; Richard Freeland, *The Truman Doctrine and the Origins of McCarthyism: Foreign Policy, Domestic Politics, and Internal Security, 1946–1948* (New York, 1985); Athan Theoharis, *Seeds of Repression: Harry S. Truman and the Origins of McCarthyism* (Chicago, 1971). For Kennan see "The Sources of Soviet Conduct," *Foreign Affairs*, 25 (July, 1947), pp. 566–82.
46 Department of State, *Bulletin*, 16 (June 15, 1947), pp. 1159–60; Leffler, *Preponderance of Power*, pp. 159–66.
47 Harry S. Truman, *Memoirs: Years of Trial and Hope* (New York, 1956); Dean Acheson, *Present at the Creation*; Joseph M. Jones, *The Fifteen Weeks: An Inside Account of the Genesis of the Marshall Plan* (New York, 1955); David Fromkin, *In the Time of the Americans: The Generation that Changed America's Role in the World* (New York, 1995); Walter Isaacson and Evan Thomas, *The Wise Men: Six Friends and the World They Made* (New York, 1986); John Lewis Gaddis, *We Now Know: Rethinking Cold War History* (New York, 1987), p. 38.
48 Michael J. Hogan, *The Marshall Plan: America, Britain, and the Reconstruction of Western Europe, 1947–1952* (New York, 1987); Alan Milward, *The Reconstruction of Western Europe, 1945–1951* (Berkeley, 1977), pp. 242–53; Melvyn P. Leffler, *A Preponderance of*

Power: National Security, the Truman Administration, and the Cold War (Stanford, 1992), pp. 10–13, 513.

49 Lacey (ed.), *The Truman Presidency*, p. 3.

50 For 1945 to 1948 in domestic politics see Hamby, *Man of the People*, pp. 361–487; Robert Donovan, *Conflict and Crisis: The Presidency of Harry S. Truman, 1945–1948* (New York, 1977). For revisionist treatments see Lacey (ed.), *The Truman Presidency*; Barton J. Bernstein (ed.), *Towards a New Past* (New York, 1968); and Barton J. Bernstein (ed.), *Politics and Policies of the Truman Administration* (Chicago, 1970).

51 Richard Polenberg, *War and Society*; Neil Chamberlain, *The Union Challenge to Management Control* (New York, 1948), p. 308.

52 David Brody, *Workers in Industrial America: Essays on the Twentieth Century Struggle* (New York, 1979), pp. 173–229; Nelson Lichtenstein, "From Corporatism to Collective Bargaining: Organized Labor and the Eclipse of Social Democracy in the Postwar Era," in Fraser and Gerstle, eds., *The Rise and Fall of the New Deal Order*, pp. 122–52.

53 Ibid., pp. 132–3.

54 William Graebner, *The Age of Doubt: American Thought and Culture in the 1940s* (Prospect Heights, Illinois, 1991), p. 10; Richard Polenberg, *One Nation Divisible*, p. 108.

55 Hamby, *Liberalism and its Challengers*, p. 61.

56 Robert Griffiths, "Forging American Postwar Order," in Lacey (ed.), *The Truman Presidency*, pp. 63–7.

57 James Judis, *The Paradox of American Democracy: Elites, Special Interests, and the Betrayal of Public Trust* (New York, 2000), p. 70.

58 Chafe, *Unfinished Journey*, pp. 83–5.

59 For black wartime experience see Richard Polenberg, *One Nation Divisible*, pp. 69–78.

60 Leuchtenburg, *In the Shadow of FDR*, p. 23–4.

61 These details are drawn from *Statistical History of the United States from Colonial Times to the Present* (New York, 1976). See also Patterson, *Grand Expectations*, pp. 10–38; Kenneth Jackson, *The Crabgrass Frontier: The Suburbanization of the United States* (New York, 1985); and Polenberg, *One Nation Divisible*, pp. 131–4.

62 Robert H. Wiebe, *The Search for Order, 1877–1920* (New York, 1967), chapter 2; Brian Balogh, "Reorganizing the Organizational Synthesis: Federal–Professional Relations in Modern America," *Studies in American Political Development*, 5 (Spring, 1991), pp. 119–72.

63 James L. Baughman, *The Republic of Mass Culture: Journalism, Filmmaking, and Broadcasting in America since 1941* (Baltimore and London, 1992), p. 11.

64 George F. Kennan, *Memoirs: 1925–1950* (Boston, 1967), p. 299. For public literary taste see Graebner, *The Age of Doubt*, pp. 50–1.

65 John Gunther, *Inside U.S.A.* (New York, 1947). For Truman quote

see Jonathan Daniels, *Man of Independence* (Philadelphia, 1950), p. 278.

66 Gunther, *Inside U.S.A., passim.* See also Jordan Schwartz, *The New Dealers: Power Politics in the Age of Roosevelt* (New York, 1993) and Numan V.Bartlett, *The New South, 1945–1980* (Baton Rouge, 1945).

67 Graebner, *The Age of Doubt*, pp. xi–xii.

68 Susan Hartman, *Truman and the 80ᵗʰ Congress* (Columbia, Missouri, 1971); Leuchtenburg, *In the Shadow of FDR*, p. 23.

69 Hamby, *Man of the People*, pp. 430–1; Clifford to the President, Memo., November 19, 1947, Clifford MSS. Truman Library, Independence, MO. See also for campaign generally Irwin Ross, *The Loneliest Campaign: The Truman Victory of 1948* (New York, 1968), pp. 29–34 and *passim.*

70 Ross, *The Loneliest Campaign*; and, more succinctly, Hamby, *Man of the People*, pp. 439–66. For Wallace campaign see Norman Markowitz, *The Rise and Fall of the People's Century: Henry A. Wallace and American Liberalism* (New York, 1973).

71 Gaddis, *We Now Know*, p. 115.

72 Ibid., pp. 46–49.

73 For final stages and immediate aftermath see Hamby, *Man of the People*, pp. 455–66.

74 For South reference see Hamby, *Man of the People*, p. 465. See also Hodgson, *America in Our Time: From World War II to Nixon,* (New York, 1976), chapter 4; and Zachary Karabell, *The Last Campaign: How Harry Truman Won the 1948 Election* (New York, 2000).

75 Schlesinger, *The Vital Center*, p. xix.

Notes to Chapter 2

1 Arthur M. Schlesinger Jr., *The Imperial Presidency* (New York, 1974) and see his article, "Parliamentary Government," *New Republic* (August 31, 1974).

2 *Public Papers of the Presidents: Harry S. Truman, 1949* (Washington D.C., 1965), pp. 112–16.

3 *New York Times* (January 6, 1949).

4 Samuel Lubell, *The Future of American Politics* (New York, 1951), p. 37.

5 Chafe, *Unfinished Journey*, chapter 4; Patterson, *Grand Expectations*, p. 164; Hamby in Lacey (ed.), *The Truman Presidency*, p. 53.

6 See generally, Walter LaFeber, *America, Russia, and the Cold War, 1945–1992*, 7th edn. (New York, 1993), pp. 86–9; William W. Stueck Jr., *The Road to Confrontation: American Policy toward China and Korea, 1947–1950* (Chapel Hill, 1981); Ross Koen, *The China Lobby* (New York, 1960).

7   Dean Acheson, "Letter of Transmittal," *United States Relations with China, 1944–1949* (Washington, 1949), pp. xiv–xvii; David McLellan, *Dean Acheson* (New York, 1976), pp. 188–209.

8   Akira Iriye, *The Cold War in Asia* (New York, 1974); Odd Arne Westad, *Cold War and Revolution: Soviet–American Rivalry and the Origins of the Chinese Civil War, 1944–1946* (New York, 1993).

9   LaFeber, *America, Russia, and the Cold War*, p. 88; William W. Stueck, Jr., *The Korean War: An International History* (Princeton, 1995); Nancy Bernkopf Tucker, *Patterns in the Dust: Chinese–American Relations and the Recognition Controversy, 1949–50* (New York, 1983).

10 David Alan Rosenberg, "American Atomic Strategy and the Hydrogen Bomb Decision," *Journal of American History*, 66:1, (June, 1979), pp. 62–87; Holloway, *Stalin and the Bomb*.

11 Lisle Rose, *The Cold War Comes to Main Street: America in 1950* (Lawrence, 1999), pp. 64–6.

12 "Editorial," *Life* (February 27, 1950). For polls see Mildred Strunk, ed., "The Quarterly Polls," *Public Opinion Quarterly*, 14:2, (Summer, 1950), p. 372.

13 NSC 68 in *FRUS*, 1950, I, pp. 235–92; LaFeber, *America, Russia, and the Cold War*, p. 96.

14 Stanley Kutler, "Introduction", in Stephen J. Whitfield, *The Culture of the Cold War* (Baltimore, 1991), p. vii; Alastair Cooke, *A Generation on Trial* (New York, 1952). See also Allen Weinstein, *Perjury: The Hiss–Chambers Case* (New York, 1978).

15 The Wheeling speech is in Thomas Reeves, *The Life and Times of Joseph McCarthy: A Biography* (New York, 1982), pp. 223–8.

16 Patterson, *Grand Expectations*, pp. 165–205; Rose, *The Cold War Comes to Main Street*, pp. 33–5, 142. Garry Wills, "Introduction," in Lillian Hellman, *Scoundrel Time* (New York, 1976), p. 19.

17 Robert Chadwell Williams, *Klaus Fuchs, Atomic Spy* (Cambridge, Massachusetts, 1987), pp. 109–17; Ronald Radosh, "More Evidence Against the Rosenbergs," *Washington Post* (October 31, 1992).

18 Rose, *The Cold War Comes to Main Street*, p. 210; Ellen Schrecker, *Many are the Crimes: McCarthyism in America* (Boston, 1998).

19 Arthur M. Schlesinger, Jr., "The Two Joes ... And Korea," *Times Literary Supplement* (September 22, 2000).

20 Rose, *The Cold War Comes to Main Street*, pp. 125–65. See also Athan Theoharis and John Stuart Cox, *The Boss: J. Edgar Hoover and the Great American Inquisition* (New York, 1990).

21 David Caute, *The Great Fear* (New York, 1978). See also Victor Navasky, *Naming Names* (New York, 1980) and congressional transcripts in Eric M. Bentley, ed., *Thirty Years of Treason* (New York, 1971).

22 Richard H. Rovere, *Senator Joe McCarthy* (Cleveland, 1960) p. 3; and Robert A. Divine, *Since 1945: Politics and Diplomacy in Recent American History*, 3rd edn. (New York, 1985),p. 34.

23   Richard Hofstadter, *The Age of Reform: From Bryan to FDR* (New York, 1955); and *The Paranoid Style in American Politics and other Essays* (New York, 1967); Daniel Bell, ed., *The Radical Right* (New York, 1964), *passim*; Seymour Martin Lipset, "The Sources of the Radical Right," in Bell, ed., *The Radical Right*, pp. 303–39; Stephen Whitfield, "The 1950s: The Era of No Hard Feelings," *South Atlantic Quarterly*, LXXIV (Summer, 1975) pp. 294–5. Richard Pells, *The Liberal Mind in a Conservative Age: American Intellectuals in the 1940s and 1950s*, (New York, 1984), p. 217. See also Martin Jay, *The Dialectical Imagination* (Boston, 1973), ch. 6.

24   Norman Pollack, ed., *The Populist Mind* (Indianapolis, 1967); Lawrence Goodwyn, *The Populist Moment. A Short History of the Agrarian Revolt in America* (Oxford, 1978), pp. vii–xxiv. Athan Theoharis, *Seeds of Repressions: Harry S. Truman and the Origins of McCarthyism* (New York, 1970); Michael Paul Rogin, *The Intellectuals and McCarthy: The Radical Specter* (Cambridge, 1967); Robert Griffiths, *The Politics of Fear: Joseph R. McCarthy and the Senate* (New York, 1970); Hamby, *Liberalism and its Challengers*, p. 112.

25   Stephen J. Whitfield, *The Culture of the Cold War* (Baltimore, 1991), p. vii; William F. Buckley Jr. and Brent Bozell, eds., *McCarthy and His Enemies: The Record and its Meaning* (Chicago, 1954); Allen Weinstein, *Perjury: The Hiss–Chambers Case* (New York, 1978); Ronald Radosh and Joyce Milton, *The Rosenberg Files: A Search for the Truth*, (New York, 1985), *passim*; Harvey Klehr, John Earl Haynes, and F. I. Firsov, *The Secret World of American Communism* (New Haven, 1995); Arthur Herman, *Joseph McCarthy: Man and Myth* (New York, 1999).

26   Schrecker, *Many are the Crimes*; Alan Wolfe, "With Friends Like These," *Times Literary Supplement* (May 26, 2000); *New York Times*, (October 23, 1998).

27   Hodgson, *America in Our Time*, p. 47.

28   Seymour Martin Lipset and Gary Marks, *It Didn't Happen Here: Why Socialism Failed in the United States* (New York, 2000).

29   Graebner, *The Age of Doubt*, pp. 63–5; Rose, *The Cold War Comes to Main Street*, p. 151.

30   Burton I. Kaufman, *The Korean War: Challenges in Crisis, Credibility, and Command* (New York, 1986), *passim*.

31   George F. Kennan, *Memoirs: 1925–1950* (Boston, 1967). For Acheson speech see, "Crisis in Asia," *Department of State Bulletin*, XXII (January 23, 1950), pp. 111–18. For its impact upon communist leaders see Sergei Goncharov, John W. Lewis, and Xue Litai, *Uncertain Partners: Stalin, Mao, and the Korean War* (Stanford, 1993). See also Bruce Cumings, *The Origins of the Korean War: The Roaring of the Cataract, 1947–1950* (Princeton, 1990), pp. 410–13; and, for contemporary skepticism, I. F. Stone, *The Hidden History of the Korean War* (New York, 1952).

32 Gaddis, *We Now Know*, pp. 70–5 synthesizes the new evidence. For a review of Soviet, Chinese, and other documentation see articles by Kathryn Weathersby in Cold War International History Project (henceforth CWIHP) *Bulletins*, 3, 5, 6, 7 (Washington D.C., 1993–96).

33 Kaufman, *The Korean War*, pp. 78–179.

34 Ibid., pp. 89–182; Cabell Philipps, *The Truman Presidency* (New York, 1966), pp. 337–47; Hamby, *Man of the People*, pp. 554–6.

35 Gaddis, *We Now Know*, pp. 77–8. For Mao's fears of wider American action see Sergei Goncharov et al., *Uncertain Partners*, p. 157 and Michael H. Hunt, "Beijing and the Korean Crisis: June 1950–June 1951," *Political Science Quarterly*, 107 (1992), pp. 458–9.

36 Kaufman, *The Korean War*, pp. 183–286; Hamby, *Man of the People*, pp. 557–98.

37 Stanley Sandler, "The First Casualty . . . ," *Times Literary Supplement* (June 16, 2000).

38 Stueck, *The Korean War*, pp. 348–53.

39 Quoted in Gilbert, *Another Chance*, p. 138.

40 Roger Dingman, "Atomic Diplomacy During the Korean War," *International Security*, 13 (Winter, 1988/89) p. 82; Gaddis, *We Now Know*, pp. 107–10.

41 Peter G. Boyle, *The Churchill–Eisenhower Correspondence, 1953–1955* (Chapel Hill, 1990), *passim*; Klaus Larres, "Eisenhower and the First Forty Days after Stalin's Death: The Incompatibility of Détente and Political Warfare", *Diplomacy and Statecraft*, 6:2 (July, 1995), pp. 431-469. See also H. W. Brands Jr., *Cold Warriors: Eisenhower's Generation and American Foreign Policy* (New York, 1988).

42 See Robert Engler, *The Politics of Oil* (New York, 1960), p. 206; Vladimir Zubok, "Soviet Intelligence and the Cold War: The 'Small' Committee of Information, 1952–53," *Diplomatic History*, 19 (Summer, 1995), pp. 466–8; and Richard Immerman, *The CIA in Guatemala: The Foreign Policy of Intervention* (Austin, 1982).

43 George Herring, *America's Longest War: The United States and Vietnam, 1950–1975*, 3rd edn (New York, 1996), pp. 47-80.

44 LaFeber, *America, Russia, and the Cold War*, p. 120.

45 For treaties see Ibid., pp. 119–20, 154.

46 Divine, *Since 1945*, p. 58.

47 Sam Tanenhaus, "Un-American Activities," *New York Review of Books* (November 30), 2000.

Notes to Chapter 3

1 Hamby, *Liberalism and its Challengers*, p. 94; David Halberstam, *The Fifties* (New York, 1993); Stephen Ambrose, *Eisenhower: Soldier and*

President (New York, 1990); Hilton Kramer, "The Fifties on Television," *The New Criterion* (January, 1998), pp. 12–15.

2   For Shannon note see Robert F. Burk, "Eisenhower Revisionism Revisited: Reflections on the Eisenhower Scholarship," *Historian*, 50 (1988), pp. 196–209. For representative surveys see Herbert Parmet, *Eisenhower and the American Crusades* (New York, 1972), p. 11 and *passim*; Hamby, *Liberalism and its Challengers*, chapter 3; J. Ronald Oakley, *God's Country: America in the Fifties* (New York, 1986); and Brands, *Cold Warriors*. See also for recent Eisenhower-era historiography Stephen Rabe, "Eisenhower Revisionism: A Decade of Scholarship," *Diplomatic History*, 17 (Winter, 1993), pp. 97–115.

3   See Stephen Ambrose, *Eisenhower: The President, Vol. 2* (New York, 1984), *passim*.

4   Patterson, *Grand Expectations*, p. 312. For further detail see *Statistical History of the United States*. For an interpretation of modern American affluence see David Potter, *People of Plenty* (Chicago, 1954).

5   John Kenneth Galbraith, *The Affluent Society* (Boston, 1958); Marquis Childs, *Eisenhower: The Captive Hero* (New York, 1958).

6   Arthur M. Schlesinger, Jr., *1000 Days: John F. Kennedy in the White House* (Boston, 1965); Eric Goldman, *The Crucial Decade – And After: America, 1945–1960* (New York, 1960); Townsend Hoopes, *The Devil and John Foster Dulles* (New York, 1973).

7   Murray Kempton, "The Underestimation of Dwight D. Eisenhower," *Esquire*, 68 (September, 1967) pp. 108–9, 156; Garry Wills, *Nixon Agonistes: The Crisis of the Self-Made Man* (Boston, 1969) p. 131; Patterson, *Grand Expectations*, chapter 9. See also Fred I. Greenstein, *The Hidden Hand Presidency: Eisenhower as Leader* (New York, 1982), pp. 155–227.

8   Arthur M. Schlesinger, Jr., "The Ike Age Revisited," *Reviews in American History*, 11 (March, 1983), pp. 1–11.

9   Samuel Lubell, *Revolt of the Moderates* (New York, 1956), *passim*; Robert Griffiths, "Dwight D. Eisenhower and the Corporate Commonwealth," *American Historical Review*, 87 (1982), pp. 82–122.

10 For a brief summary see Divine, *Since 1945*, pp. 47–100.

11 Emmett Hughes, *The Ordeal of Power: A Political Memoir of the Eisenhower Years* (New York, 1963), pp. 329, 332–5. For the view that Taft was actually more "liberal" see Patterson, *Grand Expectations*, p. 270. For the argument that Eisenhower's intentions in civil rights and judiciary reforms were little more than symbolic see Robert F. Burk, *The Eisenhower Administration and Black Civil Rights* (Knoxville, 1984), p. 253.

12 Quoted in Hamby, *Liberalism and its Challengers*, p. 121.

13 For civil rights in the 1950s see Burk, *The Eisenhower Administration and Black Civil Rights*, *passim*; Taylor Branch, *Parting the Waters: America in the King Years, 1954–1963* (New York, 1988) and David

Garrow, *Bearing the Cross: Martin Luther King Jr. and the Southern Christian Leadership Conference* (New York, 1986). For background context see C. Vann Woodward, *The Strange Career of Jim Crow*, rev. edn. (New York, 1974).

14   See Richard Davies, *The Age of Asphalt: The Automobile, the Freeway, and the Condition of Metropolitan America* (New York, 1975), p. 133.

15   Patterson, *Grand Expectations*, p. 266.

16   Ibid., p. 272; Griffiths, "Dwight D. Eisenhower and the Corporate Commonwealth," p. 102; John Kenneth Galbraith, *The Countervailing Society* (Boston, 1953).

17   A balanced account of the Eisenhower administration's foreign policy record is Robert Divine, *Eisenhower and the Cold War* (New York, 1981). An important recent study is Marc Trachtenberg, *A Constructed Peace: The Making of the European Settlement, 1945–1963* (Princeton, 1999).

18   Townsend Hoopes, *The Devil and John Foster Dulles* (New York, 1973), p. xiv; Divine, *Eisenhower and the Cold War*, pp. 11, 20–3, 153–5; Greenstein, *The Hidden Hand Presidency*, pp. 5–9, 57–72; Ambrose, *Eisenhower*, pp. 9–12, 150, 618–27.

19   Richard Immerman, *John Foster Dulles and the Diplomacy of the Cold War* (Princeton, 1990).

20   Trachtenberg, *A Constructed Peace*, pp. 125–45.

21   For "New Look" strategy see Brands, *Cold Warriors*, p. 15.

22   For details see David Alan Rosenberg, "The Origins of Overkill: Nuclear Weapons and American Strategy," in Norman Graebner, ed., *The National Security: Its Theory and Practice, 1945–1960* (New York, 1986), 173-74. See also H. W. Brands Jr., "The Age of Vulnerability: Eisenhower and the National Insecurity State," *American Historical Review*, 94 (October, 1989), pp. 988–9.

23   Trachtenberg, *A Constructed Peace*, pp. 146–7.

24   See for historical context, Geoffrey Barraclough, *An Introduction to Contemporary History* (London, 1964).

25   Gaddis, *We Now Know*, pp. 208–11, 219, 235–6.

26   Ibid., pp. 171–3. See also, for a balanced account of the Suez crisis, Keith Kyle, *Suez* (New York, 1991).

27   Divine, *Eisenhower and the Cold War*, p. 79. For the denouement in the Middle East and Europe see, respectively, Fawaz Gerges, *The Superpowers in the Middle East: Regional and International Politics, 1955–1967* (Boulder, 1994), pp. 102–22; and Trachtenberg, *A Constructed Peace*.

28   For Eisenhower's policies toward Indochina see Herring, *America's Longest War*, chapter 2; David Anderson, *Trapped by Success: The Eisenhower Administration and Vietnam, 1953–1961* (New York, 1991); and Lloyd Gardner, *Approaching Vietnam: From World War*

II through Dienbienphu, 1941–1954 (New York, 1988).

29 Gordon Chang, *Friends and Enemies: The US, China, and the Soviet Union, 1948–1972* (Stanford, 1990), pp. 116–42. But Stephen Ambrose sees Eisenhower's handling of the Quemoy–Matsu crisis as "a tour de force, one of the great triumphs of his long career," *Eisenhower*, p. 245. Robert Divine, similarly admiring, writes "the beauty of Eisenhower's policy is that to this day no one can be sure whether or not he would have responded militarily to an invasion of the offshore islands, and whether he would have used nuclear weapons." *Eisenhower and the Cold War*, pp. 65–6. See also David Alan Mayers, *Cracking the Monolith: US Policy Against the Sino–Soviet Alliance, 1949–1955* (Baton Rouge, 1986), pp. 142–9.

30 Gerges, *The Superpowers in the Middle East, passim.*

31 Stephen Rabe, "Eisenhower Revisionism: A Decade of Scholarship," *Diplomatic History*, 17 (Winter, 1993), p. 112; Richard E. Welch Jr., *Response to Revolution: The US and the Cuban Revolution, 1959–1961* (Chapel Hill, 1985), pp. 3–63; Robert McMahon, "Eisenhower and Third World Nationalism: A Critique of the Revisionists," *Political Science Quarterly*, 101 (Fall, 1986), p. 457. For recent historiographical evaluation see Gaddis, *We Now Know*, pp. 176–85.

32 For Berlin crisis see Ibid., pp. 138–43, and Trachtenberg, *A Constructed Peace*, pp. 251–97, 322–51. For U-2 affair see, most recently, Michael Beschloss, *Mayday: Eisenhower, Khrushchev, and the U-2 Affair* (New York, 1986).

33 H. W. Brands Jr., "The Age of Vulnerability," pp. 988–9.

34 Thomas F. Soapes, "A Cold Warrior Seeks Peace: Eisenhower's Strategy for Nuclear Disarmament," *Diplomatic History*, 4 (Winter, 1980), pp. 57–69.

35 Jeff Broadwater, "President Eisenhower and the Historians," *Historian*, 54 (1992), p. 53; Herring, *America's Longest War*, p. 79.

36 For economic trends in the 1950s see Frank Levy, *Dollars and Dreams: The Changing American Income Distribution* (New York, 1987); John Kenneth Galbraith, *The Affluent Society* (Boston, 1958); and Patterson, *Grand Expectations*, chapter 11.

37 See Garrow, *Bearing the Cross*; and Burk, *The Eisenhower Administration and Black Civil Rights*.

38 Jackson, *The Crabgrass Frontier*; Landon Jones, *Great Expectations: America and the Baby Boom Generation* (New York, 1980).

39 Lewis Mumford, *The City in History: Its Origins, Its Transformation and its Prospects* (New York, 1961), p. 486.

40 Herbert Gans, *The Levittowners: Ways of Life and Politics in a New Suburban Community*, rev. edn (New York, 1982), pp. 408–13.

41 Patterson, *Grand Expectations*, pp. 72–81.

42 See Cheever's short stories. For women's suburban alienation see Elaine Tyler May, "Cold War – Warm Hearth: Politics and the Family in

Postwar America," in Fraser and Gerstle, eds., *The Rise and Fall of the New Deal Order*, pp. 153–81. Todd Gitlin, *The Sixties: Years of Hope; Days of Rage* (New York, 1987).

43 Howard in Keith Kyle, "The Forty Years' Peace," *London Review of Books* (October, 1993). An internationally oriented societal analysis of the 1950s is badly needed. Osborne's point of view is expressed in his play, *Look Back in Anger*.

44 Sloan Wilson, *The Man in the Grey Flannel Suit* (New York, 1957); W. H. Whyte, *The Organization Man* (New York, 1956).

45 Alfred D. Chandler, *The Visible Hand: The Managerial Revolution in American Business* (Cambridge, 1977); Peter Drucker, *The New Society* (New York, 1940).

46 "Global Perspectives on Modern Business," Session at Organization of American Historians Convention, 1996. Halberstam, *The Fifties*, pp. 116–87; Robert Reich, *The Work of Nations: Preparing Ourselves for 21st Century Capitalism* (New York, 1991), pp. 44, 51, 58; Richard Hofstadter, "What Happened to the Anti-Trust Movement?" in his *The Paranoid Style in American Politics and other Essays* (New York, 1967).

47 *Fortune* (October, 1955), p. 81.

48 Patterson, *Grand Expectations*, p. 348. See also Erik Barnouw, *Tube of Plenty: The Evolution of American Television*, 2nd rev. edn, (New York, 1990) and Baughman, *The Republic of Mass Culture*, pp. 41–2.

49 James Twitchell, *Carnival Culture: The Trashing of Taste in America* (New York, 1992); Baughman, *The Republic of Mass Culture*.

50 Ibid., pp. 93–5.

51 See generally Halberstam, *The Fifties*.

52 See discussion in Chapter 2 and generally, Graebner, *The Age of Doubt* and Pells, *The Liberal Mind*.

53 The Frankfurt School's genesis, character, and impact are explored in Martin Jay, *The Dialectical Imagination* (Boston, 1973). For Bell, Mills, and Riesman see Pells, *The Liberal Mind*, pp. 131–6, 249–61.

54 Pells, *The Liberal Mind*, p. 246; Vance Packard, *The Hidden Persuaders* (New York, 1957).

55 Louis Hartz, *The Liberal Tradition in America* (New York, 1955); Richard Hofstadter, *The Age of Reform: From Bryan to FDR* (New York, 1955).

56 For general review see Patterson, *Grand Expectations*, chapter 12.

57 Dean Acheson, *A Democrat Looks at his Party* (New York, 1960); Walt Rostow, *The Stages of Economic Growth* (New York, 1959).

58 Halberstam, *The Fifties*, pp. 527–36; Gitlin, *The Sixties*.

Notes to Chapter 4

1 Midge Decter, "Kennedyism," *Commentary* (January, 1970), p. 20; *Life* (December 3, 1963).

2 Schlesinger, *A Thousand Days*; Theodore Sorensen, *Kennedy* (New York, 1965); Rockefeller Foundation, *Prospect for America*; W. W. Rostow, *Eisenhower, Kennedy, and Foreign Aid* (Austin, 1985), pp. 198–201; Burton I. Kaufman, "John F. Kennedy as World Leader: A Perspective on the Literature," *Diplomatic History*, 17 (Summer, 1995), pp. 447–69.

3 H. A. L. Fisher, *History of Europe* (London, 1938).

4 Chafe, *Unfinished Journey*, p. 180; Arthur M. Schlesinger Jr. quoted in Jim E. Heath, *Decade of Disillusionment* (New York, 1975), p. 119.

5 Theodore H. White, *The Making of the President, 1960* (New York, 1961).

6 *Public Papers of the Presidents: John F. Kennedy* (1961), p. 1; Burton I. Kaufman, "John F. Kennedy as World Leader: A Perspective on the Literature," *Diplomatic History*, 17 (Summer, 1995), p. 453.

7 David Halberstam, *The Best and the Brightest* (New York, 1983), pp. 93–102; Richard Barnet, *The Roots of War: The Men and Institutions Behind United States Foreign Policy* (New York, 1972), pp. 48–75.

8 Irving L. Janis, *Victims of Groupthink: A Psychological Study of the Foreign Policy Decisions and Fiascos* (Boston, 1972), pp. 14–49; Peter Wyden, *Bay of Pigs* (New York, 1979).

9 Schlesinger, *A Thousand Days*, pp. 288–339; Robert M. Slusser, *The Berlin Crisis of 1961: Soviet–American Relations and the Struggle for Power in the Kremlin, June–November, 1961* (Baltimore, 1973), pp. x–xi.

10 Michael Beschloss, *The Crisis Years: Kennedy and Khrushchev, 1960–1963*, (New York, 1991), p. 232; see also Jack M. Schick, *The Berlin Crisis, 1958–1962* (Philadelphia, 1971), pp. 137–241 and Curtis Cate, *The Ides of August: The Berlin Crisis, 1961* (New York, 1978).

11 James G. Hershberg, "Before the Missiles of October: Did Kennedy Plan a Military Strike against Cuba?" *Diplomatic History*, 14 (Spring, 1990), pp. 163–98; Thomas G. Paterson, "Fixation with Cuba: The Bay of Pigs, Missile Crisis, and Covert War against Castro," in Thomas G. Paterson, ed., *Kennedy's Quest for Victory: American Foreign Policy, 1961–1963* (New York, 1989), pp. 141–2. See also Mark J. White, "The Cuban Imbroglio: From the Bay of Pigs to the Missile Crisis and Beyond," in Mark J. White, ed., *Kennedy: The New Frontier Revisited* (New York, 1998), pp. 69–72 and Bernd Greiner, "The Soviet View: An Interview with Sergo Mikoyan," *Diplomatic History*, 14 (Spring, 1990), pp. 205–22.

12 Ernest R. May and Phillip D. Zelikow, *The Kennedy Tapes: Inside the White House During the Cuban Missile Crisis* (Cambridge, Massachusetts, 1997); *New York Times* (October 19, 1997).

13 Most narrative treatments are now inevitably rather outdated but see, for a succinct account LaFeber, *America, Russia, and the Cold War*, pp. 224–8.

14 James A. Nathan, "The Missile Crisis: His Finest Hour Now," *World Politics*, 27 (January, 1975), pp. 256–8. For more recent account see White, "The Cuban Imbroglio," pp. 63–90.

15 Ibid., pp. 81–2; Raymond C. Garthoff, *Reflections on the Cuban Missile Crisis* (Washington, 1989), pp. 94–6.

16 James A. Nathan, "The Missile Crisis," pp. 256–65.

17 Robert McNamara, "One Minute to Doomsday," *New York Times* (October 14, 1992).

18 *New York Times* (June 11, 1963); For test ban treaty see, Glenn T. Seaborg, *Kennedy, Khrushchev, and the Test Ban* (Berkeley, 1981), pp. 172–85.

19 Herring, *America's Longest War*, pp. 81–119; R. B. Smith, *An International History of the Vietnam War: The Kennedy Strategy* (New York, 1986), pp. 2–16.

20 Halberstam, *The Best and the Brightest*, pp. 12, 93–6; Richard J. Walton, *Cold War and Counter-Revolution: The Foreign Policy of John F. Kennedy* (Baltimore, 1972), pp. 34–5; Henry Fairlie, *The Kennedy Promise: The Politics of Expectation* (New York, 1973), pp. 10–12; Beschloss, *The Crisis Years*, *passim*; James G. Blight and David A. Welch, *On the Brink: Americans and Soviets Reexamine the Cuban Missile Crisis* (New York, 1989), pp. 82–4; Trachtenberg, *A Constructed Peace*, pp. 355–402; Schlesinger, *A Thousand Days*, pp. 639, 711, 713, 1006–7.

21 Tom Wicker, *JFK and LBJ: The Influence of Personality Upon Politics* (Baltimore, 1968).

22 Several of these views are summarized in James N. Giglio, "John F. Kennedy as Domestic Leader," in Mark J. White, ed., *Kennedy*, pp. 226–38.

23 Taylor Branch, *Parting the Waters: America in the King Years, 1954–1963* (New York, 1985); for a more indulgent view see Carl M. Brauer, *John F. Kennedy and the Second Reconstruction* (New York, 1977), pp. 315–20. For King, see *New York Times* (August 29, 1963). For Kennedy and civil rights generally see Patterson, *Grand Expectations*, pp. 473–85.

24 Giglio, "John F. Kennedy as Domestic Leader," pp. 230, 236–40; Hamby, *Liberalism and its Challengers*, pp. 208, 212.

25 For Kennedy's private life, see Thomas Reeves, *A Question of Character: A Life of John F. Kennedy* (New York, 1991). See also Herbert Parmet, *JFK: The Presidency of John F. Kennedy* (New York, 1983),

pp. 353–5, and essays in Paterson, ed., *Kennedy's Quest for Victory*, *passim*.

26   Larry Berman, "Lyndon Baines Johnson: Paths Chosen and Opportunities Lost," in Fred Greenstein, ed., *Leadership in the Modern Presidency* (Cambridge, Massachusetts. 1988), pp. 144–5; Robert Caro, *The Years of Lyndon Johnson: The Path to Power* (New York, 1982) and Robert Caro, *The Years of Lyndon Johnson: Means of Ascent* (New York, 1989); Robert Dallek, *Flawed Giant: Lyndon Johnson, and His Times, 1961–1973* (New York, 1998).

27   *New York Times* (November 28, 1963). For representative studies of the Johnson record see Dallek, *Flawed Giant, passim*; Robert Divine, ed., *Exploring the Johnson Years* (Austin, 1981) and Fraser and Gerstle, eds., *The Rise and Fall of the New Deal Order, passim*.

28   Patterson, *Grand Expectations*, pp. 542–7. See also Steven Lawson, "Civil Rights," in Robert Divine, ed., *Exploring the Johnson Years* (Austin, 1981), pp. 99–100.

29   Allen Matusow, *The Unraveling of America: A History of Liberalism and the 1960s*, (New York, 1984), pp. 97–107.

30   Patterson, *Grand Expectations*, pp. 535, 530–42.

31   David B. Burner, *Making Peace with the Sixties* (Princeton, 1996), p. 170; Oscar Lewis, *Children of Sanchez* (New York, 1961).

32   For 1964 politics, see Burner, *Making Peace with the Sixties*, pp. 195–6.

33   Ibid., p. 80.

34   Jane Jacobs, *The Death and Life of Great American Cities* (New York, 1961); James Baldwin, *Another Country* (New York, 1962); Rachel Carson, *Silent Spring*, (New York, 1962); Betty Friedan, *The Feminine Mystique* (New York, 1963). The four acts of Congress are discussed in Patterson, *Grand Expectations*, pp. 569–88.

35   Hugh Graham, "The Transformation of Federal Education Policy," in Divine, ed., *Exploring the Johnson Years*, pp. 155–84.

36   For Medicare see Matusow, *The Unraveling of America*, pp. 226–32. For immigration see Victor Greene, "Immigration Policy," in Jack Greene, ed., *Encyclopedia of American History*, Vol. 2 (New York, 1984), pp. 579–93.

37   The voting rights issue and law is discussed in Garrow, *Bearing the Cross*, pp. 357–430 and in Burner, *Making Peace with the Sixties*, pp. 47, 68. For Johnson's speech see *Public Papers of the Presidents: Lyndon B. Johnson, 1965* (Washington D.C., 1966), pp. 281–7.

38   Chafe, *Unfinished Journey*, pp. 235, 221–46.

39   Robert Conat, *Rivers of Blood, Days of Darkness: The Unforgettable Classic Account of the Watts Riot* (New York, 1967); Patterson, *Grand Expectations*, pp. 88–92.

40   Robert Weisbrot, *Freedom Bound* (New York, 1991), p. 173; Patterson, *Grand Expectations*, pp. 550–1, 659–68.

41 Ibid., pp. 540, 589–92.
42 Burner, *Making Peace with the Sixties*, p. 171.
43 *New York Times* (June, 1965).
44 Patterson, *Grand Expectations*, pp. 540–1.
45 For other judgments on Johnson's domestic achievements see Ibid., pp. 589–92; Chafe, *Unfinished Journey*, pp. 244–6; Burner, *Making Peace with the Sixties*, pp. 187–8; and the essays in Fraser and Gerstle, eds., *The Rise and Fall of the New Deal Order*.
46 Hamby, *Liberalism and its Challengers*, p. 265.
47 Frank Levy, *Dollars and Dreams: The Changing American Income Distribution* (New York, 1987).
48 A helpful overview is Herring, *America's Longest War*. Two historiographically oriented treatments introduce a voluminous literature: Gary Hess, "The Unending Debate: Historians and the Vietnam War," *Diplomatic History*, pp. 239–64; and Andrew Rotter, ed., *Light at the End of the Tunnel: A Vietnam War Anthology*, rev. edn (Wilmington, 1999).
49 Hess, "The Unending Debate," p. 239. The "Quagmire" characterization was popularized by David Halberstam, *The Making of a Quagmire: America and Vietnam during the Kennedy Era* (New York, 1964).
50 For figures see Rotter, ed., *Light at the End of the Tunnel*, p. xxviii.
51 Lawrence J. Bassett and Stephen E. Pelz, "The Failed Search for Victory: Vietnam and the Politics of War," in Paterson, ed., *Kennedy's Quest for Victory*, pp. 231, 242.
52 George Kahin, *Intervention: How America became Involved in Vietnam* (New York, 1986), p. 432.
53 Larry Berman, *Planning a Tragedy: The Americanization of the War in Vietnam* (New York, 1982), p. 147.
54 John P. Burke and Fred I. Greenstein, *How Presidents Test Reality: Decisions on Vietnam, 1954 and 1964* (New York, 1991), p. 261. See also George Ball, "A Dissenter in the Government," in Rotter, ed., *Light at the End of the Tunnel*, p. 119. For Humphrey, see Fredrick Logevall, "Vietnam and the Question of What Might Have Been," in White, ed., *Kennedy: The New Frontier Revisited*, p. 47.
55 Ibid., p. 45.
56 James C. Thomson, "A Bureaucratic Tangle," in Rotter, ed., *Light at the End of the Tunnel*, pp. 314–22; Barnet, *The Roots of War, passim*.
57 For Ia Drang see Hess, "The Unending Debate," p. 257. *Public Papers of the Presidents, Lyndon B. Johnson, 1965* (Washington D.C., 1966) pp. 394-9.
58 Herring, *America's Longest War*, ch. 5, 6.
59 For review of various military critiques see Hess, "The Unending Debate," pp. 242–6. See also Harry G. Summers, *On Strategy: A Critical Analysis of the Vietnam War* (Novato, 1982) and David H. Hackworth and Julie Sherman, *About Face* (New York, 1989), pp. 556, 613–14. See also Larry E. Cable, *Conflict of Myths: The Development of Coun-*

terinsurgency Doctrine and the Vietnam War (New York, 1988). For a diplomatic historian's critique of the military see Robert Buzzanco, *Masters of War: Military Dissent and Politics in the Vietnam Era* (New York, 1996).

60 See Hess, "The Unending Debate," pp. 257–8 and essays in Rotter, ed., *Light at the End of the Tunnel*, chapter 8. For a close examination, see Donald Mrozek, *Air Power and the Ground War in Vietnam: Ideas and Actions* (Washington D.C., 1989).

61 See James P. Harrison, *The Endless War: Fifty Years of Struggle for Independence in Vietnam* (New York, 1989) and Eric Bergerud, *The Dynamics of Defeat: The Vietnam War in Han Nghia Province* (Boulder, 1991).

62 Larry Berman, cited in Hess, "The Unending Debate," p. 252.

63 Baughman, *The Republic of Mass Culture*, pp. 112–15, cf. William Hammond, *Public Affairs: The Military and the Media* (Washington D.C., 1988) who downplays television's impact.

64 Ronald Spector, *After Tet: The Bloodiest Year in Vietnam* (New York, 1993), pp. 116, 313.

65 Leslie Gelb with Richard K. Betts, *The Irony of Vietnam: the System Worked* (Washington, 1978); Norman Podhoretz, *Why We Were in Vietnam* (New York, 1982); and R. B. Smith, *An International History of the Vietnam War*, 3 vols. (New York, 1983–91).

66 William J. Fulbright, *The Arrogance of Power, passim*; Frances Fitzgerald, *Fire in the Lake: The Vietnamese and Americans in Vietnam* (Boston, 1972); Loren Baritz, *Backfire: A History of How American Culture Led Us into the Vietnam War and Made Us Fight the Way We Did* (New York, 1985).

67 Gaddis, *We Now Know*, p. 189; Herring, *Longest War*, pp. 307–19; Lloyd Gardner, *Pay Any Price: Lyndon Johnson and the Wars for Vietnam* (Chicago, 1995); Gabriel Kolko, *Anatomy of a War: Vietnam, the United States and the Modern Historical Experience* (New York, 1985).

68 Arthur Marwick, *The Sixties* (New York, 1998), p. 3; Maurice Isserman and Michael Kazin, "The Failure and Success of the New Radicalism," in Fraser and Gerstle, eds., *The Rise and Fall of the New Deal Order*, pp. 212–37; Matusow, *The Unraveling of America*, supra.

69 Patterson, *Grand Expectations*, p. 451.

70 Greil Marcus, *The Mystery Train* (New York, 1982) and *The Dustbin of History* (Cambridge, Massachusetts, 1995); Pauline Kael, *I Lost It at the Movies* (New York, 1965). A good study of the relationship between culture and political radicalism is Morris Dickstein, *Gates of Eden: American Culture in the Sixties* (New York, 1977).

71 See, for SNCC, Clayborne Carson, *In Struggle: SNCC and the Black Awakening of the 1960s* (New York, 1981). For SDS see Gitlin, *The Sixties, passim*. For Young Americans for Freedom see Patterson, *Grand Expectations*, p. 455.

72 See Clayborne Carson, *In Struggle: SNCC and the Black Awakening of the 1960s* (New York, 1981), *passim*; and Howard Zinn, *SNCC: The New Abolitionists* (New York, 1965). For Mississippi in 1963/64 see Sally Belfrage, *Freedom Summer* (New York, 1965).

73 Charles Hamilton and Stokely Carmichael, *Black Power* (New York, 1967); Eldridge Cleaver, *Soul on Ice* (New York, 1968); Bobby Seale, *Seize the Time* (New York, 1974); Michael Eric Dyson, *Making Malcolm: The Myth and Meaning of Malcolm X* (New York, 1995). Terry Anderson, *The Sixties* (New York, 1999), pp. 85, 94.

74 Charles Reich, *The Greening of America* (New York, 1968); James Miller, *Democracy in the Streets: From Port Huron to the Siege of Chicago* (New York, 1987), pp. 329–74.

75 W. J. Rorabaugh, *Berkeley at War: the 1960s* (New York, 1989); Martin Seymour Lipset, *Rebellion in the University* (Chicago, 1971); Kenneth Keniston, *Youth and Dissent: The Rise of a New Opposition* (New York, 1971).

76 For casualties see Anderson, *The Sixties*, p. 91.

77 Ibid., pp. 99–100. For Tet and its impact see Herring, *America's Longest War*, pp. 203–9.

78 Matusow, *The Unraveling of America*, pp. 407–9; Lewis Chester et al., *An American Melodrama: The Presidential Campaign of 1968* (New York, 1969); Robert Weisbrot, *Freedom Bound* (New York, 1991), pp. 266–70; Patterson, *Grand Expectations*, p. 693.

79 Matusow, *The Unraveling of America*, pp. 411–22; Gitlin, *The Sixties*, pp. 320–38.

80 See Stephen Ambrose, *Nixon: The Triumph of a Politician, 1962–1972* (New York, 1989), pp. 133–222; Joe McGinniss, *The Selling of the President*.

81 Dan T. Carter, *The Politics of Rage: George Wallace, the Origins of the New Conservatism, and the Transformation of American Politics* (New York, 1998); Jonathan Rieder, "The Rise of the Silent Majority," in Fraser and Gerstle, eds., *The Rise and Fall of the New Deal Order*, pp. 243–68.

82 Dallek, *Flawed Giant*.

83 Kevin Phillips, *The Emerging Republican Majority* (New Rochelle, 1969).

84 Anderson, *The Sixties*, p. 127; Ronald Steel, *In Love with Night: The American Romance with Robert Kennedy* (New York, 2000).

Notes to Chapter 5

1 Leon Friedman and William Levantrosser, eds., *Watergate and Afterwards: The Legacy of Richard Nixon* (Westport, 1992), p. 281; Tho-

mas Edsall, "Chain Reaction," in Steven Gillon and Diane Kunz, eds., *America During the Cold War* (Fort Worth, 1993), p. 252.

2 McGinniss, *The Selling of the President*; Garry Wills, *Nixon Agonistes* (New York, 1970).

3 Leon Friedman and William Levantrosser, *Richard M. Nixon: Politician, President, Administrator* (Westgate, 1991), pp. 37, 49; Henry Kissinger, *Years of Renewal* (New York, 1999), p. 67.

4 Friedman and Levantrosser, eds., *Watergate and Afterwards*, p. 244.

5 Ibid., p. 283; Doris Kearns, *Lyndon Johnson and the American Dream* (New York, 1976), p. 286.

6 Seymour Martin Lipset, "Affirmative Action and the American Creed," *Wilson Quarterly*, 16(Winter, 1992), pp. 52, 62; Patterson, *Grand Expectations*, p. 723.

7 Friedman and Levantrosser, *Richard M. Nixon*, p. 123.

8 Joan Hoff, *Nixon Reconsidered* (New York, 1994) pp. 27, 45, and *passim*; Michael Barone, *U.S. News and World Report* (September 20, 1999); Friedman and Levantrosser, eds., *Watergate and Afterwards*, p. 326.

9 Ibid., p. 244; Patterson, *Grand Expectations*, p. 719; Hamby, *Liberalism and its Challengers*, p. 319.

10 Friedman and Levantrosser, eds., *Watergate and Afterwards*, p. 320.

11 Dan T. Carter, *The Politics of Rage* (New York, 1998) ch. 11, 12, 13.

12 Patterson, *Grand Expectations*, p. 715. See also Mary Ann Glendon, "Rights in 20th-Century Constitutions: The Case of Welfare Reform," in H. D. Graham, ed., *Civil Rights in the United States* (University Park, 1994), pp. 140–50.

13 *New York Times* (October 15, 1970); *Time* (November 16, 1970); Hamby, *Liberalism and its Challengers*, p. 299. See also Patterson, *Grand Expectations*, p. 737.

14 Ibid., pp. 737, 740–1.

15 John Rawls, *A Theory of Justice* (New York, 1971); Philip Slater, *The Pursuit of Loneliness: American Culture at the Breaking Point* (Boston, 1970); Charles Reich, *The Greening of America* (New York, 1970).

16 For 1972 see Patterson, *Grand Expectations*, pp. 758–65; Stephen Ambrose, *Nixon: The Triumph of a Politician, 1962–1972* (New York, 1989), pp. 474–583.

17 For Watergate see Stanley Kutler, *The Wars of Watergate: The Last Crisis of Richard Nixon* (New York, 1990). See also Patterson, *Grand Expectations*, pp. 771–82 and James Neuchterlein, "Watergate: Toward a Revisionist View," *Commentary* (August 1979), pp. 38–45.

18 Patterson, *Grand Expectations*, pp. 771–82.

19 *Time* (August 19, 1974).

20 Otis L. Graham Jr., *Toward a Planned Society: From FDR to Nixon* (New York, 1976), pp. 186–8, 256, 265; Friedman and Levantrosser, eds., *Watergate and Afterwards*, p. 328; *Chicago Tribune* (May 9, 1974).

21 Patterson, *Grand Expectations*, p. 780; Thomas Edsall, "Chain Reac-

tion," in Steven Gillon and Diane Kunz, eds., *America During the Cold War* (Fort Worth, 1993), p. 253.

22 Alan Wolfe, *America's Impasse: The Rise and Fall of the Politics of Growth* (New York, 1981), p. 73.

23 John Stoessinger, *The Might of Nations: World Politics in Our Time*, 7th edn. (New York, 1982), pp. 79, 85; Richard M. Nixon, "Asia After Vietnam," *Foreign Affairs*, 46 (October, 1967); Garry Wills, *Nixon Agonistes* (New York, 1970), p. 30; Herring, *America's Longest War*, p. 244.

24 Ibid., pp. 249–51.

25 William Shawcross, *Sideshow: Kissinger, Nixon and the Destruction of Cambodia* (New York, 1979), pp. 26–35, 112–27; Henry Kissinger, "Bombing Cambodia: A Defense," in Rotter, ed., *Light at the End of the Tunnel*, pp. 284–94.

26 Herring, *America's Longest War*, pp. 269–70.

27 Ibid., pp. 275–8.

28 Ibid. pp. 277–83; Kissinger, *Years of Renewal, passim*; Friedman and Levantrosser, *Richard M. Nixon*, p. 6.

29 Jeffrey Clark, *United States Army in Vietnam: Advice and Support: The Final Years, 1965–1973* (Washington, 1988), p. 521; Arnold Isaacs, *Without Honor: Defeat in Vietnam and Cambodia* (New York, 1984), pp. 493, 505; Gareth Porter, *A Peace Denied: The United States, Vietnam and the Paris Agreements* (Bloomingdale, 1975), pp. 174–95; Maynard Parker, "Vietnam: The War that Won't End," *Foreign Affairs*, 53 (January, 1975), pp. 365–6.

30 Herring, *America's Longest War*, pp. 282–3; Friedman and Levantrosser, *Richard M. Nixon*, p. 21.

31 William P. Bundy, *A Tangled Web: The Making of Foreign Policy in the Nixon Presidency* (New York, 1998), pp. 371, 376.

32 Some perceived elements of decline and other prompts to détente are succinctly summarized in LaFeber, *America, Russia, and the Cold War*, pp. 255–85.

33 Cf. Bundy, *A Tangled Web*, pp. 100–10 for argument that the Chinese took the crucial steps.

34 Kissinger, *Years of Renewal*, pp. 408–13; Paul E. Sigmund, *The United States and Democracy in Chile* (New York, 1993).

35 Raymond Garthoff, *Détente and Confrontation: American-Soviet Relations from Nixon to Reagan* (New York, 1985), pp. 404–57.

36 David Reynolds, *One World Divisible: A Global History Since 1945* (New York, 2000), p. 352.

37 John Lewis Gaddis, *Russia, The Soviet Union and the United States: An Interpretative History*, 2nd edn. (New York, 1990), p. 276; Garthoff, *Détente and Confrontation*, pp. 2, 24, 25, 1069–88.

38 Chafe, *Unfinished Journey*, p. 447; Edsall, "Chain Reaction," pp. 253–62.

39 See Peter M. Carroll, *It Seemed Like Nothing Happened: America in the 1970s* (New Brunswick, 1982).

40 Barnet, *The Roots of War*, p. 49.

41 G. M. Young, *Victorian England: Portrait of an Age* (London, 1936).

42 Baughman, *The Republic of Mass Culture*, p. 167; Chafe, *Unfinished Journey*, p. 435.

43 Christopher Lasch, *The Culture of Narcissism: American Life in an Age of Diminishing Expectations* (New York, 1979).

44 Barbara D. Whitehead, *The Divorce Culture* (New York, 1998); James Twitchell, *The Loss of Common Decency in American Culture* (New York, 1998).

45 Chafe, *Unfinished Journey*, pp. 435–8.

46 Sar Levitan and Robert Taggart, *The Promise of Greatness: The Social Programs of the Last Decade and Their Major Achievements* (Cambridge, Massachusetts, 1976).

47 Chafe, *Unfinished Journey*, pp. 440–5.

48 LaFeber, *America, Russia, and the Cold War*, pp. 282–5.

49 Jules Witcover, *Marathon: The Pursuit of the Presidency, 1972–1976* (New York, 1977); Carroll, *It Seemed Like Nothing Happened*, pp. 185–206.

50 Edsall, "Chain Reaction," p. 253.

51 Herbert Rosenbaum and Alexej Ugrinsky, eds., *The Presidency and Domestic Policies of Jimmy Carter* (Westport, 1994), p. 13.

52 Jimmy Carter, *Keeping Faith: Memoirs of a President* (New York, 1982), p. 73; Tip O'Neill, *Man of the House: The Life and Political Memoirs of Speaker Tip O'Neill* (New York, 1987).

53 John Dumbrell, *The Carter Presidency* (Manchester, 1995), pp. 14–15.

54 Douglas Brinkley, "The Rising Stock of Jimmy Carter: The Hands-on Legacy of Our Thirty-Ninth President," *Diplomatic History*, 20(4) (Fall, 1996), pp. 505–29.

55 Robert Schulzinger, *American Diplomacy in the 20th Century*, 2nd edn. (New York, 1990), p. 317.

56 Morris, *Jimmy Carter: American Moralist*, (New York, 1995), pp. 273, 290; Stanley Hoffman, "In Search of a Foreign Policy," *The New York Review of Books* (September 29, 1983).

57 J. Michael Hogan, *The Panama Canal in American Politics: Domestic Advocacy and the Evolution of Policy* (Carbondale, 1986).

58 Jimmy Carter, *Keeping Faith*, pp. 73, 74, 269–430.

59 Burton I. Kaufman, *The Presidency of James Earl Carter Jr.* (Lawrence, 1993), *passim*; Brinkley, "The Rising Stock of Jimmy Carter," pp. 505–29.

60 Carroll, *It Seemed Like Nothing Happened*, pp. 220–4; Morris, *Jimmy Carter*, pp. 261–2.

61 LaFeber, *America, Russia, and the Cold War*, pp. 298–301.

62 Martin Walker, *The Cold War: A History* (New York, 1994), pp. 244–68.

63 Carroll, *It Seemed Like Nothing Happened*, p. 224.

64 Ibid., p. 346; Morris, *Jimmy Carter*, p. 286 and *passim*; Austin Ranney, "The Carter Administration," in Austin Ranney, ed., *The American Elections of 1980* (Washington, 1981), pp. 1–36.

65 Kaufman, *The Presidency of James Earl Carter Jr.*; Brinkley, "The Rising Stock of Jimmy Carter,", pp. 505–29; Dumbrell, *The Carter Presidency*; Walker, *The Cold War*, pp. 244–68.

66 David Frum, *How We Got Here: The 70s: The Decade that Brought You Modern Life (For Better or Worse)*, (New York, 2000), pp. xv–xxiv, 353.

Notes to Chapter 6

1 Fraser and Gerstle, eds., *The Rise and Fall of the New Deal Order*, p. ix.

2 Gary Gerstle, "The Protean Character of American Liberalism," *American Historical Review* (October, 1994), pp. 1043–73; Alan Brinkley, "The Problem of American Conservatism," *American Historical Review* (April, 1994), pp. 409–29; Leo Ribuffo, "Why is There So Much Conservatism in the United States and Why Do So Few Historians Know Anything About it?" Ibid., pp. 438–52.

3 Brinkley, "The Problem of American Conservatism," p. 415; Patrick Allitt, *Catholic Intellectuals and Conservative Politics in America, 1950–1985* (Ithaca, 1993), pp. 288, 303.

4 Paul Boyer, ed., *Reagan as President: Contemporary Views of the Man, His Politics, and His Policies* (Chicago, 1990), p. 17; For Schlesinger, see Larry Berman, ed., *Looking Back on the Reagan Presidency* (Baltimore and London, 1990), p. 20; *New Republic* (January 9, 16, 1989); Michael Hogan, ed., *The End of the Cold War: Its Meaning and Implications* (Cambridge, 1992); Edmund Morris, *Dutch: A Memoir* (New York, 1999).

5 Eric Schmertz, Natalie Datlof, and Alexej Ugrinsky, eds., *President Reagan and the World* (Westport and London, 1997); John Lewis Gaddis, "Arms Control: Hanging Tough Paid Off," *Bulletin of the Atomic Scientists* (January/February, 1989); Frances Fitzgerald, *Way Out There in the Blue: Reagan, Star Wars, and the End of the Cold War* (New York, 2000).

6 Schmertz, et al., eds., *President Reagan and the World*, p. 468.

7 Anne Markusen, "Cold War Economics," *Bulletin of the Atomic Scientists* (January/February, 1989).

8 Department of Defense, *Annual Report, 1980* (Washington, 1979), p.

5; Dennis S. Ippolito "Defense, Budget Politics, and the Reagan Deficits," in Schmertz, et al., eds., *President Reagan and the World*, p. 219.

9   Sir John Hackett, et al., *The Third World War: August 1985* (New York, 1978).

10 Jonathan Schell, *The Fate of the Earth* (New York, 1982).

11 *New York Times* (March 24, 1983).

12 Fitzgerald, *Way Out There in the Blue*, p. 20; Lou Cannon in Schmertz, et al., eds., *President Reagan and the World*, p. 467; For contemporary critiques see *St. Louis Post-Dispatch*, "A Star Wars Defense" (March 23, 1983) cited in Boyer et al., *Reagan as President*, pp. 210–11.

13 Jeanne Kirkpatrick, "Dictators and Double Standards," *Commentary* (June, 1980); Robert Pastor, "The Centrality of Central America," in Berman, ed., *Looking Back on the Reagan Presidency*, p. 36.

14 Reynolds, *One World Divisible*, p. 467.

15 Walter LaFeber, *Inevitable Revolutions: The United States in Central America* (New York, 1984), p. 5; Robert Pastor, "The Centrality of Central America," pp. 36–7.

16 *New York Times* (January 17, 1984).

17 Beth Fischer, "Toeing the Hard Line? The Reagan Administration and the Ending of the Cold War," *Political Science Quarterly*, 112(3), (1997), pp. 492, 496; Douglas J. Hoekstra, "Presidential Beliefs and the Reagan Paradox," *Presidential Studies Quarterly*, 27(3) (Summer, 1997), pp. 432–9.

18 Rose, *The Cold War Comes to Main Street*, passim; Jonathan Rieder, "The Rise of the 'Silent Majority,'" in Fraser and Gerstle, eds., *The Rise and Fall of the New Deal Order*, pp. 243–68; Kim McQuaid, *Uneasy Partners: Big Business in American Politics, 1945–1990* (Baltimore and London, 1994).

19 Berman, ed., *Looking Back on the Reagan Presidency*, pp. 6, 11.

20 *Nations Business* (December, 1988); *New York Times* (January 12, 1989).

21 Fitzgerald, *Way Out There in the Blue*, p. 159.

22 David Stockman cited in Chafe, *Unfinished Journey*, p. 475.

23 Sidney Weintraub, "The 1983 Budget: Guns Up; People Down," *New Leader* (February 22, 1982); Chafe, *Unfinished Journey*, p. 475.

24 Robert Samuelson, "The Enigma: Ronald Reagan's Goofy Competence," *New Republic* (January 9, 16, 1989).

25 Reich, *The Work of Nations*, p. 199.

26 David Stockman, *The Triumph of Politics* (November, 1986), pp. 235, 355–9, 366, and *passim*; Donald Regan, *For the Record* (New York, 1988).

27 Fitzgerald, *Way Out There in the Blue*, p. 235; Berman, ed., *Looking Back on the Reagan Presidency*, p. 6.

28 Walter F. Murphy, "Reagan's Judicial Strategy," in Berman, ed., *Look-*

ing Back on the Reagan Presidency, p. 210.

29 Lewis Lapham, "The Precious Eden," cited in Boyer, ed., *Reagan as President*, pp. 34–8, and TRB, "Legacy? What Legacy?" Ibid., pp. 274–6.

30 Richard O. Curry, ed., *Freedom at Risk: Secrecy, Censorship and Repression in the 1980s* (Philadelphia, 1988).

31 Andrew Hacker, *Two Nations: Black and White: Separate, Hostile and Unequal* (New York, 1995). For Wilkins see Boyer, ed., *Reagan as President*, p. 154; for Myrdal see Sanford Lyman, *Gunnar Myrdal's American Dilemma After a Half Century: Critics and Anti-Critics: The Legacy of the American Dilemma* (Human Sciences Press, 1998); Frances Fox Piven and Richard A. Cloward, "Challenging the Great Society's Conservative Critics," in Robert Griffiths, ed., *Major Problems in American History Since 1945* (Lexington, 1992), pp. 340–51.

32 Michael Novak, "The Rich, the Poor, and the Reagan Administration," *Commentary* (August, 1983); Charles Murray, *Losing Ground: American Society, 1950–1980* (New York, 1984); Lyman, *Gunnar Myrdal's American Dilemma After a Half Century*, p. 55.

33 Hamby, *Liberalism and its Challengers*, p. 364.

34 Samuelson, "The Enigma,", p. 278.

35 Allan Bloom, *The Closing of the American Mind* (New York, 1987); Tom Wolfe, *The Bonfire of the Vanities* (New York, 1987).

36 Arthur M. Schlesinger Jr., *The Cycles of American History* (Boston, 1986); Isserman and Kazin, *America Divided*; Gitlin, *The Sixties*; Lawrence W. Levine, *The Opening of the American Mind: Canons, Culture and History* (New York, 1995).

37 Edsall, "Chain Reaction," pp. 251–62; Gilbert T. Sewall, "Revisiting the Eighties," in Sewell, ed., *The Eighties: A Reader* (Reading, 1997), p. xii.

38 Chafe, *Unfinished Journey*, p. 470; Hamby, *Liberalism and its Challengers*, p. 370.

39 Condoleeza Rice, "U.S.–Soviet Relations," in Berman, ed., *Looking Back on the Reagan Presidency*, p. 72.

40 Press conference, March 14, 1985 in *Reagan Public Papers: 1985*, p. 285.

41 Fitzgerald, *Way Out There in the Blue*, p. 267.

42 *New York Times* (April 16, 2000).

43 John Lewis Gaddis, *The United States and the End of the Cold War* (New York, 1992), p. 129.

44 Laurence Lafore, *The Long Fuse: The Origins of World War I* (Philadelphia, 1965), p. 137.

45 Caroline Kennedy-Pipe, "Getting it Right, Getting it Wrong: The Soviet Collapse Revisited," *International Affairs*, 75(2), (1999), pp. 369–75.

46 Archie Brown, "Andropov: Discipline and Reform," *Problems of Communism*, 32 (January-February, 1983), pp. 18–31.

47 Mikhail Gorbachev, *Memoirs* (London, 1996), *passim.*

48 Schmertz, et al., eds., *President Reagan and the World*, pp. 261–335;
    Chafe, *Unfinished Journey*, p. 485; Theodore Draper, *A Very Thin
    Line: The Iran–Contra Affair* (New York, 1991), pp. 108–9, 93, and
    passim.

49 *Time* (January 2, 1991); Gaddis, *The United States and the End of the
    Cold War*, pp. 123–6; David Reynolds, *One World Divisible: A Glo-
    bal History Since 1945* (New York, 2000), pp. 546–7.

50 Ibid., pp. 539–68.

51 Stephen Ambrose, *Rise to Globalism: American Foreign Policy Since
    1938*, 7th edn. (New York, 1993), pp. 366–80.

52 Reynolds, *One World Divisible*, pp. 561–8.

53 Ambrose, *Rise to Globalism*, p. 366.

54 Reynolds, *One World Divisible*, p. 569.

55 Ibid., p. 571.

56 For Feyerabend see *Times Literary Supplement* (June 23, 2000).

57 Walter A. McDougall, *Promised Land, Crusader State: The American
    Encounter With the World Since 1776* (Boston, 1997), pp. 170–1.

58 Michael Hogan, ed., *The End of the Cold War: Its Meaning and Impli-
    cations* (Cambridge, 1992), p. 5; Kenneth Adelman in Schmertz, et al.,
    eds., *President Reagan and the World*, p. 81; Genrikh Trofimenko,
    Ibid., pp. 134–45.

59 Ullman in Schmertz, et al., eds., *President Reagan and the World*, p.
    110; Thomas G. Paterson, "Superpower Decline and Hegemonic Sur-
    vival," in Thomas G. Paterson, ed., *Major Problems in American For-
    eign Relations*, 5th edn. (Boston, 2000), pp. 611–18. For Europeans
    see Daniel Deudney and G. John Ikenberry, *Foreign Policy*, 87 (Sum-
    mer, 1992), pp. 123–8, 130–8.

60 For Rodman see Schmertz, et al., eds., *President Reagan and the World*,
    pp. 32–4. For Garthoff and Barnet see Hogan, ed., *The End of the
    Cold War*, pp. 113, 136.

61 Geoffrey Barraclough, *An Introduction to Contemporary History*
    (Harmondsworth, Middlesex, 1964).

Selective Bibliography

The historical literature addressing the Cold War era is vast and rapidly growing. For a fuller and/or specialized selection the reader is referred to general textbooks. Here I simply offer a very abbreviated list of books that may be useful in allowing the reader to gain a grasp of some of the main issues.

Overviews

General studies include James T. Patterson, *Grand Expectations: The United States, 1945–1974* (New York, 1996); William Chafe, *Unfinished Journey: America Since World War II*, 4th edn. (New York, 1999); William Leuchtenberg, *In the Shadow of FDR: From Harry Truman to Ronald Reagan* (Ithaca, 1983); David Reynolds, *One World Divisible: A Global History Since 1945* (New York, 2000); John Lewis Gaddis, *We Now Know: Rethinking Cold War History* (New York, 1997); Walter LaFeber, *America, Russia, and the Cold War*, 7th. edn. (New York, 1993); Alonzo Hamby, *Liberalism and Its Challengers: From FDR to Bush*, 2nd. edn. (New York, 1992); Norman Graebner, *Ideas and Diplomacy* (New York, 1964).

See also John Diggins, *The Rise and Fall of the American Left* (New York, 1992); Harvard Sitkoff, *The Struggle for Black Equality, 1954–1992* (New York, 1983); Alan Wolfe, *America's Impasse: The Rise and Fall of the Politics of Growth* (New York, 1981); James Baughman, *The Republic of Mass Culture: Journalism, Filmmaking and Broadcasting in America Since 1941* (Baltimore and London,

1992); Richard Polenberg, *One Nation Divisible: Class, Race, and Ethnicity in the United States Since 1938* (New York, 1980); and Robert Wuthnow, *The Restructuring of American Religion* (Princeton, 1988).

Truman Era

See generally Alonzo Hamby, *Man of the People: A Life of Harry S. Truman* (New York, 1995); Hamby, *Beyond the New Deal: Harry S. Truman and American Liberalism* (New York, 1975); Alan Brinkley, *The End of Reform: New Deal Liberalism in Recession and War* (New York, 1995); Steve Fraser and Gary Gerstle, eds., *The Rise and Fall of the New Deal Order, 1930–1980* (Princeton, 1989); Barton J. Bernstein, ed., *Politics and Policies of the Truman Administration* (Chicago, 1970); Paul S. Boyer, *By the Dawn's Early Light: American Thought and Culture at the Dawn of the Atomic Age* (New York, 1985); and Tom Engelhardt, *The End of Victory Culture: Cold War Americans and the Disillusioning of a Generation* (New York, 1995).

For diplomacy see John Lewis Gaddis, *The United States and the Origins of the Cold War, 1941–1947* (New York, 1972); Walter Isaacson, *The Wise Men: Six Friends and the World They Made: Acheson, Bohlen, Harriman, Kennan, Lovett, and McCloy* (New York, 1986); George F. Kennan, *Memoirs, 1925–1950* (Boston, 1967); Wilson Miscamble, *George Kennan and the Making of American Foreign Policy, 1947–1950* (Princeton, 1992); Martin J. Sherwin, *A World Destroyed: Hiroshima and the Origins of the Nuclear Arms Race* (New York, 1987); Lloyd Gardner, *Architects of Illusion: Men and Ideas in American Foreign Policy, 1941–1949* (Chicago, 1970); Michael J. Hogan, *The Marshall Plan: America, Britain and the Reconstruction of Western Europe, 1947–1952* (New York, 1987); Melvyn P. Leffler, *A Preponderance of Power: National Security, the Truman Administration and the Cold War* (Stanford, 1992); Randall Bennett Woods, *A Changing of the Guard: Anglo–American Relations, 1941–1946* (Chapel Hill, 1990); Vladimir Zubok and Constantine Pleshakov, *Inside the Kremlin's Cold War: From Stalin to Khrushchev* (Cambridge, 1996); Fraser J. Harbutt, *The Iron Curtain: Churchill, America, and the Origins of the Cold War* (New York, 1986).

For McCarthyism see Stephen Whitfield, *The Culture of the Cold*

War (Baltimore, 1991); Richard Fried, *Nightmare in Red: The McCarthy Era in Perspective* (New York, 1990); Michael Rogin, *The Radical Specter: The Intellectuals and McCarthy* (Cambridge, 1967). For Korea see Burton Kauffman, *The Korean War: Challenges in Crisis, Credibility, and Command* (Philadelphia, 1986) and Bruce Cuming, *The Origins of the Korean War*, 2 vols., (Princeton, 1981–90).

The 1950s

Generally see David Halberstam, *The Fifties* (New York, 1993) and J. Ronald Oakley, *God's Country: America in the Fifties* (New York, 1986). For Eisenhower see Stephen Ambrose, *Eisenhower: Soldier and President* (New York, 1990); Fred Greenstein, *The Hidden-Hand Presidency: Eisenhower as Leader* (New York, 1982) and Robert Burk, *Dwight D. Eisenhower: Hero and Politician* (Boston, 1986). Diplomatic themes are discussed in Robert A. Divine, *Eisenhower and the Cold War* (New York, 1981); Townsend Hoopes, *The Devil and John Foster Dulles* (Boston, 1973); Richard Immerman, *John Foster Dulles and the Diplomacy of the Cold War* (Princeton, 1990); and Marc Trachtenberg, *A Constructed Peace: The Making of the European Settlement, 1945–1963* (Princeton, 1999).

Domestic issues are treated in Samuel Lubell, *The Revolt of the Moderates* (New York, 1956); David Garrow, *Bearing the Cross: Martin Luther King Jr. and the Southern Christian Leadership Conference* (New York, 1986); Taylor Branch, *Parting the Waters: America in the King Years, 1954–1963* (New York, 1988); Numan P. Bartley, *The Rise of Massive Resistance: Race and Politics in the South During the 1950s* (Baton Rouge, 1969); Scott Donaldson, *The Suburban Myth* (New York, 1969); Erik Barnouw, *The Tube of Plenty* (New York, 1982); and Richard Pells, *The Liberal Mind in a Conservative Age: American Intellectuals in the 1940s and 1950s* (New York, 1984).

The 1960s

For overviews see Allen Matusow, *The Unraveling of America: A History of Liberalism in the 1960s* (New York, 1984); William O'Neill, *Coming Apart: An Informal History of America in the*

1960s (Chicago, 1971); David Burner, *Making Peace With the Sixties* (Princeton, 1996); Todd Gitlin, *The Sixties: Years of Hope; Days of Rage* (New York, 1987); and Maurice Isserman and Michael Kazin, *America Divided: The Civil War of the 1960s* (New York, 2000).

For Kennedy see Arthur M. Schlesinger Jr., *A Thousand Days: John F. Kennedy in the White House* (Boston, 1965); Richard Reeves, *President Kennedy: Profile of Power* (New York, 1993); Michael Beschloss, *The Crisis Years: Kennedy and Khrushchev, 1960–1963* (New York, 1991); Thomas Paterson, ed., *Kennedy's Quest for Victory: American Foreign Policy, 1961–1963* (New York, 1989); Carl Brauer, *John F. Kennedy and the Second Reconstruction* (New York, 1977). For Johnson see Paul Conkin, *Big Daddy from the Pedernales: Lyndon Baines Johnson* (Boston, 1986); Robert Dallek, *Lone Star Rising: Lyndon Johnson and His Times* (New York, 1990); Doris Kearns, *Lyndon Johnson and the American Dream* (New York, 1976). For Vietnam see George Herring, *America's Longest War: The United States and Vietnam, 1950–1975* 2nd. edn. (Philadelphia, 1986); Frances Fitzgerald, *The Fire in the Lake: The Vietnamese and the Americans in Vietnam* (Boston, 1972); Neil Sheehan, *A Bright Shining Lie: John Paul Vann and America in Vietnam* (New York, 1988); and Andrew J. Rotter, *Light at the End of the Tunnel: a Vietnam War Anthology*, rev. edn. (Wilmington, 1999).

For domestic turbulence see additionally, Robert Conot, *Rivers of Blood and Years of Darkness* (New York, 1968); Michael Eric Dyson, *Making Malcolm: The Myth and Meaning of Malcolm X* (New York, 1995); Irwin Unger, *The Movement: A History of the American New Left* (New York, 1974); Morris Dickstein, *Gates of Eden: American Culture in the Sixties* (New York, 1977).

Nixon and the 1970s

See generally Peter Carroll, *It Seemed Like Nothing Happened: The Tragedy and Promise of American Life in the 1970s* (New York, 1982); Kevin Phillips, *The Emerging Republican Majority* (New Rochelle, 1969). For Nixon see Stephen Ambrose, *Nixon: The Triumph of a Politician, 1962–1972* (New York, 1989) and Ambrose, *Nixon: Ruin and Recovery, 1973–1990* (New York, 1993); Garry Wills, *Nixon Agonistes: The Crisis of the Self-Made Man* (New York, 1969); Joan Hoff, *Nixon Reconsidered* (New York, 1994); Stanley

Kutler, *The Wars of Watergate: The Last Crisis of Richard Nixon* (New York, 1990); and Theodore H. White, *Breach of Faith* (New York, 1975).

For diplomacy and politics see also Raymond Garthoff, *Détente and Confrontation: American–Soviet Relations from Nixon to Reagan* (Washington, 1985); William Shawcross, *Sideshow: Kissinger, Nixon, and the Destruction of Cambodia* (New York, 1979); Richard Reeves, *A Ford, Not a Lincoln* (New York, 1975); Betty Glad, *Jimmy Carter: In Search of the Great White House* (New York, 1980); Gaddis Smith, *Morality, Reason, and Power: American Diplomacy in the Carter Years* (New York, 1986); and Thomas Ferguson and Joel Rogers, *Right Turn: The Decline of the Democrats and the Future of American Politics* (New York, 1986). For other domestic themes see Phillip Slater, *The Pursuit of Loneliness: American Culture at the Breaking Point* (Boston, 1970); Christopher Lasch, *The Culture of Narcissism: American Life in an Age of Diminishing Expectations* (New York, 1979); Jo Freeman, *The Politics of Women's Liberation* (New York, 1975); Robert Heilbroner, *An Inquiry into the Human Prospect* (New York, 1975) and Walter Dean Burnham, *The Current Crisis in American Politics* (New York, 1992).

Cold War Finale

Reagan biographers include Lou Cannon, *President Reagan: The Role of a Lifetime* (New York, 1991); Michael Paul Rogin, *Ronald Reagan the Movie, and Other Episodes in Political Demonology* (Berkeley, 1987); and Robert Dallek, *Ronald Reagan: the Politics of Symbolism* (Cambridge, 1984). See also for domestic themes Garry Wills, *Reagan's America: Innocents at Home* (Garden City, 1987); Sidney Blumenthal, *The Rise of the Counter-Establishment* (New York, 1986); Jerome Himmelstein, *To the Right: The Transformation of American Conservatism* (Berkeley, 1989); Frances Fox Piven and Richard A. Cloward, *The Breaking of the American Social Contract* (New York, 1997); and Sidney Blumenthal and Thomas Edsall, eds. *The Reagan Legacy* (New York, 1988).

For diplomacy see Fred Halliday, *The Making of the Second Cold War* (New York, 1983); Strobe Talbott, *The Russians and Reagan* (New York, 1984); Thomas W. Walker, ed. *Reagan versus the Sandinistas: The Undeclared War on Nicaragua* (Boulder, 1987);

Robert A. Pastor, *Condemned to Repetition: The United States and Nicaragua* (Princeton, 1987); Michael J. Hogan, ed., *The End Of the Cold War* (New York, 1992); Raymond Garthoff, *The Great Transition: American–Soviet Relations and the End of the Cold War* (New York, 1995); Michael Mandelbaum, *Reagan and Gorbachev* (New York, 1987); George H. W. Bush and Brent Scowcroft, *A World Transformed* (New York, 1998).

Index

Brazil, 256
Bretton Woods, 229
Brezhnev doctrine, 235–6
Brezhnev, Leonid, 229, 258
Brown vs. Board of Education of Topeka, 107, 124
Brussels Pact, 57
Brzezinski, Zbigniew, 240, 253–4
Byrnes, James, 21, 25–6, 28–34
Buckley, William F. Jr., 78, 265, 283
Bulgaria, 25, 27
Bundy, McGeorge, 146, 151, 180
Burford, Anne, 284
Burger, Warren, 203, 216
Burke, Edmund, 297
Bush, George H. W., 285, 296
Business Advisory Council, 44

Califano, Joseph, 250
Cambodia, 96, 182, 221–2, 232, 247, 271
Camp David accords, 255
Carmichael, Stokeley, 170, 193
Carson, Rachel, 166
Carter doctrine, 258–9
Carter, James: general, 247–63; and Afghanistan, 258; and Africa, 256; background of, 247–9; and Camp David accords, 255; and China, 254; and "crisis" speech, 256–7; Democrats and, 248–9; and domestic policies, 250; and economic issues, 249–59; and energy policy, 251–2; and foreign policy, 252–6; and health policy, 250; and human rights policies, 252–3; image of, 261; and Iran, 257–8, 261; and Kennedy, Edward, 250, 257–9; and Latin America, 254–6; and Middle East, 255–6, 262; and 1980 election, 259–61; and OPEC,

252, 259; and Panama Canal, 254–5; and Reagan, Ronald, 259–60; and SALT II, 258; and Soviet Union, 249, 253–4, 258–9; and Vance, Cyrus, 249; and Volcker, Paul, 259; and welfare reform, 250
Casey, William 271, 277, 302, 306
Castro, Fidel, 119, 143, 146–54
Catholic Church, 52, 72, 74–5, 106, 143, 239
Ceausescu, Nicolae, 310
Central America, 271, 273, 277–80
Central Intelligence Agency (CIA), 91, 112, 123, 219, 222, 238, 279–80
Central Treaty Organization (CENTO), 96, 118
The Century of the Common Man (Wallace), 5
Cheney, Dick, 310
Chernenko, Konstantin, 281, 302
Chile, 233, 256
Chiang, Kai-Shek, 67, 117–18
The Children of Sanchez (Lewis), 171
China: communist victory in 67; and China lobby, 67; détente and, 230–1; Eisenhower and, 89, 95–6, 112, 117–18; Nixon administration and, 218, 220, 223; recognition of, 254
China lobby, 67, 86, 92, 104, 118
Chou En Lai, 229–30
Churchill Winston, 9–10, 13, 18, 27–34, 90, 316
Civil rights, 106, 140
Civil Rights Act (1957), 107, 125
Civil Rights Act (1964), 162–3
Civil Rights Act (1967), 168
Clifford, Clark, 55
Clinton, Bill, 296
Committee on the Present Danger, 258, 267
Congress of Industrial